The Church of God in Jesus Christ

ROCH A. KERESZTY, O.CIST.

The Church of God in Jesus Christ

A Catholic Ecclesiology

The Catholic University of America Press
Washington, D.C.

The paper used in this publication meets the minimum requirements of
American National Standards for Information Science—Permanence of Paper
for Printed Library Materials, ANSI Z39.48-1984.
∞

Library of Congress Cataloging-in-Publication Data
Names: Kereszty, Roch A., author.
Title: The Church of God in Jesus Christ : a Catholic ecclesiology / Roch A. Kereszty, O. Cist.
Description: Washington, D.C. : The Catholic University of America Press, [2019] | Includes
bibliographical references and index.
Identifiers: LCCN 2018047197 | ISBN 9780813231730 (pbk. : alk. paper)
Subjects: LCSH: Church—History of doctrines. | Catholic Church—Doctrines.
Classification: LCC BX1746 .K425 2019 | DDC 262/.02—dc23
LC record available at https://lccn.loc.gov/2018047197

CONTENTS

PREFACE

Humankind has reached a crucial moment. From the beginnings of history, human beings have been torn by two opposing tendencies: individualism and collectivism. In other words, the conflict between the interests of the individual and a group (a company, nation, or social class) has shaped, to a large extent, human history. At the present moment, humankind is fast approaching the climax of this drama. Either we will find a way to integrate individuals, social classes, and nations into peaceful economic, political, and cultural cooperation by accepting a multilayered, mutual dependency on each other, or the very survival of the human race will be threatened. In this dramatic time, the world needs the church as a transforming and reconciling social center in which God is to unite all of creation to himself.

More than ever before, Christians are called to be the soul of the world, as the Letter to Diognetus explained in the second century. They must show the world that the catholicity of the church does not jeopardize, but rather fully actualizes, the sacred depth of every culture. In her, all nations, groups, and cultures find a home where individuals flourish to the extent that they serve the good of the community. The church can fulfill this providential role to the extent that her members allow the one and the same Holy Spirit to inspire and unite them so that Christ's love may transform hostilities and hatred into forgiveness and cooperation.

Yet despite this high calling, the interactions of Christians seem at times only to reflect the worst of the world's divisiveness. While this is fundamentally a failure of charity, it is also a lack of faith—and this faith is nourished by true knowledge of divine realities. My motivation for writing this book came from the experience that too few of the most faithful Catholics—let alone non-Catholics—understand *what* the church is; and even less do they know *who* the church is. Some, drawing on the theology dominant from the Council of Trent to the Second Vatican Council, would recognize that the church is a hierarchical society founded by Christ and headed by the pope. Others, drawing on conciliar and postconciliar society, think of the church mainly as the people of God on march in history. The better informed have reflected on the biblical image of the church as the body of Christ, in which every member has a unique task to fulfill and a ministry to perform.

All of these notions are elements of the church's self-understanding, but viewed in isolation, they are misleading, and as understood by most Catholics, they are inadequate to the church's great tasks and its complex reality. A superficial understanding of the church often leads to a loyalty that is just as superficial and easily shaken by bitter disappointments over the sins of her members and especially of her leaders. In fact, anyone can easily rationalize abandoning a hierarchically organized institution or a people wandering and bickering on the road. But could you easily abandon your own Mother or the Bride of Jesus Christ? Who would leave the church if they were aware that by doing so they were cutting themselves off from the very life of Christ?

My intention, then, for this book is to explore and contemplate each major aspect of the mystery of the church, first, as the people of God, chosen for the salvation of the world in Christ; second, as the virginal Bride who becomes one body and one Spirit with Christ; and last, the church as Mother by the Holy Spirit of all believers and the family of God the Father. I attempt to present the mystery of the church not in a historical vacuum, but rather as from its very beginnings God's providential offer of the church to humankind. This, it seems to me, is especially important at the present hour when the church faces a dangerous stage of humankind's history: technologically interdependent but psychologically polarized, in desperate need of a spiritually reconciling and unifying force.

It is commonly observed that ecclesiology, or theology of the church, is a very young branch of systematic theology. No theologian of the patristic age wrote a comprehensive treatise on the theology of the church, even though their writings contain the building blocks of a rich, comprehensive ecclesiology. When they were writing on particular topics, as opposed to works addressing a particular controversy or scriptural commentary, their systematic reflections centered on the mysteries of the Triune God, the incarnation, redemption, baptism, Eucharist, and penance. An occasional treatise focused on church order, but not the comprehensive mystery of the church. Rather, the Fathers identified with the church and, as members of it, lived her mystery. They knew more about the church than most theologians since the late Middle Ages through the nineteenth century, but none of them organized their thoughts into one synthetic work.

During the Middle Ages, St. Thomas resumed the patristic notions on this subject, but he never formulated a single specialized treatise. The late Middle Ages saw the production of the first *summae* on the church, but these works, by John of Ragusa and Juan de Torquemada, treated only her juridical aspects. Since the Reformers wanted to diminish some or most of the church's visible structures in favor of an inward attitude of faith, the Catholic theology of the Counter-Reformation dealt almost exclusively with the marks of the visible, hierarchical church, resulting in an effective apologetics to prove that only the Roman Catholic Church is the true church of Christ. Even into the twentieth century, this one-sided trend prevailed on the theological faculties of most Catholic universities and seminaries. The treatise *de ecclesia* became part of apologetics, which collects reasons for God's existence, and presents Christ as the Revealer of God and the Catholic Church as the authentic guardian and proclaimer of this revelation. The patristic themes of the church as a participant in the life of the Triune God, and as the people of God, body of Christ, Spouse and Mother, all remained unexplained, surviving only in devotional literature.

Following a brilliant beginning undertaken by Johann Adam Möhler in the nineteenth century, Romano Guardini famously wrote in the first decades of the twentieth century that "the church awakens in the souls."[1] A wave of great theologians rediscovered and assembled the riches of biblical and patristic theology, thereby preparing for Vatican II, which has become known as the council on the church.[2] The great recovery and advancement of theology begun by the council, though, led to great dissension over its interpretation. During the first decades after the council, ecclesiological interest centered on *Lumen Gentium*, the Dogmatic Constitution on the

1. Romano Guardini, *Vom Sinn der Kirche* (Mainz: Matthias-Grünewald, 1922), 1.

2. The prevailing trend in many Catholic institutions, especially seminaries, nevertheless continued the post-Tridentine trend of defending the church as an institution.

Church, especially the second chapter, "On the People of God," a theme found congenial especially to thinkers eager to "democratize" the church. To date, the first chapter of the constitution, on the trinitarian mystery of the church, and the last one, on the relationship between Mary and the church, have not been sufficiently studied and explained.

In this study I focus on the main aspects of the mystery of the church in order to appeal to a general college-educated audience, and in particular to students of theology. The struggle to interpret *Lumen Gentium* has not yet subsided, but it is not my intention to provide the reader with every variant opinion that has appeared since the council and that fills the pages of academic theological journals. Such a survey, while useful for students intending to enter further theological study, often leaves the novice reader more uncertain and overwhelmed than enlightened. Rather, this work presents my own study of ecclesiology using a systematic approach, incorporating biblical and historical considerations, to provide the kind of comprehensive treatise often lacking since the council. My own perspective is tinged by my religious profession as a Cistercian, highlighting the important and often-neglected contributions of St. Bernard of Clairvaux, but I expect that readers and theologians of various schools of thought will find it a useful and trustworthy introduction.

Part I begins with a historical survey of the church before the birth of Israel and continues with the role of Israel in God's plan of salvation (chapter 1). Then it treats the foundations of the church in the New Testament (chapter 2) and the historical highlights of the church's self-understanding through the reception of Vatican II (chapters 3–8).

Part 2, a systematic treatment of ecclesiology, provides an explanation of the church's four essential marks: one, holy, catholic, and apostolic (chapters 9–12). Then the theme of the people of God as it participates in the priestly, prophetic, and royal office of Christ is explained (chapter 13). What has been presented to this point can be synthesized into five comprehensive notions or images: sacrament, people of God, body of Christ, virginal spouse of Christ, mother, and independent metaphysical subject (chapter 14). As the theological notion of the church is compared with its empirical reality in history, those areas and forces that can contribute to ongoing reform and renewal (chapter 15) are described. Part 2 concludes with a preview of the eschatological heavenly church (chapter 16).

To provide a more in-depth study of some particular aspects of the church's mystery, part 3 consists of several essays previously published in various periodicals. A chapter on the unity of the church in Irenaeus leads into a more detailed understanding of the beginnings of patristic ecclesiology (chapter 17). The essay on the mission of Israel seeks a theological raison d'être for the enduring existence of Judaism today (chapter 18). Chapter 19, on "Bride" and "Mother" in St. Bernard's *Sermones Super Cantica*, shows the timeliness of studying these two important images in patristic and medieval theology. Wolfhart Pannenberg was one of the few Christian theologians who responded to Pope John Paul II's call for contributions from outside the Catholic Church on how the pope could exercise his Petrine ministry in a way that is acceptable to all Christians. My essay reprinted here provides a Catholic response to Pannenberg's suggestions (chapter 20). By exploring the beginnings of the doctrine of infallibility, it connects with the Marian doctrine of virginity (chapter 21).

My hope is that the readers of this book will see somewhat more clearly the richness of the mystery of the church by discovering the light of Christ reflected on her face. However, beyond studying and reflecting, there remains one more crucial step, which is for Christ to take. He will heed the call of the Spirit and his bride and will introduce us to the wedding feast of the kingdom that has been prepared for the church from the foundation of the world (Mt 25:34; Rv 19:7; 22:20).

ACKNOWLEDGMENTS

I am very grateful to Robert Greenfield who carefully read and edited my manuscript.

A few portions of the manuscript are excerpted with minor alterations from Rev. Roch Kereszty, O.Cist., *Jesus Christ: Fundamentals of Christology* (Staten Island, N.Y.: St. Pauls, 2011).

Part 3 consists of several previously published articles relating to ecclesiology. I am thankful to the publishers for their permission to include these articles here. The chapter titles and the respective publications where these articles first appeared are as follows:

"The Unity of the Church in the Theology of Irenaeus." *The Second Century* 4, no. 4 (1984): 202–18. Copyright © Second Century. Reprinted with permission of Johns Hopkins University Press.

"'Bride' and 'Mother' in the *Super Cantica* of St. Bernard: An Ecclesiology for Our Time?" *Communio* 20, no. 2 (Summer 1993): 415–36.

"A Catholic Response to W. Pannenberg, 'Evangelische Überlegungen zum Petrusdienst des Römischen Bischofs.'" *Communio* 25, no. 4 (Winter 1998): 619–29.

"The Infallibility of the Church: A Marian Mystery." *Communio* 38, no. 3 (Fall 2011): 374–90.

"Catholicity and the Mission of the Church." *Communio* 39, no. 1 (Spring–Summer 2012): 66–81.

"A Catholic Perspective on the Mission of Israel." *Nova et Vetera*, English Edition, vol. 12, no. 1 (2013): 147–62.

"'Sacrosancta Ecclesia': The Holy Church of Sinners." *Communio* 40, no. 4 (Winter 2013): 663–79.

"The Unity of the Church." *Communio* 41, no. 4 (Winter 2014): 694–720.

ABBREVIATIONS

Ben.	Bernard of Clairvaux. *Sermon on the Feast of St. Benedict*
CDF	Congregation for the Doctrine of Faith
CF	*The Christian Faith in the Doctrinal Documents of the Catholic Church*. Edited by Joseph Neuner and Jaques Dupuis, 7th ed. New York: Alba House, 2001
Circ.	Bernard. *Sermon on the Feast of the Circumcision of the Lord*
Cl	Cetedoc Library of Latin Texts
Div.	*Sermones de Diversis*
DS	*Enchiridion Symbolorum*. Edited by Henricus Denzinger and Adolfus Schönmetzer, 36th ed. Freiburg: Herder, 1976
DV	Vatican Council II. *Dei Verbum*. Dogmatic Constitution on Divine Revelation. November 18, 1965
EG	Francis. *Evangelii Gaudium*. Apostolic Exhortation. November 24, 2013
Ep.	*Epistula*
GS	Vatican Council II. *Gaudium et Spes*. Pastoral Constitution on the Church in the Modern World. December 7, 1965
Hist. eccl.	Eusebius of Caesarea. *Historia ecclesiastica*
Hom.	*Homily*
HV	Pope Paul VI. *Humanae Vitae*. Encyclical Letter. July 25, 1968
LG	Vatican Council II. *Lumen Gentium*. Dogmatic Constitution on the Church. November 21, 1964
LN	Congregation for the Doctrine of the Faith. *Libertatis Nuntius: Instruction on Certain Aspects of the Theology of Liberation*. August 6, 1984

LXX	The Septuagint (the Greek translation of Scriptures)
MC	Pius XII. *Mystici Corporis*. Encyclical Letter. June 29, 1943
Miss.	Bernard. *Homilia super Missus est / Homilies on the Annunciation*
Nat.	Bernard. *Homilia de Nativitate*
Nat. Bapt.	Bernard. *Homilia de Nativitate Joannis Baptistae*
Nat. BM	Bernard. *Homilia de Nativitate Beatae Mariae Virginis*
NT	New Testament
OT	Old Testament
Par.	Bernard. *Parables*
PG	Patrologiae Cursus Completus: Series Graeca. Edited by J.-P. Migne. 162 vols. Paris, 1857–86
PL	Patrologiae Cursus Completus: Series Latina. Edited by J.-P. Migne. 217 vols. Paris, 1844–64
PO	Vatican Council II. *Presbyterorum Ordinis*. December 7, 1965
QH	Bernard. *Sermons on Psalm 90*
Super Cant.	Bernard. *Sermones super Cantica Canticorum*
SC	Vatican Council II. *Sacrosanctum Concilium*. constitution of the Sacred Liturgy of Vatican II
Sent.	Bernard. *Sentences*
ST	St. Thomas Aquinas. *Summa theologiae*
UR	Vatican Council II. *Unitatis Redintegratio*. November 21, 1964
V HM	Bernard. *Sermon on Holy Thursday*
Vit. Mal.	Bernard. *Vita Malachiae (Life of Malachiah)*
WA	*D. Martin Luthers Werke* (Weimarer Ausgabe). Weimar: Böhlau, 1883–2009

PART 1

Historical Survey

CHAPTER 1

The Beginnings of the Church

The Church Beginning from Abel

God's eternal plan to unite to himself all creation through his Son has not been frustrated by the fall of humankind; instead, from all eternity God has foreseen and integrated this fall into his plan.[1] He has offered the saving grace of the future Redeemer to all fallen human beings, but humankind became divided between those who rejected this grace and those who accepted it. In the latter group, among those who play a role in Genesis before Abraham are Abel, Enoch, and Noah.[2] Indeed, a portrait of the just pagan is drawn in the book of Job. These just men seem isolated without the support of a community, yet the church fathers consider them members of the church because they believed in God and in some implicit way they hoped in a coming Redeemer. The Fathers and St. Thomas explained that Christ had been revealed to some people even before the law was given; that is, before the adoption of Israel as God's people. According to Aqui-

1. This chapter owes most to Notker Füglister, "Strukturen der alttestamentlichen Ekklesiologie: Das Heilsgeschehen in der Gemeinde Jesu Christi," in *Mysterium Salutis*, vol. 4/2, *Das Heilsgeschehen in der Gemeinde: Gottes Gnadenhandeln*, ed. Johannes Betz et al. (Einsiedeln: Benziger, 1972), 23–100. This includes an abundance of biblical references for each theme in this chapter. See also Norbert Lohfink, *The Covenant Never Revoked: Biblical Reflections on Christian-Jewish Dialogue* (Minneapolis: Fortress, 1991); Michael Schmaus et al., ed., *Handbuch der Dogmengeschichte*, vols. III/3a–d (Freiburg: Herder, 1971), especially Yves Congar, vol. III/3c, *Die Lehre von der Kirche: Von Augustinus bis zum Abendländischen Schisma*, and Congar, vol. III/3d, *Die Lehre von der Kirche: Von Augustinus bis zur Gegenwart*; Maximilian Heinrich Heim, *Joseph Ratzinger: Life in the Church and Living Theology; Fundamentals of Ecclesiology with Reference to "Lumen Gentium"* (San Francisco: Ignatius, 2007); Richard P. McBrien, *The Remaking of the Church* (New York: Harper and Row, 1973). A typical example of a dangerous misunderstanding proposes to "remake" the church according to the blueprint of a successful business company.

2. According to the Fathers and some medieval authors, the church begins with Abel. See quotes in LG 2, n. 2.

nas, even those outside of Israel "were not saved without faith in a Mediator. For although they did not have an explicit faith, they did have faith in divine providence, believing that God will liberate humankind in a way he chooses and as he has revealed to some who have known the truth."[3]

In addition, every grace received before Christ came into the world through Christ's sacrifice and was received through an implicit faith in Christ that conformed the believer to him. St. Justin was aware of this in the second century when he gave the name "Christian" to Socrates and all those who came before Christ but lived according to the *logos spermatikos*, "the seed of the logos."[4] Thus, in some initial way, all the just before the coming of Christ belonged to the church as the body of Christ since they were conformed to him by his grace.

The pattern of this plan becomes intelligible if we consider the twofold structure of the human being as soul and body. As *embodied* persons, we exist in time, and therefore some of us have lived before but others after Christ. As spiritual beings, every man and woman is able in some way to transcend time and space regardless when and where he or she lives. Therefore, those before Christ could not have any explicit knowledge of him. As *spirits*, however, people of every age have been able to transcend their temporal and cultural limits and reach by faith and love in some implicit way the future reality of the incarnate Son.

Israel, the People of God

If we study in the light of Christian faith the history of Israel in the Old Testament, it presents itself as the first stage in God's plan of salvation; its historical events and its main protagonists (patriarchs, leaders, kings, prophets) can be understood as God's gradual process of education whereby he prepares Israel to live by his commandments and learn his ways so that they will be ready for the coming of the Son of God and his redemptive work. Unlike other ancient people, who claim kinship with their gods, Israel learns that she is not God's "natural offspring," but that she owes her existence to God's mysterious choice. God allows Israel to fall into situations of death and destruction, such as slavery in Egypt, drowning in the

3. Thomas Aquinas, ST II–II q. 2, a. 7 resp. to the 3rd.
4. Justin Martyr, *First Apology* 46.

sea, dying from thirst and famine in the desert, or being conquered by the surrounding great empires, which no human power could save her from. It is in such desperate situations that God shows himself to be the Savior of Israel and teaches Israel absolute trust in him. Although he severely punishes his people for their many transgressions, he subsequently saves a remnant and lavishes the love of a father and bridegroom on those he saved (see Dt 7:6–11; 14:2; 32:8–14; Mal 3:17). We might say that the entire history of Israel is a kind of "rehearsal" for the Paschal mystery, the redemption by Jesus Christ. This expectation of the final and perfect redemption from death, sin, and war ultimately makes Israel's faith identical with the faith of the New Testament church.

On this basis and in accord with patristic tradition, St. Thomas affirms a certain presence of the church within the Old Testament people of God: "By observing the sacraments of the Law, [the just men and women of the Old Testament] were brought to Christ by the same faith and love by which we are being brought to him. Therefore, the ancient fathers belonged to the same body of the church to which we belong."[5] In other words, their implicit faith and love reached Christ himself, although their understanding and expression of this trust in future redemption were limited by the time period and historical setting in which they lived. For instance, God's call for Abraham to consecrate Isaac to him enters Abraham's consciousness as a realization that he must kill his firstborn son in accord with the customs of the Near East.[6] Similarly, the ban placed on entire cities and the resulting slaughter of all of their residents was how Israel understood the radical and complete uprooting of idolatry from its midst.

If this reasoning is true, then the divine intention expressed in the words and deeds of God in the Old Testament can only be adequately grasped in the New Testament when the goal of God's plan is revealed. The spiritual meaning of Old Testament texts is not merely legitimate but necessary in order to reach the divinely intended full meaning. Without considering their New Testament fulfillment, many Old Testament events and texts seemingly present the image of an arbitrary, immoral, and cruel god.

5. Thomas Aquinas, ST III q. 2, a. 8 resp. to the 3rd. See also Vatican Council II, Decree on Ecumenism, *Nostra Aetate*, October 28, 1965, 4.

6. In fact, it is plausible that the story of Abraham's sacrifice, known in Judaism as the Akedah, the binding of Isaac, has put an end in Israel to the ritual immolation of the firstborn son. See Jon D. Levenson, *The Death and Resurrection of the Beloved Son: The Transformation of the Child Sacrifice in Judaism and Christianity* (New Haven: Yale University Press, 1995).

Abraham, Our Father in Faith

Probably sometime during the second millennium BC, God manifested his intention and began to prepare humankind for redemption by choosing Abraham to establish a nation that would become his own people. Without any merit on Abraham's part, God called him, commanded him to leave the land of his kinsfolk and his father's house and go to the land God will show him. Abraham obeys and is led to Canaan, which the Lord promises to him and his descendants (Gn 12:1–9). In spite of his old age and Sara, his wife, being beyond childbearing age, Abraham believes God's promise that his offspring will be as numerous as the stars in the sky and that all the communities of the earth shall find blessing in him (Gn 15:1–6). After the son of promise, Isaac, has been born and raised, God orders Abraham to offer his son to him in sacrifice. Again, Abraham obeys without delay and takes Isaac to the mount of Moriah (where later the temple of Israel will be built by Solomon). But before Abraham offers Isaac, God intervenes and prevents the slaying. Abraham's obedience to give back to God the child through whom all the blessings were to be fulfilled moves the Lord to effusive praise and to renew all of his previous promises:

> I swear by myself, declares the LORD, because you acted as you did in not withholding from me your beloved son, I will bless you abundantly and make your descendants as countless as the stars of the sky and the sands of the seashore; your descendants shall take possession of the gates of their enemies, and in your descendants, all the nations of the earth shall find blessing—all this because you obeyed my command. (Gn 22:16–18)

In this way, Abraham becomes not only the biological ancestor of Israel through his grandson Jacob, but also the ideal prototype of Israel's and the church's faith. Israel owes her origin to the faith of Abraham, who believed, despite all empirical evidence to the contrary, that he would beget a son with Sara and, in spite of God's command to kill the son, God's promises would be fulfilled through Isaac. By forbidding the killing of Isaac, God clearly shows that he rejects human sacrifices, but only after Abraham has proved that he trusts and obeys God unconditionally. Later, Solomon built the temple on the hill of Moriah, the place where Abraham was ready to sacrifice his son. During the period of the Second Temple all sacrifices of Israel were viewed as a reenactment of this one sacrifice, the Akedah.[7]

The full meaning of Abraham's sacrifice was only revealed in the New Testament, where he becomes a figure of God the Father who gave up for us his only beloved Son. Although Abraham was prohibited from sacrificing his son, the Father allows his Son to be sacrificed for the sake of all humankind. Thus Abraham became the privileged friend of God, the earthly image of the Father's infinite generosity.

The Birth of Israel as the People of God

Forced by famine, Jacob, Abraham's grandson, moves with his family to Egypt, where they become so numerous that Pharaoh considers them a threat to himself and his people. As a result, he subjects the Israelites to cruel slavery, which gives God the opportunity to liberate Israel under the leadership of Moses and Aaron. Compelled by God's mighty deeds, Pharaoh eventually lets Israel go into the desert to worship her God. Moses parts the sea with his staff so that Israel may cross it dry-shod, but the returning waves drown the pursuing Egyptian army. All ancient peoples understood the symbolic meaning of immersion in water: dying to one's previous existence and emerging to a new life, a new identity. In Israel's case, the exodus makes them God's own people; YHWH becomes their God and they become his special possession, his "firstborn son" (Ex 4:22; Hos 11:1). Their mutual belonging to each other is sealed by the covenant at Sinai. If Israel obeys God's laws and ordinances, God promises life as well as copious blessings on the land he has already given Abraham and his offspring. From that point, Israel is the *qəhāl* YHWH, the gathering of those who were called by God to be "a kingdom of priests, a holy nation," to proclaim God's glorious deeds to all the nations and to offer sacrifices to him and obey his commandments (Ex 19:6). In the Septuagint, the Greek equivalent of the Hebrew term, *qəhāl YHWH*, is *ekklēsia tou theou*, and this becomes Paul's favorite phrase to designate the church. Ekklēsia is also the very word Jesus uses in the ecclesiastical discourse of Matthew 16:18 and 18:17. The event of

7. See Roch Kereszty, *Wedding Feast of the Lamb: Eucharistic Theology from a Historical, Biblical and Systematic Perspective* (Chicago: Hillenbrand Books, 2004), 9. This noble theoretical view, however, has not always translated into the same interior attitude of the sacrificers. Their false ritualism provoked the harsh reactions of the prophets and Jesus.

the exodus, as interpreted in Israel's sacred Scriptures, reveals the structure of the Paschal mystery and thus prepares for the understanding of Christ's passion and resurrection. Israel's subjection to slavery is a graphic symbol of humankind's slavery to sin from which no liberation by mere human means is possible. God alone can free Israel, and he alone can forgive humankind's sins, and grant freedom and new life. Just as Moses descended to the bottom of the sea and led Israel into a new life, so does Jesus descend into death only to rise to a glorious existence and draw the new people of God to follow him into death and new life. Israel wanders in the desert before entering the promised land; the church marches through the desert of this world toward eternal rest in God's kingdom. The exodus took place within the confines of the world's history, but the Paschal mystery of Jesus Christ takes the church into the eschatological future, which transcends the dimensions of our spatiotemporal universe. As a result of the first Passover, the blood of the Lamb has saved the life of the firstborn of the Israelites; in Jesus' Passover, his blood saves us from eternal death and introduces us into God's own trinitarian life. Thus, memorializing the exodus in Christian liturgy is essential for our understanding of the Easter celebration. This pairing of promise and fulfillment, figure and reality, reveals the fidelity of God to his covenant. Through the exodus we can also understand the way God shapes and forms the individual believer. He first saves us from physical annihilation and then bestows upon us tangible gifts so that we believe that he will save us from spiritual self-destruction and introduce us into the kingdom of his Father. But most importantly, we discover here that the inner attitude of the Israelites and Christians could, in their basic nature, be one and the same. We both should have faith in God's almighty love that saves us from certain death and gives us life.

The Kingdom of David and the Kingdom of God

The conquest of Canaan was not a triumphant blitzkrieg, but rather the result of protracted battles with the inhabitants of the land, a roller coaster of defeats and victories. Israel had to learn that her destiny totally depended on obedience to God. If they called on him in faith, he liberated his people again and again through the judges, his chosen temporary leaders; but he allowed them to be defeated whenever the judges or the people themselves sinned against him. Israel's vicissitudes anticipated the spiritual struggles of the church, her history of flourishing and decline, her spring and winter, all of which depended on the faithful obedience of the leaders and the people or their lack thereof.[8]

At their best, the people understood that Israel differed from any other nation because God alone was their king, who ruled them through his law and his prophets. Yet God listened to the popular demand for a king and told his prophet Samuel to give them one, Saul (1 Sm 8:1–22; 10:1–27). However, God expected the kings of Israel to rule not in their own names, but as his visible representatives, the anointed ones of YHWH. Eventually, God rejected Saul because of his disobedience and told Samuel to anoint David, the youngest son of Jesse (1 Sm 15:1–35). David, then, became the ideal king who united all the twelve tribes into one nation, occupied Jerusalem, and made it his residence as well as the residence of the ark of the covenant. Regardless of his sins, God did not withdraw his favor from David but promised his dynasty a permanent kingship for all ages. Thus David became for Israel the embodiment of God's faithfulness to his covenant and the image of the future Anointed of the Lord, the messianic king who would usher in a paradisiac age of peace and God's rule over all the nations. Yet even David's own, initially wise son, Solomon, sowed the seeds of the nation's disintegration by oppressing the people and allowing idolatry in the land.

After Solomon's death, only Judah remained faithful to the dynasty of David. The rest of the people, the northern kingdom, fell away from the pure worship of YHWH, and eventually it was conquered and a large portion of the population deported from their land by Assyria in 726 BC.

The kingdom of Judah had a few faithful kings among several corrupt rulers, but it survived until the destruction of Jerusalem and the Babylonian exile in 587 BC. Ultimately the institution of royalty proved to be a disaster for Israel because the kings and the people were unwilling to fulfill the obligations of the Sinai covenant. Despite the repeated warnings of the prophets to trust only in God's protection and stay out of the power struggles of Egypt, Assyria, and Babylon, Israel's kings entered into fateful alliances with one power against the other, leading to the destruction of Jerusalem in 586 and the mass deportation of the Jews to Babylon. Thus the royal rule of the dynasty of David came to an inglorious end. His sons slaughtered

8. Most of the book of Judges describes these vicissitudes.

before his eyes and his eyes gouged out. Zedekiah, the last king of Judah, died in Babylonian captivity. Israel would never again become a political kingdom.[9]

However, the suppression of political independence was part of God's plan and served as a purification for Israel. Under the pressures of the exile, she was forced to become nothing more and nothing less than a cultic assembly (*qəhāl YHWH*) of God's holy people, chosen to listen to God's word and worship him as she did during the long forty years of wandering in the desert.

When King Zedekiah and his princes blindly trusted in God's protection and defied the king of Babylon, the prophets Jeremiah and Ezekiel predicted doom, death, and destruction. Yet in the face of the people's awareness of their manifold breaches of the covenant and their loss of hope in any future restoration after the exile, the prophets announced a new intervention by God that would be more glorious than anything that had happened before:

Thus, the word of the LORD came to me: Son of man prophesy against the shepherds of Israel.... "Woe to the shepherds of Israel who have been pasturing themselves!... You have fed off their milk, worn their wool, and slaughtered the fatlings, but the sheep you have not pastured...."

For thus says the Lord GOD: "I myself will look after and tend my sheep. As a shepherd tends his flock when he finds himself among his scattered sheep, so will I tend my sheep.... The lost I will seek out, the strayed I will bring back, the injured I will bind up, the sick I will heal... shepherding them rightly. (Ezek 34:1–3, 11–12, 16)[10]

This direct rule of God himself, announced by both Ezekiel and Jeremiah, also included a major role for a servant of God and a prince from David's line:

I will appoint one shepherd over them; he shall pasture them, my servant David; he shall pasture them and be their shepherd. I, the LORD, will be their God, and my servant David shall be prince in their midst. I, the LORD, have spoken. (Ezek 34:23–24; cf. Zec 9:10)

As Israel's political weight continued to shrink in the Middle East and her religion itself was threatened by extinction under Antiochus Epiphanes

9. See the rest of 1–2 Samuel and 1–2 Kings.
10. Cf. Zep 3:17–20; Pss 93; 97; 98; 99.

in the late Second Temple period, Israel's expectations increased in boldness and transcended the limits of history. The apocalyptic literature of the time hoped for a new age to come at the end of history when God's kingdom would be established. The boldest vision of this in the canonical literature is found in the book of Daniel. The Ancient One, God himself, pronounces judgement over four consecutive world powers, the Babylonian, Median, Persian, and Hellene empires. Furthermore, he will hand over the kingship, dominion, and majesty of all the kingdoms to "one like a son of man," who seems to be both one person and the "holy ones of the Most High," the eschatological Israel at the end of times (Dn 7:1–27). The kingship of the son of man and the holy people will be indestructible and everlasting.

In Jesus, an offspring of David (through adoption by Joseph), all the different threads of prophecies about him and his kingdom are synthesized. He accepts the triumphant acclamations of the crowd at his solemn entry into Jerusalem: "Blessed is the kingdom of our father David that is to come" (Mk 11:10). At the same time, he orders Peter to put back his sword into its sheath and willingly surrenders himself to his captors. The kingdom of the son of David is not of this world because in the person of Jesus God's kingdom has drawn near to Israel. In contrast to his father David, Jesus is enthroned on the cross as the king of Israel and of the entire world (Jn 19:20–22).[11] When he is lifted up on the cross and rises from the dead, those who believe in him will recognize his deepest identity. This tortured, naked, dying human being is "I AM," the God of Israel and of the entire world. From the time of his crucifixion and resurrection, he is the glorious Son of Man who is to come in judgment throughout history, discernible only through the eyes of faith, but gazed on openly and gloriously at the end of the age.

The church of the New Testament participates in the destiny of her King. She is put to death over and over again in her martyrs throughout the ages. (Their number in our age greatly surpasses their number in the first centuries.) But she rises time and again to new life, her saints acting as leaven in the dough, humanizing and uniting the nations of the world.

11. Or better, he is the king of the world qua the king of Israel since his kingship is officially announced through the Aramaic, Greek, and Latin inscription to the entire world: "Jesus the Nazorean, the King of the Jews" (Jn 19:20–22).

The People of the Covenant

At Mount Sinai, God enters into a covenant with Israel, or rather gives her the terms of a covenant. For his part, God accepts the obligation to bring the people into the promised land and to assure their peace and prosperity as long as Israel fulfills her obligation of keeping the law of the covenant that governs all aspects of her life. God sets Israel apart as a holy nation whose vocation is to praise God and stir up all the nations to join in worshiping Israel's God. The covenant is sealed when Moses splashes the blood of sacrificed bulls on the altar and the people. He declares: "This is the blood of the covenant" (Ex 24:8). Here, an archaic way of entering a symbolic blood-kinship within a tribal community is brought to a higher level. The sharing of the same blood between the altar and the people symbolizes God graciously granting a share of "consanguinity" with himself. Israel becomes God's people and God becomes Israel's God. This first covenant, however, only establishes the law, the way of life that fulfills the will of God. But the law does not by itself communicate the grace to fulfill it. Israel's whole history can be envisioned as a series of breaches of the covenant. She turns to alien gods, sheds much innocent blood, and the rich in her midst exploit the poor. In the words of Joseph Ratzinger:

> All the glory of the cult is of no avail if its condition, the observation of the *whole* Law, does not take place. This has never happened and will not happen because no human being is *wholly* good. If salvation depends strictly and exclusively on the fulfillment of moral obligations, no salvation is possible for humankind (Rom 4:14).[12]

God gave Israel this first covenant, which depended on legal obligations, to teach her insufficiency and to stir up within her a desire for his intervention, mercy, and forgiveness. Thus the Torah has served as a guide for leading Israel to Christ (see Gal 3:24). Aware of their inability to fulfill the law, the just men and women of the Old Testament prayed for deliverance from sin and death, and by doing so they received the grace of Christ before the coming of Christ (Jer 31:31–34; cf. Ezek 36:25–27). Led by this grace, these people of the Old Testament along with Christian believers have discovered that the law is a light burden, a concrete source of grace, a delight and a privilege. They and we understand that Christ did not come

12. Joseph Ratzinger, *Das neue Volk Gottes: Entwürfe zur Ekklesiologie* (Düsseldorf: Patmos Verlag, 1969), 254.

to abolish the law but to reveal its full depth and meaning as the concrete realization of the love of God and love of neighbor.

In Matthew's Gospel, which was addressed to Jewish Christians, Jesus announced that his blood is the blood of the covenant to be shed for many unto the forgiveness of sins. By using the very words of Moses ("this is my blood of the covenant"),[13] Jesus revealed that the blood of bulls splashed by Moses on the altar and the people was the sign of his own blood that he would shed on the cross the very next day. It is by participating in Christ's eucharistic blood that Jesus' disciples truly share in what the Sinai sacrifice anticipated, the divine life of the Son of God.[14]

As fulfillment of the old rite, this eternal unconditional commitment of the Son of God to nourish us with his own life was so radically new that Paul and Luke referred to it with the phrase of Jeremiah, the "new covenant."

Israel as Son of God

In addition to being a covenant partner with God, God called Israel to be his son and bride. Individual Israelites did not dare to call God their father, but addressed him as their Lord, king, and master. But God at times referred to the people as his son, or even his firstborn son. The words Moses addressed to Pharaoh in God's name reveal how dear his firstborn son is to YHWH: "Israel is my son, my firstborn. Hence, I tell you: let my son go that he may serve me. If you refuse to let him go, I warn you, I will kill your son, your first-born" (Ex 4:22–23). Through the prophet Hosea, God laments the absence of gratitude in his son, whom he has called out of Egypt:

> When Israel was a child, I loved him,
> out of Egypt I called my son.
> The more I called them,
> the farther they went from me,
> Sacrificing to the Baals
> and burning incense to idols.
> Yet it was I who taught Ephraim to walk,
> who took them in my arms;
> but they did not know that I cared for them.

13. This is the Markan-Matthean version (Mk 14:24; Mt 26:28). Luke and Paul have "new covenant in my blood" (Lk 22:20; 1 Cor 11:25), a reference to Jer 31:31.

14. This does not imply that Moses understood the full meaning of his words, which could only be fully understood in their fulfillment.

I drew them with human cords,
with bands of love.
I fostered them like those
who raise a child to their cheeks;
I bent down to feed them. (Hos 11:1–4; cf. Jer 3:19)

God also adopts the dynasty of David as his sons in a special way. Although they will be severely chastised for their sins, the royalty of David's offspring is promised to last until the end of time (see 2 Sm 7:14; 1 Chr 17:13; Ps 2:6–12). When the New Testament applies the title "Son of God" to Jesus, its meaning not only includes but also transcends both the sonship of the entire people (Mt 2:15) and the Davidic kings (Heb 1:5). The only-begotten Son of God, one with the Father, embodies and fulfills in himself both the vocation of the son of David and of the people of Israel.

Israel as Bride of God

Some of the same books of the Old Testament that speak about the father-son relationship between God and Israel also identify Israel as the bride or spouse of God. The juxtaposition of the filial and marital relationships of Israel to God makes it clear that neither one of them should be interpreted in a physical sense (see Jer 3:19–20; Hos 1:1–3:1; 11:1–4). However, the importance of the spousal imagery prevails over that of the father-son relationship. The entire history of Israel can be seen as the history of a love affair between YHWH and Israel. The peoples surrounding Israel worshiped both gods and goddesses, and conceived of fertility as a divine power. They practiced sacred prostitution in order to assure a share in the divine power of sexual fertility. In contrast, Israel's sacred books treated sexuality as a quality created by God. YHWH, then, has no need for a female partner in the work of creation. He is above sexuality. Even though he is referred to in the masculine as "he," he is also endowed with feminine qualities. He loves his people with a "womb love," more tender and more enduring than the love of a mother for her child. But once God's transcendence from sexuality is understood, the prophets begin to speak about the relationship between Israel and God not only in terms of created-Creator, servant-Master, and son-Father, but also as bride and Bridegroom. Clearly, YHWH does not need Israel to complement him, but out of his sovereign freedom, he chooses Israel as his bride and pursues her escapades into idolatry with the possessive love of a jealous bridegroom. Two books of the Old Testament especially reveal in a beautiful way these divine-human love adventures. Regardless of its original intent, the Song of Songs was soon read by Israel as an allegorical love story about YHWH and his people. In the book of Hosea, the very life of the prophet Hosea becomes a parable or allegory in action. At God's command he takes a harlot wife and their relationship demonstrates God's enduring love for Israel, who frequently commits adultery by worshiping alien gods (Hos 1:2–3; 3:1–2). God acts as a jealous lover, blocking his wife's escape routes with thorns and erecting a wall around her so that she cannot find her former lovers. Then he lures her into the desert:

> There she will respond as in the days of her youth,
> as on the day when she came up from the land of Egypt.
> On that day—oracle of the LORD—
> You shall call me "my husband,"
> and you shall never again call me "my Baal." (Hos 2:17–18)

Then the messianic wedding feast will begin and YHWH will address her wife with these words:

> I will betroth you to me forever:
> I will betroth you to me with justice and with judgment,
> with loyalty and with compassion;
> I will betroth you to me with fidelity,
> and you shall know the LORD. (Hos 2:21–22)

Only against this Old Testament background can we grasp the full weight of Jesus' statement in answer to the question of the Baptist's disciples:

> "Why do we and the Pharisees fast, but your disciples do not fast?" Jesus answered them, "Can the wedding guests mourn as long as the bridegroom is with them? The days will come when the bridegroom is taken away from them, and then they will fast." (Mt 9:14–15)

The boldest hopes of the prophets have been fulfilled. In Jesus, YHWH himself is present and celebrates the messianic wedding feast. Only after his crucifixion and resurrection will the apostles understand that the bride is the renewed people of God, the remnant of Israel united with the converted multitude of the gentiles. She has been washed clean and created anew on the cross by the divine bridegroom's sacrifice (Eph 5:25–32).

Israel, Servant of God

All individuals and all peoples, even, Pharaoh and Nebuchadnezzar, as well as Cyrus of Persia, serve God's purposes, whether they know it or not, or whether they will it or not. Israel, however, is chosen to consciously and obediently carry out God's plan of salvation. The patriarchs, Moses, David, Elijah, and the other prophets are elected to be God's servants in a special way because their mission is to teach Israel to obey the Lord's will. Yet, from the beginning, more often than not Israel rebels and refuses to serve. Despite one instance when Moses doubted God's word, he is the most trusted and effective servant of God, his chosen instrument to liberate Israel from Egypt and mediate the Sinai covenant. When God wants to exterminate his rebellious people and make Moses's offspring into a new people, Moses pleads with God time and time again. He even lies prostrate in expiation for forty days and forty nights to avert the God's rage. At Moses's intercession, God relents in his anger and has mercy on Israel. Moses's intercession both prefigures and explains the intercessory sacrifice of Jesus. Moses shows his full solidarity with his sinful people by taking the extreme step of asking God to punish him along with the sinners: "If you would only forgive their sin. If you will not, then strike me out of the book you have written" (that is, from the book of your intimate friends; Ex 32:32).

There are four mysterious songs in Deutero-Isaiah in which God's servant is both Israel and an individual.[15] In the figure of this Servant, Israel's prophetic and priestly vocation is presented in a way that expresses more clearly than any other Old Testament text the mission of Jesus in whom Israel reaches its final eschatological state. Nonetheless, Jesus never designates himself explicitly as the servant. His characteristic self-designation is "Son of Man." But according to Jesus, to be glorified, the Son of Man must fulfill the destiny of the Suffering Servant.

The Servant was chosen by God and his favor rested on him. God formed him in the womb, he gave him a name from his mother's womb, and he put his spirit on him. The Servant's vocation was not just to return a remnant of Israel to the Lord, but, more importantly, to be a light to the nations so that God's salvation might reach to the ends of the earth (Is 42:1–6; 49:1–6). He was to open the eyes of the blind, to bring out prisoners from

15. Is 42:1–9; 49:1–6; 50:4–11; 52:12–53:12.

confinement and darkness, and to establish God's justice over all the earth (42:4.7). God would give a covenant to his people in the person of his Servant (42:1, 6).

The Servant had the tongue of a disciple (50:4). God opened his ear morning after morning so that he might hear God's Word (50:5). Thus the Servant was like a sharp-edged sword, an arrow in God's quiver (49:2).

He fulfilled his vocation without any great publicity or ostentation (42:2). He was merciful:

> A bruised reed he shall not break
> and a smoldering wick he shall not quench. (42:3)

Yet his work called forth opposition, hatred, and torture. But he continued to obey God's call and perform his work. He did not return violence for violence. He gave his back to those who beat him and his cheeks to those who plucked his beard. Nor did he turn away from the buffets and spitting (50:5–6). Even though his life and work seemed to be a complete failure, he always trusted in God (50:9–10).

He was disfigured beyond human appearance, to the point that people spurned and avoided him because they thought his suffering and humiliation were due to God's just punishment (52:14; 53:3). But in reality, he was innocent (53:9), and, as a lamb led to slaughter, he remained silent before his accusers and voluntarily submitted to the punishments we ourselves deserve for our sins (53:7–8). "The LORD put upon him the guilt of us all" (53:6). He was condemned (by a court) and put to death, and it seemed that his fate would be forgotten (53:8). A grave was assigned to him among evildoers (53:9). Yet, since he gave his life as a sacrifice for sin and interceded for sinners, the saving will of God was to be accomplished through him (53:10). Because of his voluntary sacrifice, the Servant was to take away the sins of many, including those of the gentiles.[16] He would be exalted by God to the heights, and would see the light and his descendants in a long life (52:13; 53:10–11).[17]

If we keep in mind that the Old Testament leader embodies his entire people, then the leader's actions and sufferings are in some way attribut-

16. Note that the "many" in 53:12 and 52:14–15 are parallel, and therefore the "many" in 53:12 includes also the gentiles. Cf. Ben F. Meyer, "The Expiation Motif in the Eucharistic Words: A Key to the History of Jesus?," *Gregorianum* 69, no. 3 (1988): 477–478.

17. Most of the text on the Servant is taken from my *Jesus Christ: Fundamentals of Christology*, updated ed. (New York: St. Pauls, 2011), 159–60.

ed to the people. In Jesus, then, the rising of the Suffering Servant as the glorious Son of Man in some sense shows that Israel has suffered for her sins and has risen to a new life. Jesus' resurrection and glorification prophesy and anticipate the resurrection and glorification of the eschatological Israel.

CHAPTER 2

Church in the New Testament

Jesus and the Church

Mark summarizes the message of Jesus in these terms:[1]

This is the time of fulfillment. The kingdom of God is at hand. Repent, and believe in the gospel. (1:15)

As we have seen in the previous chapter, the history of Israel from its beginning appears as a series of divine promises and human disobediences, followed by a sequence of divine chastisements, and Israel's short-lived repentance. What is humanly inexplicable is the fact that, in spite of Israel's repeated breaches of the covenant, God's promises become more and more spectacular and Israel's expectations more grandiose. The Prophets and the Psalms announce not only a new Davidic king, but also the coming of God himself to rule over his people in peace. The apocalyptic texts declare that God's presence will bring an end to history, collapse our world in flames, and usher in a new world.[2] They were, however, divided over what will usher in the kingdom. The alternatives were fierce battles followed by a final victory: a miraculous conversion of Israel to the point that all of the people keep the Torah and thus compel God's coming; or a cosmic upheav-

1. Joachim Gnilka, ed., *Neues Testament und Kirche: [Festschrift] für Rudolf Schnackenburg* (Freiburg: Herder, 1974); Joachim Gnilka, *Wie das Christentum enstand* (Freiburg: Herder, 2004); Gerhard Lohfink, *Jesus and Community* (Minneapolis: Fortress, 1984); Lohfink, *Does God Need the Church? Toward a Theology of the People of God* (Collegeville, Minn.: Liturgical Press, 1999); Heinrich Schlier, "Ekklesiologie des Neuen Testaments: Das Heilsgeschehen in der Gemeinde Jesu Christi," in *Mysterium Salutis*, Vol. 4/1, *Das Heilsgeschehen in der Gemeinde*, ed. Wolfgang Beinert et al. (Einsiedeln: Benziger, 1972), 101–221; Raymond E. Brown and John P. Meier, *Antioch and Rome: Cradles of Catholic Christianity* (New York: Paulist, 1983).

2. See, for instance, Is 66; Dn 4–13; Zec 12–14, and the many apocalypses in the intertestamental period.

al that destroys all God's enemies and the entire old world. These were the dreams of Jesus' listeners, which explain their initial enthusiasm and their later disappointment with him. When the crowd wanted to make him king after the multiplication of the loaves, Jesus abandoned them (Mt 14:22–23; Jn 6:14–15). He refused to perform any grand cosmic sign and sought out the notorious sinners rather than associating with the law-abiding Pharisees.

What, then, was the kingdom Jesus proclaimed? It turned upside down all the expectations of Israel. He refused to become a warrior king or to perform a great heavenly sign. It was not earned by the good deeds of law-abiding Pharisees, but was offered as an undeserved gift to the poor, to those who mourn, to the meek, to those thirsting for holiness, to the merciful, and to the clean of heart, the peacemakers, the persecuted, the repentant sinners and lawbreakers.[3]

Jesus proclaimed that the time of fulfillment had come, that God's promises were being fulfilled here and now. In a discussion with his adversaries, Jesus pointed out: "If it is by the Spirit of God that I drive out demons, then the kingdom of God has come upon you" (Mt 12:28; cf. Lk 11:20) The kingdom of God is thus the hidden yet powerful presence of God in Jesus, forgiving sins, restoring wholeness and life to all those who accept him in faith. Surprisingly, the greatest resistance to Jesus was provoked by his love for sinners. Because he reached out to those beyond the religiously motivated social boundaries, he unsettled and upset not only the religious hypocrites but also the average, law-abiding, devout Jew, who walked the paths of righteousness and avoided the ways of the wicked. Jesus not only allowed sinners to come to him, as John the Baptist did, but he actively pursued them. He did not merely forgive their sins, but accepted table fellowship with them. Jesus' God pays the same amount to the worker hired in the last hour of the day (the sinner who repents now) as he does to the one who endured the burden and the heat of the day (the law-abiding Pharisee or Essene: Mt 20:1–15). God's love is like that of a foolish shepherd who leaves the ninety-nine sheep in order to search for the one that has been lost (Mt 18:12–14; Lk 15:4–7).[4] God is like the woman who, for the sake of

3. See Mt 5:1–12; Lk 7:36–50; 15:1–32; 19:1–10; 23:39–43.

4. Note that the Gospel of Thomas adds: "one of them went away; it was the largest" (quoted by Pheme Perkins, *Hearing the Parables of Jesus* [New York: Paulist, 1981], 30). This added remark destroys the original meaning, which shows that God's love goes after anyone who is lost: it is both gratuitous and universal.

one lost coin, sweeps every corner of the house and is not satisfied until she finds it. He is like the father watching the road for his son who had squandered his share of the family inheritance; when he spots him, he forgets his dignity, runs to meet him, and embraces and kisses him. He does not even wait until the son finishes his confession of sins before he has the finest robe put on his child and orders a splendid banquet to celebrate his return to life (Lk 15:1–32).

This festive banquet to which both the repentant sinner and the law-abiding Pharisee (who is in worse shape than the former, since he resents the Father's generosity toward his repentant brother) are invited is the central image of the kingdom (Mt 8:11; Lk 13:28; 14:15–24). The way to Jesus' *metanoia*, a complete change of heart and way of life, begins by accepting this invitation to God's banquet, which includes our grateful acceptance of God's forgiveness of our sins and our adoption of God's forgiving love toward those who have sinned against us. If we do not imitate God's forgiveness toward those who have offended us, God will deny us the forgiveness of our own sins (Mt 18:21–35). Thus love of the enemy becomes the most characteristic attitude of those who have undergone *metanoia*. Only in this way can they "prove" that they have understood and accepted the love of God, who "makes his sun rise on the bad and the good, and causes rain fall on the just and the unjust" (Mt 5:45).

Another aspect of *metanoia* is to become "like little children."[5] Children know they cannot support themselves, that they depend upon their parents for everything. They trust in their parents' care regardless of what happens and are convinced that their parents are able and willing to do what is best for them. Thus unconditional trust, love, and a joyful surrender to God as one's Father and a grateful acceptance of the kingdom as pure gift characterize the disciple of Jesus.

Those who are materially poor, hungry, and grieving are called "blessed" by Jesus, because wealth, self-satisfaction, and pleasure do not blind them to their need for God's kingdom. The poor are "at the end of their rope," or, to quote Marx's dictum: "They can lose only their chains." In other words, they don't have a stake in their present status. They don't have an excuse for refusing the invitation. Their misery helps them to cry out to God and

5. John shows the ontological aspect of this becoming like little children. It is a new birth from water and the Holy Spirit (Jn 3:3–8).

to trust in him, since everything else has failed them. In that very moment when they do so, the kingdom of God becomes theirs (Lk 6:20–21).[6]

The guests at the banquet of the kingdom of heaven are those who have accepted the undeserved invitation and have been reborn as little children. All alienation and hostility have been banished from among them, and they enjoy an intimate communion with God and with each other as children of the same family.[7] The anticipation of this heavenly banquet takes place at the Last Supper, where Jesus offers himself to the Father for the forgiveness of our sins and distributes himself as food to the twelve apostles in the form of bread and wine. This giving of the self, carried out under the signs of bread and wine in the Eucharist, is consummated the next day on the cross with Jesus' last breath. He can become true food and true drink for us because he has become a true gift to the Father in his divine-human psychosomatic self. Thus, throughout the church's history the Eucharist will be the center of the hidden presence of the kingdom.

The Eucharist is entrusted to the twelve disciples. The great importance for Jesus of the institution of this group of twelve is made clear in Luke's version: Jesus spent the entire night in prayer before he chose the Twelve from among his disciples (Lk 6:12–16). Mark's version is more concise: "He went up the mountain and summoned those whom he wanted and they came to him. He appointed [literally "made"] twelve that they might be with him and he might send them forth to preach and to have authority to drive out demons" (Mk 3:13–14). The number twelve reveals Jesus' intention. He makes them the patriarchs of the converted, a renewed Israel, each representing one of the twelve sons of Jacob and the tribe that issued from each. Since the ten tribes of the northern kingdom were deported by Assyria and virtually disappeared, the number twelve indicates that Jesus intends at this time to search out and gather together all the lost sheep of Israel. He knows that with his presence the end times have arrived, when God will restore all of Israel. Jesus chooses the Twelve with sovereign freedom unlike

6. I have followed here Luke's version of the beatitudes because it may be closer to the original wording by Jesus. According to Luke the materially poor are in a fortunate situation regarding the kingdom. Matthew's version, however, adds an important clarification: the materially poor enter the kingdom only if they become also spiritually detached from wealth and develop a hunger for God's justice and holiness (Mt 5:3–10). On the other hand, a rich man who is detached from his possessions and ready to share them with the poor also qualifies to be "poor in spirit" in Matthew's interpretation.

7. The previous few pages are excerpts from my *Jesus Christ: The Fundamentals of Christology*, new ed. (New York: Alba House, 2002), 113–15. From the immense literature on Jesus and the kingdom, see Walter Kasper, *Jesus the Christ* (New York: Paulist Press, 1976), 72–88; Ben F. Meyer, *The Aims of Jesus* (London: SCM, 1979), 111–253.

the usual rabbinic practice whereby the disciple chooses the rabbi under whom he will study. The purpose of the election is twofold: to be with Jesus and to be sent out to preach. They are not only to learn from him but also to share his life, his days and nights, his wanderings and homelessness. Only then will they be ready to be sent out to preach the good news, the *euangelion*, and to perform healings and drive out evil spirits. This last task, no matter how absurd it sounds in our age, constitutes an essential part of proclaiming the kingdom of God in power. This includes not only the exorcism of the manifestly possessed people, but also liberating believers from the effects of Satan's dominion such as sin and suffering.

Jesus' original plan was to convert all of Israel so that she might become the center for all the nations who join her in the new, extended *qəhāl YHWH*. But as Israel's leading elite observe Jesus' table fellowship with sinners, his claim to have authority to forgive sins, his healings on the Sabbath, and his thorough reinterpretation the law of Moses, they turn against him. When Jesus hears about the execution of John the Baptist, he withdraws to a deserted place (Mt 14:13; cf. Mk 6:32). He must have realized at that point that his fate also had been sealed. The crowds follow him enthusiastically, yet following the first multiplication of loaves when they want to make him king, Jesus leaves them. He declines to become the messiah of a militant uprising. All four Gospels in some way or another show him breaking with the crowds and turning to the formation of his disciples. The conflict with the Pharisees sharpens, and Jesus focuses his attention on educating his disciples in the pagan territories of Tyre and Sidon (Mt 15:21; cf. Mk 7:24). No longer counting on the conversion of all Israel, he begins building his own *ekklēsia*, an assembly of those called by God from the remnant of Israel and from the gentiles. He bases his *ekklēsia* on the twelve disciples with Simon Peter as the rock (Aramaic, *kepha*) of foundation.

The events during his last pilgrimage to Jerusalem reveal the nature of Jesus' *ekklēsia*. By driving out the merchants and money changers from the temple, he denounces its perverted worship and predicts its destruction. Then he celebrates his last Passover meal with only the twelve disciples, because it is a covenant meal. There, Jesus fulfills the Sinai covenant by establishing the new covenant in his own blood.[8] Only the twelve patriarchs

8. Each Synoptic Gospel underlines the fact that Jesus celebrates the meal with the twelve disciples: Mt 26:20; Mk 14:17. Luke writes that "he reclined at table with the apostles." We know that for Luke only the Twelve are apostles.

of the new Israel may take part in it.[9] By giving the disciples his body to eat and his blood to drink, he turns his imminent death into the sacrifice of the new covenant to be celebrated by the disciples in his memory. Thus the center of Jesus' *ekklēsia*, his church, is the Eucharist, a celebration of the community remembering (in the biblical sense: "makes present") his death and resurrection and uniting themselves to Jesus' perfect self-offering. Joseph Ratzinger points out that if we combine the words of Jesus at the Supper with the kernel of truth in the charges of the false witnesses (who asserted that Jesus would destroy the temple and rebuild it in three days), we gain further insight into the nature and task of Jesus' *ekklēsia*. She is the new temple, consisting of the personal body of Jesus and the bodies of his faithful. This is the living new temple, not primarily a material place but the ecclesial body of Christ.

At the first Eucharist we also discern the relationship between the church and the Eucharist. Jesus solemnly announces that he will not drink from the fruit of the vine until he drinks it anew in the kingdom of God (Mk 14:25). In the light of his death on the next day, this means that through his death Jesus fully enters the kingdom of God, while his disciples, especially from Luke's perspective, only anticipate it in the eucharistic meal (Lk 22:16). This, then, is the relationship between church and kingdom: The church tends toward the kingdom and enters into it "in mystery" whenever she receives—under the veil of the consecrated bread and wine—Christ, who has already fully entered into it.

In this way, the church was established at the Last Supper, but she begins her mission only after Jesus' resurrection and the descent of the Holy Spirit. The New Testament makes it clear that, by the Holy Spirit, the disciples receive the very authority (*exousia*) Jesus has received from his Father and that the outpouring of the Spirit will make the hearts of listeners accept their words as disciples of Jesus (see Mt 28:18–20; 1 Jn 2:24–27).

The Ecclesiology of Matthew

Every document of the New Testament presupposes the existence of the church and is a product of the church. The form-critical approach to the Gospels, recently renewed by the studies of Denis Farkasfalvy, has shown

9. Matthew and Mark speak about the "blood of the covenant" rather than "new covenant," since, from their perspective, the new covenant is the fulfillment of that of Sinai.

that the pericopes of the Gospels were first narrated, shaped, and reshaped within the eucharistic gatherings of the apostolic church and only later did the evangelists redact these smaller units into coherent narratives. Therefore, each narrative presents the sayings and deeds of Jesus insofar as they are relevant to the apostolic church and, at the same time, reflect the ecclesial milieu in which the pericopes were formed and handed on. In this fundamental sense, each Gospel is ecclesial. Yet the Gospels according to Matthew and to John more explicitly retroject the church of their time into the life situations of the time of Jesus. Conversely, these two Gospels show how the church of their time (and of all time) is fundamentally identical with the community of the disciples of Jesus.

In particular, Matthew has the crucified and risen Lord remaining present and active in the church until the end of this age. Through his disciples, Christ continues to forgive sins in her midst, drive out demons, heal, and raise people from the dead (Mt 8:14–15; 9:1–8). He remains the only teacher of his church, and his Sermon on the Mount, the fulfillment of the law of Moses, resounds in the church for all ages. He regulates her life and sets down the conditions of discipleship (Mt 16:24–28).

Because of his faith, Jesus chose Peter as the leader of the Twelve and the rock on which he will build his church (Mt 16:13–19). The rule of the Twelve over the church, the eschatological Israel, began in the *palingenesia*, the new age which dawned at the resurrection of the Lord (Mt 19:28).

Matthew wrote for Jewish Christians who were keeping the law of Moses. Jesus tells them to do and observe whatever the scribes and Pharisees tell them, but they should not follow their example (Mt 23:3). The righteousness of Jewish Christians should surpass that of the Pharisees; a righteousness that arises from their living of the beatitudes to the point of taking up their crosses and following Jesus. Only after his discovery of the Syrophoenician woman's great faith does Jesus turn to the pagans and perform for them the second multiplication of loaves.[10] After his resurrection, he explicitly expands his disciples' mission to all the nations after it had originally been limited to the lost sheep of Israel (Mt 28:19). Yet Jesus does not give up on Israel, although he does indict the scribes and Pharisees with a scathing sevenfold "Woe" and predicts that they will call on their

10. Moved by the Canaanite woman's faith, he healed her daughter and afterward large crowds flocked to him. He healed many of their sick so the crowd "glorified the God of Israel," indicating that they were predominantly pagans (Mt 15:21–31).

heads the guilt for the blood of all the righteous from the murder of Abel up to the recent killing of Zechariah. Foreseeing the destruction of the temple and the city, he shows his tender love for Jerusalem as he compares his love to that of a mother bird who wanted to gather her children under her wings (Mt 23:1–38). Yet, before he definitively abandons the temple, he declares: "I tell you, you will not see me again until you say, 'Blessed is he who comes in the name of the Lord'" (Mt 23:39). Jesus knows that his Father's eternal plan calls for him to rescue Israel from her sins and that this plan must be fulfilled. He knows he must shed his own blood for the forgiveness of the blood guilt of all Jewish and gentile generations (Mt 26:28).

In Matthew, the church is the kingdom of the Son of Man, where the children of the kingdom and the children of the evil one (the good seed and the weed) will live together until the end of history. Then the just will be transferred into the kingdom of the Father, where they will shine like the sun (Mt 13:43).

The Church in the Gospel of Luke and Acts

In Matthew and John, the time of the church is condensed so it coincides with the time of Jesus' public ministry and the Paschal mystery. Thus, salvation history has only two major periods: The time of promise, from Abraham to John the Baptist, and the time of fulfillment, from the conception of Jesus to his second coming. This view highlights one true aspect of the church's nature, namely, that what Jesus did and suffered (the *acta et passa Christi*, according to Aquinas) reaches all history and inserts itself—to varying degrees—into his ecclesial body and all those who are open to his transforming grace.[11]

Luke, however, divides salvation history into three periods by inserting the time of the church after Jesus' earthly ministry and passion-resurrection, and before his second coming. But even in Acts, the crucified and risen Lord is present and active through the Holy Spirit in his church. Nevertheless, Christ inspires and directs the church's leaders to become the responsible agents within the unfolding constitutive phase of church history.

The nucleus of the church exists before Pentecost. The leaders are clearly the eleven apostles. Peter is the first among the leaders, but very often

11. See Thomas Aquinas, ST III, preface.

he acts as if he were simply one of the Eleven. He organizes the election of Matthias in order to replace Judas. This shows the symbolic importance the apostles attached to the number twelve and the criteria of belonging to that select group. In addition to being a witness to the risen Lord, one of the Twelve had to be a disciple of Jesus from the baptism of John to his crucifixion, resurrection, and ascension. Therefore, Luke almost always applies the term *apostolos*, "the one who is sent," only to the Eleven (or twelve after the election of Matthias). As well as the apostles, approximately 120 other people, including Jesus' brothers and his mother Mary, stayed in the "upper room," where Jesus had celebrated the Last Supper. They persevered with one accord in prayer and expectation of the descent of Holy Spirit.

When the day of Pentecost came (the *shavuoth* feast of the Jews when the gift of the law is celebrated), the Holy Spirit descended on them in tongues of fire and as a strong, driving wind. And their audience, Jews and proselytes from many countries of the world who were at that time in Jerusalem, heard them speak in their native tongue as the Spirit enabled them to proclaim. At the building of the tower of Babel, God confused the languages of the proud builders so that no one could understand the other since they wanted to reach God by their own powers (Gn 11:1–9). At the Pentecost, the Holy Spirit did the opposite. He enabled everyone to understand the proclamation of the gospel and drew those who converted into one community. Just as in many other instances of the first twelve chapters of Acts, Peter fulfilled the role for which Jesus' prayer obtained the grace, namely, that after his conversion Peter might strengthen his brothers in the faith (Lk 22:31–32). He acted as the undisputed leader among the Twelve, explained to the crowd what was happening, and told those who were "cut to the heart" by his words to repent and be baptized in the name of Jesus. The uneducated fisherman suddenly showed a deep understanding of God's great deeds and weaved together into a convincing argument several prophetic texts of the Old Testament. Through Acts 12:17, Peter was the chief miracle worker, evangelist, and exegete and even the "chief financial officer" of the church as new members sold their property and handed over the money to the common fund of the community.[12]

In Acts, Luke describes the daily life of the community in two summaries. I quote the longer:

12. See Acts 4:5–21; 5:1–6, 15–16, 29–32; 8:20–24; 9:36–43; 10:9–49; 11:1–18; 12:1–17.

> They devoted themselves to the teaching of the apostles and to the communal life [*koinōnia*], to the breaking of the bread and to the prayers.[13] Awe came upon everyone, and many wonders and signs were done through the apostles. All who believed were together and had all things in common; they would sell their property and possessions and divide them among all according to each one's need. Every day they devoted themselves to meeting together in the temple area and to breaking bread in their homes. They ate their meals with exultation and sincerity of heart, praising God and enjoying favor with all the people. And every day the Lord added to their number those who were being saved. (2:42–47, cf. 4:32–37)

Evidently, the members of the Jerusalem church lived a very intense and joyful community life. They ate their meals "with exultation and sincerity of heart." In a parallel text they are said to have had "one heart and one soul" (4:32). They practiced a voluntary community of goods and gathered daily for prayers at the same place, the Solomon portico of the temple, and in private homes, where they participated in the "breaking of the bread," most likely a technical term for the Eucharist. The community was structured such that the apostles were the "official" teachers who explained the Christian faith in more detail and depth than was possible before baptism.

In addition to teaching the community, the apostles testified about Jesus to the people "with great power" and with "boldness" (*parrhēsia*). Their witness was full of assurance since they bore witness to what they have seen and heard (4:20) and the Holy Spirit himself confirmed their testimony (5:32).

The appearance of the risen Lord to Paul in Acts, his conversion, and his growing prominence as the most dynamic missionary indicate that Christ's church-constituting activity extends beyond the ascension and Pentecost, and was carried out through the life span of the apostles and their early disciples. In Acts, Luke upholds the complexity of Paul's position in the apostolic church as the sign of God's sovereign freedom vis-à-vis the budding "institutional church." Paul's missionary work becomes so widespread and effective that Luke centers the larger second part of his work (chapters 13–28) on Paul. The imprisoned Paul's arrival in Rome marks a providential turning point in the life of the church. At the explicit command of the risen Lord, her center has moved from Jerusalem to Rome. Since most of Israel

13. *Koinōnia* in the New Testament means the specifically Christian community life imbued by the Holy Spirit and nourished by *koinōnia*, the sharing of the eucharistic body and blood of the Lord. The fact that community life and communion in the Eucharist are expressed by the same term, *koinōnia*, shows that the Eucharist is constitutive of the Christian community.

rejected her Messiah, the church and, in particular, Paul turn to the gentiles. Paul is emphatic about being appointed and sent by the risen Christ himself, yet he places himself within the church structure, which was established by the earthly Jesus, but he is also evidence of the Lord's creative intervention during the church's foundational phase.

In spite of the rejection of Christ by a vast majority of Israel, Luke knows (just as Paul himself knew) that the eschatological future of Israel is not hopeless. The Virgin Mary and Simeon prophesied by the Holy Spirit and, therefore, their words must be fulfilled. In Jesus, God has come to the help of Israel his servant, and he will become the glory of his people (Lk 1:54; 2:32). When the apostles ask the departing Jesus: "Lord, are you at this time going to restore the kingdom to Israel?" Jesus' response implies a future restoration. He simply declines to specify the time: "It is not for you to know the times or seasons that the Father has established by his own authority" (Acts 1:6–7).

Acts also shows the beginnings of what later will be called the apostolic succession. As Paul and Barnabas travel through Lystra, Iconium, and Antioch, in each church and by the imposition of hands (14:23) they appoint presbyters to continue the apostles' ministry on the local level. Yet, when Paul speaks to the presbyters in Ephesus, he calls them *episkopoi*. The terms *presbyteros* and *episkopos* were synonyms in the second century (20:17, 28).

The narrative ecclesiology of Acts is of great importance for a better understanding of the genesis of the church. In spite of portraying a somewhat idealistic image of the Jerusalem church, Luke succeeds in showing that the church is not a mere human endeavor for it came into being through Jesus' missionary command and the Holy Spirit's guidance and inspiration. God's work cannot be destroyed by opponents and persecutors. Therefore, the history of the church is an integral part of salvation history and, once established in the apostolic age, its nature and structure may not be essentially changed by mere human initiative.

The Ecclesiology of the Johannine Writings

As with Matthew's and Luke's writings, the full breadth and depth of the ecclesiology in the Johannine writings will not be presented here. But an outline of John's work to the extent that it is indispensable for our understanding of the history of ecclesiology will be presented. Scholars disagree on the authorship of the Fourth Gospel, the three letters of John, and the book of Revelation. For our purpose, however, only the much less disputed fact matters. That is, there are remarkable similarities among the so-called Johannine writings, and this allows us to examine them en bloc.

Those who see in the church only an institution conclude that the Fourth Gospel has no ecclesiology. In fact, not even the word *ekklēsia* can be found in it. But if we concede that the Gospel of John was intended to be contemporaneous with the church, our assessment radically changes. The Fourth Gospel reveals the *Ineinandersein* (being within each other) of the mystery of Christ, the sacraments, and the church. In the first part of the Gospel, only seven signs are selected from the "works" of Jesus, and John sheds light on these by elaborating some of Jesus' words. The full meaning of John's "Book of Signs" is disclosed in the second part of John, where the Paschal mystery of Jesus' death and resurrection are presented. The patristic age and medieval monastic literature saw the special character of this "spiritual Gospel." Just as the Father reveals everything to Jesus, who rests in his bosom, Jesus does also to the beloved disciple, who rests on his breast at the Last Supper (Jn 1:18; 13:25). This Gospel in general, but especially chapters 13–17, introduces us into Jesus' inner life, his relationship to the Father, as well as to his disciples who believe in him and love him. He tells the disciples that if they love him, he and the Father will come and take their dwelling place within them. As a result, Jesus will love them as the Father loves Jesus and they shall love him and one another with this very love that comes to them through Jesus from the Father. In chapter 17 it becomes clear that this participation in the trinitarian life extends also to those who will believe in the disciples' testimony about Jesus.

The indwelling in the disciples will take place only after "a little while," but first Jesus must leave them. This "little while" will be a short period of weeping and mourning, similar to the labor of a woman giving birth who will forget the pain as soon as she sees that a man has been born into the world (16:19–21). In the perspective of John and the book of Revelation (Rv 12:1–2), this painful birth is Jesus' crucifixion and resurrection. Out of his sacrifice, the church is born. This is symbolized in the water and blood and the Spirit that Jesus releases with his last breath on the cross (Jn 19:30–37). After Jesus' death, the world will no longer see him, but the disciples will, because they will live and so will Jesus. This seeing, apparently, includes the visible encounters with the risen Lord and also the lasting vision of faith. In some real sense, the believer sees Jesus because he lives in him and is transformed by him (Jn 16:16–20, 22). Jesus' appearances after the resurrection are only short, visible manifestations in order to fully enkindle this inner vision of faith.

Jesus' return and presence within the disciples will take place through the Holy Spirit, who gives them comfort after the ordeal of the cross and becomes their advocate when they have to give an account of their faith. He will remind them of all that Jesus has done and said and will introduce them "into all truth." Thus the Spirit's revelation is no different from that of Jesus since he will take from what belongs to him (Jn 14:15–26; 16:4–15).

The boldest petition of Jesus from the Father extends explicitly to all believers in the entire church: "May [they] all be one, as you, Father, are in me and I in you, that they also may be in us, that the world may believe that you sent me" (17:21). Thus, one portion of the evidence that attests to the world the authenticity of Jesus' mission is the unity of the church, which manifests the unity of Father and Son. Those outside the church experience this in the love the disciples have for one another: "This is how all will know that you are my disciples, if you have love for one another" (13:35).

Thus the inward thrust of the Fourth Gospel does not end in an invisible, hidden church. Instead, the disciples' participation in trinitarian life and love becomes visible, authentic evidence of their authentic discipleship.

The eyewitness disciples (Jn 20:19–23, 29; 1 Jn 1:1–4) are sent to those who have not yet seen so that they can believe and in this way share in the communion with the Father and the Son. The entire future community of believers who have not seen has its foundation in the disciples who have seen and believed. The testimony of the latter as to what was made visible to them is confirmed by the invisible testimony in the hearts of the faithful by the Holy Spirit (Jn 14:15–20; 16:5–15; 1 Jn 2:20–27).

In John's Gospel, the entire mission of the disciples is summed up in the commandment to forgive and retain sins. This command cannot be restricted solely to the sacrament of reconciliation, but it certainly includes the sacrament. The paradoxical mission of Jesus, then, continues in the church. Jesus came not to judge, but to save all human beings, yet an encounter with him through the disciples ends up in judgment for those who reject him. Such an encounter separates those who believe in him from those who become hardened in their disbelief; those who come to the light from those who remain in darkness. The first group obtains forgiveness; the second remains in their sins. This separating judgment (*krisis*) and acquittal takes place among the hearers of the Gospel and also within the church as a community through public excommunication because of grave sins, only to be followed by reconciliation after repentance and penance have taken place.[14] Yet for God, the call to salvation is universal. The Son did not come to judge the world, but to save it. "When I am lifted up from the earth, I will draw everyone to myself" (Jn 12:32). Those who remain in the darkness of unbelief and hatred cause their own condemnation.

The book of Revelation is the only prophetic book in the New Testament. It sheds light on the entire history of the church from a heavenly perspective. On the one hand it is a gigantic battle between the forces of Satan and the devotees of the Lamb, but on the other it is a celebration of the splendid heavenly Eucharist, which climaxes in the wedding feast of the Lamb. The two stories do not follow one another sequentially, but rather they are simultaneous and causally connected.[15] This, then, is the heavenly liturgy and through it the blood of the Lamb obtains victory over Satan and all the kingdoms that served him. In the blood of the Lamb the martyrs wash their garments and are glorified in heaven. Thus the book of Revelation reveals the meaning of all of church history insofar as the heavenly Eucharist causes and anticipates the final victory of the Lamb. The end times of history are marked by two antithetical but apparently simultaneous banquets: the banquet of the Lamb and the great banquet of God. The central character in both is Christ.[16] In the former, he is the bridegroom of the wedding banquet (19:7, 9); in the latter, he is the King of kings and the Lord of lords who prepares a great slaughter feast for the birds of heaven by killing all God's enemies and defeating the "Beast" (19:11–21). Even though the wedding feast within the eucharistic celebration began in heaven and the outcome of the battle against the forces of Satan was decided on earth,

14. We learn about the practice of excommunication and readmission into the community of the church from Mt 18:15–18; 1 Cor 5:1–5; and 2 Cor 2:5–11.

15. Some of the liturgical passages: 4:2–5:14; 8:1–4; 14:1–5; 19:1–10; the drama of earthly history along with cosmic upheavals: 6:1–16; 8:5–21; 13:1–18; 14:8–18:24; 19:11–21. On the eucharistic meaning see Roch Kereszty, *Wedding Feast of the Lamb: Eucharistic Theology from a Historical, Biblical and Systematic Perspective* (Chicago: Hillenbrand Books, 2004), 79–90.

16. See the antithesis: *to deipnon tou gamou tou arniou* (the wedding banquet of the Lamb; 19:9) and *to deipnon to mega tou theou* (the great banquet of God; 19:17).

the Bride of the heavenly liturgy is still eagerly awaiting on earth the full visible appearance of the Bridegroom (22:17, 20).

In the Fourth Gospel, the presence of the Bridegroom and Bride are only briefly announced by John the Baptist. However, in the book of Revelation, as mentioned above, their presence plays an explicit and important role. She seems to be one subject (19:7, 9; 22:17), but also the city of the heavenly Jerusalem (21:2; 21:10). She seems to be at one and the same time descending from heaven to earth while also on earth longing for the coming of the Bridegroom from heaven. This complex imagery highlights the multiple dimensions of the mystery of the church. Her entire history centers on this dual process. On one hand, Christ, the Bridegroom, is constantly coming in every eucharistic celebration, and this marks the beginning of the wedding banquet. On the other hand, although the Bride as church has already begun the celebration, she is still being shaped and formed on earth and she longs for the definitive and manifest coming of her Groom.

At the end of the first century, when the Fourth Gospel was composed, the separation of the church and synagogue, and their mutual hostility, had already become a fait accompli. Even though John acknowledges that some Jews believed in Jesus, most of the time he means by the term "Jews" those Jews who opposed Christianity. Yet even in John Jesus emphasizes that "salvation is from the Jews" and, unlike the Samaritans, the Jews know whom they worship.

In chapter 12 of Revelation, the partial identity between the Old Testament people, the church, and Mary is symbolically revealed in the woman who is about to give birth. With the twelve stars on her crown, she is the people of the Old Testament, and the child who is born in painful travail is the royal Messiah of Israel (who will "shepherd the nations with an iron rod"). But she is also the church since she has other offspring: those who "keep God's commandments and bear witness to Jesus" (12:17). If the woman is both the Old Testament people insofar as she gives birth to the Messiah, then she must also signify Mary in whom Israel has fully realized her vocation by becoming the mother of the Messiah. However, her giving birth wailing aloud in pain is certainly not a reference to the joyful birth in Bethlehem. Because of the parallel text in John 16:2, André Feuillet believes that the painful birth pangs point to the Messiah's suffering and death, which completed his birth in Bethlehem. Through his death, he becomes the glorious king of Israel and of the whole world. Like Jesus' birth, so too Mary's motherhood is completed under the foot of the cross at the hour of Jesus' death. By accepting the last consequences of her "Yes" to Gabriel's message, she becomes, in the full sense of the word, the mother of the Messiah. Within the same process, God opens up her motherhood so wide as to embrace all believers, including the brothers and sisters of Jesus, as her own children. "Woman, behold your son," he says to Mary. And "Behold, your mother" to the beloved disciple who at the foot of the cross represents the disciples throughout all time (Jn 19:26–27). Thus Mary becomes the mother of the Messiah in the full sense of the word when she assents to being the mother of the Messiah's brothers and sisters, which is the church. But on the level of her motherly attachment, she had to fully give up her Son, so she could stretch out her love to the limit and embrace all believers.[17]

The words of the crucified Lord to his mother and the disciple he loved reveal to us the personal aspect of the church behind the institutional. As we have seen above, the beloved disciple John, the friend of Peter, symbolizes all the apostles, who received from Christ their commission to teach and to lead the faithful to Christ by celebrating the sacraments (the water pouring from Jesus' side signifying baptism, the blood, and the Eucharist). But before the apostle can start his mission, he must welcome the mother of Jesus "into his own" (*eis ta idia*), which means not merely receiving her into his home, but into all that is his, into his life, heart, and mind. He will live up to his apostolic task only to the extent that he makes Mary's motherly attitude his own. In fact, from St. Paul and St. Ambrose, all the way through to St. Bernard and John Paul II, the holy pastors of the church considered themselves fathers to their people and yet they also exhibited the tender heart of a mother who remains in travail until all her children are shaped and formed in Christ (see Gal 4:19).

The Ecclesiology of St. Paul

The Relationship of the Church to Israel

In Romans 9–11, Paul treats the theme of the church's relationship to Israel more extensively and more passionately than any other author in the New

17. For the foundation of this view in the Gospel text itself, see André Feuillet, "L'heure de la femme (Jn 16,21) et l'heure de la Mère de Jésus (Jn 19,25–27)," *Biblica* 47 (1966): 169–84, 361–80, 557–73.

Testament. He writes with "great sorrow and constant anguish" in his heart and would rather be himself accursed and separated from Christ if this would help the unbelieving Israelites, his kin according to the flesh (9:2–3). His main concern is to show that God's word, which was addressed to Israel through the words of the prophets, has not failed. Rather, the rejection of the gospel by the majority of Jews fits into both God's plan for salvation and his purpose of bestowing mercy on both Jews and pagans (11:32–36).

Paul explains that from the beginning of time, God chose the carriers of his promise not according to any fleshly line of descent, but according to his own sovereign choice. Not all who are of Israel are Israel. Not all of the descendants of Abraham are his children; only Isaac and Isaac' descendants are. Esau, the firstborn, is not; instead, Jacob is chosen (9:6–13). For this reason, God cannot be accused of injustice since, being the Creator, he is free to have mercy on whomever he wills and, conversely, harden the hearts of those he chooses (9:14–18).[18] Thus the situation Paul faces is not unusual, but rather in keeping with the general pattern of God's action. Throughout Israel's history, only a remnant of the people believed and been saved. Israel as a whole wanted to establish her own righteousness based on obedience to the law. And she failed (9:27–33).

The unbelief and the hardening of some of the people of Israel does not mean that God has rejected his people (11:1). "The gifts and the call of God are irrevocable" (11:29). They did not fall away from God's plan; they only "stumbled." In God's plan, their temporary unbelief leads to the salvation of the gentiles: "Through their transgression, salvation has come to the Gentiles to stir Israel to envy" (11:11). Paul knows that if Israel as a whole had converted to Christianity, the integration of the gentiles into the church would have been much more difficult because, in addition to the gospel, the gentiles would have had to accept the laws and culture of Israel.

Yet even under these circumstances, the believing gentiles have to be inserted into Israel as wild olive branches are grafted onto the noble olive tree. Although not entering into the ceremonial laws of Moses and Jewish culture, they would enter into the faith of Abraham, Isaac, and Jacob, and into the perennial holy remnant. We know from other texts of Paul that this "grafting unto Israel" does not mean adopting the practice of the Mosaic law, nor a racial or cultural assimilation into Israel, but a historic con-

18. Paul understands the phrase in Exodus in a sense that does not deny free will (see Ex 11:10).

tinuity and a spiritual identity with the destiny Israel received from God.

Thus Israel remains the original noble olive tree even though branches were cut from it because of unbelief and the gentiles, the wild olive branches, were grafted into it. These latter wild branches thrive off of the rich sap of the noble olive tree; in other words, their faith is enriched and deepened by sharing the sacred books and faith of historic Israel (11:17–24).

The unbelief of Israel is only temporary: "blindness has come upon part of Israel until the full number of Gentiles enters and then all Israel will be saved" (11:25–26). Paul does not specify what he means by "*pas Israēl* [all Israel]," so we can only surmise that it is the same Israel upon whom temporary unbelief and hardening fell. The following statement of Paul's does seem to confirm this interpretation: "If their transgression is enrichment for the world, and if their diminished number is enrichment for the Gentiles, how much more their full number." He also implies that their conversion will take place at the end of times: "For if their rejection is the reconciliation of the world, what will their acceptance be but life from the dead?" (11:15). Thus in God's plan everything serves as a reason for another bestowal of God's mercy on all humankind:

> Just as you [gentiles] were once disobedient to God and now have received mercy through their [Israel's] disobedience, so they have become disobedient—since God wished to show you mercy—that they too may have mercy. God has imprisoned all in disobedience that he might have mercy on all. (11:30–32)[19]

The Church of God in Christ Jesus

Paul does not use the term "people of God" (*laos theou*) as a designation for the church. The term occurs only twice (Rom 9:25–26 and 2 Cor 6:16) when Paul quotes Old Testament texts where they show the continuity and, in some sense, the identity between Israel and the church.

His favorite term for the church is *ekklēsia tou theou*, or in plural, *ekklēsiai tou theou* (1 Cor 1:2; 10:32; 11:16; 11:2; 15:9; Gal 1:13; 2 Thes 1:4). This term means the gathering of those who are called by God and so belong to God. In the Septuagint *ekklēsia* translates the Hebrew word *qāhāl*. It refers in the Old Testament to a sacred liturgical assembly, gathered by God's represen-

19. Not only Paul, but all major NT documents attest to the church's belief, which is based on Jesus' words, that the unbelief of Israel regarding Jesus is not definitive (Mt 23:37–39; Acts 1:7; Jn 11:51). He dies for the whole nation, and thus the nation of Israel cannot be definitively lost; moreover, he is enthroned over the whole world as the King of the Jews (Jn 18:33–19:22).

tative at God's command in order to listen to his voice and/or offer sacrifice to him. The first and defining *qāhāl-ekklesia* in the Old Testament took place at Mount Horeb, where, at God's command, Moses gathered the people to listen to the words of God that established the covenant and to worship him. After the exile, when Israel was refounded, Ezra orders an *ekklēsia*, a convocation or a quasi-second Mount Horeb assembly of all Israelites, men and women, to listen to the words of the law. During the long period of Israel's dispersion among all the nations, the Jewish prayer has included a supplication for a new gathering, a new *ekklēsia*. According to Joseph Ratzinger: "It is thus clear what it means for the nascent Church to call herself *ekklesia*. By doing so, she says in effect: 'This petition is granted in us. Christ, who died and rose again, is the living Sinai; those who approach him are the chosen final gathering of God's people.'"[20] The common element of the term's meaning in both Testaments emerges. It is an assembly called together by God's initiative to listen to God's word and worship him. What is radically new in Paul is the assembly's centeredness on Christ. The New Testament *ekklēsiai* are called and gathered together "in God the Father and the Lord Jesus Christ" (1 Thes 1:1). The preposition "in" (*en*) expresses a multiplicity of relationships to God the Father and Jesus Christ. Later in the same epistle Paul indicates the difference in the relationship to God and to Jesus Christ by writing: "the churches of God . . . in Christ Jesus" (1 Thes 2:14). The preposition *en* indicates the relationship of Jesus to the churches. He has acquired the churches for his Father and the churches worship the Father through the mediation of Christ. The center of this worship is the eucharistic gathering, which is the explicit meaning of *ekklēsia tou theou* in 1 Corinthians 11:22.

For Paul, then, the church is a communion of *ekklēsiai*, local communities, but not in the sense that these local communities would merely be parts of a whole, parts that together would make up the whole church. In every local community the one church of God is present and makes itself visible. For instance, the one and same church of God that is in Corinth (1 Cor 1:2) is also present and made visible in every other local community.[21]

For the Hellenistic communities, the term *ekklēsia* had an additional meaning. In the city-states *ekklēsia* referred to the official gathering of the

20. Joseph Ratzinger, *Called to Communion: Understanding the Church Today* (San Francisco: Ignatius, 1996), 31.

21. See Henri de Lubac, *Les églises particulières dans l'Église universelle* (Paris: Aubier Montaigne, 1971).

citizens in a *polis* for exercising their civic responsibilities.[22] The *ekklēsia* of the Christians does not compete with such secular gatherings, since their full rights of citizenship are in heaven (Phil 3:20). They live on earth as a "colony" of heavenly citizens in the new eschatological age where gentile Christians become fellow citizens with the saints, that is, with the members of the Jewish mother church in Jerusalem (Eph 2:12–19). Let their heavenly citizenship manifest itself in their daily lives so that they develop a certain inner freedom and detachment from the goods of this world: "Let those having wives act as not having them, those weeping as not weeping, those rejoicing as not rejoicing, those buying as not owning, those using the world as not using it fully. For the world in its present form is passing away" (1 Cor 7:29–31).

The Church as Body of Christ

We have seen that in Paul's mind the phrase "church of God" has a cultic, or more precisely, eucharistic connotation. The Christians are *ekklēsia* in the full sense of the word when they convene to celebrate the Eucharist (1 Cor 11:18, 22). Paul explains the relationship between the Eucharist and the community by showing that both are, in an analogous sense, the body of Christ (*soma Christou*), since, in the act of receiving his eucharistic body, Christians themselves become the body of Christ: "The bread that we break, is it not a participation in the body of Christ? Because the loaf of bread is one, we, though many, are one body, for we all partake of the one loaf" (1 Cor 1:16–17).[23] The fundamental meaning is: Christians are the body of Christ because they are united and conformed to the body-person of Christ.

But under closer examination, what is the meaning of the phrase "body of Christ"? In Hebrew thinking, the body is not one of two metaphysical principles (such as body and soul) that constitute human beings. Instead, the body is one's tangible, visible reality. It is in and through the body that people exist in the world, that they enter into relationships with others, that they act on the world and are acted on by it. The whole man is in his body, yet man is not simply equivalent to his body, since he has freedom over it and can oppose its tendencies. For instance, he can offer his body as

22. See this sense in Acts 19:32, 39–40.

23. Even though baptism already joins us to Christ's body, the Eucharist nourishes and builds up the ecclesial body of Christ (1 Cor 12:13).

a sacrifice (Rom 12:2), he can degrade it (1:24), he can express sin or justice in the body (6:12–13).

If we consider the analogy of the relationship of a human being to their body, we can better understand the relationship of Christ to his church. According to Heinrich Schlier, just as the body of man is man in his body, so the church as "body of Christ" is Christ in his body.[24] In other words, there is a real, albeit qualified, identity between Christ and the church. In and through the church Christ exists in this world, acts on others and suffers from others. More precisely, through the body of Christians, the real body-person of Christ is present and active in the world. Since the bodies of Christians are members of Christ, fornication is a sin against Christ's very body: "Do you not see that your bodies are members of Christ? Would you have me take Christ's members and make them the members of a prostitute? God forbid!" (1 Cor 6:15).

Yet Christ is not simply identical with his church. He also stands over against it. This is expressed in two ways in the Pauline writings. In Ephesians and Colossians, the phrase "Christ as the head of his body the church" expresses the distinction between him and the church. The image means that (1) Christ rules his church and the church is subjected to him (Eph 1:22); (2) as head, he is the principle out of which all life and growth comes into the church (Col 2:19); and (3) he is the goal toward which the church grows (Eph 4:15–16).

The analogy of head and body is clarified and enriched in another such analogy, the relationship of bridegroom and bride (2 Cor 11:2–3; Eph 5:21–32). This latter analogy shows that the unity of Christ and the church is not of nature but derives from a personal relationship of love. On the cross, Christ gave himself up to his bride, the church, "so that he might present to himself the church in splendor, without spot or wrinkle or any such thing, that she might be holy and without blemish" (Eph 5:27). The church, on her part, fully surrenders herself to Christ in love. Yet the combination of the bridegroom-bride and head-body analogies shows that the unity between Christ and the church is infinitely more real than between husband and wife, since the church as church is created by Christ and her entire life derives from him.

The church as body of Christ is a dynamic reality. In Christ the "fullness

24. Schlier, "Ekklesiologie des Neuen Testaments," 101–221.

of the divinity dwells bodily" (Col 2:9), but the church in this world is only on the road toward the fullness that is in Christ (Eph 3:19; 4:13).[25] Moreover, the church is the center that unites the whole universe in Christ. She is the "fullness of him who fills the universe in all its parts" (Eph 1:23; cf. 1:10; 4:10).

In a secondary sense the church as body of Christ means that the church is a social "organism" in which each member has a special charism to be used for the good of the whole (see Rom 12:1–8). This meaning is based on the Hellenistic-Roman idea of society as a body in which each member has an indispensable function for the whole of society.[26] This second meaning of the term is different from the first. The first explains the relationship of the entire church to Christ; the second, the different functions of the members, each cooperating for the good of the whole ecclesial body. According to the first meaning, the personal body of Christ extends his life to the Christians and makes them his own members. Christ infuses his virtues, and especially his love, into the members so that he works through them in the world, relates to those outside the church, and suffers himself in some real sense when the members suffer. Jesus asks Saul, "Why are you persecuting me?" instead of, "why are you persecuting the Christians?" (Acts 9:4). The second meaning of the church as body of Christ refers to relationships that Christians have with the ecclesial body rather than with Christ. In Paul's thought, however, these two aspects are connected and the second depends on the first. Since the body-person of Christ unites to himself, each body-person of a Christian, he assigns a different function for the good of the ecclesial body; for instance, to one an apostleship, to another prophecy, and to a third administration (see 1 Cor 12:1–12). The two meanings are joined together in 1 Corinthians 12:12–13: "As a body is one though it has many parts, and all the parts of the body, though many, are one body, so also Christ. For in one Spirit we were all baptized into one body, whether Jews or Greeks, slaves or free persons, and we were all given to drink of one Spirit." In verse 12 the social meaning of the body prevails. In verse 13 Paul explains that these parts (the Christians) are united into

25. Only the Virgin Mother of God received the fullness of God, since by her faith she received in herself the Son of God, but Paul does not draw this conclusion.

26. Cf. the famous speech of Menenius Agrippa in which he compared the city of Rome to a body where the lower classes also have an indispensable function to contribute to the health of the whole body.

one body by the Holy Spirit when they receive baptism. We, however, know from Paul's trinitarian theology that the Spirit always comes from the Father through Christ and unites us to Christ. Thus Christians are indeed one body in which there are many members with different functions (v. 12) because they are united to the one body-person of Christ (cf. 1 Cor 12:27–31; Rom 12:4–8).

The same Holy Spirit who makes the Christians one (*heis*: Gal 3:28) by joining them to the one body-person of Christ is also the principle of the members' differentiation; that is, the Holy Spirit creates both the unity of the body and the different functions of each member (1 Cor 12:4–13; Eph 4:4–16).

Living as a Member of the Body of Christ

As seen above, the Christian's conformation to and union with the risen body-person of Christ is a dynamic process. It begins in baptism, when the convert participates in the death and resurrection of Christ in faith and sacrament so that they might die to sin in their moral life and begin to live with the very life of Christ (Rom 6). This mindset needs to be maintained and nourished every day anew: "Continually we carry about in our bodies the dying of Jesus, so that in our bodies the life of Jesus may also be revealed. While we live, we are constantly being delivered to death for Jesus' sake, so that the life of Jesus may be revealed in our mortal flesh" (2 Cor 4:10–11). Even though the "body of sin" has already been destroyed in baptism, Paul exhorts his faithful not to let sin reign in their mortal bodies but to put to death by the spirit the deeds of the body (Rom 6:6–12; 8:13) and offer their bodies as a living sacrifice to God (Rom 12:2).

The more we are conformed to Christ and become *syssōma*, "one body" with him (Eph 3:6) the more we behave as members of the same body toward one another. This means that we are united in goals and ideals (*to auto phronein* or *to hen phronein*; Rom 12:1–16; 15:5; 2 Cor 13:11; Phil 2:2; 4:2), we carry one another's burdens, we share in each other's joy and sorrow, and we use our own gift for the good of all (1 Cor 12:25–26; Gal 6:2; Rom 12:15). This process of conformation is completed only at the manifest coming of the Lord, when "he will transform this lowly body of ours and remake it according to the pattern of his glorified body" (Phil 3:21).

Is Paul's Ecclesiology Catholic?

The question of whether Paul's ecclesiology is Catholic concerns not the deutero-Pauline literature (for example, Ephesians and the Pastoral Epistles), but rather those letters that are admitted by all to have been directly written by Paul (1 Thessalonians, Galatians, Romans, 1–2 Corinthians, Philippians, and Philemon). According to Ernst Käsemann, "early Catholicism" did not have its beginning in the second and third centuries as some earlier German liberal scholars had taught, but it was already taking shape in the latest writings of the New Testament, such as Acts, Ephesians, and the Pastoral Epistles. But the proto-Pauline letters, which reflect the earliest stage of the Christian communities, lack the characteristics of "early Catholicism" (namely, faith as belief in an identifiable body of doctrines vs. an existential attitude of trust and surrender to God who gives life to the sinner; sacraments vs. faith; and hierarchical authority vs. a charismatic community in which the charisms of the Spirit balance each other out and the charismatics regulate the life of the community).[27]

We cannot expect a high level of structured order in the first decades of the church that we see in Acts and the Pastoral Epistles from a later date.[28] But the alleged development from a free charismatic church to the hierarchically organized early Catholic church is an arbitrary retrojection of twentieth-century democratic models onto the beginnings of apostolic Christianity.

If apostolic authority is defined, as it is in early Catholicism, as being sent by Christ himself, then clearly Paul claims it more loudly than anyone else. He does not derive his apostolic authority from the Spirit, but from the risen Christ.[29] In spite of the fact that he was not in the company of the Twelve before the resurrection, he considers himself to be an apostle of Jesus Christ on the same level as the Twelve because he also saw the risen

27. Käsemann admits that Paul, "directly" and "indirectly," prepares for early Catholicism by introducing the theme of sacraments, but sacramentalism is counterbalanced and even contradicted by faith. Yet, faith is still trust in the God who raises the dead rather than acceptance of "salvific facts," and Paul is an "individualist" who acts independently from those who were apostles before him (Gal 1:17). See Ernst Käsemann, "Paul and Early Catholicism," in *New Testament Questions of Today* (Philadelphia: Fortress, 1969), 236–51.

28. The majority of the exegetes consider the Pastoral Epistles of deutero-Pauline origin. See a contrary position in Luke Timothy Johnson, *The First and Second Letters to Timothy*, Anchor Bible (New York: Doubleday, 2001), 35ff.

29. At the same time, Paul knows that the mission given to him directly by Christ endowed him with the power of the Spirit (e.g., 1 Cor 2:4; 7:40; 12:4–11).

Lord just as the Twelve did before him. He passes a judgment of excommunication, *kekrika* (I passed judgment) "in the name of the Lord Jesus" and acts in the "power of the Lord Jesus" (1 Cor 5:1–5). With sovereign authority he establishes order in the exercise of charisms and charges that those who will not obey his instructions should be ignored by the community (1 Cor 14:37). Clearly, he claims apostolic authority over all the charismatics. In a similar vein, he issues strict orders concerning the celebration of the Eucharist and regulates the legal and moral issues on marriage.

Paul boasts that he has received his apostolic authority and mission "not from any man or through man but from Jesus Christ."[30] Therefore, he prefers to evangelize in territories where no one else has established a community. But the same Epistle to the Galatians, which contains his most fervent insistence on his independent apostolic mission, also shows his great care and concern to confer first with Peter for fifteen days (Gal 1:18) and to work in communion with the pillars of the church, James, Cephas, and John (2:9). He laid before them the gospel he was preaching "so that I might not be running or have run, in vain" (2:2)

Paul knows also about local presiders and administrators in the communities (*proistamenos*, 1 Thes 5:12; Rom 12:8; and *kybernēseis*, 1 Cor 12:28), and even the later terminology of *episkopos* and *diakonos* appears in the Epistle to the Philippians (1:1). Unlike later terminology that distinguishes charismatic gifts from hierarchical office, Paul considers also the ecclesial office-bearers as recipients of a certain charism of their own.[31] Later Catholic theology has upheld that charismatics and those in holy orders both receive a gift from the Spirit. The difference consists in the fact that the charism (gift) of a deacon, priest, or bishop requires apostolic succession and that this gift remains permanent and irrevocable, while the gifts of the charismatics may be temporary and do not require apostolic succession.

Faith for Paul is indeed trust, but this is a trust in the God who sent his Son to save us and raised him from the dead, after which the Son appeared, and these appearances have been attested to by reliable witnesses. The risen Lord is now glorified; he rules over us, and we owe absolute obedience to him and to his teachings. Thus, from the beginning, faith is not only trust but also obedience to the gospel, whose very kernel—*pace*

30. Gal 1:1; cf. 1 Cor 9:1–5; 15:8–11; 2 Cor 12:1–12.
31. On the list of the charisms, apostle is mentioned first: 1 Cor 12:28; Eph 4:11.

Käsemann—consists of "salvific facts" (1 Cor 15:1–8; see also Rom 1:5; 16:26; 1 Cor 7:25).

Evidence of how important baptism and the Eucharist, marriage and the excommunication/readmission of the sinner, are for Paul can be found in the detailed instructions and regulations in 1 Corinthians. These rites are not just attestations of faith, but Eucharist is communion with the body and blood of Christ. In baptism, we are given a drink from the Holy Spirit. In reconciliation, the sinner returns to the church, where the Spirit dwells and grants hope of salvation.

It is to be hoped that this short survey shows that the beginnings of early Catholicism appear not only in the latest documents of the New Testament, but in the earliest texts as well.

CHAPTER 3

The Church in the Theology of the Fathers

We find no comprehensive work on the church until the fifteenth century, yet the church fathers know and unfold ecclesiological themes in their writings, themes more rich and comprehensive than the juridical treatises of the late Middle Ages. They developed their biblical themes within the context of the Hellenistic culture of their times, but at the same time they transform the meaning of the culture's Hellenistic concepts and images into expressions of the Christian mystery. I provide here only an outline of the most significant themes without dwelling on the differences among individual authors or claiming completeness. Only in the systematic section of this work will I attempt to make a sort of synthesis from among the various themes of patristic literature.[1]

In Joseph Ratzinger's words, "the Fathers take up a rabbinical theology which had conceived of the Torah and Israel as pre-existent."[2] Being convinced of the ultimate identity between Israel and the church, they were convinced that the church has existed before creation in God's eternal design. The New Testament evidence of the eternal decree of God to gath-

1. Thomas Halton, *The Church*, Message of the Fathers of the Church 4 (Wilmington, De.: Michael Glazier, 1985); Raymond E. Brown and John P. Meier, *Antioch and Rome: New Testament Cradles of Catholic Christianity* (New York: Paulist, 1983); Yves Congar, *Handbuch der Dogmengeschichte*, vol. III/3c, *Die Lehre von der Kirche: Von Augustinus bis zum Abendländischen Schisma* (Freiburg: Herder, 1971); Henri de Lubac, *The Splendor of the Church*, trans. Michael Martin (San Francisco: Ignatius, 1986); Hugo Rahner, *Symbole der Kirche: Die Ekklesiogie der Väter* (Salzburg: O. Müller, 1964). These two last works are the richest repertoire of the themes and images of patristic and medieval ecclesiology. See also Roch Kereszty, "The Unity of the Church in the Theology of Irenaeus," *Second Century* 4 (1984): 202–18.

2. Joseph Ratzinger, "The Ecclesiology of the Constitution *Lumen Gentium*," in *Pilgrim Fellowship of Faith: The Church as Communion* (San Francisco: Ignatius, 2005), 123–52.

er all creation under one head, Christ (see Eph 1:1–11; Rom 8:28–30), also contributed to the patristic belief in the preexistent church. She has existed before everything else, and everything else has been created in view of her full realization.[3]

In some sense the church has been a historical reality from the beginnings of humanity because, from Adam and Abel on, just men and women could always be found in every nation scattered throughout the world.[4] No one, however, has been justified without some form of faith in Jesus Christ, a faith longing for liberation from sin and death. With the election of Abraham, Isaac, and Jacob, God began his preparation for the advent of the Redeemer by forming and educating the people of Israel. As seen in the previous chapter, this preparatory phase has been fulfilled in Mary, the immaculate, perfect Israel, who is at the same time the archetype and eschatological realization of the church.

The church, in the full sense of the word, comes into being as the fruit of the Paschal mystery. The new Eve is born from the side wound of Christ on the cross. She who is the spotless bride of the new Adam. The Fathers often write about the birth of the church by linking Exodus 17:1–7 and 1 Corinthians 10:4 with John 7:38 and 19:34. We find the first lapidary statement in Justin: "We are the true Israel, we who have been quarried from the innards of Christ."[5] This can only be fully appreciated by those readers who are quite familiar with all four texts. Perhaps this anonymous text from *De montibus Sina et Sion* presents the most impressive theological interpretation of a conflation of all four texts:

> Struck in his side, blood mixed with water poured out profusely from his side from which he built his Church to which he dedicated the law of his passion and said: he who is thirsty, let him come and drink he who believes in me. As it was written, rivers of living water were flowing out of his side.

The formulation of this mystery in a distichon by Leo the Great and appearing on the baptistery of St. John in the Lateran deserves to be quoted in the original:

3. Cf. the gray old Lady in Hermas's *Shepherd* who was created before everything else and renews herself through the penance of her members (Vision 2) and 2 Clement 14.2.

4. Gregory the Great, *Homily on the Gospel* 19.1; Augustine, *Sermon* 341.9, 11; John of Damascus, *Against the Iconoclasts* 11.

5. Justin Martyr, *Dialogue with Trypho* 135.3.

Fons hic est vitae qui totum diluit orbem
Sumens de Christi vulnere principium.

"Here is the fountain of life which washes clean the entire earth, taking its origin from the wound of Christ."[6] This short inscription describes the sacrifice of Christ as the source of baptism, which Christ intends for the forgiveness of all sins and, thereby, the birth of a universal church. Tertullian also melds Christ's sacrifice with baptism, which creates the church: "the Church coming forth from the side of the Lord in the water of the Spirit and the blood of redemption."[7]

While the church is born from the sacrifice of Christ, her nature and life are intelligible only within a trinitarian context that brings out her different relationships to each of the divine persons. Here I will rely mostly on Irenaeus's early, yet well-developed doctrine, which for the most part is characteristic of the Fathers.

The Spirit, in Irenaeus's writings, becomes the immanent principle of divine life in the church. He penetrates and transforms the flesh, "so that the flesh forgets itself and assumes the quality of the Spirit."[8] He comes from Christ and molds us into the likeness of Christ. He does not build up separate individuals but unites them into one universal church as members of Christ. Indeed, "where the Spirit is, there is the Church." Participation in the Spirit is so real that the Holy Spirit becomes, as it were, our spirit, completes our humanity and leads us to full maturity through the vision of God. Already here and now "we see, hear, and speak" through him; that is, we know the Father, hear the voice of the Son, and bear witness to our faith.[9] Already here and now the Spirit, who is divine life itself, makes our flesh capable of incorruption and immortality.[10] Already in this life we can "mix" the power of the Spirit with the weakness of the flesh so that our weakness is absorbed by his power. Thus "spiritualized," the Christian becomes capable of martyrdom: "The weakness of the flesh once overcome, shows forth the power of the Spirit."[11] Yet this most intimate union does not abolish the distinction between the creature and God, between human-

6. For a thorough treatment of this theme, see Rahner, *Symbole der Kirche*, 208, 219–20, 221–22, 224, 231–32, 537.

7. Tertullian, *On the Soul* 43.10.

8. Irenaeus, *Against Heresies* 5.9.3.

9. Irenaeus, *Against Heresies* 5.20.2.

10. Irenaeus, *Against Heresies* 5.12; 4.18.5.

11. Irenaeus, *Against Heresies* 5.9.2.

kind and the Spirit. Even the "spiritual person" transformed by the Spirit remains a creature of God, who, through the good pleasure of the Father, participates in divine life.[12] The Spirit, however, is strictly divine and not a creature. He joins together with the Word, the "offspring" (*progenies*) of the Father.[13] Thus he is both inside and outside us (*circumdans intus et foris hominem*).[14]

The Holy Spirit has personal qualities, but unlike the Father and the Son, he lacks, so to speak, a distinct "face." He does not imprint his own image to humankind, but carves out in us the image of the Son.

Briefly, communion with the Spirit is *communicatio Christi*, an imparting of communion with Christ.[15] This means both personal communion with him and a conforming to his image. The Spirit is the agent who brings about the process of conforming to Christ.[16] However, he does not work on isolated individuals, but on the church. The whole church, being "configured to the image of the Son,"[17] participates in his sonship as adopted sons.[18] This conformation to Christ is as real and radical in Irenaeus as in St. Paul. Through the Holy Spirit, we become members of the body of Christ in the sense that Christ truly identifies himself with us: he dwells in us, he expresses his traits in us; our mortal, frail, and earthly bodies—in one word, our flesh—become members of Christ.[19]

Christ is also the head of his body, the church. This means that Christ rules over his church, and also that the body must follow its head. It must share in his passion, death, and resurrection.[20] This identification of the church with Christ's body does not blur the distinction between Christ and the church. The various types of church found in the Old Testament show that the union between the church and Christ can also be seen as a union of husband and wife. The wedding of Moses and the Ethiopian woman prefigured the wedding of Christ and the church gathered together from the gentiles.[21] Jacob's many years of labor for the beautiful Rachel

12. Irenaeus, *Against Heresies* 5.3.5.
13. Irenaeus, *Against Heresies* 4.7.4.
14. Irenaeus, *Against Heresies* 5.12.2.
15. Irenaeus, *Against Heresies* 3.24.1.
16. Irenaeus, *Against Heresies* 5.9.1.
17. Irenaeus, *Against Heresies* 4.37.7.
18. Irenaeus, *Against Heresies* 3.18.7.
19. Irenaeus, *Against Heresies* 5.6.2; cf. 3.25.7.
20. Irenaeus, *Against Heresies* 5.24.4; III.19.3.
21. Irenaeus, *Against Heresies* 4.20.12.

prefigures Christ, who endured the cross for his bride, the church.[22] Hosea's taking a prostitute for a wife and sanctifying her by this union evokes Christ, who by uniting himself to a church of sinners sanctifies her by his communion.[23] The spiritual union between Christ and the church is fertile. As explained above, Christ communicates the vital seed of the Spirit to his bride on the cross, thereby enabling the church to engender children for God.[24] Thus the church, through her union with Christ, gains, as it were, a distinct "personal" identity vis-à-vis Christ; that is, the church becomes a loving spouse and fertile mother. Because of her union with Christ through the Holy Spirit the church truly mediates salvation to the world.[25]

The participation of the church in trinitarian life does not stop at the Son. Its final goal is personal communion with the Father. The new human being, perfected by the Spirit, conformed to the image of the Son, ascends to the Father, becomes filled with his vision and life, and begins an eternally new dialogue of friendship with him (*novus homo . . . semper nove confabulans Deo*).[26]

As seen above, the church born from the wound in the side of Christ is not a passive recipient of grace and salvation, but cooperates with Christ in giving birth to Christ.[27] Thus the baptismal pool is called in antiquity the womb of the church. The relationship between the moon and the sun is for many Fathers a symbol of the life-giving activity of the church. As the moon diminishes and dies into the sun, so the church dies into the blinding light of Christ's splendor.[28] In Ambrose's words: "The moon is being diminished so that it may fill all." The moon imitates Christ, who "has emptied her [the moon-church] in order to fill her, just as Christ emptied himself that he may fill all [things]."[29] Maximus of Turin explains that "the Church is rightly compared to the moon since she also besprinkles us with the dew of a bath and makes alive the soil of our body by the dew of bap-

22. Irenaeus, *Against Heresies* 4.21.3.

23. Irenaeus, *Against Heresies* 4.20.12.

24. Irenaeus, *Against Heresies* 4.31.2; 3.25.7.

25. On the theology of the church as mother, see Karl Delahaye, *Ekklesia Mater chez les Pères des trois premiers siècles* (Paris: Cerf, 1964); Boniface VIII, *Unam Sanctam* 46.

26. "The new man conducting with God an always new conversation" (Irenaeus, *Against Heresies* 5.36.1; cf. 3.18.7; 5.362; 5.36.1.

27. The church's role is to prepare the candidates by teaching them and strengthening their faith through her community life, making them members of Christ's body, the church, through baptism.

28. The union of moon and sun as cause of the moon's fertility is part of ancient mythology, which the church applies to the relationship of church and Christ.

29. Ambrose, *Hexaemeron* 4.8.32.

tism."[30] Thus, through union with the Son, the virginal spouse becomes virginal mother.

In fact, there is only one virginal mother, the church, whose perfect embodiment and archetype is Mary, the Mother of God (Clement of Alexandria, Origen). Origen goes on to explain that Mary has only one son, Jesus, but she is also the mother of the members of the church in the sense and to the extent that Jesus is born in them as they conform to Christ.[31] Just as the woman clothed with the Son in the book of Revelation is at once the people of Israel, Mary, and the church, so too in Irenaeus are the womb of Mary and the womb of the church are seen in a mutual "perichoresis":[32] "the Pure One opening purely that pure womb which regenerates men unto God and which He himself made pure."[33] It is Jesus who opened from inside the pure womb of Mary the same pure womb that gives birth to the members of the church.

The birth of Christ in us through baptism is only the beginning of a lifelong process in which every virtuous deed results in a continuous birth of Christ within us. As St. Ambrose said: "He who gives birth to justice, gives birth to Christ," and "He who gives birth to wisdom gives birth to Christ."[34] This continuous birth of Christ in us is a reflection in the church of the Son's eternal generation from the Father. For the Fathers, then, Christian virtues are not just abstract general notions of behavior, but a gradual participation in the virtues of Christ; in fact, participation in Christ's very being.[35] In the words of Origen: "It is Christ who is said to grow within us and for us.[36]

Another way to express the relationship of the church with Christ is based on the Pauline notion of the body of Christ. In particular, St. Augustine unfolds the riches of this *Realsymbol*. The later scholastic theologians considered the personal presence of Christ in the Eucharist as the primary spiritual effect (*res et sacramentum*) of the eucharistic celebration, and the unity of the mystical body as its final effect (*res*), but for Augustine these two appear as equally direct and simultaneous. The object of spiritual eat-

30. Maximus of Turin, *Hom.* 101.

31. Origen, *Against Celsus* 6.79.

32. The word is primarily applied to the Trinity, meaning that the divine persons are within each other.

33. Irenaeus, *Against Heresies* 4.33.11.

34. Ambrose, *Commentary on Luke* 10.24–25.

35. Ambrose, *Commentary on Luke* 10.14.25.

36. Origen, *Commentary on the Canticle of Canticles*, Prologue.

ing, the *manducatio spiritualis*, is Christ *and* the church. This is the reason for Augustine's saying: "It is your mystery which is on the altar" and for telling the communicant that "it is you yourself whom you receive."[37] On account of the unbreakable unity between Christ and the church, only those who are within the ecclesial body of Christ can spiritually eat his body. The excommunicated and heretics who attempt to receive sacramental communion cannot receive the *res*, the spiritual reality. Theirs is not a spiritual eating but only a sacramental one whose result is condemnation rather than life.[38]

The cause of this intimate union between Christ and the church is the charity of Christ. The Eucharist is the *vinculum unitatis* because it is the *vinculum caritatis*. Through the cross, Christ has purified the church and joined her to himself so as to become *una caro*, one flesh with him, bridegroom and bride bound together by perfect virginal *caritas*. At the same time this *caritas* is inseparable from the Holy Spirit because it is the gift of the Spirit.

As we have seen, the spiritual eating of the body and blood of Christ unites us with both Christ and the church. The union with Christ integrates us into his body-person and joins us to his ascent to heaven. Two texts serve as illustration:

> The Teacher of humility came not to do his own will, but the will of him who sent him. Let us come to him, let us enter into him, let us be incorporated into him so that we, too, might do not our will, but that of the Father.[39]

The incorporation of the church into Christ's body is so real that the church and Christ are truly one subject:

> The head is the body's savior, he who has already ascended to heaven. The body is the Church who is still laboring on earth. Had this body not adhered to its head by the bond of charity so much so that one being [*unus*] has become from the head and the body, he would not have reprimanded a certain persecutor from heaven by saying: "Saul, Saul, why do you persecute me?"[40]

The same act of charity that unites us to Christ unites all the members together into one body; in fact, into one man. Consider: "we are one [*unus*] in Christ," "we are one in the one" [*unus in uno*], the unity of Christians is

37. Augustine, *Sermon* 272.

38. So, for instance, Augustine, *Ep.* 34.2, 141.5; Augustine, *In Evangelium Johannis tractatus* 26.13, 26.15, 26.18, 27.11.

39. Augustine, *In Evangelium Johannis tractatus* 25.18.

40. Augustine, *Enarrationes in Psalmos* 30.2.

one [*unus*] man."[41] Thus we are in some real sense one subject along with Christ. Out of the two is one person (*una quadam persona*); that is, out of the head and body, out of the bridegroom and bride.[42] Therefore, we speak with the same tongue and with the same words.[43]

Some Fathers compare the role of the Holy Spirit in the church to that of our created spirit in our body. He is the source of divine life within us, and he inspires our actions. Irenaeus describes the Holy Spirit as the *vas Spiritus*, "the vessel of the Spirit," who constantly rejuvenates the church.[44] In the full sense of the word, the church is the *Columba immaculata*, the immaculately pure church, the temple of the Holy Spirit, the bride of Christ for whom Christ died.[45]

> to sanctify her, cleansing her by the bath of water with the word, that he might present to himself the church in splendor, without spot or wrinkle or any such thing, that she might be holy and without blemish. (Eph 5:26–27)

This entirely pure church is an eschatological reality, but it is already fully realized in the present in heaven because Mary and the saints are in full communion with God. Yet the church's earthly members also belong to this communion of the saints, although not yet fully purified. Here on earth she is the *casta meretrix*, the chaste whore foreshadowed in Rahab of Jericho, who on account of her faith receives the forgiveness of God and is changed from a whore into a chaste bride. This process of the prostitute becoming a chaste bride is an unceasing process in history.

To make sinners face their own reality, in the first six centuries the church excommunicated those who sinned gravely because they had lost the presence of the Holy Spirit. They were cut off from the very life of the church, the temple of the Holy Spirit. Yet the church did not disown her sinful members. The entire community prayed for them during the (usually) long purification process. It was especially the duty of the bishop to support the penitents, to comfort and prepare them for reconciliation.

St. Cyprian exemplifies the compassionate but conscientious bishop who wants to balance the demands of God's justice and mercy with regard

41. Augustine, *Enarrationes in Psalmos* 2.23, 2.5.
42. Augustine, *Enarrationes in Psalmos* 30.2.4.
43. Augustine, *Enarrationes in Psalmos* 37.6.
44. See Irenaeus, *Against Heresies* 3.24.1.
45. See Roch Kereszty, "'Sacrosancta Ecclesia': The Holy Church of Sinners," *Communio* 40, no. 4 (2013): 669–70.

to penitents. When imposing penance, he felt a deep solidarity with the sinners.

I mourn, brothers, I mourn with you and find no comfort in my own personal integrity and health, for the shepherd is wounded more by the wound of his flock [than the flock itself]. I join my heart with each one of you, I share the weight of your sorrow and mourning. I grieve with those who are grieving, I weep with those who are weeping, with the fallen I feel I have fallen myself. My limbs too were struck by the arrows of the raging foe; his savage sword has pierced my body too. No mind can remain free and unscathed from the raging persecution. When my brothers fell, my heart made me fall, too.[46]

St. Ambrose also asked God for the highest virtue, compassion, with penitents.

Give me first of all that I may know how to grieve with the deepest love with those who sin, for this is the highest virtue; it is written: "you shall not rejoice over the sons of Judah on the day of their destruction and you should not talk haughtily on the day of their affliction" (Obadiah 12); but whenever the sin of someone who has fallen comes to light, may I feel with him; may I not condescendingly reprimand him; may I rather mourn and cry over him so that, while I weep over him, I may cry over myself, saying: "Thamar is more just [in the eyes of God] than I am myself" (Gn 38:26).[47]

While set apart from the world, the church is spread through the whole world, and at the end of history she will be identical with the whole renewed human race. But she exists in the local communities, each of which is centered on the bishop's eucharistic celebration. Local church communities are seen not as an administrative part of a whole, but as the local presence of the one indivisible church of God in Christ Jesus. In the lapidary statement of St. Peter Damian: *est tota in toto, et tota in qualibet parte*: "the whole [church] is in the whole, and the whole is in each [local church]."[48] The universal church exists as the communion of all the local churches, and the term *ecclesia* does not refer to the hierarchy alone, but to everyone in the eucharistic assembly.[49]

46. Cyprian, *De lapsis* 4.

47. Ambrose, De paenitentia 2.73. While the Fathers have maintained that sinners in some real way still belong to the church, heretical and near-heretical tendencies (e.g., Donatists, Cathari, Wyclif) denied this and claimed that the only true church is the church of the pure, spiritual church.

48. Peter Damian, *Dominus vobiscum* 6.

49. See Henri de Lubac, *The Church: Paradox and Mystery*, trans. James R. Dunne (Staten Island: Alba House, 1969).

Nevertheless, the *ecclesia* does not exist without her bishop, who stands in the line of apostolic succession and thus continues the mission of Christ. While representing Christ, the bishop also incorporates the church into himself and acts in her name. The bishop, however, was not imposed by the pope on the local assembly, but in principle the entire local church, clergy and people all, elect the bishop, who will always act together with his people. This does not mean that episcopal governance is purely democratic to the point that the bishop follows majority opinion. His role is to teach, shape, and form his people so that they may carry out St. Paul's injunction to develop the same mind and heart.[50]

The following text of St. Cyprian is a concise summary of the relationship between bishop and his people:

> The Church are people united to the bishop and the flock clinging to its shepherd; hence you should know that the bishop must be in the Church and the Church in the bishop. Whoever is not with the bishop is not in the church.[51]

His authority is entirely spiritual. The bishop is to build up the church by preaching, celebrating the liturgy, and being the protector and father of the poor, widows, and orphans. "Act not like a judge but as a bishop" was the advice given to Ambrose when, still a layman, he was sent to calm down the rioting at the episcopal election in Milan.[52]

The relationship of episcopal authority to Christ is twofold: horizontal and vertical. The bishop stands in succession to the apostles, who were sent by Christ, and he is the image, the visible, sacramental representation of Christ in his church.

Even though every local church embodies the universal church, each church is not fully herself without communion with the other churches and, in particular, with the church in Rome. Communion with the church in Rome soon began to be seen as constitutive of communion with the universal church and excommunication by the church of Rome to result in being excommunicated from the universal church of God.[53] Moreover, if

50. For instance, Rom 12:3; 2 Cor 13:11; Phil 4:2.

51. Cyprian, *Ep.* 69.8.

52. See Paulinus, *The Life of St. Ambrose* 6.

53. Cf. Tertullian, *Contra Praxean* 1.5.n. Tertullian, even in his Montanist period, acknowledges the decisive influence of the church of Rome over the universal church. He is convinced that if the bishop of Rome had accepted the "new Prophecy" (Montanism), by that acceptance all the bishops of Asia and Phrygia would have established communion with it.

a doctrinal or disciplinary controversy could not be solved on the local or regional level, it was often transferred to Rome for final adjudication.[54]

54. Due to the great political influence of the Byzantine emperors and the growing cultural differences with the West, the defining role of the church of Rome was much less understood and accepted in the East than in the Western church. Nevertheless see the Synodal Letter of the Council of Chalcedon to Leo the Great (451): "You yourself have protected it [the faith] like a golden chain that comes down to us by the order of the Master, since you are the interpreter of the voice of blessed Peter and the one who procures for all the blessing of his faith. . . . you were their leader [of the fathers of the Council of Chalcedon], as the head is [the leader] of the limbs in the persons who represented you."

CHAPTER 4

The Medieval Synthesis and Great Thinkers

The Symbiosis of Church and Empire

The patristic themes outlined above were preserved and further unfolded by the Fathers after the "Constantinian turn."[1] Nevertheless, the close association and gradual symbiosis of church and empire, of the church hierarchy and political rulers, that developed during the Middle Ages brought new, more juridically articulated ecclesiological terms into the papal and episcopal courts as well as in the universities. Instead of being the *populus Dei*, the people of God, the church was seen more and more as the *populus christianus*, the Christian people, a geographically limited sociological reality whose boundaries coincided with those of the empire.

Instead of being persecuted by the empire, the empire began to persecute the heresies that opposed the church. The enemies of the church became the enemies of the empire and vice versa. When, however, heretical emperors came to power, they persecuted Catholics and tried to win over the bishops to their heresy. Constantine considered himself the "bishop for those outside the church" and the church's protector. He and his successors assumed the right to call together ecumenical councils whose decrees would become laws of the empire. The bishops took over state functions and privileges. They received judicial powers and senatorial rank.

Thus, from a persecuted minority, the church became the *domina genti-*

1. See Yves Congar, *Handbuch der Dogmengeschichte*, vol. III/3c, *Die Lehre von der Kirche: Von Augustinus bis zum Abendländischen Schisma* (Freiburg: Herder, 1971); Congar, *Power and Poverty in the Church* (Baltimore: Helicon, 1965).

um, the ruler of the peoples. Her doctrine and moral values began to shape culture, legislation, and public morality in the empire. Many at the time thought that the kingdom of God, so ardently awaited in early Christianity, had indeed arrived and was taking shape in the triumphant symbiosis of church and empire.

When Constantine transferred the imperial court and capital from Rome to Constantinople, a great power vacuum resulted in Italy. The growing threat of invading barbarian hordes forced the bishop of Rome to take on more and more of the functions of a secular ruler in Rome and central Italy because the distant imperial power could not halt barbarian armies from looting cities and massacring the population on a whim.

However, at the same time the Constantinian alliance between church and state posed grave dangers for the church. It persuaded the church to justify violence for the uprooting of heretics. Moreover, millions joined the church not out of inner conviction, but to enjoy the privilege of belonging to the official state religion of the empire.[2] As previously stated, the support of the state proved to be a double-edged sword; that is, heretical emperors persecuted Catholics and promoted their heresy through violence.

Fortunately, this deterioration of the quality of Christian life produced its own antidote within the church, the monastic movement. Those who wanted to return to the purity of the *vita apostolica*, or who wanted the fellowship of those who had given up wealth and power to follow Christ in poverty and celibacy, moved to the deserts of Egypt and Asia Minor. They established monasteries in Italy and Gaul in order to live either in loosely united settlements as hermits or in closely organized communities.[3] This served the renewal of the church universal by providing heroic examples of Christian lives and holy bishops for the church at large.

The alliance between empire and church developed in different ways in the East and the West. Being closer to the seat of imperial power, the Eastern churches could not emancipate themselves from the supreme control of the emperor. But Rome's distance from Constantinople allowed greater freedom for the bishop of Rome.[4] He remained the only stable authority

2. By the decree of Theodosius in AD 380 the Catholic Church became the sole accepted religion of the empire. The Jews were merely tolerated.

3. The most famous among the hermits was St. Anthony in the deserts of Egypt. The cenobitic monastery of St. Pachomius flourished in Egypt; in Asia Minor, St. Basil the Great protected and guided monasteries of men and women.

4. In 1054 mutual excommunications by the papal legate and the patriarch of Constantinople,

in the West to face the onslaught of the barbarian tribes without help from the emperor in Constantinople. Thus, this dangerous power vacuum compelled, as it were, the popes to take up the challenge and play a key role in assuring some level of political and economic stability in Italy. Moreover, Pope Leo III transferred the title of emperor to Charlemagne (AD 800), because he alone was capable of defending Italy and uniting most of Europe under one rule. Charlemagne promoted the preservation and the handing on of classical culture, the conversion of the migrating barbaric tribes, the establishment of bishoprics and monasteries, and he made great strides in Christianizing Europe. But he took for granted that he had the right to appoint bishops in his empire. At the same time, the fact that the pope crowned Charlemagne emperor alienated the Byzantine emperor and, indirectly, the Byzantine church.

When Charlemagne died, his empire fell apart. Rome and the papacy were subjected to the bloody rule of rival Roman warlords who fought each other, and deposed and imposed their rival popes, each a puppet of one of the warring factions. As a result, the papacy lost prestige and influence in the Western church.

In the second half of the tenth century, Otto the Great established order and stability in a large swath of the lands that had been included in the Carolingian Empire and was crowned by the pope as emperor of the Holy Roman Empire. He restored order in Rome and imposed a German pope (Henry III) who rescued the papacy from corruption.

During the eleventh century, the popes, who came from the monastic reform movement of Cluny—the greatest among them being St. Gregory VII—thought that the church was strong enough to oppose its subjection to the secular rulers and to treat this subjection as a grave abuse to be uprooted. These popes could not tolerate remaining under the tutelage of the emperor and that local bishops could only receive investiture by the symbols of their office from the emperor or from some other secular ruler. Of course, the emperor justified the practice of imperial investiture by the fact that he granted land and political power to the bishops and, therefore,

based on mutual misunderstandings and high-handedness, further alienated the two sides of Christianity. The hostility of the Greeks was further aggravated and became long-lasting because of the siege and sack of Constantinople by the Crusaders in 1204. See Yves Congar, *After Nine hundred Years: The Background of the Schism between the Eastern and Western Churches* (New York: Fordham University Press, 1998). See also Joseph Famerée, "Le ministère du pape selon l'Orthodoxie" [The ministry of the Pope according to the Orthodox churches], *Revue théologique de Louvain* 37, no. 1 (2006): 26–43.

he was empowered to choose them and hand over to them their spiritual insignia, the miter, staff, and ring. The popes saw this as an enslavement of the church and certain to end in decay and corruption. Thus began the "investiture controversies" to free the church from the control of the feudal rulers.

Ironically, the church appropriated the vocabulary and use of secular power to liberate itself from the secular powers. At this time, canon lawyers began to use terms like *regimen papae* and *potestas papae* (the rule and power of the pope). The statement of Paul, "the spiritual man judges everything" (1 Cor 2:15), was applied in patristic theology to the discerning power of the spiritually mature person. But a new interpretation was applied, one with a juridical sense regarding the supreme power of the pope. It held that no one is allowed to judge the pope, but he is competent to judge the moral actions of all rulers. The "theory of the two swords" was developed to justify papal supremacy. That is, Christ gave both the sword of spiritual power and the sword of secular power to St. Peter. The first sword the pope keeps for himself, and the second he gives to the emperor. But if the emperor abuses his power and becomes morally unworthy, the pope has the right to take back the sword and give it to another worthy individual.[5] Even the moon-sun symbolism, which in the patristic age referred to the relationship of Christ and the church, was appropriated during the Middle Ages to signify the belief that the emperor (the moon) receives his power from the pontiff (the sun).

As long as the popes were saintly men and/or they were inspired by reform movements such as the Benedictines of Cluny and later the Cistercians, Franciscans, and Dominicans, this system worked to an extent. The best popes did in fact ensure some order in the Christian commonwealth, and they serve as a counterweight to the whim and violence of secular rulers. Nevertheless, this firm subjection of the secular power to the spiritual eventually led to the secularization of the spiritual sphere and the gradual corruption of the hierarchy.

Since the papacy led the fight against the feudal state and ensured the freedom of election for local bishops, the scope of its operations was con-

5. In Luke's Gospel, the two swords episode concerns Jesus' Farewell Discourse, in which he encourages his listeners to be resolute and strong in facing enemies. The two swords became a metaphor to illustrate the autonomy and relationship of temporal and spiritual power to each other. See Pope Gelasius's *Letter to Emperor Anastasius* (AD 494) and the bull *Unam Sanctam* by Pope Boniface VIII (AD 1302).

stantly expanding and eventually led to greater and greater centralization. The pope had to intervene so often to decide among competing candidates in an episcopal election that gradually most bishops were simply appointed by the pope with varying degrees of input from the secular rulers. Thus the bishop was often regarded as simply representing the pope in his diocese.

The *ecclesia* no longer meant the local Christian community, but the complexus of rights and privileges embodied in the pope and bishops. In fact, in the mind of some canon lawyers of the Roman curia, the whole church was seen as one big diocese and the bishops merely as vicars of the pope. One extreme formulation at the time of Boniface VIII was the following: *papa qui potest dici ecclesia*, "the pope who may be called the church."[6]

Instead of speaking of the church as *corpus Christi mysticum*, the phrase *corpus ecclesiae mysticum*, meaning a structured, organized social body with a system of spiritual powers, was used. The first systematic ecclesiologies in the fifteenth century, those of Juan de Torquemada[7] and John of Ragusa,[8] treated only the legal aspect of the church.

Yet this curial ecclesiology was counterbalanced first by a monastic theology that continued the ecclesiology of the Fathers and later by the ecclesiology of the mendicant orders. From among the many significant representatives of these two trends, only three of the most influential are treated here: St. Bernard, St. Francis, and St. Thomas.

St. Bernard

For St. Bernard the most important image of the church is as spouse.[9] The whole church is one spouse, and also the individual soul is spouse insofar as she participates in the mystery of the Church: "For what we all together possess fully and integrally, we participate individually without any contradiction."[10] Every individual soul is called to embody in herself the one spouse of Christ:

6. See Marsilius of Padua, *Defensor civitatis*, 1324.

7. Juan de Torquemada, *Summa de Ecclesia*, 1550.

8. John of Ragusa, *Tractatus de Ecclesia*, finished in 1440, published in its entirety only in 1986.

9. Yves Congar, "L'ecclésiologie de saint Bernard," in *Saint Bernard théologien: Actes du Congrès di Dijon 15–19 sept 1953* = *Analecta Sacri Ordinis Ciserciensis* 9 (1953): 136–90; Roch Kereszty, "'Bride' and 'Mother' in the *Super Cantica* of St. Bernard: An Ecclesiology for Our Times?" *Communio* 20, no. 2 (1993): 415–36.

10. "Quod enim simul omnes plene integreque possidemus, hoc singuli sine contradictione participamus" (Bernard, *Super Cant.* 12.11).

For we all are called to a spiritual wedding feast in which, of course, Christ the Lord is the bridegroom. That is why we sing the Psalm: "And he, as a bridegroom, comes forth from the bridal chamber." We ourselves are the bride. And all of us together are one bride and each individual soul is, as it were, an individual bride.[11]

It is the love of Christ that joins the many spouses into one spouse, into the one church, *carissima illa est una uni* (this dearest one is one [spouse] for the one [groom]).[12] Yet the soul that is dedicated completely to God alone knows that God sees her and loves her as if she alone were seen and loved by God.[13] Note that the bridegroom of the church is Christ the Word, not the Son prior to or abstracted from his incarnate state. The bridegroom is the incarnate Word risen and glorified, whose humanity is no longer a screen, but who is completely transparent to the divine glory of the Word.

While the prevailing image for the church in St. Bernard is the church as the spouse of Christ the Word, he also writes of the "church as body of Christ." He distinguishes the personal body of Christ from his ecclesial body, the church. The point of the distinction is to show that by the passion of his crucified body, he acquired his body, the church, which is *universum Christi corpus* (the universal body of Christ).[14] Thus his body the church is dearer to Christ than his "other body," since he delivered the latter to death in order to prevent his body the church from tasting death: "The Church is the Body of Christ which is dearer to him; all Christians know that he gave his other body unto death lest [the ecclesial body] taste death."[15] Writing about Paul's persecution of the church, Bernard charges that those who persecute Christ's members on earth persecute him more gravely than those who crucified him on the cross, because the souls for whom he shed his blood are dearer to him than his own blood.[16] The persecution Bernard refers to is not the torture and murder of Christians, but the sacrilegious attempt to lead souls for whom Christ shed his blood into sin. St. Bernard thinks that the *universitas populi christiani* (the whole Christian people) is sick through sin "from the sole of the foot up to the head" and that they

11. "Omnes enim nos ad spirituales nuptias vocati sumus, in quibus utique sponsus est Christus Dominus; unde canimus in Psalmo: Et ipse tamquam sponsus procedens de thalamo suo. Sponsa vero nos ipsi sumus . . . et omnes simul una sponsa, et animae singulorum quasi singulae sponsae" (Bernard, *2nd Sermon on 1st Sunday after the Octave of Epiphany*).

12. Bernard, *Super Cant.* 6.4.

13. Bernard, *Super Cant.* 7.8.

14. Bernard, *Super Cant.* 12.10.

15. Bernard, *Super Cant.* 12.7.

16. Bernard, *Super Cant.* 12.10.

all have conspired against Christ and have persecuted him by snatching away his members through scandalous example and evil suggestions. Yet he singles out the hierarchy for special criticism: "They are the first in your persecution who seem to hold primacy and principality in the Church." He especially inveighs against the sale of sacred orders to make money: *In occasionem turpis lucri.*[17]

Thus St. Bernard knows that the church here on earth is not completely purified. "The Church is not without stain in those who are struggling [on earth]."[18] The sinners remain in the church through faith and the sacraments so that they may convert and receive life while here on earth.

He acknowledges the *plenitudo potestatis* (the fullness of power) of the pope, yet he severely criticizes the state of the papacy. The popes, he said, had become closer to successors of Constantine than of Peter; their tribunals were full of the laws of Justinian rather than those of the Lord. He also defends the rights of the bishops against the pope. He writes to Pope Eugene III: "You are mistaken if you think that your supreme apostolic power was alone established by God. You create a monster if you remove the fingers from the hand and attach them to the head.[19] According to Yves Congar,[20] the most original contribution of Bernard to our understanding of the role of spiritual power in the church centers on the image of the minister as the "friend of the bridegroom," whose role is to present the church as a chaste virgin to Christ.[21] Nowhere does the classic image of "the bishop-bridegroom of his church" appear in Bernard. For Bernard, Christ is the bridegroom, and the role of the abbot, priest, bishop, and pope is to announce the coming of the bridegroom and yield the place to him. Thus the members of the hierarchy have the *potestas* but not the *dominium*. They have a spiritual power to facilitate the encounter of the spouse and the bridegroom, but they do not possess the bride (*dominium*).

He warns Pope Eugene III, his former monk:

If you are a friend of the bridegroom, you should say not "his beloved is my princess," but "his beloved is a princess," claiming for yourself nothing of what is hers,

17. Bernard, *Super Cant.* 2–3. The sin Bernard chastises is simony, the sale of church offices.

18. Bernard, *Sermon 3.2 on All Saints Day*.

19. Bernard, *De consideratione* 3.4.17.

20. Congar, "L'ecclésiologie de saint Bernard," 171–73. Most of this section is based on Congar's article.

21. "Tibi commissa est sponsa Christi, amice Sponsi: tuum est tandem uni viro virginem castam exhibere Christo" (*Ep.* 191.2). Notice the conflation of Johannine and Pauline texts, a general characteristic of Bernard's style and an indication of the foundations of his theology (Jn 3:29; 2 Cor 11:2).

save only the privilege of dying for her if necessary. If you have come from Christ, you have come, don't forget, not to be served but to serve. Let the successor of Paul be able to say with Paul: "We have come, not because we exercise dominion over your faith, but because we are helpers in your joy" (2 Cor 1:23). Let the heir of Peter be able to say with Peter: "We have come, not to lord it over the household of God, but to be an example of the flock" (1 Pt 5:3). So shall the bride, no longer a servant, but beautiful and free, be delivered by you into the arms of her fair bridegroom. From whom else can she expect the liberty to which she is entitled if you (which God forbid) seek your own profit from the inheritance of Christ, you, who long ago learned not to call anything your own, not even your own body.[22]

St. Francis

St. Francis was not a theologian, but his example, his preaching, and his order (along with the order founded by St. Dominic) renewed the church at a time when she was lapsing into a sorry state. The wealth of the higher clergy and their princely lifestyle alienated the poor from the church, especially the poor in the growing cities of Italy. Francis and his friars, by their voluntary poverty and by serving the poor, manifested the church as the servant church of the poor. "Little brother Francis," as he called himself, made present and visible again to the world Jesus Christ who, though rich, became poor for our sake.

Unlike the heresies (Cathari and Albigenses), Francis and his authentic followers did not separate themselves from the hierarchical church, whose sins they saw very clearly. But Francis knew that the clergy has been given the ministry of the holy body and blood of the Lord as well as his holy Word:

Afterward the Lord gave me and still gives me such faith in priests who live according to the manner of the holy Roman Church because of their order, that if they were to persecute me, I would still have recourse to them.... And I do not wish to consider sin in them because I discern the Son of God in them and they are my masters. And I act in this way since I see nothing corporally of the Most High Son of God in this world except His Most Holy Body and Blood which they receive and which they alone administer to others.[23]

22. Bernard of Clairvaux, to Pope Eugenius III, Letter 205 in the *Letters of St. Bernard*, trans. Bruno James (Kalamazoo, Mich.: Cistercian Publications, 1998), 276.

23. Francis of Assisi, *The Testament*, in *Francis and Clare: The Complete Works*, Classics of Western Spirituality (New York: Paulist Press, 1982), 152.

Thus he and his movement were able to reform the church from inside without causing a schism or heresy.[24]

The life story of Francis is a powerful illustration that there is no contradiction between charismatic saints and the hierarchical church. Innocent III, the most exalted pope of the Middle Ages, in his golden robes and jeweled triple crown, recognized in the poor, dirty beggar the ambassador of Christ and supported him and his brothers in the renewal of his church.

The Ecclesiology of St. Thomas

While using the language and the categories of scholastic theology as well as those of curialist ecclesiology, St. Thomas synthesized many elements of the patristic tradition.[25] Neither the *Summa theologiae* nor any other work of Thomas has a treatise on the church. His ecclesiology must be gathered from all of his writings. He often defines the church as the *congregatio fidelium*, the assembly of those who believe in Christ. Since faith in Christ may also be implicit (implied by believing in God's existence and in his providing of everything necessary for our salvation),[26] all who have ever explicitly or implicitly believed, those who believe now and those who will believe in Christ in the future belong to the same "body of the church." Faith in Christ is expressed by some outward sign. Even in the Old Testament and among the pagans this was achieved by offering sacrifices and, beginning with Abraham, by circumcision.[27] This must be so since the faith of the Fathers in the Old Testament did not terminate in the rituals of the law, as if these rituals were the ultimate object of their faith. By seeing and performing the rituals they embraced in and through these images the reality they symbolized: "Thus, observing the sacraments of the Law, the Fathers were carried unto Christ by the same faith and love by which we are carried unto Him. And so the ancient Fathers belonged to the same body of the Church to which we belong."[28]

24. It should be added that later, mainly because of the growing secularization of the hierarchical church, a branch of the radical Franciscans developed an ambiguous, and in some cases even hostile, attitude toward the institutional church.

25. For a more detailed treatment, see Avery Dulles, "The Church according to Thomas Aquinas," in *A Church to Believe In: Discipleship and the Dynamics of Freedom* (New York: Crossroad, 1982), 149–70; Thomas F. O'Meara, "Theology of the Church," in *The Theology of Thomas Aquinas*, ed. Rik van Nieuwenhove and Joseph Wawrikow (Notre Dame: University of Notre Dame Press, 2005), 303–25; Yves Congar, *Thomas d'Aquin, Sa vision de théologie et de l'Église* (London: Variorum Reprints, 1984).

26. Aquinas, ST II–II q. 1, a. 7.

27. Aquinas, ST III q. 68, a. 1, ad 1.

28. Aquinas, ST III q. 8, a. 3, ad 3.

Another of Thomas's phrases for the church is *corpus Christi mysticum*, the "mystical body of the Christ," which expresses the mysterious unity between the members of the church and Christ, her head. He is head of the church for three reasons:[29] (1) Christ is the closest to God and through grace we are conformed to him; (2) he is head of the church since he has the plenitude of all graces; (3) as head, he has the power to communicate grace to all the members of the church. Those members of the church who belong to Christ the head most perfectly are united to him by faith and charity. But even those who do not believe are potentially members of the mystical body and thus, in some sense, Christ is the head of all human beings.[30] In fact, he is also the head of the angels and so the angels also belong to the same one church. The one church exists in two states. Insofar as she is on the road, she is the assembly of believers, but insofar as she is in the heavenly homeland, she is the assembly of those who see God face-to-face (*congregatio comprehendentium*). The two states are joined together by the same Christ, who has both the fullness of grace and the fullness of glory.[31] Both the church on the road and the church in heaven may be called kingdom, but the former only because she is modeled on the latter. "The true Church is the heavenly Church, which is our mother, and to which we tend; upon it our earthly Church is modeled."[32]

Christ is not only the exemplary cause of the church, insofar as through his grace the members of the church are conformed to him, but his passion is also the instrumental cause of the church. This the Fathers expressed through the image that the church has been born from the wound in the side of the crucified Christ.

St. Thomas explains in detail the juridical and institutional aspect of the church (hierarchy, teaching office, sacraments, church laws), but he never loses sight of the primary aspect outlined above, that the church is primarily a community of believers united to Christ through faith and love, and conformed to him. The relationship between the external and internal aspect of the church is beautifully illustrated in Thomas's treatment of the new law:

> What is most preponderant in the Law of the New Testament and in which all its power resides is the grace of the Holy Spirit which is given through faith in Christ.

29. On the grace of Christ as head of the church, see Aquinas, ST III q. 8, a. 1–6.
30. Aquinas, ST III q. 8, a. and 3.
31. Aquinas, ST III q. 8, a. 4, ad 2.
32. Aquinas, *Lect.* 3 on Eph 3:10.

And therefore, the law of the New Testament is chiefly the grace itself of the Holy Spirit given to those who believe in Christ....

Nevertheless, the New Law contains certain things which dispose us to receive the grace of the Holy Spirit and those which pertain to the use of that grace. These are, as it were, secondary in the New Law about which the faithful of Christ need to be instructed both by words and writings, both as to what they should believe and as to what they should do. Consequently, we must say that the New Law is primarily a law inscribed in the heart, but that secondarily it is a written law.[33]

From this short summary of the essential aspects of the new law, the dynamism of St. Thomas's ecclesiology emerges. All that belongs to the church as institution—the preaching, sacred Scriptures, code of laws, sacramental signs—are necessary, but justified only insofar as they point beyond themselves to the grace of the Holy Spirit. They dispose the members to receive the grace of the Holy Spirit, or they are means of that grace and instruct us how to live those virtues for whose practice we received the grace of the Holy Spirit.

The church, however, doesn't possess the created grace of the Holy Spirit only. In the words of Avery Dulles,

In an even deeper sense, however, the Spirit unifies the Church by bestowing himself as uncreated grace. He is numerically one in all the faithful and thus unites them very intimately to one another and to Christ their head. Identically the same person of the Holy Spirit is present and active both in Christ the Head and in all the faithful as members.

The personal indwelling of the Holy Spirit is so intimate that it makes Christ and the Church, in a certain sense, "one mystical person."[34]

We then understand why the true church is the heavenly church. The church on earth, as means of grace, as an institution, leads us to heaven, and it will cease there while the church as communion with God and with one another will be perfected in heaven.[35]

33. Aquinas, ST I-II q. 106, a. 1.
34. Dulles, *The Church according to Thomas Aquinas*, 154.
35. Cf. Dulles, *The Church according to Thomas Aquinas*, 155.

CHAPTER 5

The Ecclesiology of the Reformation and Counter-Reformation

Even though the institutions of the church were threatened several times by decadence and corruption before the end of the sixteenth century, charismatic saints and their followers succeeded in effectively curtailing the decline by injecting powerful energies into reforms and spiritual renewal. The Benedictines of Cluny during the tenth and eleventh centuries, and the Cistercians during the twelfth, provided exemplary abbots, bishops, and even several popes to the contemporary church. In the thirteenth century, the Dominicans and Franciscans showed the increasing number of urban poor that the church cared about them. A crucial factor in this success was the support of the papacy. As a result, heretical or semiheretical reform groups remained on the sidelines, outside of the church universal. However, by the sixteenth century, the state of Western Christendom had reached a critical stage. Although Europe had its saints and fervent Christian communities, as well as spiritually healthy religious, these positive forces did not have sufficient momentum to reverse the general trend of decline and corruption. As the Reformers put it, the church needed *reformatio in capite et membris* (reform in head and members), but, except for short intervals and for conciliar decrees that typically went unimplemented, the head of the church was distracted by matters other than reform and renewal.[1] The

1. Pius II (1458–64) set up plans to reform the church but died soon after his election. Even Alexander VI (1492–1503), the openly immoral pope, had a short episode of repentance, when he drew up an effective plan for reform, though he never implemented it. The Fifth Lateran Council (1512–17) listened to blunt expositions of the abuses by reform-minded prelates and issued several reform decrees, but Leo X (1513–21) did not have the will to implement them.

main concerns of the Renaissance popes centered on beautifying Rome, promoting the arts, and defending and expanding the papal states rather than the pastoral care of the faithful and uprooting the abuses in the papal curia and the church at large. The openly immoral and criminal life of Pope Alexander VI is well known even by those who otherwise are completely ignorant of church history. The following are brief descriptions of several of the main causes of the Protestant Reformation in the middle of the sixteenth century.

One rather remote but important cause of the Reformation was the exile of the papacy to Avignon, France, for more than seventy years. The proximity of the popes to the French kings weakened the papacy and rendered it dependent on the secular power of the state (1305–78). Multiple schisms in the church involving first two and later three claimants to the papal throne further undermined the popes' prestige and authority. Eventually, an ecumenical council (Constance, 1415–17) put an end to the divisions in the Western church, and as a result the doctrine of conciliarism became popular even among influential theologians. Conciliarism holds the principle that the ultimate authority in the church is not the pope but the ecumenical council. Adding to the impact of these events were the blatant abuses in the life of the clergy, abuses that increased and spread as the fifteenth century progressed. Among the most egregious were the negligent and at times immoral behavior of popes and bishops who did not or could not exercise their pastoral ministry, morally corrupt and uneducated priests, abuses in sacramental practice, and indulgences, all of which resulted in the corruption of the visible, institutional church. This, in turn, eroded the credibility of the sacramental view of the church. Patristic and Thomistic ecclesiology had taught that the institutional church is an effective sign, which in various ways, such as preaching, administering the sacraments, and giving testimony of Christian life, mediates the invisible reality of grace with the hearts of the faithful. And this grace establishes communion with Christ and with each other in the Holy Spirit. Therefore, being a member of the church is necessary to receive such graces. Yet belonging to the institutional church is not the goal of a Christian life journey. It is only the beginning. On earth we are in the *ecclesia viatorum*, a pilgrim church on the road toward the glorious church in heaven. The sacramental dynamism whereby the institutional leads to the spiritual and the spiritual expresses itself in community—a community that is on a journey toward the heavenly church—was to a large extent compromised before the Reformation. Unfit prince bishops, greedy clergy, and defective preaching could hardly build up a holy community. One of the first responses to this situation was Luther's respectful attempt to attract the attention of his own bishop and of Pope Leo X to the abuses, but Luther was ignored. So Luther and his rapidly growing party began to build up their own congregations under the protection of Elector Prince Frederick the Wise. Thus, in their effort to renew the church, Luther and the other Reformers ended up abandoning, partly or totally, the Catholic sacramental vision of the church.[2]

Martin Luther

As mentioned above, Luther at first did not intend to establish a new church, but rather reform the one church of Christ. He also acknowledged the authority of the popes and, when his calls for reform to his own bishop went unheeded, he appealed for help to Pope Leo X. Nevertheless, his personal religious experience "in the tower" had changed his life and predisposed him to what would later become the Lutheran view of the church. Dreading the condemning justice of God, he sought protection under the cross of Jesus. There, while meditating alone on the Letter to the Romans, he discovered the gracious God of mercy. He believed that God forgave his sins and made him just as a result of the infinite merits of Jesus Christ. As much as he had worried beforehand about his own salvation, now he believed in it with absolute, unshakeable trust. Questioning the certainty of his own salvation became tantamount to questioning the efficacy of Christ's sacrifice. Belief in one's personal salvation became part and parcel of faith itself.

Since solitary reading of Scripture led him to discover God's mercy for those who believe in Christ's atoning sacrifice, the personal interpretation of Scripture gradually became for Luther the one ultimate guarantor of true belief.[3] He seems unaware that official Catholic teaching has also affirmed

2. See Paul D. L. Avis, *The Church in the Theology of the Reformers* (London: Marshall, Morgan and Scott, 1982; repr., Eugene, Ore.: Wipf and Stock, 1982).

3. At the Diet of Worms Luther sums up his stand in these powerful and passionate words: "Unless I am convinced by the testimony of the Scriptures or by clear reason (for I do not trust either in the pope or in councils alone, since it is well known that they have often erred and contradicted themselves), I am bound by the Scriptures I have quoted and my conscience is captive to the Word of God"

that we are justified not by good works, but by undeserved grace not caused by any previous merit of ours, but through faith, which brings with it trust and love. However, the Catholic Church maintains that while the church's faith in the efficacy of Christ's grace ensures the salvation of the church, the individual believer cannot have absolute certainty of his or her own salvation without special revelation. Despite discussions with the excellent Catholic theologian Cardinal Cajetan, Luther clung to his own version of salvation. He was unwilling or unable to give up his conviction of the certainty of salvation for the individual believer, a certainty he came to after the great anguish of his "discovery."[4] For this reason, he gradually rejected the divine authority of the pope and ecumenical councils. The only authority he felt bound to became the written Word of God, Scripture alone, which every believer can understand by their own reasoning with the help of the Holy Spirit. He also rejected the special powers that only the clergy received through ordination. All Christians are priests, he believed; that some are selected by the church to preach the gospel and celebrate the Lord's Supper is only a practical matter of church order. Of the sacraments, he retained only baptism, Eucharist, and the optional sacrament of "holy absolution" or "the office of the keys." The other sacraments he rejected as lacking a basis in Scripture.

Even though Luther and his circle organized in a short span of time an institutional church with a vigorous community life and attractive liturgy in the vernacular, he maintained that the true church is the invisible hidden church: "The Church is hidden; it lives in spirit and inaccessible light; God has buried it under errors, infirmity, and sin so that it appears nowhere to the secondary senses."[5] Yet he also asserted that "the Church must appear in the world. But it can only appear in a covering (larva), a veil, a shell of some kind of clothes which a man can grasp, otherwise it can never be found."[6]

Thus a certain sacramental structure was retained because the outward

("Luther at the Diet of Worms," in *Luther's Works: Career of the Reformer, II*, ed. George W. Forrell and Helmut T. Lehmann [Fortress: Philadelphia, 1970], 112). Thus the sole criterion of Luther's faith is Scripture as understood by himself, and he is obligated to it by his own conscience.

4. Luther required that the penitents be absolutely certain that their sins are forgiven, otherwise they do not receive fruitfully the sacrament of penance. Cardinal Cajetan pointed out that this belief "instituted a new religion" (*Opuscula* [Lyons, 1562], 111a).

5. Martin Luther, *Galaterbriefvorlesung von 1535* (WA 40/2:105).

6. Martin Luther, *Briefwechsel 1509–1522* (WA 9:608).

signs of baptism and Eucharist could lead those who have the right kind of faith to membership in the invisible church.[7] But since the hidden church is covered over by errors and has no magisterial authority, the content of faith to a large extent becomes the private conscience of the believer. In spite of writing two catechisms based on his beliefs, Luther could not avoid the consequences of this position. Beginning in his lifetime, the Protestant denominations continued to splinter. While Luther retained much of the Catholic substance, the followers of Zwingli and the Anabaptists went much further, discarding the visible structures of the church. Later the Quakers drew the most radical conclusions from the belief in a "hidden church" by retaining only the spiritual meaning of baptism and Eucharist without the external rites.

Vilmos Vajta and other twentieth-century Lutheran theologians claim that Luther discovered the spiritual-sacramental character of ecclesial communion. If we are aware of the rich sacramental-spiritual ecclesiology of the Fathers and Aquinas, we must qualify their conclusion. Luther may have rediscovered the tradition of ecclesial communion for his age. He asserted that the church's communion with Christ is realized through the believing acceptance of Christ's Word and through the Lord's Supper, both of which are received in faith. Not only his words, but Christ himself is received in his full human, divine, and spiritual reality. A true exchange comes about between him and the recipients. He gives us all that he is and takes on himself all that is ours: our weakness, our sins, and our struggles with the devil. Since he sacrificed himself for us, we must also sacrifice ourselves for our neighbors. As he carried our sins, we too must carry the sins of others.[8]

Unlike later Protestant denominations that abolished infant baptism on the grounds that infants are incapable of the act of personal faith, Luther kept the Catholic practice. This fact shows that Luther's understanding of faith has not become exclusively individualistic. He believed in the church as communion based on the faith of the ecclesial assembly that an infant

7. Luther opposed the true church with the false church, which teaches salvation to be gained not through faith but through works. "But even the Roman church was not a wholly false church for the mere presence of Scriptures and baptism, even in perverted forms, held Roman Catholicism back from complete capitulation to human and demonic forces" (Mark A. Noll, "Martin Luther and the Concept of a 'True' Church," *Evangelical Quarterly* 50, no. 2 [1978]: 82).

8. See in detail: Vilmos Vajta, *Communio: Krisztus és a szentek közössége Luther teológiájában* (Budapest: Magyarországi Luther Szövetség, 1993).

could participate in. The assembly "comes to aid the children through its faith and aids even those who offer the children.... In this way, through the almighty prayer of the offering and believing church, the faith poured out changes, cleanses and renews the child."[9] Unaware of the christological interpretation of the *ex opere operato*, the efficacy of the sacraments, Luther does not accept this Catholic teaching since he equates it with belief in magic.[10] He insists that "the sacraments achieve what they do not by their own power, but through faith."[11]

Luther's friend Philipp Melanchthon was less radical than Luther, and he tried to heal the rift with Rome. The Confessio Augustana (Augsburg Confession of Faith of 1530) became the official creed of the Lutheran Church and was mainly Melanchthon's work. Its ecclesiology is closer to the Catholic faith than many of Luther's own formulations:

> They [followers of Luther] teach that the one Holy Church will remain forever. Now this Church is the congregation of the saints, in which the Gospel is rightly taught and the sacraments rightly administered.
>
> And for that true unity of the Church it is enough to have unity of belief concerning the teaching of the Gospel and the administration of the sacraments. It is not necessary that there should everywhere be the same tradition of men, or the same rites and ceremonies devised by men.[12]

John Calvin

Calvin's ecclesiology resembles that of Luther; that is, "the one Holy Catholic Church" is invisible. It is "the body and society of believers whom God hath predestined to eternal life." Yet he acknowledges that "there is indeed also a visible Church of God, which he has described to us by certain signs and marks, but here [in this catechism] we are properly speaking of the assemblage of those whom he has adopted to salvation by his secret election.

9. Martin Luther, *De captivitate Babylonica Ecclesiae. Preludium* (WA 6:538).

10. On the christological interpretation of the *ex opere operato* principle, see Edward Schillebeeckx, *Christ the Sacrament of the Encounter with God* (New York: Sheed and Ward, 1963), 68–73, 82–89.

11. Schillebeeckx, *Christ the Sacrament*, 68–73, 82–89. If Lutherans had understood that the sacraments are the sanctifying actions of Christ that touch every recipient throughout the centuries, and if Catholics had heeded Karl Rahner's suggestions and discovered that the sacraments are the almighty Word of God embodied in material signs just as Christ is the incarnate Word himself, then a significant rapprochement could have been achieved.

12. "The Confession of Augsburg," in *Documents of the Christian Church*, ed. Henry Bettenson (London: Oxford University Press, 1963), 210.

This is neither at all times visible to the eye nor discernible by signs."[13] Yet, in another text, Calvin affirms the presence of the church of God in the Reformed churches:

> But although it is not lawful to judge individually who belongs to the Church and who does not, since we do not yet know the judgment of God, nevertheless wherever we see that the word of God is sincerely preached and heard and the sacraments instituted by Christ administered, it is not to be doubted in any way that there is a Church of God, since his promise cannot fail: "Wherever two or three are gathered in my name there I am in the midst of them."[14]

Calvin, moreover, knows the patristic tradition on the visible church:

> Let us learn from her single title of Mother, how useful, nay, how necessary the knowledge of her is, since there is no other means of entering into life unless she conceives us in the womb and give us birth, unless she nourish us at her breast, and, in short, keep us under her charge and government, until divested of mortal flesh, we become like the angels.[15]

The Catholic tradition also distinguishes between the visible and the invisible church, but believes that every human being is offered sufficient grace for salvation, while according to Calvin it is offered only to those whom God has predestined to eternal life.

The Ecclesiology of the Counter-Reformation

The Council of Trent did not treat solely the church, but also questions closely linked with it, such as the relationship of Scripture and tradition, and the sacraments.[16] At the same time, however, the council exposed and condemned the abuses in the life of the church, while subsequent popes and devout bishops such as St. Pius V and St. Charles Borromeo, to name the most important, implemented crucial reforms and renewed the vitality of the church. By defining the real, substantial presence of Christ in the Eucharist, the council assured the ultimate ontological basis for the uni-

13. "Catechism of the Church of Geneva," in *John Calvin: Selections from His Writings*, ed. John Dillenberger (Garden City, N.Y.: Doubleday, 1971), 260–61.

14. John Calvin, "The Institutes of the Christian Religion—1536 [Selections]," in Dillenberger, *John Calvin*, 301.

15. John Calvin, *The Institutes of the Christian Religion*, trans. Henry Beveridge (Grand Rapids: Eerdmans, 1983), 2:283. See the entire chapter on the church, 279–314.

16. Yves Congar, "Die Ekklesiologie der Gegenreformation," in *Handbuch der Dogmengeschichte*, vol. III/3d, *Die Lehre von der Kirche vom Abendländischen Schisma bis zur Gegenwart* (Freiburg: Herder, 1971), 52–65.

ty of the church. The Eucharist is the real and effective symbol "by which our Savior intended to bind and unite the Christians in his Church."[17] By emphasizing the sacramental character of church orders and the bishops' authority over the presbyters, the council defended the institution of the "external and visible priesthood," which was denied by Protestants. The council did not treat the primacy of the bishop of Rome so that the controversy within the Catholic Church over conciliarism would not be reignited. As stated earlier, the council fathers focused on defending those Catholic doctrines that had been attacked by Protestants, and did not present the entirety of Catholic teaching on the controverted issues.[18] At the council, the absence of historical knowledge and the council's overall defensive atmosphere prevented a comprehensive treatment of the subjects discussed. For instance, the council defended the sacramental nature of the hierarchical priesthood, which the Protestants denied, but we do not find a single reference in the council proceedings to the biblical and patristic notion of the universal priesthood of all baptized Christians, a doctrine much cherished by Protestant theologians. The church had to wait four hundred years, until the Second Vatican Council, for the conditions to be ripe for a more comprehensive treatment of the church, her liturgy, her Scriptures and tradition. As a result, in the documents of Vatican II, Protestants discovered much of their own doctrine, transformed yet present in a Catholic synthesis.

The ecclesiology of the Post-Tridentine period was by and large reduced to an apologetics intended to prove what the Reformers denied, namely, that the church is essentially a visible hierarchical society. St. Robert Bellarmine would go as far as to say that the "Church is such a visible and tangible society of people as the society of the people of Rome or the kingdom of France."[19] Bellarmine's definition of the church became normative for Post-Tridentine theology. "The Church is a society of men [and women] joined together by the profession of the same Christian faith and by participation in the same sacraments under the rule of legitimate pastors, chiefly, the only vicar of Christ, the Roman Pontiff." Bellarmine, however, is fully

17. CF 1512.

18. The Decree on Justification, however, was more comprehensive in scope, and in particular it showed how Catholic doctrine insists on the absolute gratuity of the grace of justification (CF 1924–83).

19. Robert Bellarmine, *De controversiis*, tom. 2, lib. 3, cap. 2 (Naples: Giuliano, 1857), 2:75. Cited by Avery Dulles, *Models of the Church*, expanded ed. (New York: Image, 2000), 26.

aware that the visible church is not the entire Church. Yet, in the same treatise he also wrote about the "soul" of the church because he knows that there are people who are outside the visible church yet belong to his soul through sanctifying grace.[20]

Bellarmine's definition is not false, but one-sided. He does not treat the church as mystery nor her trinitarian, christological, and pneumatic dimensions. As a result, in post-Tridentine theology, his treatise on the church became part of fundamental theology, the goal of which was to demonstrate that the Roman Catholic Church is the only true church established by Christ. This was done by explaining the scriptural and patristic texts that deal with church authority, and by showing that the marks of the one true church of Christ, as defined by the First Council of Constantinople (one, holy, catholic, and apostolic), can only be found in the Roman Catholic Church. Evidently, this kind of apologetics, which stressed only what the Reformers denied rather than explaining how the Reformers' partial truths could be integrated into a Catholic synthesis, did not promote any ecumenical rapprochement between the two sides, but rather hardened their mutual lines of defense.

20. Bellarmine, *De controversiis*, tom. 4, lib. 3, cap. 2.

CHAPTER 6

Ecclesiology before and after Vatican I

The Church on the Defense against the Modern World

Beginning in the second half of the eighteenth century, the church felt obliged to defend herself not only against Protestants but also against the growing influence of the Enlightenment, which had developed into a militant anticlericalism. It portrayed the church as an opponent of any kind of scientific or social progress, a remnant of the "Dark Ages" (Middle Ages) and the defender of the privileges of the "ancien régime."

In general, the church adopted a defensive posture, while those Catholic thinkers who saw the errors but also the truths and values in the modern world and who tried to integrate these (more or less successfully) into Catholic theology remained a minority. In fact, these Catholic thinkers were, at times, silenced and disowned by Rome. Instead of examining their critics' partial truths, such as rationalism and, from the political movements of the time, *liberté*, *égalité*, and *fraternité*, and determining how these ideas could be integrated into the Catholic worldview, most of the church hierarchy fell back on a certain kind of siege mentality. The church saw herself as beleaguered on every side and the last bastion of truth. As a rule, she did not tolerate any internal criticism or any sort of compromise with the enemy. The best illustration of this age was the papacy of Blessed Pius IX. He began his reign in 1846 as a supposed "liberal" pope, who seemingly sympathized with the democratic ideas of the times. He even approved a moderately democratic constitution for the papal states. However, when his own parliament declared war against Catholic Austria, he refused to fight against a Catholic emperor. His people then rebelled against him, forcing him to escape from Rome and only returning with the help of French troops. After this experience, he turned completely against the modern age and became the defender of the status quo not just in politics but also in theology. At the same time, however, in 1854 he defined the dogma of Mary's immaculate conception, which largely contributed to the flourishing of Marian devotion. During his papacy, several new religious orders, such as the Salesians of Don Bosco, were founded and older religious orders were revitalized. There was a general resurgence of religious piety in the church.

In the nineteenth century, the most important books on ecclesiology to break through the narrow confines of treating the church merely as an institution were the two works of Johann Adam Möhler, *The Unity in the Church* (1925) and *Symbolik* (1932).[1] Under the influence of Romanticism, the first presented the church as a supernatural "organism," the second as the extension of the incarnate Word in time and space. Möhler's works greatly influenced the next generation of important theologians, who included Giovanni Perrone, John Henry Newman, and Matthias Scheeben.

Amid the intensifying anticlerical climate of the secular nation states, such as France, Prussia, and Italy, the church needed to strengthen its Catholic center, the authority of the papacy, so the independence of the local episcopacy could be more effectively defended against the controlling influence of the state. The church also needed to clarify the doctrine of her infallible magisterium; namely, it asked, What are the criteria for determining the enduring, living truth, which the church is able to discern in revealed truth, and how is this distinguished from opinion or error?

To address these two issues, the condemnation of current errors and clarification of papal authority, Blessed Pius IX called together the First Vatican Council (1869–70). To avoid a one-sided emphasis on the papacy, the preparatory commission planned to deal with all the aspects of the church through two theses: (1) The church is a true, perfect, spiritual, and supernatural society. (2) The church is the mystical body of Christ. Because of

1. Johann Adam Möhler, *Die Einheit in der Kirche oder das Princip des Katholicismus, dargestellt im Geiste der Kirchenväter der drei ersten Jahrhunderte* (Tübingen, 1825); English translation: *Unity in the Church, or the Principle of Catholicism: Presented in the Spirit of the Church Fathers of the First Three Centuries*, trans. Peter C. Erb (Washington, D.C.: The Catholic University of America Press, 1995). Möhler, *Symbolik oder Darstellung der dogmatischen Gegensätze der Katholiken und Protestanten nach ihren Öffentlichen Bekenntnisschriften* (Mainz, 1832); English translation: *Symbolism or, Exposition of the Doctrinal Differences between Catholics and Protestants as Evidenced by their Symbolical Writings*, trans. James Burton Robertson (London: Charles Dolman, 1843).

the approaching Italian army, which intended to abolish the papal states and create a unified Italian state, the council was suspended in 1870 after dealing with the primacy of the Roman pontiff.

In the introduction of the decree *Pastor Aeternus,* the council stated that the purpose of the Petrine ministry is to assure that all believers "might be united together in the bond of one faith and one love." The ecclesial unity for which Christ prayed is expressed in his high priestly prayer before his arrest: that "all might be one, as he, the Son and the Father are one."[2] This was a concise anticipation of *Lumen Gentium*'s trinitarian foundation. The Petrine ministry's goal is to promote this spiritual unity, a communion of faith and love, which participates in the unity of the Father and the Son. For this purpose, Christ bestowed on St. Peter "a perpetual principle and visible foundation of this twofold unity" of faith and love.[3] The council upheld the ancient tradition according to which the popes represent "Peter, Prince and Head of all the apostles, who 'even to this time and forever lives' and governs, and exercises judgment in his successors, the bishops of the holy Roman See, which he established and consecrated with his blood."[4] In order to avoid errors and misunderstandings as well as strengthen the centripetal forces in the church, the council defined a twofold truth about the Petrine ministry:

1. The pope, as successor of Peter, has supreme, immediate, ordinary, and full power of jurisdiction over the universal church not only in matters of faith and morals but also in matters that pertain to discipline and government.[5]

2. The pope possesses under certain conditions "the infallibility with which the divine Redeemer willed His Church to be endowed in defining doctrine concerning faith or morals" and that these definitions of the Roman pontiff "are therefore irreformable of themselves not because of the consent of the Church [*ex sese non ex consensu Ecclesiae*]."[6]

The first canon, directed primarily against Gallicanism, rejects any interference from secular authority and any curtailment by bishops of the

2. CF 818. Cf. Jn 17:20–21.

3. CF 818.

4. CF 822, quoting from the discourse of Philip, the legate of the pope at the Council of Ephesus (July 11, 431).

5. CF 830.

6. CF 839.

pope's legal power to intervene in the affairs of a diocese.[7] The supreme, immediate, full, and ordinary power of jurisdiction of the pope was not meant to stand in the way of the ordinary and immediate jurisdiction of the diocesan bishop over his diocese. According to Vatican I, the bishops were appointed by the Holy Spirit and were successors to the apostles. The pope, as supreme and universal shepherd, rather affirms, strengthens, and vindicates their power.[8] However, this short paragraph in *Pastor Aeternus* on bishops was not sufficient to dispel the false impression that diocesan bishops were mere delegates of the popes, agents of a foreign power, and unable to be loyal citizens of the state. Especially in England and in Germany, this misunderstanding caused enormous difficulties. Newman in England and the bishops in Germany attempted to dispel this erroneous interpretation.[9]

At the council, the "ultramontanist" party did not achieve its objective of defining without qualifications that papal infallibility is a personal charism of the pope.[10] They held that whatever the pope teaches on matters of faith and morals is infallible. At the intervention of a thoughtful minority, the council finally agreed on these points: (1) The pope has no right to define a new doctrine, but only explain what has been revealed. (2) Under some definite conditions, such as when he speaks *ex cathedra*, the Roman pontiff "possesses through divine assistance the infallibility promised to him in the person of Blessed Peter, the infallibility with which the divine Redeemer willed his church to be endowed in defining the doctrine concerning faith or morals."[11] (3) "That such definitions of the Roman Pontiff are therefore irreformable of themselves, not because of the consent of the Church."[12]

The conditions under which the pope speaks *ex cathedra* were also defined as follows: (1) "He acts in the office of shepherd and teacher of all Christians," rather than addressing a private person or a particular audi-

7. Gallicanism approved of the French practice by which papal decrees could not be promulgated in France without the king's permission.

8. CF 827.

9. CF 841.

10. Ultramontanist bishops at the council wanted to define that any declaration of the pope on matters of faith and morals is infallible.

11. CF 839. "Romanum Pontificem cum ex cathedra loquitur ... per assistentiam divinam ipsi in beato Petro promissam, ea infallibilitate pollere, qua divinus Redemptor Ecclesiam suam in definienda doctrina de fide vel moribus instructam esse voluit."

12. CF 839.

ence. (2) The object of his teaching is a doctrine concerning faith and morals. (3) The pope makes clear that he is defining a doctrine to be held by the universal church rather than exercising his ordinary magisterium through a discourse, encyclical, or message.[13] (4) Since these dogmatic definitions are necessarily true, they are not reformable; that is, they cannot be reversed or negated. But, as the history of the church amply demonstrates, mysteries of faith will always need to be penetrated further or be better articulated. (5) Such dogmatic definitions are in and of themselves true, rather than conditionally true and reliant on the acceptance of the church. That is, they are not bills introduced into a democratic parliament, bills that become valid laws of a nation only upon the approval of a parliamentary majority.[14]

While defeated in the council, the ultramontanist view on the papacy is present to this day among Protestants and rank-and-file Catholics. Although the narrow focus of Vatican I on the papacy triggered an exaggeration of the pope's importance, these definitions proved to be providential in the life of the church, especially during the storms of the twentieth century. By crystallizing a traditional tenet of faith, they provided the church with a strong center concerning matters of doctrine and its own discipline. Moreover, the far-reaching renewal and reforms of the church orchestrated by Vatican II would have been impossible without a strong papal office whose ultimate authority every Catholic recognized. As a Protestant theologian remarked, such thorough changes would have splintered any Protestant denominations into antagonistic groups.

The Renewal of Ecclesiology

Following in the footsteps of Otto Dibelius, the noted Protestant exegete and bishop, Yves Congar titled the chapter of his ecclesiology on the twentieth century "The Century of the Church."[15] Romano Guardini famously

13. Thus the definition of *Pastor Aeternus* implies what LG 25 of Vatican II makes explicit: infallibility is a charism of the church, which is present in the pope in a unique way under some definite conditions ("in quo [Papa] charisma infallibilitatis ipsius Ecclesiae singulariter adest").

14. *Lumen Gentium* specifies that "the assent, however, can never fail to be given to these definitions on account of the activity of the same Holy Spirit, by which the whole flock of Christ preserved in the unity of the faith and makes progress" (no. 25). By no means does this imply that the validity of the definitions can be measured by statistical surveys among those who identify themselves as Catholic.

15. Yves Congar, *Handbuch der Dogmengeschichte*, vol. III/3d, *Die Lehre von der Kirche: Von Augustinus bis zum Gegenwart* (Freiburg: Herder, 1971), 114.

proclaimed: "A religious process of incalculable magnitude is happening: the Church begins to wake up in the souls."[16] The renewal of ecclesiology in the first half of the twentieth century was part of a general renewal of the church and her theology, a process that culminated in Vatican II.[17]

As the philosophy of personalism focused interest on the person and their relationships, so ecclesiology began to describe the church as a communion of persons united by the power of the Holy Spirit into the mystical body of Christ as well as a hierarchically ordered society. In the first half of the century, Catholic scholars and even some educated Catholics in German- and French-speaking countries rediscovered the long-buried riches of biblical and patristic theology, including the biblical and patristic images and notions of the church.[18] What has been discussed in previous chapters concerning biblical and patristic ecclesiology began to shape Catholic thinking, experience, and practice in these countries. Catholics became aware that in the liturgy the biblical word is actualized as the Word of Christ that awakens our faith in order to celebrate the Eucharist, which transforms us into his mystical body.[19] The church is not fused into Christ, but rather she becomes the spouse of Christ so that her virginal union with Christ forms Christ's ecclesial body. In spiritually mature souls, the church also becomes a spiritual mother by conceiving Christ in these souls and by carrying Christ to those who do not know him.

The study of the church's biblical-patristic heritage has also refreshed the trinitarian foundations of ecclesiology, which holds that the church is a trinitarian communion. At the same time, the expanding historical horizon of the age rediscovered the various stages in the history of the church, such as the church beginning with Abel, developing in the Old Testament, being established in its current state by Christ, and ultimately arriving at its perfect stature in eschatology. The biblical-patristic renewal also introduced into ecclesiology the notion of the people of God; that the church is

16. Romano Guardini, *Vom Sinn der Kirche* (Mainz: Matthias-Grünewald, 1922), 1.

17. See Stanislas Jáki, *Les tendances nouvelles de l'ecclésiogie* (Rome: Herder, 1957). The most comprehensive and judicious evaluation of the new ecclesiological trends can be found in the works of Yves Congar: See Joseph Famerée, "L'ecclésiologie du Père Yves Congar: Essai de synthese critique," *Revue de sciences philosophiques et théologiques* 76, no. 3 (1992): 377–419. Another great theologian of the church at that time was Henri de Lubac. See Marc Pelchat, *L'Église mystère de communion: L'Ecclésiologie dans l'oeuvre de Henri de Lubac* (Paris: Les Éditions Paulines, 1988).

18. Henri de Lubac, *The Splendor of the Church*, trans. Michael Mason (San Francisco: Ignatius, 1986); Hugo Rahner, *Symbole der Kirche: Die Ekklesiogie der Väter* (Salzburg: O. Müller, 1964); Rahner, *Our Lady and the Church* (Bethesda, Md.: Zaccheus Press, 2005).

19. Emile Mersch, *Theology of the Mystical Body* (St. Louis: Herder, 1951).

God's pilgrim people from Abraham until the present time, and as such she shares in Christ's prophetic, kingly, and priestly dignity.

Even though further splintering into diverse groups has continued, a large number of Protestant denominations discovered they needed some form of union that would, at very least, foster cooperation and friendship with other Christians. In 1948, when the World Council of Churches (WCC) was founded as a loose assembly of various Protestant denominations, all of the churches in the Anglican Communion and the ecumenical patriarchate of Constantinople joined. A few years later, other churches also joined. The goal of the group was to develop closer relationships among churches and promote visible unity. Its most important agency, which discusses doctrinal issues, is the Faith and Order Commission. The Catholic Church is not an official member of the WCC, but she sends observers to the meetings, has full membership rights, and actively participates in the Faith and Order Commission. Through Pope Pius XII's papacy, the holy see looked with suspicion on any ecumenical activity that was not solely a theological discussion. The WCC has always tacitly supposed that the church of Christ is only partially present in the institutional churches. Therefore, the holy see reasoned, formal membership would contradict the Catholic Church's self-understanding as the one true church founded by Christ. With John XXIII, however, the ecumenical climate changed so that Catholic theologians no longer looked on their Protestant counterparts as willfully rejecting what they believed to be revealed truth. Rather, Catholic theologians regarded their Protestant peers as separated Christian brothers and sisters who were born into a non-Catholic community and are sincerely open to embrace all that they recognize to be God's revelation. Another factor for the interest in dialogue was the fact that the *ressourcement* had spread beyond the Catholic Church to include Protestant churches, which rediscovered their own Catholic heritage in the thought of their great reformers. For mainly psychological reasons, dialogue with the Orthodox churches was more difficult. Nevertheless, a shared patristic tradition, the West's interest in the Eastern liturgies, and their common minority status in the Middle East soon overcame the Orthodox churches' initial aversion to dialogue.

As global interaction increased across the continents, Christians became acutely aware of their diminished stature amid the great multiplicity of world religions. The question of the salvation of non-Christians and atheists, and the obvious human and religious values of non-Christian religions, caused much consternation and speculation among Catholic theologians and, in particular, missionaries.

The missionary thrust of the church gained new direction and energy during the papacy of Pius XI. For the first time in history, Chinese bishops were ordained for Chinese dioceses. Unfortunately, the Communist terror would later enslave the country and expel all foreign missionaries. The theory and practice of inculturation also gained momentum at that time. Missionaries, supported and later replaced by native bishops and priests, had clearly realized they needed to separate Christian faith from some elements of European culture that could prevent Christianity's implantation into the non-European cultures.

The church's relationship to the world also began to change. As previously stated, the twofold attacks by Protestants and Enlightenment thinkers, coming as they did at different times and from different directions, forced the church to close ranks, withdraw into a defensive position, and behave as if she were under siege in a beleaguered fortress. The ecclesial awakening inspired a new, positive attitude toward the world. The church should welcome all the positive developments in modern civilization and reinterpret the *Syllabus of Errors*, which was promulgated by Pius IX and appeared to proscribe "any progress, the entire liberal agenda and modern civilization."[20] According to the famous program of Hans Urs von Balthasar, the church must erase her defensive bastions and embrace the vocation of the Suffering Servant in order to serve the real needs of the world and accept the resistance and sufferings caused by hostile forces.[21] The church should welcome the values of science and technology and even the partial truths of opponents' views. Christianity does not destroy, but rather purifies, fertilizes, and perfects a culture, bringing to light its hidden treasures.

Three important encyclicals by Pius XII were intended to recognize and encourage the renewal in scriptural studies (*Divino afflante Spiritu*, 1943), ecclesiology (*Mystici Corporis*, 1943), and liturgy (*Mediator Dei*, 1947). Although Vatican II subsequently transcended these documents by attempting a syn-

20. DS 2980. Pope Pius IX in fact did not reject all progress or the entire liberal agenda, just its errors, which the rest of the *Syllabus* proscribes. Nonetheless, contemporary readers interpreted it on its face value. At any rate, the *Syllabus* was by no means an infallible document.

21. Balthasar's famous book was *Schleifung der Bastionen* (Einsiedeln: Benziger, 1952).

thesis of the church's recovered tradition and the needs of contemporary culture, these encyclicals at the time of their issuance were milestones that marked the positive results of renewal.

Mystici Corporis explains the biblical image of the mystical body of Christ for the first time in a magisterial document. It praised the unfolding theology of the mystical body, but criticized how some theological works separated the institutional church from the church of love. The encyclical explained that the invisible mission of the Holy Spirit (Jn 20:22) and the juridical commission of rulers and teachers established by Christ (Jn 20:21; Lk 10:16) complement and perfect each other and relate like soul and body.[22]

The pope beautifully unfolds the role of the Holy Spirit in the mystical body of Christ by showing that the whole Spirit dwells in Jesus, in the church, and in each of the faithful of the human race. He, the Spirit, is the "soul" of the church, existing in each member and in the whole organism.[23] Thus the nature of the mystical body of Christ is qualitatively different from the mere moral union of a society, which merely shares the same goals, and also different from a physical body, whose members have no personal identity. In the mystical body of Christ, the Holy Spirit preserves each member's personal identity while uniting each in the closest possible unity.[24]

According to *Mystici Corporis*, those are in reality (*reapse*) members of the church "who have been baptized and profess the true faith and who have had not the misfortune of withdrawing from the body or for grave faults been cut off by legitimate authority."[25] The partial or analogous ecclesial reality of other Christian churches is not yet recognized; and the encyclical stresses that the state of separation from the Catholic Church of these Christians means that they cannot be assured of their eternal salvation. Yet the encyclical admits that they may be ordained by an "unconscious desire and vow to the mystical body of the Redeemer."[26]

To evaluate *Mystici Corporis* fairly, we must underline its positive significance, namely: (1) Although not using the term, *Mystici Corporis* demonstrates the sacramental nature of the church by emphasizing that her visible and invisible aspects belong together. (2) *Mystici Corporis* builds the

22. CF 853.

23. CF 852. Vatican II does not call the Holy Spirit "soul of the church" but merely says that the Fathers compared the role of the Holy Spirit in the church to what the soul does in the human body (LG 7).

24. CF 847.

25. CF 849.

26. DS 3821 ("inscio quodam desiderio ac voto ad mysticum Redemptoris Corpus ordinentur").

theology of the church on the notion of the mystical body of Christ, which is ultimately a Pauline and patristic notion.[27] (3) It presents the indwelling of the whole Spirit in Christ, in the church as a whole, and in each member as the foundation for the mysterious unity of the church and as the arbiter of her hierarchical functions and charismatic gifts.

Yet, when compared to the Dogmatic Constitution on the Church of Vatican II, *Mystici Corporis* is an excellent example of the way that magisterial teaching develops in the church. The next chapter shows how much *Lumen Gentium* of Vatican II was able to enrich and correct the ecclesiology of *Mystici Corporis* just twenty-two years later.

27. Note that the Fathers qualified the eucharistic body of Christ by the adjective "mystical." It was first applied to the church as the "mystical body of Christ" in the Middle Ages.

CHAPTER 7

The Ecclesiology of Vatican II

On January 25, 1959, after celebrating the feast of the Conversion of St. Paul in the Roman Basilica of San Paolo fuori le mura, John XXIII stunned his entourage by announcing he had decided to convoke an ecumenical council.[1] To his surprise and great disappointment, the cardinals and other church dignitaries present, rather than responding with enthusiastic applause, as is customary after papal pronouncements, fell into complete silence and some allegedly shot icy glances in his direction. "Why do we need a council?" some were surely thinking. After all, papal infallibility had been solemnly defined. If he wanted to, the pope could make new doctrinal definitions on his own and, by doing so, save considerable money, controversy, and time. Others were reluctant to approve because most other ecumenical councils throughout history had been convoked only when heresies had to be identified and rejected. At that point in time, no heresy threatened the church.

Pope John, however, had been pondering and debating with several trusted aides the idea of a council ever since he had been elected to Peter's chair. Yet, as he confessed later, a sudden inspiration provided the impetus for his decision, after which no opposition or delaying tactics could prevent him from opening the council in less than three years. The pope himself had no clear idea about the specific program for the council, so he asked for input from the Catholic bishops of the entire world. However, during

1. Matthew L. Lamb and Matthew Levering, eds., *Vatican II: Renewal within Tradition* (Oxford: Oxford University Press, 2008); Commentary on *Lumen Gentium* by Avery Dulles, *My Journal of the Council* (Adelaide: ATF Theology, 2012); Giuseppe Alberigo and Joseph A. Komonchak, eds., *The History of Vatican II*, 5 vols. (Maryknoll, N.Y.: Orbis; Louvain: Peeters: 1998–2006).

his radio message a month before and again in his speech at the opening session of the council on October 11, 1962, he outlined in general terms an ambitious program of renewal that would follow these guidelines: (1) The council should be pastoral council, responding to the needs of the church and the world today. (2) No new doctrinal condemnations are intended but a positive presentation of the gospel in a language that modern men and women understand. (3) The pope asked God that the council act as a new Pentecost, an outpouring of the gifts of the Holy Spirit on the church. (4) Official observers from every Christian denomination were invited and granted access to all the documents of the council, and their input on the conciliar documents was solicited. (5) The renewed church, as a result, would be able to work more effectively with other Christians from other churches for the restoration of Christian unity. (6) The church would thus be able to give credible witness to the power of Christian love and truth.[2]

John XXIII lived only through the council's first session, which lasted from October 11 to December 8, 1962. After his death on June 3, 1963, Paul VI was elected. At the beginning of the council's second session, Paul VI formulated a more concrete program for the council: (1) The church should awaken to a deeper understanding of herself and articulate this for herself and the world. (2) The church must renew herself by looking on Christ as a mirror in which she can identify her stains, shadows, and shortcomings. (3) She should seek the "recomposition" of unity with each baptized Christian brother and sister who believes in Christ. (4) Even though she sees the many forms of evil in the world, the church should also embrace the world with the redemptive love of Christ. "She does not want to dominate the world, but to serve it; not to scorn, but to increase the dignity of human beings; not to condemn, but to comfort and save it."[3]

At the recommendations of Cardinal Suenens of Belgium, all the schemata of the council were organized around the theme of the church. Of the sixteen documents the council voted on, the following is a list of those most important with regard to ecclesiology: *Lumen Gentium*, a dogmatic treatise on the church; *Unitatis Redintegratio*, a decree on Catholic ecumenism; *Ad*

2. John XXIII, *Radio Message to All the Christian Faithful One Month before the Opening of the Second Vatican Ecumenical Council* (September 11, 1962); John XXIII, *Address on the Occasion of the Solemn Opening of the Most Holy Council* (October 11, 1962). Both are available at vatican.va.

3. Paul VI, *Address at the Solemn Opening of the Second Session of the Second Vatican Council* (September 29, 1963), 149–90.

Gentes, a decree on missions; and *Gaudium et Spes* (GS), a pastoral constitution on the church's role in the modern world.

According to the famous French theologian Yves Congar, the council worked toward two interrelated goals: *ressourcement*, a return to the sources; and *aggiornamento*, an updating or reforming of the church.[4]

The former task involves the rediscovery and reassimilation of the treasures of the Christian tradition, especially the theology of the Bible, the Fathers, and the ancient Christian liturgy. This recovery of the past, however, would enrich only the libraries if it were not combined with *aggiornamento*. The church must renew and reform herself, must become aware of the joys and hopes, tragedies and errors of our age so that she may find a new language for the "eternal gospel" that speaks to men and women of our times.

Because from the beginning of the council most of the curia were less than enthusiastic about the convocation and some were strongly opposed to it, John XXIII staffed the many preparatory commissions with leading members of the curia. In this way, he attempted to win their support. At the same time, he knew that the church needed a spiritual, theological, and pastoral renewal, so he appointed to these committees several bishops and consultors who understood and supported both *ressourcement* and *aggiornamento*. But this group was in the minority on most of the council's commissions. As a result, most of the schemata[5] prepared by the commissions reflected the narrow outlook of those who—with some cosmetic changes—wanted to maintain the status quo. Only the Liturgical Commission and the Secretariat for Christian Unity presented draft schemata that "could serve well as a basis for the conciliar discussions.

The schema on the church had been prepared by the Doctrinal Commission, headed by Alfredo Cardinal Ottaviani, prefect of the holy office. He was chiefly responsible for criticizing or censuring some of the best theologians of the time. These same theologians would eventually play a decisive role in shaping the council's agenda and documents.[6] The secretary of the Theological Commission, Fr. Sebastian Tromp, SJ, who had previously drafted for Pius XII the Encyclical *Mystici Corporis*, produced the schema on the church, which was proposed for discussion in the General

4. Yves Congar, *Vrai et fausse réforme dans l'église* (Paris: Cerf, 1950), 57, 335–37.

5. Texts to be discussed, amended, and voted upon by the council fathers.

6. The most famous theologians he had denounced were Henri de Lubac, Yves Congar, and Marie-Dominique Chenu.

Conciliar Assembly. The significance of the final document, *Lumen Gentium*, can only be appreciated when one compares the outline of Tromp's preparatory document to the outline of the final product, which was approved and promulgated by the council.[7] The chapter titles for the preparatory schema reveal its orientation and content. These titles were (1) "The Nature of the Militant Church"; (2) "The Members of the Church and the Necessity of the Church for Salvation"; (3) "The Bishops"; (4) "The States of Perfection to Be Acquired" (*status perfectionis acquirendae* of the religious communities); (5) "The Laity" (6) "The Magisterium"; (7) "Authority and Obedience" (8) "Relationship between State and Church" (9) "The Necessity for the Church to Announce the Gospel Everywhere to All Creatures."

Although accepting the schema *De Ecclesia* for discussion, the interventions of the fathers in the conciliar aula at the end of the first session and during the second soon revealed the need for a thorough rewriting. The debate still continued through the end of 1964, when on November 21 the Fathers voted on the final text of the Dogmatic Constitution *de Ecclesia*, approving it almost unanimously, with only five opposing votes.

The chief objections to the first draft were as follows: (1) The phrase "militant church" evokes the defensive ecclesial posture of the post-Tridentine age. (2) The only biblical image treated in the draft was the mystical body; notions such as people of God, spouse, and mother were missing. (3) Legal language prevailed at the expense of a biblical and patristic approach. (4) The sequence bishops-religious-laity suggested a hierarchical ecclesial membership with successively lower status at each level. The structure of the final document reveals a substantially different theological outlook.

The Mystery of the Church

The biblical, patristic, and liturgical understanding of the church as mystery becomes the key notion of the Dogmatic Constitution on the Church. The church is mystery primarily because it participates in the mystery of the Holy Trinity.[8] The specific relationship and role of each divine person to the church is delineated and a crucial amendment was introduced into the final text. The clause: *Lumen Gentium cum sit Ecclesia*, "since the Church

7. See Joseph Ratzinger, "The Ecclesiology of the Second Vatican Council," in *Joseph Ratzinger in Communio*, vol. 1, *The Unity of the Church* (Grand Rapids: Eerdmans, 2010), 62–77.

8. LG 1–7.

is the light of the nations,"[9] was changed to *Lumen Gentium cum sit Christus*, "since Christ is the light of the nations." This improvement defined the perspective and direction of the entire document by emphasizing the sacramental structure of the church. The church is no source of light in herself, but, to use the patristic image, she is simply the moon, which receives all its light from Christ, the sun. She is the effective sign of humankind's union with Christ and, for that reason, the sign and anticipation of the unity of humankind. Whoever sees only the sign, the impressive ceremonies, majestic buildings, or the persons of the office-holders, will lose the reality to whom the sign points, Jesus Christ.

Instead of speaking only about the "militant church" of the present, *Lumen Gentium* articulates the perspective of the Fathers who spoke about a church that is coextensive with the entire history of humankind. Foreshadowed in Abel and all the just from the beginning of the world, prepared for in the history of Israel and the ancient covenant, established in these last times, manifested by the outpouring of the Holy Spirit, the church will be gloriously consummated at the end of time. This first chapter of *Lumen Gentium* uses all the biblical images of the church rather than that of the mystical body alone.

Lumen Gentium does not simply identify the kingdom of God with the church on earth, but the church is described as a dynamic process to be consummated in eschatology. The church is "the initial budding forth of that Kingdom. While she slowly grows, the Church strains toward the consummation of the kingdom and, with all her strength, hopes and desires to be united in glory with her King."[10]

Unlike *Mystici Corporis*, *Lumen Gentium* deemphasizes the issue of membership in the church, since this might be interpreted to completely exclude non-Catholic Christians from her. Instead of a simple identification of the hierarchically organized Catholic Church and the mystical body, *Lumen Gentium* explains that a visible assembly and a spiritual community, a society, equipped with hierarchical structure, and the mystical body of Christ "must not be considered as two things, but as forming one complex

9. *LG* 1.

10. *LG* 5. Even though several texts in Matthew and most of the parables in chapter 13 identify the church with the kingdom (Mt 16:19), *LG* emphasizes an eschatological interpretation. Thus the entire church strives toward the kingdom: the apostles are sent to preach the kingdom of God (*LG* 19) and the Lord uses also the service of laypeople to extend his kingdom on earth, which he himself will consummate and hand over to the Father (*LG* 36).

reality." This formulation allows the assertion that the church of Christ "set up and organized in this world as a society, subsists in the Catholic Church . . . although outside its structure many elements of sanctification and of truth are to be found which as proper gifts to the church of Christ, impel towards catholic unity."[11]

The People of God

In the New Testament, the phrase "people of God" is rarely applied to the church and only in the sense of expressing the continuity with the people of God in the old covenant. But in *Lumen Gentium*, it becomes the church's most important designation. In this way, the council eliminated the dominance of the one-sided notion of the "mystical body."[12]

Lumen Gentium declares also the equal dignity of all baptized Christians, whether laypeople or members of the hierarchy.[13] Everyone in the church participates in the priestly, prophetic, and royal dignity, as well as the role of Christ.[14] The distinction between laity and clerical hierarchy is secondary, and both the hierarchical and charismatic gifts are necessary for the upbuilding of the church. Consequently, *Lumen Gentium* treats the special roles of the hierarchy and laity (chapters 3 and 4) only after what is common to the entire people of God has been explained.

The Hierarchical Constitution of the Church and, in Particular, the Episcopate

Lumen Gentium included the teaching of *Pastor Aeternus* from Vatican I on papal primacy, but counterbalanced it by explaining the sacramental nature of episcopal ordination and by articulating the meaning of the doctrine of episcopal collegiality. Until the publication of *Lumen Gentium*, theologians were legitimately divided over the nature of episcopal ordination: is it the imparting of the fullness of the sacrament of orders or an actualization of the juridical (governing) authority already bestowed potentially at priestly ordination? Although the council had declared it did not intend to define

11. LG 8.

12. See Rose Beal, *Mystery of the Church, People of God: Yves Congar's Total Ecclesiology as a Path to Vatican II* (Washington, D.C.: The Catholic University of America Press, 2014).

13. LG 32.

14. LG 10–12, 36.

any new infallible dogma, it solemnly taught "that the fullness of the sacrament of orders is conferred by episcopal ordination."[15]

The doctrine of collegiality caused perhaps the hottest debates in the Doctrinal Commission and in the conciliar aula. A nervous minority of bishops and theologians were convinced that the principle of collegiality would mean an end to papal primacy. Between the second and third sessions, Pope Paul had to intervene to convince this militant group that he did not consider collegiality a threat to papal authority. The commission finally composed a *Nota explicativa praevia*, an official commentary on paragraphs 22–23 of *Lumen Gentium*. This declared that the college does not exist without its head, the Roman pontiff, who retains his full freedom of speaking and acting either collegially or personally. But it pointed out that the college acting with its head, the Roman pontiff, "is the subject of full power over the universal church."[16]

The Laity

The traditional definition of laypersons, sanctioned by the Codex of Canon Law of 1917, was purely negative. That is, anyone is a layperson who is neither a cleric nor a religious.[17] The only right of a layperson mentioned in the codex is the right to receive spiritual goods from the clergy.[18]

According to *Lumen Gentium*, laypeople, made one body with Christ and established among the people of God by baptism, share in their own way the priestly, prophetic, and royal office of Christ and carry out his threefold mission in the church and the world. The council stresses that "a secular quality is proper and special to the laity . . . the laity, by their very vocation, seek the kingdom of God by engaging in temporal affairs and by ordering them according to the plan of God."[19]

The Call of the Whole Church to Holiness

What sacred Scriptures and saints such as Francis de Sales and Thérèse of Lisieux have taught, but most Christians have not realized, *Lumen Gentium* solemnly affirmed. Everyone in the church, not only priests and religious,

15. *LG* 21.
16. *LG*, *Nota explicativa praevia* 3–4.
17. Codex of Canon Law of 1917, canon 948.
18. Codex of Canon Law of 1917, canon 682.
19. *LG* 31; cf. Yves Congar, *Lay People in the Church* (London: Geoffrey Chapman; Westminster, Md.: Christian Classics, 1985).

is called to holiness and the fullness of Christian life. Although holiness is obtained in various ways and exists in many forms, it essentially consists in the perfection of charity.[20] From among the many ways Christians attain to holiness, *Lumen Gentium* describes in greater detail conjugal holiness and the practice and/or vow of the evangelical counsels of chastity, poverty, and obedience, lived alone or in religious communities.

Religious

In order to give greater weight to religious communities, the council dedicated a special chapter to them. This chapter extols the example and practice of religious for all Christians, who can see in them the indissoluble bond of love that unites Christ and the church. They follow more closely the life of Jesus on earth, have greater freedom from attachment to worldly goods, and thus have more energy for serving their neighbors. They can more easily develop an undivided love for God and anticipate already on earth the goods of eternal life.

In spite of this special chapter on the religious, which was added belatedly, and the Decree on the Appropriate Renewal of Religious Life (*Perfectae Caritatis*), the council's overriding interest, as shown in the documents it produced, focused on the collegial role of the bishops, on the beauty of marriage and parenting, as well as on the laity's mission in the world; the council attempted to correct the false impression that only the clergy and religious were called to holiness.

The Eschatological Nature of the Pilgrim Church and Her Union with the Heavenly Church

Pope John XXIII insisted that the council develop and insert a chapter into *Lumen Gentium* that treated explicitly the eschatological nature of the church, a pilgrim people on march toward heaven. The church militant on earth is only one phase on the journey and one class of members, inseparable from the suffering church in purgatory and the triumphant church in heaven. We venerate the church in heaven and its members, try to imitate their virtues, and ask for their prayers. We are most closely united with them in the liturgy, especially in the eucharistic celebration, when we praise and thank

20. LG 40.

God the Father along with all the angels and all the saints in heaven; we sing with one voice the Sanctus, the song of the seraphim, and the acclamations of the jubilant crowd that celebrated the solemn entrance of Jesus into the holy city of Jerusalem. Unfortunately this chapter has almost been forgotten in the postconciliar period. It still awaits adequate commentary and reflection.

The Role of the Blessed Virgin Mary, Mother of God, in the Mystery of Christ and the Church

This chapter, which was at first a separate document, was inserted into *Lumen Gentium* by a very narrow majority vote following a heated discussion. Almost half of the fathers wanted a separate document on Mary for they feared that its insertion into *Lumen Gentium* would signal to the world that the council intended to minimize Mary's importance. The other side argued that, from the perspective of the New Testament and the patristic tradition, the mystery of Mary becomes intelligible only within the larger mystery of Christ and the church. In her, the history of the world and Israel is fulfilled. She is the woman promised by God after the fall, the new Eve, whose offspring will crush the ancient serpent's head; she is the exalted virgin daughter of Zion, who will bear Emmanuel, "God with us." Mary gave birth to the Messiah and Redeemer not only physically but primarily by her faith. The text quotes the frequent assertion of the Fathers: "Death came through Eve, but life through Mary."[21] Moreover, as she is the mother of Christ, she is also the mother of all believers, assisting them until they are fully born into eternal life with God. In this way, she is the model, the perfect realization of the church; virgin, spouse, and mother. Her immaculate conception is the anticipation and guarantee of that immaculate holiness that will belong to the whole church in heaven at the end of times.

21. LG 56.

CHAPTER 8

Ecclesiology after the Council

Crisis and Renewal

Even before the conclusion of the last session of the council, the initial signs of an alarming postconciliar crisis began to surface.[1] At the beginning of the first session, several great theologians, including Henri de Lubac, Yves Congar, Jean Daniélou, Joseph Ratzinger, and Karl Rahner, who had advocated the rediscovery of the biblical and patristic heritage, were in serious danger of being excluded from the work of the council by curial manipulations. But with time, as more bishops discovered the necessity of both *ressourcement* and *aggiornamento*, these theologians became the prime movers in shaping the direction and the content of the conciliar documents. During the last session, however, these progressive bishops and theologians found themselves in opposition to those who, in the name of renewal, began to clamor for a different kind of "progress," a thorough secularization of society, culture, and politics. Fr. de Lubac, for instance, caricatured a bishop who fell into "ecstasy" as he declared that the church must learn everything from the world.[2] He also observed that a priest, trying to appear "progressive," complained that Paul VI practiced "clericalism" at the United Nations because he mentioned God and the gospel in his speech.[3]

1. Yves Congar summarized the postconciliar trend in these terms: "Before the Council [theologians] looked at the world from the perspective of the Church. But now they tend to understand the Church from the perspective of the world, which carries with it the danger to secularize and misunderstand the Church. In reality, although the Church is very much for the world, it is still something other than the world: it is the fruit of God's intervention which cannot be reduced to creation and history" (Yves Congar, *Handbuch der Dogmengeschichte*, vol. III/3d, *Die Lehre von der Kirche: Von Augustinus bis zum Gegenwart* [Freiburg: Herder, 1971], 126–27).

2. Henri de Lubac, *Carnets du Concile* (Paris: Cerf, 2007), 428.

3. De Lubac, *Carnets du Concile*, 429.

Pope Benedict XVI in his last discourse to the clergy of Rome pointed out one of the main sources of the postconciliar crisis:

There was the Council of the Fathers—the real Council—but there was also the Council of the media. It was almost a Council apart, and the world perceived the Council through the latter, through the media. Thus, the Council that reached the people with immediate effect was that of the media, not that of the Fathers. And while the Council of the Fathers was conducted within the faith—it was a Council of faith seeking *intellectus*, seeking to understand itself and seeking to understand the signs of God at that time, seeking to respond to the challenge of God at that time and to find in the word of God a word for today and tomorrow—while all the Council, as I said, moved within the faith, as *fides quaerens intellectum*, the Council of the journalists, naturally, was not conducted within the faith, but within the categories of today's media, namely apart from faith, with a different hermeneutic. It was a political hermeneutic.[4]

Unfortunately, not only the faithful and the lower clergy but also many bishops, who did not understand Latin and/or were not familiar with the issues, learned only from the media about what happened in the council aula on a given day. For instance, the English-speaking cardinals and bishops became avid scrutinizers of reports in *Time* magazine and *Newsweek*. Priests and laity all over the world depended on the media reports even more so than the bishops. Thus, as a result of this communications disaster, the council of the media prevented the world for a considerable period of time from learning about the real council of the fathers. The secular media tends to interpret everything in political terms. Even Catholic journals in America were, by and large, unprepared for perceiving and communicating the theological dimension of the conciliar events. In this context, then, the phrase "people of God," by which the Dogmatic Constitution on the Church expressed the continuity between the peoples of the two Testaments as well as the Christians' share in Christ's priestly, prophetic, and royal office, became a sociological catchword.[5] Other biblical and patristic titles for the church, such as participation in trinitarian communion, body of Christ in the primary sense of an extension of Christ's personal body, spouse of Christ and mother, were ignored or forgotten by the so-called

4. Benedict XVI, *Address to the Clergy of Rome* (February 14, 2013).

5. To counteract a secular understanding of the church, the Congregation for the Doctrine of the Faith issued *Letter to the Bishops of the Catholic Church on Some Aspects of the Church Understood as Communion* (May 28, 1992).

cutting-edge theologians, who scrambled to be in the avant-garde of progressive theology. Only the title "body of Christ" became widely used, but in a secondary, sociological sense as the unity and equality of the diverse members with diverse ecclesial functions. The terms "spouse" and "mother," which were used but sparingly by the council, were later not only avoided but also sharply criticized by some feminists as the harmful residue of an oppressive patriarchal theology.

The relationships between the pope, the college of bishops, and the laity were interpreted as a power struggle, a fight for the church's democratization. So the storyline went that the laity was struggling for more power over the clergy, and the bishops were grasping for more power over the pope.

We as Catholics must not, however, belittle the positive fruits of authentic renewal in the theology and life of the church, although every positive development comes with its own distorted extreme.

Many of the great theologians, who were responsible for the conciliar documents on the church, have continued their work, and they have influenced a small but dedicated segment of Catholic intelligentsia. Of great importance was the recovery of the role of the Holy Spirit and along with it the notion of the church as a communion that participates in the trinitarian communion.[6] Equally significant and fundamental was the articulation of the church's sacramental and eucharistic structure,[7] as well as the unfolding of her spousal and maternal aspects, which are fully exemplified in the Blessed Virgin Mary.[8]

Regarding the life of the church, there has never been so many laypeople active in the life of a parish and diocese as in the postconciliar age. Today in a well-organized parish, lay ministers typically run a multiplicity of services, such as the liturgy, catechesis, charity, care of the sick, baptism and marriage preparation, care for the divorced and for the grieving,

6. See Heribert Mühlen, *Una mystica Persona: Die Kirche als Mysterium der heilsgeschichtlichen Identität des heilgen Geistes in Christus und in den Christen* [The Church as the mystery of the identity of the Holy Spirit in Christ and in the church in salvation history] (Paderborn: Bonifatius, 1968); Jean Rigal, "Trois approaches de l'ecclésiologie de communion: Congar, Zizioulas, Moltmann" [Three approaches to the ecclesiology of communion: Congar, Zizioulas, Moltmann], *Nouvelle revue théologique* 120, no. 4 (1998): 605–19; Joseph Ratzinger, *Called to Communion: Understanding the Church Today* (San Francisco: Ignatius, 1996); Marlé, René, "L'Eglise, quel type de communion?" [What kind of communion is the church?], *Etudes* (October 1993): 371–73; Yves Congar, *I Believe in the Holy Spirit*, 3 vols. (New York: Crossroad-Herder, 2000).

7. See Otto Semmelroth, Henri de Lubac, Edward Schillebeeckx.

8. Louis Bouyer, Joseph Ratzinger, Hans Urs von Balthasar, Henri de Lubac.

financial matters, youth ministry, and others. The danger, however, is that the pastor does not take overall responsibility for what is happening in his parish and simply reduces his role to the "sacramental minister." And the bishop should not limit himself to a few selected issues in the diocese.

Much progress has been made in the area of Catholic-Orthodox, Catholic-Anglican, and Catholic-Protestant relations. A Secretariat for Christian Unity, later reorganized as the Pontifical Council for Promoting Christian Unity, has been established to further the unity of all Christians by clearing up false conflicts as well as promoting mutual understanding and unity on divisive issues.

In January 1964, Pope Paul VI went on pilgrimage to the Holy Land to meet with Patriarch Athenagoras of Constantinople and asked for forgiveness of sins committed by Catholics. The two embraced on the Mount of Olives, recited together the Our Father, and lifted the mutual excommunications between Constantinople and Rome.

Pope John Paul II visited Constantinople at the very beginning of his papal ministry. He and Ecumenical Patriarch Demetrios set up a joint Catholic and Orthodox doctrinal commission to discuss several divisive issues and began working toward a target date of the year 2000 for full ecclesial union, a goal that obviously has not yet been achieved. Nevertheless, some progress has been made. A joint document issued after the last session of this commission in 2007 in Ravenna, titled "Ecclesial Communion, Conciliarity and Authority," declared for the first time in an ecumenical Catholic-Orthodox dialogue that there is a need for one "first" (*protos*) of ecclesial authority on both the local and regional level, as well as the universal level of the church. The two sides also agreed that this function of a united Catholic-Orthodox Church should be exercised by the bishop of Rome. They were, however, far from agreeing on what the authority of this primate would entail.[9]

After the collapse of communism, great tension arose between Rome and the Orthodox Church of Russia over the rights of Eastern Catholics. The very existence of these churches, united with Rome, has been a lasting irritation for Orthodox sensitivity, which questions the legitimacy of their

9. A major step for rapprochement was the omission from the traditional Orthodox position that the bishop of Rome may have only a *primus inter pares* (first among equals) standing in a reunited church. A major problem with the document is the absence of the endorsement of the Moscow patriarchate, whose delegates, because of an intra-Orthodox disagreement, walked out of the discussion.

existence. In Russia and Romania, the Eastern Catholic churches had been suppressed by the state, their clergy forced to join the Russian Orthodox Church, and anyone who resisted this pressure was persecuted and driven underground. As these people regained their freedom, the Eastern Catholics asked that their churches be returned to them, but the Orthodox resisted or used delay tactics. Rome's support for them, especially for the large Ukrainian Catholic Church, became a great obstacle to a closer relationship with the patriarch of Moscow.[10]

Joint ecumenical commissions were set up also between Catholics and many Protestant denominations (such as Lutheran, Anglican, Methodist, and Presbyterian) on national and international levels. These commissions issued common declarations on fundamental points of Christian faith.[11] The Faith and Order Commission of the World Council of Churches, consisting of theologians from Protestant churches, and the Orthodox and Catholic churches produced in 1982 the most promising document resulting from this dialogue, the document known as *Baptism, Eucharist, and Ministry*, the result of meetings held in Lima, Peru. The text was discussed and agreed on by theologians from all major Christian denominations. It articulates surprising convergences on the teachings of baptism, Eucharist, and Holy Orders. It lists points of basic agreement and also major differences. In spite of this real progress, crucial disagreements remained on a wide range of the issues treated by the Lima document, in addition to issues relating to ecclesiology, sacramental theology, and moral issues such as abortion, homosexuality, divorce, and the ordination of women.

Perhaps even more positive than a single document were the diverse ecumenical interactions, a reduction in mutual misunderstandings, and the formation of many ecumenical friendships. At the same time, many rank-and-file Catholics came to believe that Christian denominations, including the Catholic faith, are only culturally different expressions of the same Christian faith and that everyone is free to choose any one of them, depending on their personal likes and dislikes.

Underlying all other issues, a basic divergence regarding church unity

10. Long awaited by the Catholic side, a historic first meeting between Pope Francis and Kirill, the Patriarch of Moscow and all of Russia, took place in Cuba on February 12, 2016.

11. Walter Kasper, *Harvesting the Fruits: Basic Aspects of Christian Faith in Ecumenical Dialogue* (New York: Bloomsbury, 2009). It provides a balanced evaluation of the common effort to achieve the unity of all Christians.

has emerged among Catholics and Protestants. For Protestants in general, the church is primarily an inward spiritual reality of faith, while for Catholics she is a sacrament in which the visible, institutional structures are, in diverse ways, effective signs of grace. Thus, for most Protestants, essential unity has already been achieved for all those who believe and trust in Jesus Christ, Son of God and Savior, and who are reconciled to each other in mutual love. Unity in the sacraments, doctrine, and church order are important goals, but not vitally urgent;[12] whereas the Catholic Church believes that disunity in these matters manifestly contradicts the will of Christ. Yet, beyond a partial convergence on a number of questions, and although problems certainly still remain, many personal interdenominational friendships have developed, and these have removed many of the misunderstandings and psychological obstacles that previously were held against each other's religion.

Pope Francis has recently proposed "the ecumenism of blood," a shared witness of martyrdom that has taken on global dimensions in our age. Just as the baptism of blood has always been the most powerful form of baptism, the communion achieved by shedding blood or being tortured for the same Christian faith may have unforeseeable providential results for the future of church unity.[13]

Not only has the council promoted dialogue and friendly relationships among Christian denominations, but it has also done so with non-Christian religions. Popes John Paul II, Benedict XVI, and Francis have continued in this direction. All three have emphasized the unique closeness between Judaism and Christianity. They even went beyond the Declaration on Non-Christian Religions (*Nostra Aetate*) by declaring that the Jews are our older brothers and Judaism is part of the church's own mystery. John Paul II had also stated that the covenant of God with Israel has never been repudiated by God. During their pontificates, both John Paul and Benedict successfully invited representatives of all religions to Assisi for the purpose of praying for peace and for signing a common declaration in which they would condemn any involvement of their religion in promoting violence.[14]

12. I came to this opinion not so much as the result of explicit declarations by Protestant theologians, but as a tacit presupposition that determines their attitudes in ecumenical discussions.

13. John L. Allen Jr., one of the most respected American journalists, has documented the frightening worldwide dimensions of the persecution of Christians: *The Global War on Christians: Dispatches from the Front Lines of Anti-Christian Persecution* (New York: Image, 2013).

14. The first day of common prayer for peace was convoked by John Paul II in 1986. Another day

Thus, for the first time in history, the Catholic Church could awaken and give voice to the most positive elements in every religion. That is, those who came to Assisi agreed to pray for peace. Even if officially they did not believe in a personal god, their prayer implied his existence. For the Jewish-Christian tradition, this seems obvious, but not so much for those religions whose prevailing notion of the divine is impersonal. But this agreement to pray, each in its own way, uncovered a hidden depth in all of these traditions, a depth of which the participants were previously unaware.

One negative result of frequent and close contacts with non-Christian religions has been the growing number of theologians who have developed a relativist understanding of all religions. They find the exclusive claim of Christianity that it is the one full self-revelation of God no longer credible, and they interpret such a claim by the Bible as the caressing language of the lover for his beloved. On the objective level, however, they hold that religions are only different culturally speaking and that they are equal in religious value for reaching the divine. For these people, religious pluralism as described above is the only credible option in our age. Wherever this view has been adopted, the need for missionary work is also questioned because if every religion is an equally valid way to the Absolute, then evangelization is not only unnecessary but positively harmful because it is an exercise in cultural imperialism.

The longest and perhaps most time-specific document of Vatican II is known as the Pastoral Constitution on the Church in the Modern World or *Gaudium et Spes*. Even though it articulates the dangers and moral problems in the world, its overall outlook is optimistic, emphasizing the mutual contributions of the church and the modern world. Since the time of its writing, the world has dramatically changed. Wars and civil wars with increasing subhuman cruelty have occurred with increasing frequency, and the fertility index of Europe presages the disappearance of European culture unless a radical reversal to larger families takes place. Abortion on demand, euthanasia, and gay marriage are on their way to becoming legalized almost everywhere in the Western world.

Unfortunately, many Catholics, lay and clergy alike, misinterpreted

of common prayer was planned and carried out by Pope John Paul II after the 9/11 attack on New York City in 2001.

Gaudium et Spes and have encouraged an uncritical assimilation of the value system of contemporary culture. Hoping to become relevant, these individuals have compromised the integrity of the gospel. In response, the magisterium of Popes John Paul II, Benedict XVI, and Francis, as well as that of the bishops, has articulated a consistent humanism, a culture of life in opposition to a culture of death that threatens the dignity and even the life of the human person and human civilization. In doing so, the church has emerged, even more visibly than before, as the chief guardian of the family, the sacredness of human life from birth to natural death, the champion of social justice in defense of the poor and marginalized, as well as the defender of the inalienable rights of the human person, who is threatened by the totalitarian state and laissez-faire capitalism.

In Latin American countries, where the exploitation and dehumanization of the lowest layers of society have reached a very high level, several different forms of liberation theology have developed. Liberation theology started in Latin America, but has spread to Africa, North America, and Asia. Especially before the collapse of Communism in Eastern Europe and the Soviet Union, a number of liberation theologians experimented with a contradictory hybrid of Marxist and Christian ideas, provoking a sharp critique from John Paul II. Instead, he promoted an integral liberation theology in which the universality of charity and the fullness of the Christian message have been combined with a preferential option for the poor. By his own example and teaching, Pope Francis attests to the unbreakable connection between the central Christian mysteries and a commitment to the poor and marginalized, to the unborn and to the elderly. This happy balance also dominates Francis's post-synodal exhortation, *Evangelii Gaudium*, as well as the joint publication on liberation theology by the prefect of the Congregation for the Doctrine of Faith, Gerhard Ludwig Müller, and the father of liberation theology, Gustavo Gutiérrez.[15]

Closely linked to liberation theology is feminist theology, which has as its goal the liberation of women from an oppressive patriarchal society. A branch of this movement is faithful to the church, while it fights for full equality of women in civil society and the church, as well as their full representation in leadership roles. At the same time, members of this movement point out the distinctive role and contribution of women. The extremists

15. Gustavo Gutiérrez, *Taking the Side of the Poor: Liberation Theology* (Maryknoll, N.Y.: Orbis, 2015).

among them, however, aim at abolishing any distinction between male and female roles and refuse to attribute any name to God, such as Father and Son, that is not gender neutral.

When dealing with the moral aspect of the socioeconomic issues, Pope Benedict XVI and Pope Francis have called attention to the growing global ecological crisis. In particular, Pope Francis's prophetic encyclical *Laudato si'* analyzes the imminent danger of exhausting the earth's resources, devastating the environment, and especially exposing the poor masses to the destructive effects of global warming: "The earth, our home, is beginning to look more and more like an immense pile of filth."[16] The pope explained that God's command to man and woman to subdue the earth and to have dominion over all living things does not mean exploitation, but rather responsible stewardship (Gn 1:26, 28). Humankind's future depends on restoring the harmony between God, humanity, and nature. Francis has pointed out that the rupture of our friendship with God and man's usurping of God's place has resulted in a breakdown of the harmony among human beings and in our destructive relationship with the environment:

> The creation accounts in the book of Genesis contain, in their own symbolic and narrative language, profound teachings about human existence and its historical reality. They suggest that human life is grounded in three fundamental and closely intertwined relationships: with God, with our neighbor and with the earth itself. According to the Bible, these three vital relationships have been broken, both outwardly and within us. This rupture is sin. The harmony between the Creator, humanity and creation as a whole was disrupted by our presuming to take the place of God and refusing to acknowledge our creaturely limitations. This in turn distorted our mandate to "have dominion" over the earth (cf. *Gn* 1:28), to "till it and keep it" (*Gn* 2:15). As a result, the originally harmonious relationship between human beings and nature became conflictual (cf. *Gn* 3:17–19).[17]

The pope calls for an ecological conversion that begins with reconciliation with God, and a universal solidarity with both our fellow human beings and the earth. Ecological and social development are inseparable: "Today . . . we have to realize that a true ecological approach *always* becomes a social approach; it must integrate questions of justice in debates on the environment, so as to hear *both the cry of the earth and the cry of the poor*."[18]

16. Francis, Encyclical Letter *Laudato si'* (May 24, 2015), 21.
17. Francis, *Laudato si'*, 66.
18. Francis, *Laudato si'*, 49.

As mentioned previously, the Second Vatican Council formulated the doctrine of collegiality and highlighted the church's episcopal authority by, in particular, calling for the formation of national and regional bishops' conferences. The role of these conferences was the application of Christian doctrine and the discipline of the universal church to a particular situation of a nation or region. A problem, however, arose as many of these conferences developed an extensive bureaucracy of consultative and executive commissions consisting of clerics and laypersons. These experts had the tendency to influence the bishops' conferences. In reaction, the Congregation for the Doctrine of Faith (CDF) under Cardinal Ratzinger's leadership emphasized the unavoidable responsibility of every single bishop in his own diocese versus an impersonal bishops' conference. Later, Pope John Paul II restricted the competence of the conferences.

The root cause of this postconciliar crisis is found in the one-sided and distorted view of "renewal." Due largely to the communications disaster regarding the authentic teaching of the council, many understood renewal as mere *aggiornamento* and ignored *ressourcement*. Henri de Lubac's profound insight on genuine renewal and reform went unnoticed by many theologians whose ideal was to adjust Christian doctrine to the ever-changing contemporary cultural trends. These theologians nonetheless attempted to remain within the church by trying to avoid manifest heresy. De Lubac's comments on ressourcement must be quoted in full:

> Before it can be adapted in its presentation to the modern generation, Christianity in all necessity must, in its essence, be itself. And once it is itself, it is close to being adapted. For it is of its essence to be living and always of the time.
>
> The big task consists then in rediscovering Christianity in its plenitude and in its purity. A task which is always and ceaselessly called for, just as the work of reform inside the Church itself is called for always and ceaselessly. For even though Christianity is eternal, we are never once and for all identified with its eternity. By a natural leaning we never cease losing it. Like God Himself, it is always there, present in its entirety, but it is we who are always more or less absent from it. It escapes us in the very measure that we believe we possess it. Habit and routine have an unbelievable power to waste and destroy.
>
> But how should we rediscover Christianity if not by going back to the sources, trying to recapture it in its periods of explosive vitality?[19]

19. Henri de Lubac, *Paradoxes of Faith*, trans. Paule Simon, Sadie Kreilkamp, and Ernest Beaumont (San Francisco: Ignatius, 1987), 57–58. In a similar vein, Yves Congar, *True and False Reform in the Church* (Collegeville, Minn.: Liturgical Press, 2011). The first edition of Congar's book had to be withdrawn

In many places and institutions where recovery of the integral Christian heritage went hand in hand with reform, true renewal has taken place. The vibrant parishes in the United States; the flourishing and rapid growth of the church in Africa and several Asian countries; and the ecclesial movements such as Focolare, Communione e Liberazione, the Neo-Catechetical Movement, charismatic communities, and Bible study and prayer groups all reflect the face of the spouse of Christ to the world in renewed splendor.

from bookstores in the 1950s at the directive of the holy office, but later it became a guiding light for the reforms of the council. Compare Congar's and de Lubac's view with that of Richard P. McBrien, who proposed to "remake" the church according to the pattern of an efficient contemporary corporation (*The Remaking of the Church* [New York: Harper and Row, 1973]).

PART 2

Systematic Ecclesiology

CHAPTER 9

The Unity of the Church

Why Do We Need a Church?

The ultimate and adequate reason for the existence of the church is the will of Jesus Christ as it was attested to in the books of the New Testament. Theology, however, always explores—as far as it can—the meaning of the divine will and action.[1]

The earthly life, passion, and resurrection of Jesus has not been just one great historical event that belongs only to the past, but is indeed the center of all history, a theandric (divine-human) event that, in a real sense, transcends all times and is made present to all human beings, past, present, and future. Thus everyone is offered the grace of Christ through the Holy Spirit, which shines through our encounters with fellow humans. Nevertheless, respecting the social and psychosomatic character of human beings, Christ wanted to extend his presence not just through the invisible, universal mission of the Holy Spirit, but also through a visible community of eyewitnesses and their successors, who would preserve and proclaim his teaching and extend his sanctifying presence through ritual activity.

We are psychosomatic beings, receiving and communicating spiritual realities through physical signs, such as speech, writing, and actions. Thus it is most appropriate that the teaching and sanctifying action of Christ is mediated to us by the physical, ritual signs of the sacraments.[2]

1. See Vandevelde-Dailliere, "Nécessité de l'Eglise, salut des non-chrétiens, théologie des religions: options et enjeux" [The necessity of the church, the salvation of non-Christians, theology of the religions: options and stakes], *Nouvelle revue théologique* 123 (2001): 204–17.

2. See Charles Journet, *The Theology of the Church* (San Francisco: Ignatius, 2004), which shows the "logic" of the incarnation in ecclesiology; Guy Mansini, "Ecclesial Mediation of Grace and Truth," *The*

We are also social beings. Our natural life, psychological development, and intellectual growth depend on community. We cannot be conceived, born, survive, and mature without a community of people, such as parents, teachers, friends, and society at large. So it is quite appropriate that divine life and its growth comes to us through the mediation of community.

The importance of the physical and social dimensions of Christianity is confirmed by recognizing what happens to Christians, individuals or denominations, when these external structures are diminished or almost entirely missing. Typically, with the disappearance of external signs, the inner reality is also obscured or entirely lost.[3]

All that has been said so far does not prevent, but rather promotes, for every Christian direct intimacy with God. According to the Letter to the Hebrews, we are invited to enter through the flesh of Jesus into the heavenly sanctuary (Heb 10:19–22). The Gospel of John tells us that the Son and the Father intend to dwell in us. And Paul declares that Christians are the temple of the Holy Spirit, the body of Christ, and the children of the Father. The external, sacramental structure of the church enables direct intimacy with God. Moreover, the action of the Holy Spirit in the soul is not solely the end point but also the preceding inspiration for the process of ecclesial mediation. That is, no one would go to the sacraments or join a church community, and no one would be moved by the preached word, unless they were inspired by the Holy Spirit. Thus the charge that the Catholic Church prevents her faithful from direct access to God stems from a fundamental misunderstanding. She leads those who have been directly inspired by God to an even deeper intimacy with him through her preaching and sacraments, and through the personal witness and community life of her members.

The need for the church derives from the demands of human nature and from the very purpose of God's plan of salvation. The Father's goal is to gather all of us into his own family in heaven by perfecting in us a likeness to his Son. Our earthly life, then, consists of preparing, training, and struggling to become ready for entering fully into the trinitarian communion. Thus we must learn how to live in God's family as brothers and sisters. The

Thomist 75 (2011): 555–83; Benoit Dominique de la Soujeole, "The Economy of Salvation: Entitative Sacramentality and Operative Sacramentality," *The Thomist* 75 (2011): 537–53.

3. See Henri de Lubac, *The Splendor of the Church*, trans. Michael Mason (San Francisco: Ignatius, 1986), 179–313.

church community helps us to love one another with the very love of Christ and anticipate the joys and consolations of eternal life as we discover in each other the features of Christ, his love, mercy, patience, joy, and peace. At the same time, we also learn to forgive one another, to carry each other's burdens of sin and immaturity so that ultimately we may become fit for perfect communion in heaven.

In the church community, we also learn how to become an open circle, attracting outsiders by our love and joy. In this way, we can overcome our tendency to exclusive, possessive relationships. If we had not gone through this school of love, if we had not learned to accept others into our hearts and share with them our own heart, heaven would place unbearable burdens on us.

The Four Marks of the Church

We find the four marks of the church, one, holy, catholic, and apostolic, mentioned together for the first time in the Nicene-Constantinopolitan Creed. They shed light on the nature of the church and lead to a better understanding of her mystery. Post-Tridentine polemical theology used these marks only as part of the proof that only the Catholic Church is one, holy, catholic, and apostolic. The discussion here follows Yves Congar's masterly treatise that saw these marks primarily as a manifestation of the essence of the church and relegated their apologetic aspects to secondary importance.[4]

A fashionable trend in academic circles in the twenty-first century is to consider the unity of the church as a later product of development; as it were, a unity forged through the suppression of alternative (in traditional terms, heretical) Christian communities. Many scholars maintain that at the beginning of the "Jesus movement," there was no unified Christian church, but rather, diverse groups of Christians often with opposing views, each group claiming to derive its teaching and legitimacy from Jesus of Nazareth. What later became the early Catholic Church, these scholars say, was the result of a power struggle, the outcome of which was that one group prevailed and excommunicated the rival groups, which in particular

4. Yves Congar, "Die Wesenseigenschaften der Kirche" [The essential marks of the church], in *Mysterium Salutis*, vol. 4/1, *Das Heilsgeschehen in der Gemeinde*, ed. Wolfgang Beinert et al. (Einsiedeln: Benziger, 1972), 357–600. Congar's study provided the foundations for this section of this work.

had various forms of Gnostic tendencies. Thus, in the general contemporary climate of celebrating diversity, the unity of the church is looked on as a later, purely accidental result, as is the traditional distinction between orthodox and heterodox Christianities; the ancient church, in other words, "sinned" against the tacit but all-pervading contemporary principle of inclusivity.[5]

It is not possible to respond here to the many aspects of this problem, but two issues should be addressed: first, the historical link between Jesus of Nazareth and the development of unity in what is widely called catholic or mainline Christianity. Second, I will provide a brief outline of a Catholic theology of ecclesial unity.

The One Church at the Beginning of Her History?

Scholars readily admit that the dates of the proto-Pauline letters precede the written forms of the Gospels by one or two decades and that Paul passionately insisted in his letters that he received his gospel (the only authentic gospel) not from any human authority, but through God's revelation of Jesus Christ directly to him (Gal 1:12–15). What, however, is often forgotten is that this same Paul, according to his own words, went up to Jerusalem twice, first to confer with Peter when he met James as well, and then again, after fourteen years, to present his gospel to the "pillars," James, Cephas, and John. His avowed purpose was to make sure that he "might not be running, or have run, in vain." He proudly announced that "those of repute made me add nothing" and gave him "the right hand of partnership [*koinōnia*]" (Gal 1:11–2:10). In 1 Corinthians, Paul quotes a summary of the gospel he had received from those before him and that he transmitted to the Corinthians in AD 50–51 (15:3–7). This Gospel regards Jesus, his death for our sins, his burial, and his resurrection as the fulfilment of Scriptures. In addition, he lists the appearances of the risen Lord (1 Cor 15:1–7).[6]

As Bill Farmer has often expounded, Paul's handshake with the three pillars, James, Peter, and John, is of paramount significance for assessing

5. For example, Helmut Koester, *From Jesus to the Gospels: Interpreting the New Testament in Its Context* (Minneapolis: Fortress, 2007); Elaine Pagels, *The Gnostic Gospels* (Minneapolis: Fortress, 1989); Bart Ehrman, *The Orthodox Corruption of Scripture: The Effect of Early Christological Controversies on the Text of the New Testament* (Oxford: Oxford University Press, 2011).

6. In the same epistle, Paul also condenses the rite of the Lord's Supper as learned from the church and confirmed by revelation from Jesus Christ (1 Cor 11:23–26).

the earliest phase of catholic Christianity. Most of the books of the New Testament were either written by one of these four people or the text depended on the traditions derived from one of them. Peter is the chief witness for the Synoptic tradition, Paul for the proto- and deutero-Pauline Epistles; John for the Fourth Gospel, the three Letters of John, and, more remotely, for the book of Revelation; and James for the letter bearing his name. If this is true, the content and genesis of the canonical books of the New Testament cannot be attributed to an uncontrolled growth process of Jesus folklore because these four apostles/disciples were clearly in charge of discerning the genuine Jesus traditions from the distortions. These four appear to be the guardians and authenticators of the gospel of Jesus Christ.

For an adequate treatment of the canonical Jesus traditions, a lengthier and separate study would be needed, but even this short summary suggests that what the canonical Gospels and Acts say about the beginnings of the church has the backing of some of the first disciples of Jesus. Thus the historical link between Jesus and the origin of the church, composed of mainline or catholic Christianity, appears quite strong.

Even though there was a diversity of different and mutually antagonistic Christian communities in the early Christian centuries, this discussion only treats the nature and unity of that form of Christianity that, under the control of these four disciples, produced the books of the New Testament and, thus, directly determined the church's further development.

The Synoptic Gospels present the Twelve as the beginning of the church. They were chosen personally by Jesus, gathered around him in the "house" (most likely the house of Peter in Capernaum), were instructed and trained by him, and then were sent out alone on missions throughout Israel during Jesus' earthly life.[7] The number twelve indicates that Jesus planned to gather into one all of converted Israel, including the ten lost tribes of the north. When it gradually becomes clear that Israel as a nation either misunderstands and/or rejects Jesus' message, he establishes his *qāhāl/ekklēsia* out of the remnant of Israel built on Peter, who receives his rock-like solidity from faith in Jesus. He celebrates the new covenant in his own blood with these twelve patriarchs of the renewed Israel. And these Twelve will be sent out to proclaim the gospel to the entire world after the resurrection.[8] At the appearances of the Risen One and at Pentecost,

7. See Mk 2:1; 3:20; 7:17; 9:28; Mt 10:5–6.
8. See Mk 14:17; Mt 26:20; Lk 22:14.

the one universal church is already present in the small group of disciples, ready to embrace the whole world with all its diversity of languages and cultures in order to integrate each one of these into the converted "Israel of God." Thus the one universal church is not an abstraction or a later creation, but the concrete historical reality of the apostolic group trained and sent by Jesus, equipped with one gospel and one Eucharist, in which the same Jesus in the same Holy Spirit will be present in the world unto the end of the ages.[9]

This early self-understanding of the one church explains the belief that is expressed in some of the Pauline epistles and in early Christian authors, who attest that the same church exists throughout the whole world. Paul, for instance, writes "to the church of God that is in Corinth" (1 Cor 1:2; 2 Cor 1:1), while Clement begins his letter with an even more expressive formula: "The church of God which lives in Rome to the church of God which lives in Corinth." This awareness that the one church is present in every local church where a local bishop gathers the community around the Eucharist has survived, despite being periodically eclipsed, throughout the entire history of the church.[10] This awareness has been threatened not only by the nationalist centrifugal tendencies of the Eastern churches but also by the growing centralization of the Western Latin-rite church. Paradoxically, too much emphasis on juridical unity has often eclipsed not only the importance of diversity in local churches, but also the deeper inner unity that derives from the local churches' participation in the trinitarian communion. The following investigates the theological principles of the church's inner unity derived from her participation in the mystery of the Trinity and the incarnation.[11]

The One Church Sharing in the Unity of the Father

From all eternity, the Father has decided to extend the unique filial relationship of his eternal Son to an innumerable multitude of human beings.[12]

9. See Congregation for the Doctrine of the Faith, *Letter to the Bishops of the Catholic Church on Some Aspects of the Church Understood as Communion*, May 28, 1992, 2, 9.

10. Congregation for the Doctrine of the Faith, *Church Understood as Communion*, 3, 9.

11. An important source for this chapter on the unity of the church was Yves M. Congar, "Die eine Kirche" [The one church], in Beinert et al., *Das Heilsgeschehen in der Gemeinde*, 368–439.

12. Evidently, all decisions of the Father take place through the Son and in the Holy Spirit, but the decision to establish the church originates from the Father.

This eternal fatherly love is the ultimate source for the creation of humankind and its home, the material universe. The fall of humankind has not altered the plan of the Father who has foreseen it and made the realization of his plan depend on the cross of his Son. In this way, the Father revealed an even greater depth of his love by sending his Son to rescue fallen humankind through his incarnation, passion, and resurrection. The *Exultet* of the Easter Vigil expresses with astonishing realism this *inaestimabilis dilectio caritatis*, the love that exceeds all rational understanding: *ut servum redimeres, Filium tradidisti* (in order to rescue the slave, you handed over the Son). On the cross, then, we see the perfect revelation of the Father's sacrificial love by which he glorifies the Son, so that the Son may glorify him. Here is the ultimate source of the church's all-encompassing and transcendental unity; it results from the Father's drawing of all humankind to the Son, so that all may share in the Son's filial relationship and, at the same time, love and glorify the Father in union with the Son.

The Church Sharing in the Unity of the Incarnate Son

The participation in the Son's divine filiation by all who open themselves to the Father's call is not a metaphor; all of tradition has understood it in an analogical sense, one in which the *primum analogatum* is the filial relationship between God the Father and the eternal Son. We are by grace what the Son is by nature. According to Paul, the first Christians addressed God as "Abba," Father, in the Spirit:

> For those who are led by the Spirit of God are children of God. For you did not receive a spirit of slavery to fall back into fear, but you received a spirit of adoption, through which we cry, "Abba, Father!" The Spirit itself bears witness with our spirit that we are children of God. (Rom 8:14–16; see Gal 5:18)[13]

Paul's entire theology of Christian life shows that for him our "adoption" is more than a legal notion. John, however, is even more explicit. He avoids the term "adoption" altogether, and speaks rather about our birth

13. No subsequent criticisms could substantially change the thesis of Joachim Jeremias that calling on God as Abba (rather than Lord or King) reveals the unique filial relationship of Jesus with the Father. This was so characteristic of Jesus that Mark quotes it in the original Aramaic when recording Jesus' prayer in Gethsemane: "Abba, Father, all things are possible to you. Take this cup away from me, but not what I will but what you will" (Mk 14:36). Thus the fact that Christians address God by the word "Abba" reveals that, by the outpouring of the Spirit, they are taken up into the same relationship with God as Jesus was. The Spirit himself testifies to the reality of their *huiothesia*, their adoption as children of God.

"of God" (Jn 1:13). In his typical combination of crassly materialistic and sublimely spiritual language, John explains that the believer cannot sin, because he is born from God and the seed of God remains in him (1 Jn 3:9). To be born of God, however, is equivalent to being born of the Spirit (Jn 3:5–6), and we know that we remain in God by the gift of his Spirit (1 Jn 4:13). John summarizes the mystery of our filial nature in these terms: "Beloved, we are God's children now; what we shall be has not yet been revealed. We do know that when it is revealed we shall be like him, for we shall see him as he is" (1 Jn 3:2).

Just as every gift comes ultimately from the one Father, and every member of the human race is a child or called to become a child of the same Father, we give thanks to him, worship and glorify him through the Son in the Holy Spirit, with one heart, mind, and voice. The eucharistic anaphoras of the church are directed to the one Father and include a trinitarian doxology that glorifies the Father through the Son in the Holy Spirit. The church has originated from all eternity in the plan of the Father. The Son will hand over the glorified church, his kingdom, to the Father, and thus God will be all in all (1 Cor 15:24–28).[14]

As previously stated, on the one hand, it is the Son who hands over all creation, restored and sanctified, to the Father. But on the other hand, this giving is mutual and returned by the Father. According to a biblically based patristic tradition, the parable involving the banquet that the rich man organized for his Son is an allegory of the wedding feast for the incarnate Son and the eschatological church with all of creation united to it. This church is the purified and beautified bride whom the Father has prepared for the Son from all eternity. The Father thus returns the Son's gift to the Son, so that the reciprocal gift of all creation is taken up into the process of eternal generation and filiation; the giving and receiving between Father and Son in the Holy Spirit.[15]

The above explanation jumps forward to the completion of the Son's work in God's plan. However, to see the full work of the Son in our redemption we must start from the very beginning of salvation history. Since human beings are the substantial unity of body and soul, flesh and spirit,

14. See LG 2.

15. See Gregory the Great, *Forty Homilies* 38.1, 3–4; Gregory of Nazianzus, *Theological Orations* 30.5; Hans Urs von Balthasar, *Theo-drama: Theological Dramatic Theory*, vol. 5, *The Last Act*, trans. Graham Harrison (San Francisco: Ignatius, 1998), 506–21.

and since God the Father wanted to respect the needs of the human nature he created, he united humankind to himself in a twofold unity carried out by the twofold mission of the Son and the Holy Spirit. For the Son's incarnation to be a real entrance into human history, a definite place and a definite point in time were necessary. A limited number of human beings, peoples, and individuals must also have prepared for this event and foreshadowed it. Thus, while the Father and the Holy Spirit aim for a universal unity that embraces the entire human race, the Son assumes one concrete and limited human nature as his own. He could not accept full solidarity with us unless he became one of us, bone from our bones and flesh from our flesh. Understandably, then, all of salvation history is directed at that one particular point in time and space when and where the eternal Logos of the Father became human. Before Christ, salvation history is a gradual process of narrowing the number of those who carry the promise of salvation through God's subsequent elections and rejections, starting with the fallen Adam, the head of original humankind, through Noah, Abraham, Isaac, Jacob, Israel, the kingdom of Judah, the exiles in Babylon, the builders of the Second Temple, and the poor of YHWH (*ănāvîm*), and leading up to Mary and her son Jesus.[16] This narrowing line of elections does not mean that the rejected are necessarily doomed to damnation. This is rather a process of divine pedagogy whereby God gradually accustoms humankind to live in his presence and through different figures shows them the many different features of the coming Messiah and the saving event he brings. For instance, some of these teaching figures are Isaac, Moses, David, the heavenly Son of Man, and the Suffering Servant, as well as the exodus from Egyptian slavery and the return of the remnant from the Babylonian exile.

The central event, however, toward which salvation history leads, the incarnation of the Son of God and his redemptive work, is raised up by Jesus' resurrection into God's eternity, a realm that transcends time and thus becomes contemporaneous to universal human history through the Holy Spirit, who reaches into both the past and the future, all times and all places.

Regarding church unity, the essential point is to realize that if God wanted to enter into the fullest solidarity with sinful humankind, he would ap-

16. See Oscar Cullmann, *Christ and Time: The Primitive Christian Conception of Time* (London: Westminster, 1950).

propriately have become, in patristic terminology, the *Verbum abbreviatum*, the *Verbum infans*, the little child who is unable to speak yet contains in himself the fullness of divinity (Col 2:9). All of the other finite limitations of Jesus' life and mission in Judea, Galilee, and the outskirts of the surrounding territories derive from this one concentration of God in a limited human being, Jesus of Nazareth. The limitations of the incarnation continue in the limitations of church history, such as the following: We have only one Holy Bible in its original languages of Hebrew, Aramaic, and Greek. We have only one Holy Land and twelve original apostles with the one leader, Cephas, with whom (through his successors) we must remain in communion if we want to remain in communion with Jesus of Nazareth. Nor can we substitute tea and rice, or whiskey and crackers, for the eucharistic bread and wine, regardless of the culture in which we celebrate the Eucharist. These restrictions point to the one contingent reality of the incarnation, which sets limits to the necessary process of expressing the one gospel within the context and language of different cultures. Thus inculturation and tradition are in a fruitful tension, the former allowing various adaptations to different cultures, and the latter setting limits on the differentiations.[17]

The Church Sharing in the Unity of the Holy Spirit

While the mission of the Son, his incarnation, and his redemptive work require a restrictive unity of concentration, the mission of the Spirit (as mentioned above) extends the presence and saving action of the incarnate Son to all times and all places. The Holy Spirit is the one person who is fully and equally present in the Father and the Son and, according to the Fathers of both East and West, he is the bond of unity in the church.[18] Jesus sends the Holy Spirit to the church, and the Spirit renews and transforms all those who receive him by making them into his temple, which is the ecclesial body of Christ in whom he chooses to dwell. As the encyclical *Mystici Corporis* asserts, the Spirit is *numerice idem* with the Father and the Son, but also in the (spiritually) living members of the church. *Numerice idem* means that one and the same Spirit is present in each member in his unique personal reality.[19]

17. See Congar, "Die Wesenseigenschaften der Kirche," 496–99.

18. See Heribert Mühlen, *Una mystica Persona: Eine Person in vielen Personen* [One mystical person in many persons] (Munich: F. Schöning, 1968).

19. MC 62, quoting St. Thomas, *De veritate* [On the truth] q. 29, a. 4.

The unifying action of the Spirit works in different ways in the different activities of the church. Since the same Holy Spirit inspires the different texts of the entire Bible, the entire Bible opens up its full meaning in Christ. The Spirit assures that the church remains faithful to the Word of God and protects the definitions of the ecumenical councils and those of the pope from error. At the same time, the Spirit is also present in the members of the church and in those non-Christians who listen to the preaching of the church and are inspired to accept her teachings as the unfolding and application of the teaching of Christ. Were the Spirit to deny his help to a person who is trying to accept the church's teaching as coming from God, even the words of the most eloquent preacher would remain ineffective; at best, his words would be received as human wisdom. The invisible mission of the Holy Spirit extends beyond the reach of the visible church and prepares receptive souls all over the world to seek the truth and yearn for love.

By the Holy Spirit the sacramental prayers of the church become the prayers and sanctifying actions of Christ. At the same time, the Holy Spirit also works in those who have received the sacraments and enables them to receive the grace of Christ fruitfully. This twofold action of the Spirit is shown most clearly in Holy Eucharist. By the invocation of the Holy Spirit (*epiclesis*), the words of Jesus recited in the eucharistic institution account become the very words of Christ, who changes the bread and wine into his own body and blood. Analogously, by the power of the same Spirit, recipients of Eucharist are built up into the body of Christ, the church.

Being himself the communion of the Father and the Son, the Spirit also builds up the community of the church. He unites the many members into the communion of the one church by conforming to the Son individual persons of every color, language, and culture. They become the body of Christ in the sense that Christ is present and active in them, so that his members share in his filial relationship to the Father, his love of the Father, and his love of people. They also appropriate the prayer of Jesus: "Abba, Father" (Mk 14:36). They form a unity with each other that surpasses the strength and intimacy of any natural bond, since one and the same Spirit inspires their wills and enlightens their minds. In Paul's letters, *to auto phronein*, to think and desire the same thing, is a recurrent refrain (Rom 12:16; 2 Cor 13:11; Phil 2:2). The source of this unanimity is the one Spirit, who unites their thinking and willing with that of Christ (Phil 4:2; Rom 15:5). In the same way, Christians today should share the same love (Phil 2:2) and are of one heart and one soul. The first believers in Jerusalem lived in a community of shared material goods; each sold what he or she had and gave the proceeds to the apostles, who distributed to everyone according to their needs (Acts 4:32).

Even though the Holy Spirit unites the many into one, personal distinctions are not abolished. As the uniting Spirit affirms the distinct persons of both Father and Son in the immanent Trinity, so also in salvation history the Spirit joins the many members of the church by perfecting their unique individuality in a transcendent unity. He inspires the unique vocation of each individual in the church, and distributes a variety of gifts for the building up of the church. The Holy Spirit is not the principle of uniformity, but of unity in diversity within the church. St. Paul explains this mystery in the following terms:

> There are different kinds of spiritual gifts but the same Spirit; there are different forms of service but the same Lord; there are different workings but the same God who produces all of them in everyone. To each individual the manifestation of the Spirit is given for some benefit. To one is given through the Spirit the expression of wisdom; to another the expression of knowledge according to the same Spirit; to another faith by the same Spirit; to another gifts of healing by the one Spirit; to another mighty deeds; to another prophecy; to another discernment of spirits; to another varieties of tongues; to another interpretation of tongues. But one and the same Spirit produces all of these, distributing them individually to each person as he wishes. (1 Cor 12:4–11; see also 1 Cor 12:27–14:40; Rom 12:3–21)

External Forms of Unity in the Church

The unity of the Triune God isn't the only determinant of the unity of the church. Human nature plays a role as well. In the incarnation, God the Son became flesh, one visible and tangible human being who speaks, listens, and acts in the world through his bodily actions and suffers through his human body and soul. The church continues the sanctifying action and passion of Christ in her sacraments, teaching, and community life. Just as Christ had one personal body, so too does his one mystical body express his presence and activity in visible, tangible, and audible forms that express in a variety of rites the one faith. In this sense, *Lumen Gentium* declares that "the Church is in Christ as a sacrament or instrumental sign of intimate union with God."[20] A concise summary of this sacramental activity is found in Acts 2:42: "They [the first community in Jerusalem] devoted themselves to the teaching of the apostles and to the communal life, to the breaking of the bread and to the prayers."

The unity of faith requires common external structures, such as written documents (creed, Scripture, episcopal, conciliar, and pontifical documents), a commonly accepted magisterium, unity of faith in preaching, and unity within a plurality of theologies. These structures express the one object of faith (the Triune God insofar as he shares his life with us in the history of salvation), but they also aim at forming one and the same inner attitude, the "obedience of faith," consisting of a personal surrender in trust to God. This point touches on the paradox of faith. Faith, as the trusting surrender of mind, will, and heart to God, is in the biblical sense the most personal act of an individual, since it elevates the person's unique subjective center to God. Yet faith is also a profoundly communitarian act, since individuals actualize in themselves (to varying degrees and intensity) the loving surrender of the one spouse of Christ. This is also true of the act of faith for those in non-Christian religions, who respond positively to the offer of grace, yet remain unaware of their profound inner relationship with the one church-spouse.

The empirical forms of community life, such as the shepherding activity of the pope, bishops, and priests, as well as parish and diocesan communities, international gatherings, and smaller ecclesial communities all serve the formation and intensification of the communion of love whose source is the Holy Spirit. This communion is an open circle, perennially growing, attracting, and embracing by its mystery of mutual love and support all those who are still outside it. The ultimate aim of this communion is to let the dough of all humankind rise so that all who accept the inspiration of the Holy Spirit are united in one universal and visible brotherhood. Thus the church, precisely because she is the sacrament of union with God, is also the sacrament of the unity of all humanity. The more the members of the church are united to Christ in the Holy Spirit, the more their love will attract outsiders as they see that this unity encourages and actualizes the unique values of each nation, culture, and individual. This all-embracing love gives birth to and nourishes the missionary activity of the one church.

20. LG 1.

Divided Christianity and Unity

The doctrine regarding the unity of the church seems to stand in irreconcilable opposition to the empirical fact of separated Christian communities, each with claims to being the church founded and willed by Jesus Christ (or at least one in basic accord with his intention).[21] After centuries of insisting on either the evil of this mutual separation or its insignificance (many Protestants think that spiritual unity alone is necessary), a great number of Christian denominations during the first half of the twentieth century acknowledged, to varying degrees, the need for some form of visible unity. The resulting ecumenical movement sought greater unity among churches, but this unity took on several substantially different forms. Most Protestant denominations envision a visibly united one church of Christ only as a future task. In contrast, the Roman Catholic and Orthodox churches considered themselves the always existing one true church of Christ and each other as sister churches, since both possess apostolic succession and, therefore, the same sacraments, including especially the full reality of the Holy Eucharist. The Anglican Communion has traditionally considered herself as the *via media*, the authentic middle way, between Catholics and Protestants.

The Second Vatican Council had the complex task of formulating the Catholic Church's self-understanding in the presence of non-Catholic observers, who held the diversity of views mentioned above. Understandably, the council debated the relationship between the one church of Christ and the Roman Catholic Church at great length, as well as the relationship between the Catholic Church and other Christian denominations.[22] The final statement was very carefully formulated:

> This Church [the unique church of Christ] constituted and organized in the world as a society, subsists in the Catholic Church which is governed by the successor of Peter and by the bishops in union with that successor, although many elements of sanctification and of truth can be found outside her visible structure. These elements, however, as gifts properly belonging to the Church of Christ, possess an inner dynamism toward Catholic unity.[23]

21. Joseph Ratzinger, "What Unites and Divides Denominations? Ecumenical Reflections," in *Joseph Ratzinger in Communio*, vol. 1, *The Unity of the Church* (Grand Rapids: Eerdmans, 2010), 1–9; Ratzinger, "Luther and the Unity of the Churches: An Interview with Joseph Cardinal Ratzinger," in *Unity of the Church*, 44–61.

22. Unlike MC, which spoke in an undifferentiated way about those who are "truly members of the Church," LG 14 admits various degrees of belonging to the one church of Christ.

23. LG 8.

The teaching of the council in this text and other related passages may be summarized in the following points:

1. The church of Christ exists as a recognizable and visible historical reality. This position is opposed to the prevailing Protestant view, which believes that the church of Christ will exist only in the future as a result of the union of the churches, and that all Christian churches are more or less equally the church of Christ.

2. The verb "*subsistit* [in English, "subsists"] in the Catholic Church" was chosen over *est* or *adest* (the unique church of Christ is [*est*] the Catholic Church; or, the unique church of Christ is present in [*adest*] the Catholic Church) to stress the qualitatively unique realization of the church of Christ in the Catholic Church. The verb *est* would have been misunderstood as if only the Catholic Church had ecclesial reality; the term *adest* would have left the way open to the interpretation that the church of Christ may be present in other churches as well. The term *subsistit* was known by most of the conciliar fathers to denote a subject that or who exists in itself. According to Joseph Ratzinger, the fathers were saying, "The being of the Church as such extends much farther than the Roman Catholic Church, yet in the latter she has in a unique way the character of an independent subject."[24] The Decree on Ecumenism *Unitatis Redintegratio* uses a different conceptuality than subsistence to describe the unique character of the Catholic Church; she possesses "the fullness of grace and truth," as well as "all the fullness of the means of grace."[25]

3. Nevertheless, non-Catholic Christian churches and ecclesial communities have also some ecclesial reality, because they have elements of truth and sanctification.[26] The Decree on Ecumenism explains this in greater

24. Quoted by Maximilian Heinrich Heim, *Joseph Ratzinger: Life in the Church and Living Theology; Fundamentals of Ecclesiology with Reference to Lumen Gentium* (San Francisco: Ignatius, 2007), 317. The noted ecclesiologist Francis Sullivan has reviewed the different interpretations by different theologians and basically sided with Ratzinger's interpretation. At the same time, however, he insisted on the importance of the change in official church doctrine and did not advert to Ratzinger's further explanation, which made the point that the nonexclusive identification of the church of Christ with the Catholic Church had already been implied in the ancient practice of the church of Rome, which maintained the validity of heretical baptism in the controversy with Cyprian. See the three articles by Sullivan in the *Theological Studies* on the meaning of *subsistit*: "Response to Karl Becker, SJ, on the Meaning of *Subsistit In*," *Theological Studies* 67, no. 2 (2006): 395–409; "The Meaning of *Subsistit in* as Explained by the Congregation for the Doctrine of the Faith," *Theological Studies* 69, no. 1 (2008): 116–124; "Further Thoughts on the Meaning of *Subsistit In*," *Theological Studies* 71, no. 1 (2010): 133–47.

25. *LG* 3.

26. The Declaration *Dominus Iesus* by the Congregation for the Doctrine of the Faith (August 6, 2000) clarified the theological distinction between non-Catholic churches and ecclesial communities:

detail: "Some, even very many, of the most significant elements and endowments which together go to build up and give life to the Church herself can exist outside the visible boundaries of the Catholic Church: the written word of God, the life of grace, faith, hope and charity, along with other interior gifts of the Holy Spirit and visible elements."[27] Therefore, the Holy Spirit can use these Christian churches and ecclesial communities as a means of salvation.

4. The ecclesial reality of these Christian churches and ecclesial communities, however, derives from the fullness of grace and truth entrusted to the Catholic Church, and impels these Christian churches and ecclesial communities toward catholic unity.[28]

Thus, a doctrine of analogous participation is implicit in the conciliar teaching. The church of Christ is realized in a qualitatively unique way in the Catholic Church, but not only with regard to the church as the means of salvation (as it has often been misunderstood); the Catholic Church is also the rightful "possessor" or subject of the "fullness of grace and truth."[29] Nevertheless, the one church of Christ is participated in to varying degrees by other Christian churches and ecclesial communities as well. According to *Dominus Iesus*, only the churches that possess apostolic succession and, therefore, a valid episcopacy and the valid Eucharist are "true churches," while those preserving other elements of the church are referred to as "ecclesial communities."

The conciliar teaching leaves open a way to affirm the empirical fact that non-Catholic Christian individuals can grow to a greater perfection of faith, hope, and love than a Catholic person, and, indeed, a non-Catholic local community may also have a more intense life of grace, faith, hope, and love than a particular Catholic church.

"Therefore, there exists a single Church of Christ, which subsists in the Catholic Church, governed by the Successor of Peter and by the Bishops in communion with him. The Churches which, while not existing in perfect communion with the Catholic Church, remain united to her by means of the closest bonds, that is, by apostolic succession and a valid Eucharist, are true particular Churches. Therefore, the Church of Christ is present and operative also in these Churches, even though they lack full communion with the Catholic Church, since they do not accept the Catholic doctrine of the Primacy, which, according to the will of God, the Bishop of Rome objectively has and exercises over the entire Church.... The lack of unity among Christians is certainly a *wound* for the Church; not in the sense that she is deprived of her unity, but "in that it hinders the complete fulfilment of her universality in history" (17).

27. Vatican Council II, Decree on Ecumenism *Unitatis Redintegratio* (November 21, 1964), 3 (hereafter abbreviated UR).

28. UR 3; LG 8.

29. Obviously, we cannot speak of the church as a perfect institution in the customary sense of the word. The conciliar text means only that this church has the full ecclesial order, all the sacraments, and the entire gospel of Christ and, consequently, the fullness of grace and truth.

Unitatis Redintegratio: The Recomposition of Christian Unity

This is the title of the Second Vatican Council's decree on ecumenism. The word "recomposition" better expresses the Latin *redintegratio* than the usual translation as "restoration." By the term, the council intended to express its intention to work for corporate unity, in which the liturgical and organizational structures of other Christian denominations (to the extent that they conform to the nature of the unity willed by Christ) could be integrated into the one Catholic Church of Christ. The special status of those Anglican clergymen and laity who have recently established full communion with the Catholic Church has shown how far the Holy See is ready to go in respecting and accepting most of the Anglican liturgy and church order.[30]

Even though the last fifty years of ecumenical relations have been highlighted by significant achievements, substantial roadblocks remain, and hope for their removal in the near future is diminishing. While the main impediments to full communion between the Catholic and Orthodox Churches are of a historical and psychological nature, the major obstacle in the dialogue with Protestant Christians is a disagreement over the understanding of church unity. For most Protestants, the unity willed by Christ is primarily and essentially the invisible unity of the one true faith in Jesus Christ. They believe that the unity of external forms (such as the same creed, sacraments, and ministry) are desirable goals to achieve, and that only when this goal is reached will the one visible church begin to exist. However, most Protestants do not see the urgency of this task, since they are convinced that what is really important is the unity of hearts and minds, and this has already been achieved to a large extent. Nevertheless, these denominations are most ready to forge with Catholic Christians personal friendships and join in some common projects for promoting human rights and, in particular, social justice.[31]

Prior to its preparation for the Second Vatican Council, the Catholic Church scrupulously avoided any official involvement in ecumenical work because the popes believed that formal membership in the World Council of Churches would give the impression that the Catholic Church was one of many denominations seeking to establish the one church of the future.

30. See Pope Benedict XVI, Apostolic Constitution *Anglicanorum Coetibus* (November 4, 2009).

31. Nevertheless, few Protestants, except for evangelicals, share the full measure of the pro-life stance of the Catholic Church.

The Catholic policy of having only official observers at the World Council of Churches was continued after the council as well, but in 1968 the Catholic Church became a member of and substantial contributor to the Faith and Order Commission, which has successfully worked toward a rapprochement among the beliefs of many different denominations.

Beginning with John XXIII through Paul VI, John Paul II, Benedict XVI, and now with Francis, each pope has considered visible Christian unity a most urgent and essential task. At times, the ensuing Catholic ecumenical activity has been influenced by a desire to seek the lowest common denominator in faith and practice, but its best manifestations have been motivated by genuine Catholic faith in church unity. For Catholics, Christ and the church, as well as faith in Christ and the church, stand or fall together. The incarnation and redemption are not only past historical events, but theandric (divine-human) acts of the God-man. Jesus did not simply return to heaven from where he sent the Holy Spirit to inspire the New Testament books and dwell in our hearts. He has extended his incarnate, risen presence through time and space by a visible and organized community built on the apostles, who were with him and witnessed his teaching, passion, and resurrection. After receiving the Holy Spirit, they were sent by him to the ends of the earth. Christ will continue his sanctifying action through the sacraments and teaching of the church until the end of time. As Jesus is the sacrament of God in the sense that his humanity is the visible expression of his Godhead, so is the church analogously the sacrament of Christ, his visible sign communicating his presence and sanctifying action to the world. Therefore, just as the humanity of Christ is essential to our redemption, so too is the visible church indispensable to the extension of his redemptive work in space and time. The visible mission of the apostles as his successors, as well as the invisible action of Christ in the Holy Spirit, together form the one church built by Christ. The Holy Spirit's action is, of course, universal, and his grace is offered to each human being, but the radiating center of his activity is the Holy Eucharist, through whom Christ continues to breathe his Holy Spirit on the world. Thus we can understand the urgency that animates the Catholic Church to work for this visible sacramental unity and to draw all men and women through the preaching of the Word of Christ to the one Eucharist, in which Christ remains present with us until the end of this age.

At the same time, we are aware, as we saw earlier, that "some, even very many, of the most significant elements and endowments which together go to build up and give life to the Church herself can exist outside the visible boundaries of the Catholic Church." The Holy Spirit does not refrain from using these "elements and endowments" as "means of grace," which "must be held capable of giving access to the communion in which is salvation." However, the council fathers add that their "efficacy comes from that grace and truth which has been entrusted to the Catholic Church."[32]

One wonders what kind of suprapersonal subject the church is, when its significant elements exist in separation from her? In the natural realm, no such ontological subject exists whose essential components could live and "generate eternal life" in separation from its subject. This contradiction results from the sins of her members, but it also reveals God's power and mercy. Sin cannot fully destroy unity, only wound it.[33] The "means of salvation" in other churches and ecclesial communities are life-giving because of their inseparable union with the Catholic Church. Similarly, those who belong in good faith to a separated community may receive a greater measure of the fullness of grace that radiates from the Eucharist of the Catholic Church than a lukewarm Catholic would.

The Experience of the Unity of the Church

In the post-Tridentine period, catechisms stressed the apologetical value of unity in the Catholic Church just as much as the marks of holiness, catholicity, and apostolicity. Only the Catholic Church, the catechisms explained, teaches and professes everywhere the same doctrine, celebrates the same sacraments, and has the same unified church order of priests, bishops, and pope. Such an argument retains some value even today, but it omits what is most meaningful for our age, which prefers experience to abstract knowledge. If the church is one suprapersonal and active subject whose every member is animated by the same Spirit and united to the personal body of Christ as members of his ecclesial body, then her unity must also be partially experienced.

At the same time, the Christian theologian knows that in this life God

32. UR 3.

33. Joseph Ratzinger, "The Ecclesiology of the Constitution *Lumen Gentium*," in *Pilgrim Fellowship of Faith: The Church as Communion* (San Francisco: Ignatius, 2005), 148.

and his grace cannot be directly experienced, but only mediated by the direct experience of our own body and soul as they are affected by the action of Christ on us through his Holy Spirit. These effects of the spiritual experience are not unique in themselves. Very similar feelings, moods, and even religious visions can be produced by drugs or electronic stimulation of the brain. Thus, only if we discern the actions and attitudes that Paul calls the fruits of the Holy Spirit in the realm of experience can we conclude that the Holy Spirit is at work in a person or community. These fruits are "love, joy, peace, patience, kindness, generosity, faithfulness, gentleness, self-control" (Gal 5:22–23). Our conclusion would be confirmed if we found that an individual or a community practices these virtues while being the object of hatred and persecution. Wherever the cross is accepted, not only in passive resignation but in hope and love, and wherever it generates a deeper faith and love, then the Spirit of Christ is most likely at work. Additional signs of the presence of the Holy Spirit are the unanimity in which every member of a community believes the same mysteries of the Christian faith and embraces the same moral ideals. Paul never stops exhorting his faithful to "think in harmony . . . with Christ Jesus" (Rom 15:5), and to "have the same attitude in yourselves that is also in Christ Jesus" (Phil 2:5; see also Rom 12:16; 2 Cor 13:11; Phil 4:2). In brief, wherever we see the attitude of Christ and perhaps some features of his personality realized, we can conclude that this individual or community is inspired by the Spirit of Christ.

The experience of unity in history has always been weakened by the offenses of church members, both lay and clerical, who disturbed the peace of the church through power struggles, dissensions, and at times by separating themselves from the one body of Christ. Human sinfulness and petty disagreements have prevented many from finding their way to the one church of Christ. Yet those who travel to different countries and continents experience the universal and catholic character of the church's unity. They find everywhere that the pattern of the cross of Christ, as well as an abundance of life flowing from the cross, is experienced by persons and communities of different races, cultures, and age groups. From Jesus' postresurrection commands in Matthew, Mark, Luke, and Acts, through the prayer of the captured Polycarp of Smyrna for the church scattered throughout the world, to Augustine's insistence on one church, which speaks the languages of each nation, to the "world church" today, which in fact has spread all over the world, the unity of the church has always been all-embracing, that is, catholic.[34]

Conclusions

The church is simply one and, in a special way, uniquely one: *una et unica*. Its unity transcends that of any other community or institution, since she participates in the trinitarian communion and extends the mystery of the one incarnation and redemption in space and time to the ends of the earth and the end of human history. All who belong to the church belong to the one family of the Father, because they have been reborn by grace as one of his own children. They are inserted into the one body of the incarnate and risen Son, who is the head of his body, the church. He lives, acts, and suffers in and through his body, prays to the Father, and offers himself to him in, through, and with his church.

However, the union between head and body is not a pantheistic oneness, but the result of the loving personal union of Christ the bridegroom with his bride, the church, and enabled by the power of the Holy Spirit. Far from absorbing the church into himself, the Spirit's love creates the bride out of the immaculate Virgin Mary and the innumerable multitudes of forgiven sinners. Thus the church is an autonomous ontological subject, the beloved of Christ whom he associates with all his activities. In fact, Christ sustains her existence, finds delight in hearing her voice, preserves her purity of mind and heart (teaching and morality), listens infallibly to her petitions, and lifts her up to himself.

The creation of the bride, her union with Christ, and her ontological cohesion as one bride out of many individual brides is the work of the Holy Spirit. As the Holy Spirit is wholly in the Father and wholly in the Son, uniting both while preserving their unique personhoods, so is his unifying presence within the church. He is fully in Christ and fully in the church while personally present in every (spiritually) living member of the church. His activity unites Christ with the church and every member with Christ and with each other while preserving and actualizing each member's personal uniqueness and differences. His radiance and call reach every human being, and it is either accepted or rejected. This uniting and individualizing

34. Mt 28:18–20; Mk 16:15; Lk 24:46–49; Martyrdom of Polycarp 8.

work of the Spirit begins on earth, but fully penetrates, purifies, and transforms the members of the church only in heaven. The heavenly church, featuring Mary and the saints, is the immaculate bride in full beauty and splendor; on earth the living members are only imperfectly and partially bride, because sin is not quite extinct in them, nor are our bodies glorified.

Since the Son himself has become flesh and his spouse consists of human beings, who are spirit and flesh, the union between the church and Christ must also be both spiritual and fleshly, a visible community that expresses and mediates an invisible, direct, spiritual relationship. This church, the body of Christ, his spouse, "set up and organized in this world as a society, subsists in the Catholic Church."[35] Her external organs of community life and service operating on the universal, regional, and local levels express and mediate her inner attitude of love. The inner acts of faith are expressed and reinforced by corresponding professions and documents of faith, while the sanctifying action of Christ and the church is communicated by the common signs of the sacraments and sacramentals.

Although the assistance of the Holy Spirit ensures that the church cannot lose the sanctifying action of the sacraments and the gospel of Christ, love of God and neighbor can be frozen in many of her ministers and people, such that even their faith grows cold. The church bars those who are in grave sin from the very heart of the church, the Eucharist; at the same time, however, she prays for sinners, carries the burden of their sins, confesses them to God as her own, and bears their shame. In this way, sinners are both separated from and embraced by the church with a special love.

A contradiction similar to that of sin is introduced into the church by heresy, the stubborn rejection of some of the truths that have been revealed by God. For this reason, groups or communities have separated themselves from the unity of the church, yet they have retained "many elements of truth and sanctification" of the Catholic Church. Those persons who have joined or have lived in good faith in these separated communities may obtain salvation through the means of grace available to them, such as baptism, Scripture, and the ecclesial community itself. Even on earth they may already be in invisible spiritual union with the Catholic Church if the same Holy Spirit, which animates the Catholic Church, is present and active in them. This, then, is the paradox: The church established by Christ sub-

35. LG 8.

sists as one autonomous subject in the Catholic Church, yet many of her own "elements of truth and sanctification" also exist outside of the visible boundaries of the Catholic Church. These elements are separated from the Catholic Church yet somehow still belong to her. Sins on both sides caused the separation, but the grace operating in them draws everyone toward catholic unity.

CHAPTER 10

The Holiness of the Church

In the Catholic churches throughout the world, every Holy Saturday night the deacon intones the ancient hymn *Exultet*, by which the most holy church (*sacrosancta ecclesia*) offers to the Father the praise of the Paschal candle. The Latin of the original *Sacrosancta Ecclesia* expresses the holiness of the church more emphatically than *sancta ecclesia*, yet, regardless of the former's apparently unrealistic meaning, it is often found in the liturgy and ecclesial documents. Even though *sacrosancta* seems an almost absurd term at first, its repeated use in these documents points out just how important holiness is for the church's self-understanding. In the past, pious Catholics also spoke of "Holy Mother Church." However, many pious Catholics in recent years have been deeply shaken in their inherited belief regarding the church's holiness. Although most of these people remained loyal Catholics, they no longer refer to the church as "Holy Mother." The recurring stories of the sexual abuse scandal made their childhood catechism lessons on the holy church less credible. While mindful of this situation, I will review the broader theme of holiness and sin in the church as it appears in the Scriptures, tradition, and experience of the church.

The Experience of God's Holiness in the Old Testament

Holiness resists any attempt at a definition since it refers to what is divine and, therefore, is marked by the unfathomable depth of the mystery of God. Holiness marks God as God, in contradistinction to all that is not God. Everything else is holy to the extent that it belongs to God. Thus, everything that has been removed from the sphere of the profane (the secular, "this-worldly" realm)[1] and dedicated to God—such as the temple, the city of Jerusalem, the priests and the commandments, the people of Israel, and in fact the whole earth—is holy in the ontological sense of belonging to God.

Although we cannot grasp and express the reality of God's holiness, we can describe its effects on the people who experience it. In the desert, Moses is attracted to the burning bush that is not consumed. As he draws closer, he is stopped by the voice: "Come no nearer. Remove the sandals from your feet for the place where you stand is holy ground" (Ex 3:4–5). Yet the mysterious fire of God's holiness does not harm Moses, and God sends him on a saving mission to his people. God does not reveal his name to Israel through Moses, yet this nonrevelation ("I am who am") will be the sacred name by which the Israelites can call on him.[2] He is absolute and unapproachable mystery; nonetheless, he is present in a pillar of cloud during the day and in fire at night as he leads Israel through the desert. He does not disdain to dwell in the midst of these erring people with hardened hearts and is not ashamed to be called their God. But Israel's stubborn disobedience stirs up his wrath to destroy the sinners.

In the call of Isaiah, the same polarity regarding the experience of holiness is present. Isaiah is struck with terror when he sees God seated on a lofty throne in the temple. He thinks he will die, for he is sinful and he lives among a sinful people. And now he has seen God! He is convinced of the Old Testament belief that "one cannot see [God] and live" (Ex 33:20). Yet, as soon as his lips are cleansed with a burning piece of coal by a seraph, he volunteers to be God's messenger: "Send me" (Is 6:1–8), he exclaims. Rudolf Otto is right when he points out that the experience of holiness is the experience of a *mysterium tremendum et fascinans*, a mystery both frightening and irresistibly fascinating.[3] We find the same polarity in the experience of Jacob's night-long wrestling with God (Gn 32:23–31), a terrifying and yet uplifting event. It forecasts the entire history of Israel as a painful and gradual educational process in which Israel has to learn how to live in the presence of the holy God and act according to his will. We find the climax

1. "Profane," "secular," and "this-worldly" do not mean "sinful"; rather, they means created realities in their relative autonomy as distinguished from what is divine.

2. The sacred name YHWH, translated in the LXX as *Ho ōn*, has also an implicit ontological meaning of "the One Who Is." But the analogical meaning of being, if understood in the sense of greater dissimilarity than similarity, preserves the mystery.

3. Rudolf Otto, *The Idea of the Holy*, 2nd ed. (London: Oxford University Press, 1958).

of this revelation in the book of Hosea. After God punished Israel for all her breaches of fidelity, he reveals to her the inmost secret of his holiness:

> My heart is overwhelmed
> My pity is stirred.
> I will not give vent to my blazing anger,
> I will not destroy Ephraim again;
> For I am God and not a man,
> The Holy One present among you;
> I will not come in wrath. (Hos 11:8–9)

Here it becomes clear that God's holiness is different from any human quality not because it is an alien and destructive force, but because it is an infinitely intense fire of love. He is God and not man, so his love is incomparably greater than ours and unshakably faithful despite the accumulating infidelity of his people.

The holy God of Israel demands that his people live up to his holiness: "Be holy as I am holy" (Lv 11:44; 20:26). Exactly because God has chosen her and consecrated her to be holy in an ontological sense, Israel must become holy also in the ethical sense, that is, in her hearts and in her actions. Yet she has failed time and again. In fact, God has often complained through his prophets that Israel, his spouse, became a harlot by following alien gods. As punishment, God first destroyed the kingdoms of Israel and then Judah. Nevertheless, in Isaiah's words, he left for himself a "holy trunk," a holy remnant (Is 6:13).

Jesus Christ, the "Holy One of God"

While the just men and women of the Old Testament anticipate the outpouring of the Holy Spirit and the holiness of the renewed people of God, the form of their holiness is the yearning for, and the expectation of, a new beginning, a new creation in which the law of God will be inscribed in the hearts of his people and he will espouse the remnant of the former harlot Israel forever in justice, love, and fidelity (Hos 2:13).

When through Jesus Christ God begins to fulfill these promises, he does not save Israel and humankind from outside or above, or, as it were, by a totally foreign divine intervention. Rather, he saves from within by becoming man, a man of Israel, the son of Joseph and Mary, the offspring of great men and women, saints and sinners, the son of David, Abraham, and Adam. However, Jesus is not conceived by Joseph's seed, but by the Holy Spirit; therefore, he is the *hagion gennōmenon*, the "holy thing," the Holy One of God (Lk 1:35). In him the fullness of divinity and, therefore, the fullness of holiness dwells among his people in a bodily form (Col 2:9). This presence is no longer conditioned by Israel's fidelity to the covenant, as it was in the temple of the old covenant. God left the temple before the Babylonians occupied and destroyed it (Ezek 10:18–23). In Jesus, however, the Holy One of Israel is inseparably and unconditionally united with his people for all eternity. His body is now the center and source of God's holy presence, dwelling on the earth and becoming holy food for all believers. Yet, apart from some anticipated revelations of his glory as power and majesty (Mt 14:33; 17:2),[4] Christ's body before the resurrection reveals his glory as weakness and lowliness, as compassionate love that accepts the ultimate desecration of his body on the cross. It is no accident that the church kneels and sings at the foot of the cross on Good Friday: "Holy God, holy and immortal, have mercy on us."

Jesus came not only to manifest his divine holiness but also to share it with us. He prays to the Father that his disciples may be consecrated in the truth (Jn 17:17–19), and on the cross he hands himself over for her, the church, so that "he may sanctify her, cleansing her by the bath of water with the word, that he might present to himself the church in splendor, without spot or wrinkle or any such thing that she might be holy and without blemish" (Eph 5:25–27). Thus the ultimate humiliation of the crucifixion brings about the messianic wedding feast, the transformation of the harlot into the chaste bride of the Lamb. Jesus and the church are so intimately united in the most perfect spiritual marriage as bridegroom and bride that they become one body and one spirit (see 1 Cor 6:17; 12:12). The church, then, becomes holy through the holiness of her heavenly spouse.

The Gospel of John completes this Pauline teaching by showing the role of the Holy Spirit in the birth of the church. Jesus hands over the Spirit with his last breath on the cross, and out of his pierced side blood and water flow, baptism and Eucharist, the two church-constituting sacraments (Jn 19:34–37). During his first postresurrection appearance to the disciples, Jesus breathes into them the Holy Spirit, the source of all forgiveness and

4. The glory of God is synonymous with holiness; it means the manifestation of God's holiness.

sanctification. The entire mission of the church (including the sacrament of reconciliation) is foretold here as the continuation of the breathing of the Holy Spirit into all those who are receptive to it. The forgiving and sanctifying mission of the Holy Spirit through the apostolic mission extends the realm of light and holiness into the darkness of the world, which is still in the grasp of the evil one (Jn 20:19–23; 1 Jn 5:19).

The Holy Church of God

In the New Testament, the adjective "holy" is not applied to the church, but to her members. St. Paul writes to his faithful as to "the chosen holy ones" (*klētois hagiois*) (1 Cor 1:2). Since they belong to the mother church, the Christians in Jerusalem are in a special way the "holy ones" (Rom 15:25–26). Closely following the Old Testament, the term has a twofold but interrelated meaning. All Christians are holy because they are chosen out of this world and transferred to the possession of God. "Having been registered" through baptism to the name of the "Father, the Son, and the Holy Spirit," their persons and in particular their bodies no longer belong to this world but are Christ's possession.[5] This ontological holiness, their becoming one body and one spirit with the Lord and with each other, calls for ethical holiness. Since Christ died for us, we belong not to ourselves but to him. So we should live not for ourselves, but for the one who died for us (Rom 14:7–8). This is the foundation and compendium of the Christian's moral life. Paul's priestly ministry aims at the same goal; that the self-offering of the gentiles may be sanctified by the Holy Spirit and become an acceptable sacrifice to God (Rom 15:16).

From the beginning of the church, the first occurrences of the phrase *hagia ekklēsia* (holy church) are found in the following: a letter of Ignatius of Antioch to the Trallians, the account of the martyrdom of Polycarp, and three times in writings of the *Shepherd* of Hermas. All of these date from the second century. In the Nicene-Constantinopolitan Creed a reference to the holy church occurs along with the three other essential marks, "one, holy, catholic, and apostolic church."

For the Fathers, the church in the full sense of the word is the "glorious

5. The baptismal formula of Mt 28:19, "baptizing them in the name [*eis to onoma*] of the Father and the Son and the Holy Spirit," denotes the original meaning of registering something or someone to the name of the owner. The one who is baptized becomes the possession of the Triune God and, therefore, is holy.

church without spot or wrinkle," the spouse whom Christ washed clean by his sacrifice on the cross. They called this perfect church, the church of those who are spiritually mature, "the bride without blemish" (*sponsa sine macula*) in reference to Ephesians 5:27. Beginning with Origen, the church-bride is identified with the bride in search of the bridegroom in the Song of Songs, where the "beautiful soul" (*anima decora*), the perfect Christian, refers to the bride. Using the titles that refer to the bride in the Song of Songs, the church and the perfect soul are both called "dove without any blemish, a unique dove, my immaculate dove" (*columba sine macula, columba unica, columba mea immaculata*). The Fathers put these words of invitation from the Song of Songs onto the lips of the bridegroom:

> See the winter is past,
> the rains are over and gone.
> The flowers appear on the earth,
> the time of pruning the vines has come,
> and the song of the turtledove is heard in our land.
> The fig tree puts forth its figs
> and the vines, in bloom, give forth their fragrance.
> Arise my love, my beautiful one, and come! (Song 2:11–13)

Christ has only one immaculate spouse, the church, to whom he is always faithful. Therefore, no soul may be united to Christ in holiness without the church. She must embody the church-spouse in herself; in Origen's words, she must become an *anima ecclesiastica*, an ecclesial soul, who realizes in herself the spousal relationship of the church and participates in the intimate union between Christ and the church.[6] In this context, we can understand why St. Bernard and many other Fathers held forth that Christ has both one spouse and many spouses. The many spouses participate in the relationship to Christ of the one perfect spouse, the church.[7] The individual is sanctified to the extent that he or she becomes that one unique spouse. For this reason, there is no holiness outside the church, and growth in holiness means a growing identification with the disposition and activity of the one church-bride.[8]

6. "Therefore, if you are an ecclesial soul, you are better than all other souls; if you are not, you are not an ecclesial [soul]" (Origen, *Homilies on the Song of Songs* 1.10).

7. "We ourselves are the Spouse, and, if this does not seem to you unbelievable, we all are one spouse and the souls of each are individual spouses" (Bernard of Clairvaux, *Sermon on the First Sunday after the Octave of Epiphany*).

8. The insistence of the Fathers on the one church-bride without whom there is no sanctification is not incompatible with the teaching of Vatican II, which admits the possibility of salvation outside the

What has been intuited from the beginning is articulated conceptually only much later, following a process of development that culminates in the dogma of the immaculate conception. This church of the perfect, the immaculate dove, can only be in the fullest sense the heavenly church, the immaculate Virgin Mary in the most perfect way and, arrayed around her, all the saints, sharing in her holiness.[9] The church on earth is always in process, transitioning from harlot to chaste harlot, from black beauty to white dawn, from young girl to perfect bride. It is the bridegroom who effects this purification, as Blessed Isaac of Stella explains:

> Whatever he found repugnant in the bride, he took away and affixed it to the cross. He took away through the tree where he endured her sins on the tree. What was naturally hers, he assumed and put on himself; what was his own and divine, he gave [to his bride] . . . so that all that belongs to the Bridegroom may belong to the Bride.[10]

Through her union with the bridegroom, the bride becomes mother and, thus, associated with the sanctifying action of the bridegroom. The active originator of sanctification is Christ, but Mother Church receives and nurtures the "seed" of the bridegroom to full growth by her prayers, sacraments, and teaching. Isaac continues: "Every faithful soul is understood to be a spouse of the Word of God, the mother, the daughter and the sister of Christ, both virgin and fertile."[11] According to Isaac's wonderful formulation: "The almighty Christ is able to do everything by himself; that is, to baptize, consecrate the Eucharist, ordain [ministers] and so on. But the humble and faithful Bridegroom does not want to do anything without the Bride. Therefore, what God has joined, man should not separate."[12] The implications of this unbreakable marriage are far-reaching. The divine office is the prayer of the church not just by a legal decree of church authority. When we, as members of the church, pray it, we truly share the prayer of the one spouse, Mary, and all the saints, who already enjoy the vision of God, as well as those on earth in whom the Holy Spirit is present and ac-

---

church. The grace offered to those outside the church is the grace of Christ, and therefore, to the extent it is accepted, it conforms the non-Christians to Christ and thus joins them in some real sense to the church, who in her saints reflects Christ to the world.

9. Cf. Hans Urs von Balthasar, *The Office of Peter and the Structure of the Church*, trans. Andrée Emery, 2nd ed. (San Francisco: Ignatius, 2007), 227–28.

10. Isaac of Stella, *Sermo* 11.10.

11. Isaac of Stella, *Sermo* 51.8.

12. Isaac of Stella, *Sermo* 11.14.

tive. Moreover, when the priest prays before Holy Communion that Christ "may not look at my sins, but at the faith of your church," the *fides ecclesiae* is not an abstract notion. It is the faith of the one spouse, that of Mary and of all those in heaven and on earth who possess the supernatural virtue of faith.[13]

Perhaps the following distinction can be made regarding what traditional theology calls the two types of efficacy among the sacramental activities of the church: first, sacramentals, or the prayers and blessings instituted by the church, work *ex opere operantis ecclesiae*; and second, the sacraments, instituted by Christ, work *ex opere operato*.[14] So the sacramentals are primarily the prayers of the holy church accompanied by Christ, who gives weight and efficacy to his bride's prayer. The sacraments, on the other hand, are primarily Christ's sanctifying actions, mediated for us by the faith of the church.[15]

In light of these considerations, the popular Catholic notion of the sacraments as merely visible signs of invisible grace is simply an impoverishment of sacramental theology. The prevalent formula is true, but inadequate and potentially misleading. It can lead to neglect of the personal structure of the sacraments. The principle of *ex opere operato* in St. Thomas's theology literally implies the unconditional presence of the personal sanctifying activity of Christ through the performance of the rite as well as the receptive action of the faith of the church.

Sin and Holiness in the Church

While the authors of the New Testament and the Fathers were aware of the lofty vision of the church as the Holy Spirit-filled bride, they also had to acknowledge the reality of sin in the church. Apparently, none of the local churches of that time could be seen as fully embodying the spotless spouse of Christ. Paul's letters to the churches and, in particular, his two letters to

13. Balthasar in several texts interprets 1 Cor 13:13, "so faith, hope, love remain," in the sense that all three theological virtues remain in heaven, but operate in a different way. If faith is sharing in the knowledge of God here on earth, in heaven this sharing will be perfected. We will see the Father by sharing in the face-to-face vision of the Son.

14. The free translations of *ex opere operantis Ecclesiae* is: it is effective by what the church does; *ex opere operato*: it is effective by the rite performed.

15. In what de Lubac calls the "Great Tradition," the faith of the church does not mean only what the church believes, but also the subject of that faith, the holy church, the spouse of Christ, Mary, and the saints. This is the reason why the faith of the church is always informed by love, according to St. Thomas (*De veritate* q. 14, a. 11), since it is the faith of the saints.

the Corinthians, deal with cases of grave sin, which called for temporary exclusion of some from the community. St. Augustine and other Fathers explained this conflict between belief in the immaculate bride-church and the presence of sinners in the church with the following distinction: The sinners only appear to be within the church for they are there only "by body" and not "by heart"; and so they do not belong to the holy church of God, to "that unique dove, modest and chaste, the spouse without blemish or stain."[16] However, this view that sinners only appear to belong to the church led to heretical or near heretical beliefs before and after Augustine. Many who succumbed to the temptation of restricting church membership to a pure church of the Spirit omitted Augustine's concession that sinners belong by body (*corpore*) to the church. Montanists, Donatists, Novatianists, the Cathari, and the followers of Wyclif all reduced the church in one way or another to "the pure" ones or the "spiritual" elect. The Catholic view has always maintained that even the faithful who are in grave sin still, in some sense, belong to the church; moreover, the holy church prays for them and calls them to penance and full participation in her life.

Lumen Gentium, the Dogmatic Constitution on the Church promulgated during the Second Vatican Council, avoided the term "church membership" because it does not express the many different ways of belonging to the Catholic Church. According to *Lumen Gentium*, members are "fully incorporated into the society of the Church who, possessing the Spirit of Christ, accept its whole structure and all the means of salvation that have been established within it, and within its visible framework are united to Christ."[17] Thus the council restored the role of the "possession" of the Holy Spirit and union with Christ as essential to the nature of the church. The perennial *sensus fidei* has now been confirmed by the magisterium, the *sensus fidei*, which has always maintained that the church is most intensely present among those in whom the Holy Spirit dwells and so belong to Christ. On the basis of *Lumen Gentium*, it can be shown that the objective holiness of the church as an institution is based on her union with Christ, who upholds the institution until the end of history.

16. See Augustine, *De baptismo* 6.3, 28.39. He, however, acknowledged the validity of the baptism of heretics and of grave sinners so that in the event they return to the church, they will not need to be baptized again. Thus he implied that sinners belong to the church in some way: *corpore* but not *corde* (in a visible, bodily way but not in their hearts).

17. LG 14.

Since it is Christ who works through the church's rites, the sacraments sanctify the worthy recipients regardless of the holiness of the minister. The teaching of the church is preserved in the church in spite of, and at times through, unworthy bishops and popes. The church offices of deacon, priest, and bishop, and in particular that of the bishop of Rome, remain sacred despite the sinfulness of the office holders. In this context, it becomes evident that the belief mentioned above has nothing to do with magic, but is rooted in the christological and pneumatological mystery of the church. Christ has given himself over to the church completely and irrevocably. He has united a renewed Israel to himself so that, as stated earlier, he has become one body and one spirit with her. As a result, the basic structures of the institution, the sacraments, teaching, and daily office, are sacred and indestructible because they are ways by which the one bride of Christ operates, the bride mother with whom and through whom Christ sanctifies through the Holy Spirit all those who are open to his grace.

All graces come from Christ's sacrifice, which is present in the Church's Eucharist. These graces are also given to those outside the institutional structures of the church, who always prays for all men and women. We may even speak of non-Christian saints who, for reasons not of their own making, have not found the church. Yet since they were sanctified by the grace of Christ, they reveal some of Christ's virtues. Two examples may suffice. According to Chinese sources, Confucius (K'ung-Fu-tzu) was such an honest and irreproachable public servant of a certain prince that the prince could not tolerate his righteous deeds and fired him. Confucius then wandered around the provinces of China and offered his services to various rulers, but not one was willing to hire him. Thus he became a relatively unknown master of a few disciples. Only after his death was he acknowledged as the unparalleled moral master of Chinese history. He taught that one should strive for goodness (*jen*) and heaven gives everyone the power of virtue (*Te*) to obtain goodness. But he also acknowledged that neither he nor others whom he knew have ever realized this goodness in their lives.

Another example is Mahatma Gandhi of India, who preached nonviolent resistance and nonhatred of the British oppressors. He was killed by one of his compatriots because he opposed the war between India and Pakistan. Gandhi had a special love for the Dalits, the outcasts of Indian society, whom he called the children of God. Both of these men had certain features of Christ, including an indomitable courage to teach and live justice and goodness, and, in the case of Gandhi, the courage to die as a martyr for preaching peace and love.[18] If it is true that these "saints" are conformed to Christ in some important ways, they must have been molded by the Spirit of Christ, the "finger of God" who carves out the features of Christ in us. These "saints" who are outside the institutional boundaries of the church must belong in some real sense to the church, the body of Christ.[19]

Having seen the indestructible holiness of the bride-church rooted in the spousal love of Christ, we are now in a better position to appreciate what *Lumen Gentium* says about sin in the church: "The Church containing sinners in her own bosom, is at one and the same time holy and always in need of purification and it pursues unceasingly penance and renewal."[20] Confirming the perennial tradition of the church, the Second Vatican Council refused to exclude sinners from the church, but at the same time it refrained from calling the church herself sinful. The council evidently could not do otherwise, because, according to Ephesians 5:25–27 and her constant tradition, the church is the spotless bride of Christ and thereby his body itself. Thus the church, insofar as it is the holy bride of Christ, cannot commit a sin. Nevertheless, she accepts full solidarity with her sinful members, does penance for them, and thus constantly purifies and renews her earthly countenance, disfigured and soiled as it is by sinful Christians. It is important to see that the holiness of the spotless bride has nothing to do with scorn or indifference toward sinners. Since her holiness is the holiness of Christ, she continues in history the mission of Christ who has come to seek what has been lost, to pursue the straying sheep, to take on himself not only the sins of her members but the sins of the world, and to accept to be counted among the wicked by hanging on a cross between two criminals. God made Christ to be sin, according to Paul, so that we may become God's righteousness in him (2 Cor 5:21). According to St. Thomas, Christ, "as it were, ascribes to himself all the sins of the human race."[21] Thus the church fully purified in heaven and on the way to purification on

18. Cf. Roch Kereszty, *Christianity among Other Religions: Apologetics in a Contemporary Context* (New York: Alba House, 2006), 79–85, 152–53.

19. I present these two men as highly probable examples of some Christic features in their attitudes and actions rather than suggesting their canonization.

20. LG 8.

21. Thomas Aquinas, ST III q. 46, a. 6.

earth (and probably also in purgatory)[22] unites herself in compassion and prayer with her sinful members on earth and with all sinners. In addition to compassion and prayer, the church on earth also does penance for her sinful members and, as her divine master, carries the burden of all the sinners of the world. Joseph Ratzinger beautifully summarizes the relationship between the church of sinners and the holy church. He asks the rhetorical question: If the church is the manifestation of the holiness of Christ, who enters into full solidarity with sinners, then

> is it not appropriate that the Church appear in inseparable communion with sin and with the sinners in order to continue the destiny of the Lord and his carrying of us all with him? If so, then the proper, new and true holiness of God's love would manifest itself in the unholy holiness of the church in contrast to the human expectation of Purity. This holiness would not stand in aristocratic distance from the untouchable Pure One, but would mix itself with the filth of the world in order to overcome it. It would express itself—in opposition to the ancient notion of purity—as essentially love, which means standing for the other, taking over the burden of the other, carrying the other and thereby redeeming him.[23]

The Holy Church and Evangelization

Today, many would answer the question, "Why did you leave the church?" by saying, "I left because of the church." Some may have left because they found the church too holy, calling for a moral life they consider too demanding. Others, however, whose sincerity we can hardly call into question, may say that they left because they found in the church only a soulless bureaucracy or a scandal-ridden institution. Still others may have had a bad experience with a priest; not necessarily sexual abuse, but a lack of personal care or understanding. In short, these people left because they did not find Christ in the church.

On the other hand, if we interview those who have found Christ, we discover, in a great variety of ways, some form of ecclesial mediation. Even those who had come to Christ by a spiritual experience apart from any visible ecclesial setting likely searched afterward for a Christian community where they could find the Christ they encountered in their private expe-

22. There is no consensus among theologians as to whether souls in purgatory can help the rest of the church while they are totally dependent on the help of the church in heaven and on earth.

23. Joseph Ratzinger, *Das neue Volk Gottes: Entwürfe zur Ekklesiologie* (Düsseldorf: Patmos Verlag, 1969), 245.

rience. The story of Paul is paradigmatic of a certain type of conversion; he experienced a personal encounter with the risen Christ, but he was instructed to go to the church in Damascus, where he would be told what to do. Had these individuals not found a community that convinced them of the permanent presence of Christ in their midst, their faith would not have grown beyond a lonely yearning for the presence of Christ in this world.

In other cases, encounters with holy Christians gave the first impetus to the process of conversion. For instance, searching for God or for some ultimate meaning in their lives, they met a person or a community that radiated goodness, peace, joy, and a readiness to forgive and love. Such an encounter has the potential to draw the one searching to discover the "secret" that makes possible such a life. Once they find that faith in Jesus is what enables them to be who they are, they conclude that Jesus must be real, alive, and powerful. Yet not everyone who comes in contact with holy people senses their mystery. A fruitful encounter always presupposes a prior working of grace in the heart of the eventual convert.

Thus, in each of these two types of conversion are found two kinds of causes, one inner and the other external: an inward experience of grace and a visible encounter with the church through some of her members or her communities. In each such encounter with the church, the searchers must find Christ present in that church member or church community. In other words, the searchers must encounter the holy church.

Conclusions

God's holiness refers to what characterizes God as God. He reveals his holiness in the Old Testament both as a deadly threat to sinful humankind and, simultaneously, as an infinitely attractive mystery. Israel learns through the prophet Isaiah that God's holiness is dreadful not because it is destructive, but because it is a love that exceeds human endurance, a love whose fire mortal humankind cannot bear. In spite of Israel's infidelities, God does not disdain to become the Holy One of Israel who dwells in the temple among his people. Yet Israel's sins eventually arouse God's wrath and his glory abandons the temple. Jerusalem is devastated by Babylon. Although God's glory returns after the exile, Israel's future is far from clear at the time.

God's presence becomes unconditionally guaranteed in Jesus of Nazareth, the Holy One of God, in whom the fullness of divinity and thus the fullness of holiness dwells. In Jesus' passion, death, and resurrection God's holiness or glory reveals itself as infinite humility, a compassionate search for sinners and a vicarious suffering for them. He thus obtains forgiveness and sanctification for his bride, the immaculate dove composed of Mary and the saints in heaven and on earth. It is this holy bride, the *sacrosancta ecclesia*, that Jesus associates to himself in his work of extending forgiveness and divine life to the world and all those who open up to him. The association of this bride with Jesus and his sanctifying activity through her is signified by the fact that the priests or bishops who preach and especially when they administer the sacraments represent both Christ and the church. This immaculate church is definitively sanctified in those who have been consummated in heaven and is in the process of sanctifying those who belong to her on earth. Members, who remain within the church by being joined to Christ in the Holy Spirit, will be infallibly sanctified.

The objective structures of the church, the gospel, the sacraments, and church office are indefectibly holy not in and of themselves, but through Christ, who with the cooperation of his holy church-bride safeguards their holiness. Ratzinger, then, is right in saying that "in theology, it is not the person that is reducible to the thing, but the thing to the person."[24]

The holiness of the immaculate bride-church is the holiness of her bridegroom who carries the stray sheep on his own shoulders and takes on himself all the sins of the world on the cross. Therefore, the bride embraces her sinful members in her bosom, supports them with her prayer, and offers them the sacrifice of her groom. Sinners, who have lost the Holy Spirit by mortal sins, and the saints on earth, who are still not fully purified, disfigure the face of the holy bride on earth, yet none of their impurities can deface the church in heaven. Nor can sin destroy the sanctifying power of the sacraments, falsify the teaching of the gospel, prevent the emergence of saints, or eliminate the presence of the Holy Spirit, who in the words of Irenaeus and *Lumen* Gentium, rejuvenates the church, continually renewing her and leading her to perfect union with her spouse."[25]

24. Joseph Ratzinger, "Thoughts on the Place of Marian Doctrine and Piety in Faith and Theology as a Whole," in Hans Urs von Balthasar and Joseph Ratzinger, *Mary, Church at the Source* (San Francisco: Ignatius Press, 2005), 27.

25. Irenaeus, *Against Heresies* 3.24.1, quoted by LG 4.

CHAPTER 11

The Catholicity of the Church

The Historical Foundations of Catholicity

The word "catholic" is not in the Bible.[1] We find it first in the letter to the Smyrnaeans by Ignatius of Antioch: "Where the bishop is, there must also the community be; just as where Jesus Christ is, there is the catholic church."[2] Scholars are divided over whether "catholic" here means universal or authentic. The letter on Polycarp's martyrdom states that after his capture he was allowed to pray for two hours, during which time he remembered everyone he had encountered in his long life and "the whole catholic church which is spread out over the whole world."[3] Here the meaning is geographic universality. For St. Augustine, catholic means the true, authentic church which shows itself in geographic and anthropological universality, while heretical or schismatic assemblies are limited to a certain locale.[4] The most comprehensive definitions of catholicity come from St. Cyril of Jerusalem and Aquinas. Here is Cyril's definition:

> The Church is called Catholic because it is spread throughout the world, from end to end of the earth, also because it teaches universally and completely all the doctrines which man should know concerning things visible and invisible, heavenly and earthly; and also because it subjects to right worship all humankind, rulers and ruled, lettered and unlettered; further, because it treats and heals universally every sort of sin committed by soul and body, and it possesses in itself every conceivable virtue, whether in deeds, words or in spiritual gifts of every kind.[5]

1. For greater detail, see Avery Dulles, *The Catholicity of the Church* (Oxford: Clarendon, 1985).
2. Ignatius of Antioch, *Letter to the Smyrnaeans* 8.2.
3. Martyrdom of Polycarp 8.1.
4. See Augustine, *Enarrationes in Psalmos* 147.19; *De catechizandis rudibus* 22, 39; *De unitate Ecclesiae* 11, 30.
5. Cyril of Jerusalem, *Catechetical Lectures* 18.22.

Cyril introduces this third meaning of "catholic," fullness as a basis for its geographical and anthropological universality. The church is catholic because she has the fullness of Christ's revelation and self-communication; she can heal the sins of all human beings and adorn them with all the virtues and charisms.

To geographical and anthropological universality St. Thomas adds the dimension of history. The church is catholic because it extends to the full course of human history and beyond. It started with Abel and includes not only the earthly members of the church but also those in purgatory and heaven. And it continues in heaven through all eternity.[6] He also explains that the church's laws apply "to the whole life of man and to everything that in any way pertains to that life."[7]

According to St. Thomas, people belong in different ways to the ecclesial body whose head is Christ. Those who most perfectly belong to the church are those who are united to the body by faith and charity. They belong so perfectly that the Holy Spirit fills them as *unus numero*, meaning that the same Holy Spirit is present in each member.[8] Nevertheless, Christ is also the head of unbelievers, since here on earth every unbeliever is capable of being united to the body of the church.[9] St. Thomas, then, is not very far removed from *LG* 16, which speaks about the varying ways and the extent to which those "who have not yet accepted the Gospel belong to the people of God."

After the Council of Trent, the catholicity of the church was used mainly for apologetic purposes, along with the three other marks of the church, one, holy, and apostolic. The term "catholic" had already been restricted by the Roman Catechism to mean geographical and anthropological universality.[10]

This short sketch of the tradition shows that the Second Vatican Council did not invent any new notion of catholicity. Such a claim would make sense only if one thought that the post-Tridentine restricted notion of cath-

6. Aquinas, *Opusculum* 7. Of course, many of the Fathers speak about the *Ecclesia ab Abel* and take for granted that the church is both on earth and in heaven, but they do not connect this notion with her catholicity.

7. Aquinas, *In Boethium*, part 2, q. 3, a. 3, co. 3.

8. Aquinas, *Super Sententias Lombardi*, lib. 3, d. 13, q. 2, a. 2, qc. 2, co.

9. Aquinas, *Super Sententias Lombardi*, lib. 3, d. 13, q. 2, a. 2, qc. 2, co.

10. Roman Catechism, art. 9. Interestingly, the Baltimore Catechism's definition is somewhat richer. In addition to the geographical and anthropological university of the church, it also claims that that the church teaches "all the truths revealed by God" (*New St. Joseph Baltimore Catechism*, ed. Bennet Kelley, rev. ed. [Totowa, N.J.: Catholic Publishing Company], 1991, no. 131).

olicity captured the whole tradition. In reality, the council documents have recovered the threefold interconnected meaning of catholicity from the Fathers and St. Thomas: fullness, universality, and authenticity. She has the fullness of God's revelation and self-communication. Therefore, her mission extends to the whole world and to every human being. For these reasons she is the authentic, true church of Christ.[11]

However, a significantly new notion in the council documents is the explanation of the trinitarian and anthropological basis of the Church's universal, catholic mission, and an articulation of the church's relationship to the autonomous structures and values of the created order (what the French liked to call *la théologie des réalités terrestres*, "the theology of earthly values"). At the same time, the council fathers were aware of the relevance of catholicity for the new situation of humankind.

Only today can the world be spoken of as a "global village," in which each person's life is interconnected with everyone else's, socially, technologically, economically, and politically. Many dramatic events have already given us a firsthand experience of our interdependent destiny. An economic crisis in any major country affects the world economy; the pollution of the atmosphere and waters in one country or a nuclear catastrophe in another may result in tragic global effects. For the first time, humankind is capable of destroying itself, but we are also, for the first time, able to feed every human being on the planet. In fact, we could feed more than the present population, if only the international community had the will to organize and finance the effort. We are also aware of the danger of an eruption of violence that may result from the forced interdependence of many people. At the same time though, this may be a moment of grace when people discover a universal brotherhood of mutual love and solidarity within the Catholic Church.

The Foundation of the Church's Catholicity in the Triune God and in Human Nature

For a deeper understanding of the church's catholicity we need to take a closer look at the "catholicity" of the trinitarian God. In other words, we

11. See *Catechism of the Catholic Church* (New York: Doubleday, 1995), 8320–21, which admirably summarizes the council's teaching and thereby the whole tradition.

need to examine the fullness and universality that characterize God's intratrinitarian relationships and how this fullness and universality are reflected in salvation history.

By eternally generating the Son, the Father gives over to him all that he has and all that he is, the fullness of his divinity. Throughout salvation history, the eternal generation of the Son is reflected in the Father's sending him into the world so that the Son may acquire an innumerable multitude of human brothers and sisters, bringing them back home to the Father as the Father's own children,[12] the universal "family of God."

The eternal Son, born in time as the son of the Virgin Mary, "contains" in himself the absolute *fullness* of divinity. He lives and dies for *all* human beings so that he may make us share in the *fullness* of his divine life. He offers his body and blood as the perfect sacrifice on behalf of, and for, *all* human beings. And he wants to "distribute" his sacrificed and glorified body and blood, which are inseparably united with his divinity, as spiritual food and drink to *all* humankind. He sends his disciples to teach and baptize *all* nations and gather them together into one church. By the church's sacraments, by God's written and preached Word, by the church's ministers and loving community, Christ wants to reach beyond the geographical and temporal boundaries of his historical existence into *all* times and places. Just as in his earthly life he carried the burden of *all* sins, in the *universal* compassion of his glorified existence he shares in *all* our joys and tragedies. Pascal's words echo a long tradition: Christ's agony lasts to the end of the ages.[13]

The Holy Spirit, with whom Father and Son eternally share the *fullness* of divinity, is the bond who unites Father and Son even while preserving their distinction. In salvation history, we appropriate Christ's redemption by the power of the Holy Spirit. By him, the Father draws *all* men and women to Christ. In him, those drawn to Christ are also united in the one body of Christ while retaining—or rather, realizing—their unique individuality in this one body.

12. The Pauline notion of "adopted sons" in the light of the Johannine writings in which God's adopted children are "born from God" and "the seed of God" remains in them makes it obvious that our adopted status as God's children infinitely transcends all legal notions. We are simply God's true children out of a sheer undeserved gift of grace.

13. Christ exists in the glory of the Father, yet in his members on earth, he is in agony until the end of history. We do not know how this is possible. All we know is that this is a miracle of his almighty compassion.

As quoted in the historical introduction, St. Ignatius of Antioch wrote: "Where Jesus Christ is, there is the catholic Church."[14] We may interpret this phrase in the most radical sense. Where the sacrifice of Jesus Christ is celebrated, he is truly, substantially present; there, then, is the catholic (that is, the authentic) church. This and many other biblical and patristic texts imply that local churches are not simply parts of the universal Catholic Church, but also that each local church makes the one Catholic Church present in a particular celebrating community. In some sense, even the individual Catholic in whom the indivisible Holy Spirit, and thereby Christ himself, is dwelling, has, in the words of Origen, an *anima ecclesiastica*, a churchly soul. In other words, he who wants to progress in spiritual life must have a catholic soul that embraces the entire church with his love; a soul that lives the mystery of the church's betrothal to Christ. Beginning with Origen, the bride in the Song of Songs is seen as both the church and the individual soul, yet the many brides are only one bride since Jesus Christ remains faithful to his one bride, the church. Therefore, the individual Christian in her most personal, intimate union with Christ fulfills and manifests the vocation of the entire Catholic Church. Our intimate spiritual life, then, is not that of an isolated individual, but rather catholic, a personal living out of a universal vocation.

From the catholicity of the Trinity follows the church's universal mission of evangelization, which extends the fullness of divine life unto the entire world. In other words, the catholicity of the intratrinitarian love ensures the catholicity of the church, a universal community created by God that embodies in herself the fullness of the all-embracing love of the Holy Trinity. It follows that whoever opposes or neglects evangelization under the pretext that salvation is possible outside the visible boundaries of the church, that person then opposes the will and the love of the Father, the Son, and the Holy Spirit.

In fact, those who are saved without an explicit knowledge of Christ and God are not saved without accepting in some way or another the grace of the Holy Spirit, which conforms them to the Paschal mystery of Christ.[15] This conformation may often manifest itself both in religious and nonreligious terms, or only in nonreligious terms, such as true self-giving in a

14. Ignatius of Antioch, *Letter to the Smyrnaeans* 8.2.
15. See GS 22.

lifelong marriage, yearning for the truth and accepting suffering or even death for the sake of truth or love of neighbor. This unconscious grace of the Holy Spirit impels the recipient to seek and yearn for a better understanding of the object of their own desires. In other words, all grace impels one to search for Christ and to be united with him in the church.[16] Therefore, ceasing to or neglecting evangelization is resistance to, or neglect of, this longing of the Holy Spirit to guide searching souls into full belonging in the "family" of the Father.

In addition to the trinitarian foundation, the catholicity of the church also has an anthropological base. If humankind did not share one and the same human nature, the universality of the church's mission would only lead to tragic attempts to squeeze radically different individuals into a strangulating straightjacket. It would justify the frequent charge in intellectual circles that the church is practicing a form of cultural imperialism. In reality, however, as the Second Vatican Council and Popes John Paul II and Benedict XVI insist, by revealing to us the mystery of Christ, God has also "fully disclosed humankind to itself."[17] If, however, a common human nature exists, and in one instance an individual human nature has been lifted up to the state of the human nature of God the Son, then every human being is *capax Dei*, capable of receiving divine life out of sheer undeserved, divine love. Thus the divinization of a human being does not distort but rather perfects and fulfills our humanity. Then Aquinas's insistence that God's revelation transforms every level of human nature does not lead to the suppression of the individual, but to our supreme flowering. St. Ignatius of Antioch expressed this mystery in the early second century. He knew that only upon arriving in heaven would he become "a [perfect] human being."[18]

The Catholic Church and the World

Since the very nature of the church is catholic, she embraces all human beings and all human values, art, science, technology, and literature. Therefore, her missionary character cannot be reduced to some accidental sec-

16. Often, however, the entrance into the church of these graced people is prevented by cultural barriers or not encountering an authentic witness to Christian faith.

17. GS 22.

18. Ignatius of Antioch, *Letter to the Romans* 6.2.

ondary feature, as if it were a particular vocation of only certain Catholics. Since the church is missionary in her very nature,[19] every Catholic community and every faithful Catholic ought to be concerned about evangelization and bear witness to those "outside" the church in a way that is compatible with each of our life situations. A local church that turns completely inward and cares only about its own members and its own self-preservation betrays its mission. One of the best critics of this self-protecting ecclesial attitude is the Lutheran pastor Dietrich Bonhoeffer, who in his prison correspondence pointed out that just as Christ's divine transcendence revealed itself in his existing entirely for others, so should the church exist entirely for the world rather than restrict herself to self-preservation.[20] The moment that a local church becomes self-absorbed in her concerns, her life and activities, that's when her catholicity, the fullness of her ecclesial reality, is compromised.

The church's missionary nature, her catholicity as the sacrament of the unity of all humankind, is one of the defining factors for the right relationship between the church and the world. As a result of the Reformation and the Enlightenment, the church in Europe was threatened in her freedom of activity, in her doctrine, and in her very existence. As a result, she took up a largely defensive, self-protecting posture. Hans Urs von Balthasar and others compared the church of that time to a beleaguered fortress that tried to shut all her doors and windows in order to keep out the poisonous air of the world. Vatican II rejected this defensive posture. Not a single anathema of condemnation came from the council, but rather it emphasized the church's complete solidarity with the world: "The joys and hopes and the sorrows and anxieties of people today, especially of those who are poor and afflicted, are also the joys and hopes, sorrows and anxieties of the disciples of Christ, and there is nothing truly human which does not also affect them."[21]

A huge number of Catholics, including theologians, have not paid atten-

19. See Vatican Council II, Decree on Missionary Activity *Ad Gentes* (December 7, 1965), 2; Pope Paul VI, Apostolic Exhortation *Evangelii Nuntiandi* (December 8, 1975); John Paul II, Encyclical Letter *Redemptoris Missio* (December 7, 1990); Francis, Apostolic Exhortation *Evangelii Gaudium* (November 24, 2013). Cf. Roch Kereszty, "Why a New Evangelization? A Study of Its Theological Rationale," *Communio* 21 (1994): 594–611.

20. See Dietrich Bonhoeffer, *Letters and Papers from Prison*, ed. Eberhard Bethge (New York: Macmillan, 1967). Bonhoeffer writes about the Lutheran Confessing Church in Germany during the Nazi regime, but his critique, mutatis mutandis, applies also to the Catholic Church.

21. GS 1.

tion to the balanced approach of the council documents, but only to its general openness and respect for the modern world and human progress. The ensuing uncritical embrace of the modern world and an a priori hostility to, or at least suspicion of, the teachings and practices of the post-Tridentine church, coupled with a certain ignorance of the rich fruits of patristic and biblical *ressourcement*, resulted in confusion among many Catholics and in the total or partial loss of faith in a significant number.

The council, on the contrary, adopted a truly catholic approach in clear continuity with the biblical theology of the world. While the world is the object of the Father and Son's self-sacrificing love, Christians, at the same time, ought not to love "the world" (Jn 3:16), insofar as it is "the craving of the flesh, the craving of the eyes, and the pride of life" (1 Jn 2:16). On the one hand, the council emphasized that no human value, nothing created by God, is alien to the church. In fact, the kingly office of the Christian laity includes a commitment to their secular jobs and their work in society. The laity is called to improve the structures of society, to increase the respect for the dignity and rights of the human person, to reach a more equitable distribution of goods, and thus to promote universal progress.[22] The laity should bear witness to its faith and imbue society with the spirit of Christ, but at the same time they should respect the autonomy of the created order.

From the fact of being created everything possesses its own stability, truth and goodness, and its own laws and order, which should be respected by us in recognizing the methods which are appropriate to the various sciences and arts.... And whoever tries humbly and perseveringly to explore the hidden depth of reality, is being led, even unawares, by the hand of God who upholds everything and makes it what it is. One can, therefore, legitimately regret attitudes to be found sometimes even among Christians, through an insufficient appreciation of the rightful autonomy of science, which have led many people to conclude from the disagreements and controversies which such attitudes have aroused, that there is opposition between faith and science.[23]

On the other hand, the council acknowledged the powerful presence of evil in our society, and proclaims:

All human activity, which is daily jeopardized through pride and self-love, needs to be purified and completed by the cross and resurrection. Only in the spirit of

22. LG 36.
23. GS 36.

poverty, in freedom from craving possessions can we use and enjoy created things and so attain to a true possession of the world, "as having nothing yet possessing everything."[24]

In this way the catholicity of the church will be lived according to Paul's great program: "All are yours, and you are Christ's, and Christ is God's (1 Cor. 3:22–23)."[25]

Appendix: The Relationship of Earthly Progress and the Kingdom of God

The church's catholicity includes her concern for human progress and its relationship to the kingdom of God. As an appendix to this chapter, I intend to summarize here the most important points of the council's teaching along with comments by later magisterial documents.

1. The eschatological reality that is already present in the world and transforming the world is the love of God present in Christ and poured out into our hearts through the Holy Spirit. The progress of Christ's kingdom in the world is proportionate to the increase of this love in the hearts of people.[26]

2. Earthly progress (scientific, technological, and cultural) is different from the progress of Christ's kingdom. Higher levels of scientific and technological knowledge, even higher levels of culture, do not necessarily translate into purer and greater love. Science and technology are ambivalent and, in the hands of sinful people, may serve demonic purposes, possibly destroying the humanity of man and even the world.[27]

3. Yet insofar as this earthly progress promotes a better order of society and the perfection of humanity, both in its personal and social dimensions ("the good of human dignity, brotherly communion and freedom"), it is of vital concern for the kingdom. These values and all the goods of nature and our enterprise, "we will find again, but freed of stain, burnished and transfigured" in the eschatological consummation.[28]

4. The unjust political, social, and economic structures of society are

24. GS 37.
25. GS 38.
26. GS 38–39.
27. GS 35, 37.
28. GS 39.

a threat and obstacle to humankind's true destiny and, consequently, they need to be changed, but by just means.[29]

5. True liberation must begin with the transformation of hearts by accepting God's transforming grace. Without a change of heart, without man being inwardly re-created in the Holy Spirit, no structural change in society will produce true "liberation."[30]

6. Unjust societal structures may jeopardize and restrict, but cannot completely destroy human freedom, in particular the freedom from sin and the freedom to love God and neighbor. In fact, any suffering caused by these structures and endured out of love becomes a share in the cross of Christ through which the love of God and neighbor may grow to a heroic degree.[31]

7. We can and should improve economic and social structures, but these will remain imperfect and none will be the full expression of God's kingdom, which remains an eschatological gift rather than an earthly accomplishment.[32]

The best illustration of how true human progress, "the work of human hands," will be taken up into God's kingdom is to be found in the Holy Eucharist. The bread and wine represent ourselves and all our work by which we try to live and improve this world. The bread and wine are necessary elements for the Mass, yet in themselves are perishable and earthly. They need to be offered to God so that they may be ontologically transformed (transubstantiated) into the body and blood of Christ by God's gratuitous gift of consecration. Thus the final reality of the Eucharist is God's gift, Jesus Christ in his divine-human reality, in his crucified and risen body. Yet this gift cannot take place without "the work of human hands," without the elements of bread and wine that man has prepared for the Mass. In an analogous way, the kingdom, even in its final definitive reality, will be a pure gift of God, yet human progress must precede and prepare it. Nevertheless, the two—God's gift and our progress—are incommensurate since our gift to God, Jesus Christ under the signs of bread and wine, is the gift of God and not the result of human work.[33]

29. Congregation of the Doctrine of the Faith, *Instruction on Christian Freedom and Liberation* (March 22, 1986) 42, 44 (below cited by CL).

30. CL 23, 27, 31.

31. CL 52, 99.

32. CL 32, 64.

33. Cf. GS 38 and John Paul II, Encyclical Letter *Sollicitudo Rei Socialis* (December 30, 1987), 48.

8. The transformation of societal structures remains the task of laypeople rather than that of the church hierarchy. The rejection of this distinction would lead us to ignore the relative autonomy of secular realities (state, politics, etc.) and ultimately would lead to the secularization of the sacred and the idolization of the secular. The history of the church starting with Constantine has given too many frightening examples of what happens if this distinction is not respected.[34]

Conclusions

The catholicity of the church means both universality, fullness, and therefore authenticity. The church is universal geographically, racially, and culturally. She extends herself to all lands, nations, and cultures.

However, her universal dimensions do not diminish or water down the fullness she brings to the world. She is constantly mediating the fullness of divine life and love to her members and prays for all human beings. She respects the autonomy and promotes the progress of culture, but also purifies it and brings to light each culture's transcendent depth.

34. Cf. GS 42–43.

CHAPTER 12

The Apostolicity of the Church

History of Apostolicity

The term *apostolos* means "the one who is sent."[1] Some scholars think that the institution of apostleship has its origins in Jesus, who applied the Hebrew term *shalia* to the twelve chosen disciples. Among other meanings, the term *shalia* referred to authorized delegates of the Jerusalem authorities to the Jewish congregations of the Diaspora.[2] The *shalia* had the same authority as the one who sent him. "The one sent by a man is as the man himself" is an often repeated rabbinic rule.[3] However, the majority of scholars do not trace the term's use back to Jesus, but think the term originally referred to an itinerant missionary sent out by a church. Only later was it restricted to the Twelve (see Rom 16:7; 2 Cor 8:23; Acts 14:4, 14).

It is, however, certain that Jesus chose and instituted the Twelve from

1. See in greater detail Yves Congar, "Die apostolische Kirche" [The apostolic church], in *Mysterium Salutis*, vol. 4/1, *Das Heilsgeschehen in der Gemeinde*, ed. Wolfgang Beinert et al. (Einsiedeln: Benziger, 1972), 535–600; Francis A. Sullivan, *From Apostles to Bishops: The Development of the Episcopacy in the Early Church* (New York: Newman Press, 2001); Karl Rahner and Joseph Ratzinger, *Episcopate and Primacy* (New York: Catholic Publications Society, 1962); Richard De Clue, "Primacy and Collegiality in the Works of Joseph Ratzinger," *Communio* 35 (2008): 642–70; Walter Kasper, "Das zweite Vaticanum weiterdenken. Die apostolische Sukzession im Bischofsamt als ökumensisches Problem" [A further implication of Vatican II: The apostolic succession in the episcopacy as an ecumenical problem], *Kerygma und Dogma* 44 (1998): 207–18 (see its condensation in *Theological Digest* 47 [2000]: 203–10); Edward Schillebeeckx, *The Church with a Human Face* (New York: Crossroad, 1985); Albert Vanhoye, "Le ministère dans l'Église: réflexions à propos d'un ouvrage recent," part 1, "Les données du Nouveau Testament," *Nouvelle Revue Théologique* 104 (1982): 722–38; Henri Crouzel, "Témoignages de l'Église ancienne" [Testimonies from the church of the Fathers], *Nouvelle revue théologique* 104 (1982): 723–48. The article offers a thorough critique of Schillebeeckx's *The Church with a Human Face*.

2. Cf. Mt 10:2, Mk 6:30, Lk 6:13.

3. Karl Heinrich Rengstorf, "Ἀπόστολος," in *Theological Dictionary of the New Testament*, ed. Gerhard Kittel and Gerhard Friedrich, trans. Geoffrey Bromiley (Grand Rapids: Eerdmans, 1999), 1:415, see also 407–45.

among his disciples as his own representatives, whom he sent out after his resurrection to all nations; they were to be eyewitnesses to his earthly ministry, passion, and resurrection, and were endowed with Jesus' own power and authority (*exousia*) to proclaim the good news to all nations (Mt 28:18–20).[4]

In the Pauline writings, the beginnings of a theology of apostleship can already be discerned. Paul finds great pride in referring to himself as one "called to be an apostle" (Rom 1:1) or as "apostle of Christ Jesus" (1 Cor 1:1; 2 Cor 1:1) sent "not by men but by Christ Jesus and God the Father who raised him up from the dead" (Gal 1:1). In another text he defends his apostleship by calling attention to the fact that he has seen the risen Lord: "Am I not an apostle? Have I not seen Jesus our Lord?" (1 Cor 9:1). In the Pauline lists of charisms, the first—without exception—is the charism of apostleship (1 Cor 12:28–29; Eph 4:11).

Thus, at least when he speaks about an "apostle of Christ Jesus" and also in several other instances, Paul calls an apostle someone who saw the risen Christ and was personally sent by him to proclaim the good news with full authorization from the Risen One. Paul is aware that his own apostolic authority places him clearly above all the charismatics, even above the prophets, who are closely associated with the term "apostle" in the Pauline literature (1 Cor 14:37–38).

The theology of apostleship developed when the first generation of eyewitnesses was passing away and the church was searching for criteria of authenticity so that she could identify the authentic teachings and the authentic churches over against spurious doctrines, traditions, and assemblies. In the New Testament, the writings of Luke have the most developed form of the theology of apostleship.

Luke tries to restrict the term apostle to the Twelve (but does not fully succeed as Acts 14:4, 14, shows) and claims that Jesus gave this title to the Twelve (Lk 6:13). They are sent by Jesus and are eyewitnesses to his earthly life and resurrection.[5] Just as the twelve tribes of Israel are the extension of the twelve sons of Jacob, so is the church the extension of the Twelve.

4. The "Twelve" became such an important group that even after Judas's betrayal, they were known as Twelve, and according to Luke their number was again filled up by the addition of Matthias (1 Cor 15:5; Acts 1:15–26).

5. Since Paul was not an eyewitness to Jesus' earthly life but only to his resurrection, he does not qualify to be called an apostle by Luke.

Everyone else is "added" to the original group of apostles and to those who are with the apostles (Acts 2:41:47; 5:14; 11:24).

The mission of the twelve apostles is to preach the good news beginning with Jerusalem until the ends of the earth and maintain the identity of the church between the resurrection and the parousia (Acts 1:8–11). They are to be clothed by the power of the Holy Spirit, who will enable them to perform this mission (see also Mt 28:18–20; Rv 21:14).

John presupposes that his readers know about the Twelve, their names and election. Yet without using the term "apostle," he has worked out a definite theology of apostleship. The Twelve remain with Jesus after the crisis among the disciples, a crisis caused by the eucharistic discourse (Jn 6:66–71). Judas leaves them on the night of the betrayal, but the risen Christ appears to the remaining eleven, whom he sends on a universal mission (Jn 20:19–29; see especially v. 24!). The Father sends Jesus, and the risen Jesus sends the Twelve. They are empowered to forgive and retain sins through the power of the Holy Spirit. In a general way, the forgiveness and retention of sins describes their entire mission, but in a special and particular way, the remission of sins committed after baptism within the community characterizes what they will be doing. These disciples are the witnesses who have seen and believed while the rest of the church consists of those who have not seen but believed in the testimony of those who had seen (Jn 20:29). All future generations of believers are to enter into communion with this original group of eyewitness disciples and thereby enter into communion with the Father and the Son (1 Jn 1:1–4).

The church of the second and third centuries further develops the theology of the apostolate into the theology of apostolic succession. The apostles, especially Peter and Paul, moved from city to city, from region to region. They were itinerant missionaries who established new churches and encouraged the believers in their faith, but who also assured that the apostolic witness to Jesus would be correctly handed on so that the new Christian communities would share the same faith as the apostles. More restricted was the mission of Timothy and Titus, who were commissioned by Paul to found and supervise churches, not all over the world as Paul did, but in a definite region defined by Paul that was larger than the mission of the local bishops, who would come later.

The prevailing majority opinion today is that the earliest phase of church organization after the passing of the apostolic generation consisted of several church leaders (*presbyteros* or *episkopos*, the two terms being synonyms) equal in authority to each other and each heading a household church within the same city. With time, however, one emerged as the leader of the rest of the presbyter-bishops, analogous in authority to our contemporary local bishops. In fact, such is most likely the church order in Corinth in 96, the date of Clement of Rome's letter to them. More probable is the hypothesis which holds that at the beginning there were two types of church order: several presbyters ruling over a particular church or one bishop governing a local church. An example of the presbyteral order is the church in Corinth; of the monepiscopal, the church in Jerusalem. Around the turn of the first century, the letter of Clement, the bishop of Rome, clearly formulates the doctrine of apostolic succession: "From land to land, accordingly, and from city to city they [the apostles] preached, and from among their earliest converts they appointed men whom they had tested by the Spirit to act as bishops and deacons for the future believers."[6] To move from the first generation of successors to all subsequent generations, Clement again appeals to the authority of apostolic practice to claim that the men appointed by the apostles were in their turn to appoint successors:

> Our apostles knew from Jesus Christ our Lord that there will be strife regarding the episcopal office. For this reason, equipped with perfect foreknowledge, they appointed the men mentioned before [i.e., bishops and deacons], and afterwards laid down a rule once for all to this effect; when these men [i.e., first-generation successors] die, other approved men [i.e., second-generation successors] shall succeed to their sacred ministry.[7]

I believe we need to question the prevailing majority opinion that the presbyteral order of churches was everywhere the oldest form of government.[8] More likely is the hypothesis that from the beginning there were two church orders existing next to each other in the second century.[9] After Peter's departure, James was clearly the one overall leader, a *monepiskopos*, in the church of Jerusalem surrounded by a body of presbyters. Each of the churches of Asia Minor, Ephesus, Tralles, Smyrna, Philadelphia, and

6. 1 Clement 42.

7. 1 Clement 44.

8. Francis A. Sullivan in *From Apostles to Bishops*, 217, agrees with this majority opinion.

9. See Jean Colson, *Tradition Paulinienne et tradition Johannique de l'épiscopat des origines à saint Irénée* [The Pauline and Johannine tradition on the episcopacy from the beginnings to Irenaeus] (Paris: Cerf, 1951).

Magnesia certainly had one *monepiskopos* at the beginning of the second century. Since Ignatius's letters enunciate the principle of the one bishop in each city or region as a self-evident truth to the faithful, this structure must have been in place prior to Ignatius's term. The bishop is envisioned as the visible image (sacrament) of Christ and God in his church. He is the focal point and the guarantee of the church's unity and faith, and the president of the eucharistic assembly.

A great majority of historians suppose that in the second century a presbyteral structure functioned in the church of Rome. These are their most important arguments: (1) Ignatius's *Letter to the Romans* does not mention any bishop in Rome. (2) The letter of Clement to the Romans is anonymous, addressed "to the Church of God which is a stranger in Corinth" and sent from the "Church of God which resides as a stranger at Rome." It was attributed to Clement only by a second-century tradition initiated by Irenaeus. (3) The *Shepherd* of Hermas, written in the first half of the second century, speaks of presbyters in the plural at Rome.

One decisive piece of evidence, however, reveals how shaky the above hypothesis is. We know from a letter fragment of Irenaeus written in the second century that there was in Rome a monepiscopal bishop, Anicetus, whom Bishop Polycarp from Smyrna visited to discuss the difference between the quartodeciman and Roman date of the celebration of Easter. Irenaeus was Polycarp's disciple, a firsthand witness to Polycarp's intentions. It is hardly imaginable that Polycarp would have discussed this important issue with Anicetus and would have concelebrated only with him had Anicetus been just one of the presbyters equal to the others.[10] Moreover, Ignatius of Antioch may not have mentioned the name of the bishop of Rome because the Roman church has been acutely aware for centuries of the active presence in her midst of the two martyr apostles Peter and Paul. Ignatius, in fact, mentions Peter and Paul as if they were giving commands even at that time to the Romans.[11] As for the *Shepherd* of Hermas, the Muratorian canon, around AD 200 mentions Pius as the bishop of Rome at the time Hermas's *Shepherd* was composed.

10. See Eusebius, *Hist. eccl.* 4.24.12; 4.14.1. Note that the same Irenaeus, whose teacher was Polycarp, appointed by the apostles gives a complete list of the monepiscopal bishops of Rome until his own times: Linus (after the martyrdom of Peter and Paul), Clement, Evaristos, Alexander, Xistus, Telesphoros, Hygin, Pius, Anicet, Soter, Eleutheros (*Hist. eccl.* 5.6.1–4).

11. See Ignatius, *To the Romans* 4.3.

Around the end of the second century, the monepiscopal church order prevails almost universally.[12] The resident local bishop emerges everywhere as the undisputed leader of the community, preaching, shepherding, and presiding over the Eucharist as the representative of Christ and the embodiment of the local church. This at least indicates an awareness within the church of the second century concerning the origin of the episcopal office. The apostolic succession assures the oneness of the church through time. Through the apostolic succession, the church of the second century understands herself to be identical with the church of the apostles, who were eyewitnesses to Christ. This gives the second-century church the assurance that its faith and grace must be authentic.[13]

When defining the limits of the scriptural canon, the church accepts those writings as the inspired Word of God that are, in a broad sense, of apostolic origin; in other words, those books become part of the canon that are authored by an apostle, or depend on, or are guaranteed by, an apostle.

When determining authentic teaching versus heretical distortions, Irenaeus and Tertullian point to the teaching of the churches founded by an apostle and where the present presbyters or bishops can trace back their succession to the apostles.[14] In the words of Irenaeus:

> Everyone who wants to see the truth can perceive the Tradition of the apostles which has been made manifest in every Church and we are able to enumerate the bishops who were established by the apostles in the Churches and their successors up to our own times. They did not teach anything similar to the delirious phantasies of these people [the Gnostic heretics]. . . . [They did not keep any secrets from the bishops] whom they left as their successors and to whom they transmitted their mission of teaching [*suum ipsorum locum magisterii tradentes*].[15]

According to Tertullian, the other churches borrowed and continue to borrow the "transplant of faith and the seed of doctrine" (*traducem fidei et*

12. On this fact, Francis A. Sullivan (*From Apostles to Bishops*) and Alistair C. Stewart (*The Original Bishops: Office and Order in the First Christian Communities* [Grand Rapids: Baker Academic, 2014]) agree with Congar ("Die apostolische Kirche," 538–43) even though they disagree on the function and character of the original ecclesial community leaders.

13. This "natural" development was indirectly helped by the claim of the Gnostic sects, which based their authority on secret apostolic traditions. The Catholic Church responded by remembering the apostolic origins of her *episkopoi* and *presbyteroi*, who guaranteed the authenticity of the church's traditions.

14. In the first two centuries, *presbyteros* and *episkopos* (in later usage priest and bishop) alternatively referred to the same office.

15. Irenaeus, *Against Heresies* 3.3.1.

semina doctrinae) from the churches founded by the apostles. Only through this relationship to the churches founded by the apostles can new offshoots also become churches and may also be called apostolic. Thus apostolicity expresses the identity of the churches spread out in space and time with the original church of the apostles. As Tertullian explains: "Everything must be judged in relationship to its origin. Therefore, the Churches may be many and large, nevertheless they are that one first Church founded by the Apostles from which all derive. Thus, they are all first, all apostolic as they are all one [*Sic omnes primae et omnes apostolicae, dum una omnes*]."[16] What the apostles handed over to the bishops was not only doctrine, but also "the Church at every place."[17] In the words of Tertullian, the object of transmission is "the same sacrament," meaning the entire Church.[18]

The bishop-presbyters truly succeeded the apostles and possessed the *charisma veritatis certum* when teaching with authority.[19] "It is through this order and through succession from the apostles that the apostolic tradition in the Church and the preaching of the truth has come down to us."[20]

Yet the apostles do not simply yield their chair of teaching to the presbyter-bishops. In the theology of the patristic church, the bishops do not simply succeed to the apostles. Their role can be understood only in the context of the theology of the kingdom and the Holy Spirit. The apostles do not "retire" after their martyr death; on the contrary, they enter fully into the kingdom and begin to exercise their role as eschatological judges, sitting on twelve thrones and judging the twelve tribes of Israel (Mt 19:28). Just as the kingdom is present in the church throughout history, so are the apostles present in a new way in the church. They "govern" the church until the end of times. (Cf. the ancient Preface of the Apostles: the eternal shepherd continues to govern and protect the church by means of the blessed apostles throughout history.) One important way the apostles exercised their leadership role in the church after their deaths is the bishops' ministry.

That Christ continues to govern his church through the apostles and that the apostles themselves remain present in the church through the

16. Tertullian, *Prescriptions against Heretics* 20.7.
17. Irenaeus, *Against Heresies*, 4.33.8: "eam quae in unoquoque loco est Ecclesiam tradiderunt."
18. Tertullian, *Prescriptions against Heretics* 20.9: "eiusdem sacramenti una traditio."
19. Irenaeus, *Against Heresies* 4.26.2.
20. Irenaeus, *Against Heresies* 3.3.3.

bishops is due to the Holy Spirit. He is the ultimate principle who assures that the kingdom is present, inchoatively but really, in the church, and that the church of all times and places is constantly rejuvenated so that she remains identical with the church of the apostles.[21]

Although church order developed in different stages in the various parts of the world, the church government of bishop, presbyter, and deacon, which is exhibited in the letters of Ignatius of Antioch, prevailed almost everywhere in the church around the end of the second century. Ignatius insists on the unity between the bishop and his congregation. The bishop and his congregation must be of one mind so that, like a harmonious chorus, they might sing with one voice through Jesus Christ to the glory of God the Father:

> Therefore, it is fitting that you should live in harmony with the will of the bishop, as indeed you do. For your justly famous presbytery, worthy of God, is attuned to the bishop as the string is to a harp. Therefore, by your concord and harmonious love Jesus Christ is being sung. Now each of you, join in this choir so that being harmoniously in concord you may receive the key of God in unison, and sing with one voice through Jesus Christ to the Father, that He may both hear you and may recognize through your good works that you are members of his Son. It is, therefore, profitable for you to be in blameless unity in order that you may always commune with God.[22]

Union with one's bishop is analogous to the union between Christ and the church.[23] Separation from the bishop means separation from the "bread of God," and from God himself.[24] Communion with the bishop is the necessary prerequisite for any celebration of baptism or the Eucharist. Indeed, one should consider the church to be wherever the bishop is and recognize that the bishop is the guardian of right teaching and conduct:

> See to it that you all follow the bishop, as Jesus Christ follows the Father, and the presbytery as if it were the Apostles. And reverence the deacons as the command of God. Let no one do any of the things appertaining to the church without the bishop. Let that be considered a valid Eucharist which is celebrated by the bishop or by one whom he appoints. Wherever the bishop appears, let the congregation be present; just as wherever Jesus Christ is, there is the catholic Church. It is not lawful either

21. See Irenaeus, *Against Heresies* 3.24.1.
22. Ignatius, *To the Ephesians* 4.1–2.
23. Ignatius, *To the Ephesians* 5.1.
24. Ignatius, *To the Ephesians* 5.2.

to baptize or to hold an *agape* without the bishop; but whatever he approves, this is also pleasing to God, that everything which you do may be secure and valid.[25]

We find presbyters and deacons hierarchically ranged under one bishop. As the representative of Christ in a local community, the bishop assures that the community worships God in harmony and unity.

Some claim that this development of a Catholic, hierarchical church structure, along with emphasis on the sacraments and faith as belief in an identifiable body of teachings, stands in opposition to the charismatic, nonsacramental, existential attitude of trust and surrender that is allegedly reflected in Paul's authentic, early epistles. However, opposing this "free, charismatic church" model with that of the early Catholic model fails to respect the evidence of the New Testament. The church order, implicit in the Pastoral Epistles, does in fact differ to some extent from what we find in the earlier Letters of Paul. Nevertheless, in 1 Corinthians and Romans we see Paul's emphasis on the sacraments of baptism, Eucharist, and the excommunication and readmission of sinners (1 Cor 5:1–5; 10–11; 14:37). More than an act of self-surrender to an unknown God, for Paul the act of faith is an act of trust and self-surrender to the God of Jesus Christ, to the God who, according to the Scriptures of the Old Testament, accepted the sacrifice of His Son, raised him from the dead, and saw to it that reliable witnesses attested to the appearances of the risen Son. Faith for St. Paul also includes obedience to the teachings of Christ (Rom 1:5; 1 Cor 7:25; 15:1–58). Finally, Paul does indeed recognize the value of various charisms, such as prophecy, healing, and speaking in tongues. But he always lists as the first among charisms that of apostleship (1 Cor 12:28). As apostle, he also claims the authority and responsibility of imposing order on the charismatics so that all charisms build up the church (1 Cor 14, esp. v. 37). Although church structures developed further during the subapostolic generation, the foundations are already evident in Paul

If one is searching for the authentic apostolic faith and church, they should consider the testimony of Irenaeus, who early in the life of the church acknowledged a unique normativity to the church of Rome:

But since it would be very long in such a volume as this to enumerate the successions of all the churches, I can, by pointing out the tradition which that very great,

25. Ignatius, *To the Smyrnaeans* 8.1–2.

oldest and well-known church, founded and established at Rome by those two most glorious apostles, Peter and Paul, received from the apostles, and the faith she has announced to men, which comes down to us through the successions of bishops, put to shame all of those who in any way, either through wicked self-conceit, or through vainglory, or through blind and evil opinion, gather as they should not. For every church, that is, the faithful from everywhere, must be in harmony with this church because of its most excellent origin, in which [church] the tradition coming from the apostles has always been preserved for the faithful from everywhere.

After the blessed apostles had founded and built up the church, they handed over the ministry of the episcopate to Linus.[26]

As Emmanuel Lanne convincingly shows from an analysis of this text and its parallels in other early patristic writings, the normativity of the church of Rome derives in the first two centuries from the fact that both apostles Peter and Paul founded this church and died as martyrs there.[27] Later, more and more weight would be given to Peter's association with Rome because he was appointed by Christ as the "rock" of the church and the shepherd of all the faithful, and that he gradually came to be remembered as the first bishop of Rome. Nevertheless, Paul's cofounding role and the importance of their joint martyrdom has never been forgotten.[28]

Theology of Apostolicity

On the basis of the historical information mentioned above and Yves Congar's study, the following is an outline for a systematic theology of apostolicity.[29]

1. Apostolic succession means a continuous "chain" of missions: the Father sends Christ; Christ sends the apostles with his own authority (*exousia*)

26. Irenaeus, *Against Heresies* 3.3.2. Translation from Cyril C. Richardson, ed., Early Christian Fathers (New York: Touchstone, 1996), 372. The clause: "since the tradition coming from the apostles has always been preserved in it for the benefit of the faithful from everywhere" has been emended according to the French critical edition: *Contre les hérésies, Livre III*, Source Chrétienne 210 (Paris: Cerf, 2002), 233–36. Cf. Tertullian, *Prescriptions against Heretics* 34.3.

27. Emmanuel Lanne, "L'Église de Rome, a gloriossimis duobus apostolis Petro et Paulo Romae fundatae et constitutae Ecclesia," *Irénikon* 49 (1976): 275–322. Note that, historically, neither Peter nor Paul "founded" the church of Rome. The Fathers are aware of the fact that Paul wrote his Letter to the Romans to an already existing church. Thus "founding" for them was a theological notion, meaning that the apostolic preaching and martyrdom of Peter and Paul in Rome established the church of Rome in its uniquely normative character.

28. For more on this, see William R. Farmer and Roch Kereszty, *Peter and Paul in the Church of Rome: The Ecumenical Potential of a Forgotten Perspective* (Mahwah, N.J.: Paulist, 1990).

29. Congar, "Die apostolische Kirche," 535–70. See also Francis Sullivan, *From Apostles to Bishops: The Development of the Episcopacy in the Early Church* (New York: Newman Press, 2001).

to proclaim the good news in a comprehensive sense of establishing the church; the apostles in turn appoint or approve successors who will succeed and represent the apostolic college until the end of times.[30]

2. The purpose of the apostolic succession is to maintain an identity with regard to doctrine, sacraments, and church order between the local churches that spread out in space and time, and the church of the apostles.

3. Not only does the college of bishops succeed the college of the apostles, but the latter is present and active in the former. This distinguishes the Catholic doctrine of apostolic succession from the merely juridical model that describes many institutions besides the church.

4. What makes this unique "being in one another" possible is the Holy Spirit. As the transcendent principle of unity in the church, he enables the apostles, perfected in heaven, to continue their ministry in multiple ways, but especially through the ministry of the bishops of every generation. Through the Holy Spirit's presence, the church of the apostles and the church of every age constitute more than just a single legal person; the churches derived through apostolic succession are, in some sense, identical with the church of the apostles.[31]

5. However, the apostolic college and the college of the bishops differ in some ways. First, the apostles were eyewitnesses sent and empowered by Christ to found the church. Peter is the rock on which the whole church is founded, but the Twelve are also foundation stones (Rv 21:14). In contrast, the bishops are not eyewitnesses, but transmitters of the apostles' eyewitness testimony. Therefore, in a theological sense, the bishops do not found the church, but rather build it up and assure their diocese's identity with the church of the apostles. Second, except for the bishop of Rome, who was the successor of Peter, no individual bishop succeeded an individual apostle, but the college of bishops does succeed the college of the apostles.

Congar unfolds the implications of the theology of apostolic succession in the following four points.

30. As we have seen, the belief of the Catholic Church in apostolic succession is based on historical facts. Succession from apostles (in a broad sense, including all who were commissioned by Christ or by his direct disciples) took place in different ways in different regions, but eventually around the end of the second century, monepiscopacy became the norm. We cannot prove that from the beginning and everywhere all local leaders were appointed by an apostle, but, the strict control of Paul over the churches he founded makes it very probable that he at least approved all of them. Nor can we ascertain that each office holder was installed by an ordination rite, even though Acts (14:23) and the Pastoral Epistles (2 Tm 1:6–8, Ti 5:17) testify to its early practice. Suffice it to know that from the beginning local churches derived their authenticity from their link with an apostle in a broad sense.

31. This, of course, is a qualified identity and can only be fully perceived in the light of the Holy Spirit.

1. The essential mark of the church's apostolicity follows from the permanent significance of the Son's incarnation for all times and places. The churches of all times and places extend this historically contingent "church" of Peter and Paul and the other apostles since all subsequent generations must be in communion with this original group of eyewitnesses who were sent by the incarnate Son of God, Jesus of Nazareth.

2. In every act of episcopal ordination, the laying on of hands by a successor of the apostles establishes a historical connection with the earthly Christ. But only through his resurrection and glorification do Christ's earthly church-founding actions transcend time and bestows the grace of the Holy Spirit in the sacrament of holy orders on all the successors of the apostles throughout the end of history.[32]

3. The classic Protestant view is different. The only indispensable visible link connecting the earthly Jesus and apostles with a contemporary believer are the books of the New Testament, which the believer reads under the inspiration of the Spirit of the risen Christ. The contemporary visible church structures with which Protestant believers may be comfortable take diverse forms, but they lack apostolic succession. The document *Baptism, Eucharist, and Ministry*, also known as the Lima Document, composed by the Faith and Order Commission of the World Council of Churches, went a long way toward acknowledging the importance of episcopal succession. It affirmed that in the first centuries, episcopal succession was understood as serving, symbolizing, and guarding the continuity of the apostolic faith and communion.[33] As the evangelical response to the Lima Document shows, the largest segment of Protestant Christians is still far from accepting the necessity of apostolic succession as a safeguard for faith: "What is important is that churches live 'in faithful continuity with the apostolic faith and mission [and] have a ministry of Word and sacrament.'"[34] For them, however, the "faith and mission and ministry of Word and sacrament" can be established by their understanding of Scripture; traditions are secondary.

32. These two dimensions of one and the same act of Christ reveal the nature of what theology calls a theandrical act: Christ's saving acts take place in time since he is a human being, but these acts have transcendent effects because they are the acts of God the Son.

33. *Baptism, Eucharist, and Ministry*, Faith and Order Commission 11 (Geneva: World Council of Churches, 1982), para. 35.

34. *Baptism, Eucharist, and Ministry*, para. 53. See the response of the World Evangelical Fellowship (Paul Schottenboer, ed., "An Evangelical Response to BEM," *Evangelical Review of Theology* [1989]: 291–313) to *Baptism, Eucharist, and Ministry*.

4. The apostles bear witness not only to the incarnation but also to the resurrection and ascension of Christ. They testify to the risen body of Christ, in whom God has already consummated his work and made Christ's body the pledge and cornerstone of the new eschatological creation. Thus the presence of the apostolic witness in the church through the apostolic succession assures not only the fidelity of the church to her origins, but also her faithful expectation of the parousia. The witness of the apostles connects the church both with her origins in the earthly ministry of Jesus and with her consummation in the glorious appearance of the risen Lord.

The Petrine Ministry in the Church

The Leadership Role of Peter in the Gospels and in Acts

The way Peter's role is described or alluded to in many different instances indicate a special leadership role for Peter among the Twelve.[35]

1. Every list of the Twelve begins with Peter as the first.

2. From Jesus, Peter receives the name *kepha* ("rock" in Aramaic), a name that, evidently, cannot refer to his character; it designates a mission or vocation (Jn 1:42).

3. He acts as a spokesman for confessing the faith of the Twelve (Mt 16:16; Mk 8:29; Lk 9:20; Jn 6:68).

4. He asks questions from Jesus in the name of the others (Mk 10:28; Mt 15:15; 18:21; Lk 12:41).

5. He alone is ordered to come to Jesus on the water (Mt 14:28).

6. Jesus pays the temple tax for himself and Peter (Mt 17:24–27).

7. Jesus heals in the house of Peter (Mt 8:14–15).

8. Jesus teaches the crowds from Peter's boat. Peter fishes with companions, yet he lowers the net at the word of Jesus and Jesus tells only him: "from now on you will be a fisher of men" (Lk 5:1–11).

9. In Mark, the angel's words at the tomb indicate that, in spite of his denial, the special role of Peter is to continue after the resurrection: "Go now and tell his disciples and Peter . . ." (Mk 16:7).

35. Yves Congar, *Église et papauté: Regards historiques* [The Church and the papacy: Historical aspects] (Paris: Cerf, 2002); Hans Urs von Balthasar, *The Office of Peter and the Structure of the Church*, 2nd ed. (San Francisco: Ignatius, 2007); J.-M. R. Tillard, *The Bishop of Rome* (Wilmington, De.: Michael Glazier, 1983); Stephen Otto Horn, "The Petrine Mission of the Church of Rome: Some Biblical and Patristic Ciews," *Communio* 18 (1991): 313–21; Farmer and Kereszty, *Peter and Paul in the Church of Rome*; Ratzinger, Joseph, "The Primacy of the Pope and the Unity of the People of God," *Communio* 41 (2014): 112–28.

The many individual texts that reveal a special leadership role of Peter describe also his cowardly denial of his Master and his emotional volatility. Matthew and Mark quote Jesus' harsh reprimand of Peter: "Get behind me Satan" (Mt 16:23; Mk 8:33). Such a compromising presentation can hardly be the creation of Peter's "PR group," which instead would attempt to legitimize his apostolic authority. Interpreted against this general background, three key texts on the leadership role of Peter are very significant.

Matthew 16:13–23 This text from Matthew shows many Aramaisms,[36] which indicate its Palestinian origin and reveal that the passage likely relied on a tradition of Aramaic provenance.[37] Many exegetes point out that the likely background of Paul's insistence on his apostolic credentials in 1 Corinthians 3:11, 9:1–26, 15:8–11, and Galatians 1–2 are an effort to prove his equality with Peter, which, however, presupposes that the audiences of 1 Corinthians and Galatians knew about the "*kepha* tradition" of Matthew 16:16–19.[38]

Thus, *pace* other scholars, I side with the magisterial commentary of W. D. Davies and Dale Allison, who hold that the origin of these sayings was the earthly Jesus' reaction to Peter's confession of faith. In the name of the Twelve, Peter confesses Jesus to be the Messiah, the "Son of the living God." Jesus' response points out that this confession of faith cannot come from human beings but only from his heavenly Father. The parallelisms in Jesus' words in Matthew 16:17 and in Matthew 11:27 about the exclusive mutual knowledge between Father and Son, a knowledge only the Son or the Father alone can reveal to whom he wills, shows the parallelism between the two texts and thereby the depth of Peter's confession. Going beyond the messianic dignity, it points to the unique depth of the relationship between Father and Son and ultimately to the Son's divine status. This conclusion is

36. For interpreting Matthew's text, I rely to a large extent on W. D. Davies and Dale C. Allison, *The Gospel according to St. Matthew*, International Critical Commentary (Edinburgh: T&T Clark, 1991), 2:602–47.

37. I mention only a few: the wordplay between the new name given to Peter by Jesus and the function of his becoming rock is understood only in Aramaic (*Kepha/kepha*); in Greek there is only a similarity (*Petros/petra*). the Aramaic phrase: *bariona* (son of Jonah) remains untranslated. The phrase "flesh and blood" means here a human being, "bind and loose" either imposing/removing a legal obligation or imposing/lifting the ban of excommunication.

38. For instance, he points out that he received his apostolic commission and the gospel not from human beings but from the Father, who *revealed* his Son to him (Gal 1:11, 15). He also emphasizes that he did not consult with *flesh and blood*. In 1 Corinthians Paul claims that he has laid down the *foundation* of the church in Corinth while others were building on that foundation. Paul, however, immediately notices a possible misinterpretation of his claim to be the foundation and declares that there is no other foundation for the church but Jesus Christ (1 Cor 3:10–11).

confirmed by the meaning of the phrase "living God." According to Davies and Allison, the phrase stresses that "God has life in and of himself, and alone gives it to others." The Son "stands on the side of God vis-à-vis man" and "shares his quality of 'living' so completely that he can promise his community that the powers of death cannot prevail against it."[39]

There has been much debate over whether the rock on which Jesus intends to build his church is Peter's person or faith, or actually Jesus himself. Davies and Allison rightly call attention to the parallelism in Jesus' words to Peter, "you are *Kepha* and on this *kepha* . . ." and Peter's confession addressing the person of Jesus, "you are the Messiah." Thus Jesus' promise designates Peter *in* his confession of faith, a faith that is an exclusive gift of the Father to him. It is on account of his faith that Jesus designates him as the foundation rock or stone of the church, which will not be defeated by the jaws of the netherworld. In other words, the powers of evil, death, and sin, and all machinations of the devil, will not prevail against her. The word we translate as "church" is *ekklēsia*, which is one of the usual translations of the Hebrew *qāhāl*, or *qəhal YHWH*. In the LXX it stands for the community of YHWH, the liturgical assembly of Israel called together by God to listen and sacrifice to him.[40] If we take into account Matthew's dramatic structure, it is perfectly understandable that after Jesus has failed to convert Israel as a nation and her leaders have rejected him, he turns to building his community. However, that he chooses the emotionally unstable Simon son of Jonah to be the church's solid foundation is puzzling; this is the same person who did not trust Jesus' support when he was walking to him on the water, the impetuous enthusiast who deserves Jesus' sharp rebuke for trying to prevent him from fulfilling the Father's plan, the self-confident coward who denies him three times after vowing to go with him into prison and death. But precisely this contrast between the personal qualities of Peter and his commission to be the invincible rock enlightens for the reader that the solidity of the rock comes from Jesus and from the Father, who revealed to Peter the mystery of his Son. Thus Paul is right when he contends that there is no foundation for the church but Jesus Christ. Tertullian explains this apparent contradiction by pointing

39. Davies and Allison, St. *Matthew*, 2:621.

40. On account of this well-known OT usage and the Aramaic background of the pericope, there is no need to suppose the Hellenistic origin of *ekklēsia*, a legal assembly of a city's citizens empowered to vote.

out that Jesus "wanted to share lovingly with his dearest disciple a name taken from his own symbols."[41] Since name and symbol mean more than an arbitrary designation for Tertullian, this text implies a doctrine of participation between Jesus and Peter. Peter can receive the name and symbol "rock" from the names and symbols of Jesus himself because Jesus makes him participate in his own rocklike quality.

The meaning of "the keys of the kingdom of heaven" is disputed. It might refer to binding, authoritative teaching (Lk 11:52), or, more likely, to a delegated supreme power over the church, the community of Jesus, in which the dynamism of the kingdom is already present. Viewing the phrase in the context of Isaiah 22:15 and Revelation 1:18, 3:7, reveals that as Shebna and Eliakim, masters of the royal palace, held power over the house of David, the risen Lord holds supreme power over the heavenly house of David and Peter is his representative on earth.

Of the many different meanings of "bind" and "loose," two are relevant to our text: "impose an obligation or cancel it" and "impose the ban of excommunication or lift it." Here, unlike Matthew 18:18, the second meaning is more likely. In other words, Peter is *the* ultimate authority in the *ekklēsia*.

However, Matthew's presentation of Peter is not completed with these passages. He goes on to paint a diptychon of a scene of exaltation followed by a most dramatic humiliation. As Jesus predicts his passion and resurrection, Peter reacts as an anxious friend would: "God forbid, Lord! No such thing shall ever happen to you" (Mt 16:22). Jesus' response must have been devastating for Peter: "Get behind me, Satan! You are a *skandalon* to me" (Mt 16:23). Led by human considerations of saving his master from suffering, Peter became the mouthpiece of Satan, a *skandalon*, a stumbling block to the fulfillment of God's plan.

These episodes can be seen as a preview of the entire history of the church. The bishop of Rome with the bishops in communion with him has guarded and preserved the apostolic faith up to the present day, but at the same time the papacy has been a scandal from time to time, an obstacle to the fulfillment of God's plan and a strong temptation for many to fall away from the unity of faith.

41. Tertullian, *Adversus Marcionem* 4.13.6.

Luke 22:24–34 The context in Luke for Jesus' words to Peter is a dispute among the disciples at the Last Supper. Only a few hours are left before the arrest of Jesus, and he has already told them that one of them will betray him, yet they are debating who among them should be regarded as the greatest (22:24). Jesus does not deny that there is a leader among them, but he explains that leadership among them should turn the standards of this world upside down; the greatest should become as the youngest, and the leader as the servant, just as Jesus, their master, is among them as the one who serves (vv. 25–27). After he has promised that all of them will become judges, that is, rulers in his kingdom (vv. 28–30), he turns to Peter and reveals the crisis that awaits the disciples and Peter's subsequent role among them. With the arrest of Jesus, the eschatological tribulation begins: Satan plans to attack his disciples to "sift all of you like wheat." To counter Satan's attack, Jesus plans to save his disciples by praying for Peter: "I, however, have prayed *for you*." The object of his prayer is to safeguard Peter's faith so that, after his conversion, he may strengthen his brothers (22:31–32).

Comparing Luke 22:30–33 to the Matthean text, we notice how they relate and mutually enlighten each other. Both texts point out the crucial role of Peter's faith for the church. In Matthew, the promise of leadership takes place as Jesus responds to Peter's confession of faith and Peter is designated as the rocklike foundation of the church on account of his faith. Thus the reader concludes that the faith of the church will not be destroyed because it is built on Peter. In Luke, the task of Peter will be to strengthen the faith of the incipient church amid the eschatological upheaval that begins with the arrest of Jesus. In both texts, the loftiness of Peter's role is counterbalanced by a sharp critique by Jesus. In Matthew, Peter is rebuked as speaking Satan's message; in Luke his self-assured vow to follow Jesus into prison and death is called into question by Jesus' prediction of his threefold denial. In both texts, the magnitude of the commission and the inadequacy of the person commissioned are in glaring contrast. Both texts show that Peter will be able to accomplish his mission only through a gift of God. In Matthew, Peter draws his faith from the Father's revelation; in Luke, Jesus' prayer enables Peter to confirm his brothers in faith.

John 21:1–19 In the Gospel of John, the anonymous disciple "whom Jesus loved" has a special prominence. Unlike Peter, he has never been singled out for any criticism, he has never denied Jesus, and at the Last Supper he rests his head on Jesus' chest. Peter is curious to find out who will betray the Master, so he signals the beloved disciple to ask Jesus. He alone stays close to Mary under the cross and Jesus entrusts his mother to him. He is the disciple who believes in the resurrection of Jesus before he sees him. As he enters the empty tomb and spots the burial cloths and the cloth that has covered Jesus' head rolled up in a separate place, "he saw and believed" (20:8) Yet Peter also has an important place in the Fourth Gospel. He confesses his faith in Jesus at the critical moment when, after the eucharistic discourse, many disciples abandon the Master. In the name of the Twelve, he pledges loyalty to Jesus and proclaims him the Holy One of God (Jn 6:68–69). Although "the other disciple" arrives first at the empty tomb, he waits and lets Peter enter first. Then, at the end of the book in chapter 21, the "competition" is clearly decided to Peter's advantage.

The Fourth Gospel is well-known for its twofold levels of meaning. The narrative is based on history, but a deeper, second meaning is revealed to the believer in a subsequent discourse or dialogue. Thus the narrative must first be analyzed. Simon is presented as the leading fisherman among the seven disciples who joined him for a nighttime fishing expedition. While the anonymous disciple is the first to recognize Jesus standing on the shore in the morning twilight, the impulsive Peter jumps into the water to reach Jesus before any of the others. He then drags to shore the net full of 153 large fish, which the disciples caught by following Jesus' directions. Some commentators think that the number 153 designates the 153 different kinds of fish that had been known in the ancient world. Hence, they conclude that by this number the evangelist is hinting at the universality of the community Peter will have to lead.

Jesus' threefold questioning of Peter corresponds to Peter's threefold denial. However, following his denials, Peter experiences a deep conversion. He no longer boasts of his fidelity, nor does he even dare to say that he loves Jesus more than the others, but instead he places his assurance in Jesus rather than in his own virtue: "Lord, you know everything; you know that I love you" (21:17). In 6:68–69, he had already confessed the faith of the twelve disciples; now he must confess his own love in Jesus before receiving his commission to shepherd the sheep and lambs of Jesus. No other disciple receives such an all-encompassing leadership role. In Matthew, he received his commission on account of his faith; here faith is presupposed and love is called for. Jesus wants Peter to love him more than any other disciple because he received an office that no one else received. But Peter does not dare to claim that greater love. There must always remain a gap between the requirements of the Petrine office and the holiness of the office bearer.

Peter's role, as the shepherd of Jesus' sheep, must be linked to the parable of the Good Shepherd. Until Jesus comes again, Peter will represent him, the Good Shepherd, and become responsible for the sheep and lambs of Jesus. He must also follow him in giving his life for Jesus' sheep. Thus the "office" of Peter does not end, but is rather consummated in his death as a martyr. Only through his martyrdom will he become the perfect representative of the Good Shepherd. From John's perspective, then, any successor to Peter is irrelevant, since Peter's role continues in the church.

The Relationship between Peter and Paul on the Basis of Paul's Letters

The relationship between Peter and Paul is complex and charged with dramatic tension. Paul is aware that he is not an apostle of Jesus Christ in the same way as the Twelve. Paul states that he was "born abnormally," not even "fit to be called an apostle," since he "persecuted the church of God" (1 Cor 15:8–9). Yet he still claims to be an apostle (1 Cor 9:2) and boasts that he has worked harder than all the others (1 Cor 15:10). His companion Luke, who centers the second part of Acts almost exclusively on Paul (Acts 12:25–28:31), avoids calling his hero an apostle. Paul, however, insists that his experience of the risen Christ was of the same kind as that of Cephas and of the Twelve. As we have seen in Matthew, Paul is aware of the "Peter, rock of the church" tradition and, perhaps to counter a misunderstanding on the part of the Corinthians of Peter's role, he emphasizes that Jesus is the foundation of the church. Yet in the previous sentence he nonetheless affirmed that *he*, Paul, laid down the foundation of the church in Corinth (1 Cor 3:10–11).

Quite remarkably, Paul attempts to prove his equality with Peter by measuring himself against the standards by which Peter is measured in the church. His status is based on the fact that he received his commission not from men but from God, who "revealed" his "Son" to him. As a result, he did not feel the need after this experience to consult "flesh and blood." In some way, nevertheless, he acknowledges the unique importance of Peter. Three years after his conversion, he goes to Jerusalem to get to know (*historēsai*) Cephas and stays with him for fifteen days. We can safely assume that they did not waste much time in small talk, but discussed and compared what each was teaching, since Paul wanted to be certain that he was not preaching a gospel that differed from Peter's, James's, and John's so that he "might not be running, or have run, in vain" (Gal 2:2). Clearly it is crucially important for him to be in accord with the pillars, and yet, in the same breath, he trivializes them by saying that "what they once were makes no difference to me" (Gal 2:6). Still, Paul acknowledges that the first "official" appearance of the risen Lord happened to Cephas.[42]

In conclusion, Paul's own letters do not prove that he acknowledged Peter's authority over himself, but they do not prove that he did not. His concern to confer with Peter at the beginning of his ministry, his acknowledgment that Cephas is the first official witness to the resurrection of Christ, his insistence that his gospel and divine mission were accepted by Peter and the other pillars in Jerusalem, may suggest he did acknowledge Peter's authority, but Paul also shows a remarkable freedom in his relationship with Peter. He openly rebukes Peter when he judges that Peter did not act in accord with the truth of the gospel (Gal 2:11–14).[43]

The Relationship between Peter and Paul on the Basis of the New Testament Canon

While the first half of the New Testament canon, the Synoptic Gospels, shows the dominating influence of Peter as the chief witness to Jesus' earthly life and resurrection, the second half is certainly dominated by the Pauline corpus. Yet the Gospels of Mark and Luke also show a Pauline and/or deutero-Pauline influence, while Acts, situated in the middle of the New Testament canon, presents a diptychon. The first half of Acts is dominated by the figure of Peter (chaps. 1–12) and the second by Paul (chaps. 13–28).

42. See 1 Cor 15:5 and Jn 20:16. The appearance to Mary Magdalene does not count as "official," that is, as usable in court, since women's testimonies were unacceptable before the law.

43. It seems, however, that the two separate fields of apostolate did not prove practical (Gal 2:7–10). Once the persecution in Judea started, the Christians escaped from Jerusalem and so did the three pillars. Peter sojourned for a while in Antioch, most likely also visited Corinth, and finally ended up in Rome. Besides, Peter addressed himself to the gentiles just as Paul did. The faction of Cephas in Corinth most likely was not a Jewish-Christian group (1 Cor 1:12).

Thus, at first glance, the canon shows an effort to balance out the figures of these two important apostles and to put them on an equal footing. However, a more careful inquiry reveals a tendency in the New Testament documents and in the formation of the New Testament canon to have Peter "above" Paul, not on the level of theological depth and effective apostolic work, but above on the level of pastoral and magisterial authority.

For example, John is accepted into the canon only with its appendix (chap. 21), which affirms Peter as universal shepherd by deciding in his favor the "competition" between him and the beloved disciple, which runs throughout the Fourth Gospel.

The author of 1 Peter presents Peter as the one who, in possession of a (deutero)-Pauline theology, writes letters to the churches Paul founded. (Whether this letter was written during the lifetime of Peter or after is irrelevant.) The authority of Peter is based on the fact that he is an apostle of Jesus Christ (1:1) and witness (*martys*) to his sufferings. (The word *martys* may imply that Peter himself has already become a witness to the passion of Christ by his own martyrdom.) In this capacity, Peter has the right and obligation to present the ideal of the presbyter to all the presbyters so that they may be rewarded when the chief shepherd, Jesus Christ, appears (1Pet 5:1–4).

The author of 2 Peter presents Peter as superior to Paul since Peter was an eyewitness to the Lord's majesty on the holy mountain (2 Pt 1:16–18) during his earthly life, whereas Paul saw him only after the resurrection. Second Peter acknowledges the God-inspired wisdom of "our beloved brother Paul" (3:15) but, at the same time, warns against those who misinterpret his writings. Thereby, 2 Peter implies that Peter holds the key to the correct interpretation of Paul. By implying the Pauline corpus (3:15–16) is closed and by excluding further letters in the name of Peter (the author, in 1:14–15, reveals that Peter's death is imminent), 2 Peter effectively closes the canon of the New Testament.[44]

Thus, as long as the documents of the New Testament are viewed as providentially coalescing *concordia discors*, "a discordant harmony," Peter appears as the apostle whose witness extends to and guarantees the whole span of the Christ event, that central phase of salvation history that began with Jesus' public ministry and lasted through the resurrection and the

44. For more on these matters, see Denis Farkasfalvy, "The Ecclesial Setting of Pseudepigraphy in Second Peter and Its Role in the Formation of the Canon," *Second Century* 5 (1985–86): 3–29.

foundation of the church, eventually culminating in the closing of the New Testament canon. This canonical interpretation of the New Testament, which understands each document in the light of the whole and attempts to resolve the contradictions in some higher "harmony," can hardly avoid the conclusion that Peter attained a certain "primacy" even above Paul; at the same time, it confirms the superiority of Paul on the level of theological depth and missionary work.

The Emerging Role of the Bishop of Rome

Even several non-Catholic exegetes conclude that Peter had a leadership role in the New Testament, but they do not find scriptural evidence that Peter's position has been transmitted to any successor.[45]

In fact, no mention is made of successors to Peter in the New Testament. Some attribute this fact to Jesus' mistaken conviction that the eschatological kingdom of God will end history in Peter's lifetime. Others think that Peter received only a personal leadership charism.

For a more adequate response, however, one must consider the date of the Gospels' composition and their literary genre. At least in their present form, all the Gospels were written after Peter's death. They do not claim to be a complete biography or a complete repertoire of Jesus' sayings. As the exegetical school of *Formgeschichte* has convincingly shown, the Gospels report what is of significance for the life of the contemporary church. Therefore, it is right to conclude that Peter features so predominantly in them because he remained important for the church even after his death. John 21 even goes a step further. Jesus links his bestowal on Peter of the authority to be the shepherd of his lambs and sheep with the necessity of his martyr death. This suggests that Jesus envisions Peter's martyrdom not as the end of his role but rather as the consummation of his being constituted as the worthy and permanent vicar of the Good Shepherd. The likelihood of this interpretation is confirmed by Matthew 16:18, where the "rock" symbolizes a strong and permanent support rather than a short-lived personal role.[46] More light is shed on the meaning of Peter's death by comparing it with

45. Oscar Cullmann is an exception. His book on Peter claims that after Peter left Jerusalem, he gave over his leadership to James, who remained in the city. See Oscar Cullmann, *Peter, Disciple, Apostle, Martyr: A Historical and Theological Study*, trans. Floyd V. Filson (London: SCM, 1953).

46. Even in Matthew the promise of primacy is linked with following Jesus on the way of the cross (16:18–20, 21–25). Peter will become the rock only when he accepts Jesus' invitation to lose his life for him.

the early church's developing theology of martyrdom. St. Ignatius of Antioch declares that if a Roman Christian prevents his martyrdom, he will be merely an empty "voice"; but through his martyr death he becomes the "word of God."[47] According to the book of Revelation, where this theory is developed further by the early church, the martyrs reign in heaven and share in the kingship of Jesus Christ (20:1–6). Perhaps because of this theology of martyrdom, the early church turned to the martyrdom in Rome of the chief apostles, Peter and Paul, rather than the Petrine texts of the New Testament, as the basis for the *potentior principalitas* of the Roman church.[48] Addressing a letter to Pope Sylvester, the Synod of Arles praises Rome as the place where the two "apostles sit every day in judgment and their blood every day attests God's glory."[49] If one considers their martyrdom and its consequence, which ensures the permanent presence of Peter and Paul in the Roman church, then one understands why the issue of succession to Peter has not surfaced either in the New Testament or in the subapostolic church. Peter and Paul themselves are guarding the faith of the Roman church.[50]

Nevertheless, beginning with Clement, the bishops of the Roman church, where Peter and Paul had poured forth their teaching along with their blood, were convinced of their responsibility for churches outside of their own.[51] The first known occasion when the church of Rome intervened authoritatively in the internal affairs of another church was the "rebellion" against the leaders of the church of Corinth. A faction of the church attempted to remove their presbyters from office. A letter of Clement from Rome intervened to reestablish order and remind the Corinthian church of the importance of "apostolic succession" (AD 96). The Father has sent Christ, Christ the apostles, and the apostles their successors, the presbyters.[52] Therefore, those who want to depose the presbyters commit a grave sin. He kindly appeals to the charity of the rebel leaders to leave the church of Corinth so that the community may live in peace with the presbyters.[53] But those who disobey this letter will entangle themselves

47. Ignatius, *To the Romans* 2.1.

48. See Farmer and Kereszty, *Peter and Paul in the Church of Rome*, 83.

49. Farmer and Kereszty, *Peter and Paul in the Church of Rome*, 146.

50. On the permanent personal presence of the martyrs at their tombs, see Peter Brown, *The Cult of the Saints* (Chicago: University of Chicago Press, 1981).

51. Tertullian, *Prescriptions against Heretics* 36.3.

52. 1 Clement 42, 44.

53. 1 Clement 54.

in transgression and no small danger (for their souls). In other words, the directive of Clement along with the entire Roman church mediates God's command.[54]

The first time that the bishop of Rome is known to have acted with an awareness of his universal authority to settle a disciplinary (although in his mind it was a doctrinal) issue for the entire church was the intervention of Bishop Victor at the end of the second century. After initiating a wide-ranging consultation among all the bishops, he decided to extend the date of the Roman tradition for celebrating Easter (Sunday after the Jewish Passover, the 14th of Nisan) to all the churches. His decision went against an ancient custom of some churches in Asia Minor, which, referring to a Johannine tradition, celebrated Easter together with the Jews on the 14th of Nisan (hence the name "quartodeciman party"). Victor threatened with excommunication all the churches who resisted his decree. Many protested, including Irenaeus, but their protest only underlines the fact that Victor believed he had the authority to settle an issue for the universal church.[55]

Beginning in the third century the number of instances increases when the intervention of Rome in doctrinal and even in disciplinary matters is regarded as decisive throughout the West, and often also in the East. Some important examples are the letters of Stephen I to Cyprian against the "rebaptism" of heretics[56] and the letter of Agatho against monotheletism.[57] The letter of Boniface to Bishop Rufus in 422 exemplifies the self-understanding of the bishops of Rome: "We addressed these writings to the synod of Corinth. By these writings all the brothers [bishops] should understand that one ought not to reverse that on which we had already passed judgement. For it has never been allowed to treat again a matter which had already been decided by the Apostolic See."[58] In many cases, the bishops of Rome, as a rule, did not provide theological arguments for their doctrine. They simply justified their intervention by restating the apostolic tradition.

In the first four centuries, no centralized papal power structure had yet been established. The bishops of Rome intervened in crisis situations and passed judgments on doctrinal and disciplinary matters that were brought

54. 1 Clement 59.

55. See the letters of Polycrates representing the quartodeciman party, and that of Irenaeus exhorting Victor to toleration, both quoted by Eusebius, *Hist. eccl.* 5.24.1–17.

56. DS 110–11, in AD 254–57.

57. DS 542–45, in AD 680; see also DS 181, 218.

58. DS 232.

to their attention. For various reasons, a tendency to centralize power in the Western church began in the fifth century. One important factor was the presence of three apostolic churches in the East (Alexandria, Antioch, and Jerusalem) and only one, the see of Rome, in the West. According to tradition, Alexandria was founded by Mark, Peter's interpreter; Antioch served for a while as the headquarters of both Peter and Paul; and the Jerusalem church was led first by Peter followed by James, the brother of the Lord.[59] These apostolic churches had been considered as depositories of apostolic doctrine and thereby had great influence on the regions around them.

Another reason for the development of two different models of church order was the presence of the emperors in the Eastern half of the empire. They tried to rule the Eastern churches and discouraged their dependence on Rome. On the other hand, Rome was the only apostolic see in the West, and as the place of the martyrdom of the chief apostles Peter and Paul it enjoyed unparalleled prestige and doctrinal weight. Moreover, the great distance from the imperial center of Constantinople also encouraged the development of papal power as a stabilizing influence during the barbarian invasions of Italy. For better or worse, the emerging Carolingian and the ensuing German-Roman Empire assumed supreme authority over the church in these territories. After a long struggle, however, the popes were able to assert their independence vis-à-vis imperial power. In order to weaken the influence of feudal rulers over the election of bishops by diocesan chapters, the popes asserted their own authority to appoint bishops over more and more dioceses. At the same time, the differences in church structures contributed much to the weakening of the communion between the two halves of Christianity. Yet, even in this first phase of church history, although often forgotten or hindered in the East, the essential primacy of the bishop of Rome had been acknowledged and practiced in the universal church. This essential primacy can be summarized in two theses:

1. Both the church of the East and the West were generally aware that communion with the church of Rome is essential for being in communion with the universal church.[60]

59. The foundation of the church of Constantinople by the apostle Andrew was artificially created for political reasons in the seventh century in order to enhance the dignity of the new imperial capital. Eventually the pentarchy theory of church leadership developed in the East: the patriarchs of the five apostolic sees were the leaders of the church universal, each having limited authority only within a certain region. But even within their territories, the diocesan bishops were the true leaders of the local church.

60. This has been held in a modified form even by the Orthodox churches up to the present day.

2. The bishop of Rome had been widely acknowledged (often even in the East) as the last appellate authority in matters of faith and discipline.

These two theses logically imply the dogmas of the pope's supreme, universal, and immediate jurisdiction in the church and his charism of infallibility, the two essential decrees of the First Vatican Council regarding the papacy.[61]

These dogmas allow for a variety of organizational models in the church. The current centralization in the Latin church is only one possibility. The Code of Canon Law for the Oriental churches that are in communion with Rome is different from that of the Latin church and so is its current organizational structure. Pope John Paul II invited all non-Catholic Christian theologians to suggest to him a way acceptable to all Christians for the exercise of his universal ministry of unity.[62]

The Pope and the Episcopal College

From its very beginning, the nascent church has practiced certain forms of collegiality, or special kinds of collective leadership. Paul subjected his gospel and mission to the scrutiny of those who were considered pillars of the church: James, Peter, and John (Gal 2:9). Even though he was recognized as the primary leader, Peter *always acted within and often with the active participation of the group of the Twelve* throughout the Synoptic Gospels and Acts. At one point, the Twelve send Peter and John to complete the Christian initiation of the Samaritans whom Philip has baptized (Acts 8:14–17).

When facing momentous decisions, the bishops of Rome convened a synod of bishops of the surrounding areas. But the bishops of Rome considered their office as a merging of the heritage of both Peter and Paul. They often described their mission as vicars of Peter in Pauline terms like this: "blessed Peter carries in us [his] solicitude for all the churches."[63] In his important book *The Bishop of Rome*, J.-M. R. Tillard calls the pope a *perso-*

The pentarchy theory holds that the validity of an ecumenical council requires the participation of all five of the patriarchs. Thus without the bishop of Rome one cannot convoke an ecumenical council, and since the Eastern schism this has become impossible.

61. As part of the excited protest movement against the Encyclical *Humanae Vitae*, Hans Küng published his book that questioned the dogma of papal infallibility: *Unfehlbar? Eine Anfrage* [Infallible? An Inquiry] (Zürich: Benziger, 1970). See a response organized by Karl Rahner: *Zum Problem der Unfehlbarkeit* (Freiburg: Herder 1971).

62. John Paul II, Encyclical Letter *Ut Unum Sint* (May 25, 1995).

63. E.g., DS 218 (citing 2 Cor 11:28).

na composita, a composite or collegiate person, because his office embodied both Petrine and Pauline features. He is the "vicar" or representative and successor of Peter, but he also represents Paul and through him the entire Pauline heritage.

Throughout church history there have been many indications that bishops considered themselves part of an episcopal college just as the apostles constituted a college. Here are a few examples:

1. Bishops exchanged letters with each other wherein they testify to their common faith and love and offer assistance to each other to solve common problems.

2. Bishops included the names of other bishops in the eucharistic prayers.

3. Many regional or national synods have been convoked to discuss common problems and agree on common resolutions.

4. Ordination to the episcopacy has been from ancient times celebrated by three bishops to symbolize that the new bishop is incorporated into the episcopal college.

5. Ecumenical councils, which have been convened from time to time throughout the history of the church, prove decisively that collegiality has always been a characteristic of the church. These (theoretically) universal gatherings of bishops have always been considered to have full and supreme power over the universal church, but not one has ever been approved as truly ecumenical unless it was later accepted as such by the bishop of Rome; nor was a decree of an ecumenical council accepted as valid unless it was approved or accepted freely by the bishop of Rome. Moreover, the fathers of every council have always been considered not mere counselors to the bishop of Rome, but true "judges" in matters of faith, morals, and church discipline.

To ensure the freedom of local churches against the dominating influence of nation-states, papal authority became increasingly centralized to the point where bishops appeared to be no more than mere functionaries of the pope. Vatican I did not have the time to take up the issue of the episcopacy and so it strengthened the false impression, especially in Protestant countries, that the Catholic Church is an absolute monarchy. To correct this error, the German bishops issued a collective declaration in 1875 which explained that both the episcopate and the papacy have been divinely instituted. The bishops are not papal officials, but true shepherds appointed by the Holy Spirit to feed and rule the particular flock assigned to each of them.[64]

The Teaching of Vatican II (*Lumen Gentium* as Interpreted by the Explanatory Note) on Collegiality The first time collegiality was treated in a magisterial document was at Vatican II (LG 19–27), as follows.

1. The episcopal college succeeds the apostolic college, which will continue to exist in the church through the college of bishops until the end of time.

2. "Just as by the Lord's decree, St. Peter and the rest of the apostles constitute one apostolic college, in a similar way, the Roman Pontiff, Peter's successor, and the bishops, successors of the apostles, are joined together."[65] This episcopal college has supreme and universal power over all aspects of church life: teaching, sacraments, and governing. (Even though every bishop must have a concern (*affectus collegialis*) for the universal church, yet no bishop by himself alone has authority over the universal church or over the diocese of any other bishop.) By fostering the faith and sacraments as well as the morality of the universal church in his diocese, every bishop builds up the unity of the church.

3. "A person is constituted member of the episcopal body by virtue of sacramental consecration and by hierarchical communion with the head and members of the college."[66] Consequently, he is inserted into the college by the very act of episcopal consecration. Then his being a member of the episcopal college belongs to the very structure of the episcopal office whose collegial nature derives from the nature of the church as communion. The great number of bishops shows the universality of the church; that they make up one college under the head of the college, the bishop of Rome, demonstrates the church's unity. Therefore, an individual bishop cannot exercise his episcopal functions without the canonical and jurisdictional determination of the head of the college.[67]

64. *CF* 841.

65. *LG* 22. Note that the college of the apostles and that of the bishops are not the same, but only of similar natures. The power of each apostle extended over the universal church; that of a bishop, only over a given territory. The apostles were eyewitnesses to Christ; the bishops, witnesses to what they received from the apostles, the deposit of faith. The former established the church; the latter rule the church established by the apostles.

66. *LG* 22.

67. See the *Nota explicativa* of the Theological Commission, 2. The council did not intend to decide

4. This college is of divine institution. It cannot be abolished by any human authority, because it was established during the constitutive phase of church history.

5. The college is constituted as a college only in union with its head, the bishop of Rome. Without him, it does not exist and, consequently, cannot act as a college. Every valid act of the college requires at least the consent or free acceptance of the pope.

6. While the college does not exist without the pope and cannot act without his consent or free acceptance, the pope may act freely without the college of bishops.[68]

7. The only strictly collegial acts to this point in church history have been the acts of the ecumenical councils. However, *Lumen Gentium* foresees other possible acts of collegiality, but does not provide examples: "The same collegial power can be exercised by the bishops throughout the world in conjunction with the pope provided that the head of the college calls them to collegial action or at least approves of, or willingly accepts, the united action of the dispersed bishops in such a way that the result is a truly collegial act."[69]

Theological Reflections on Collegiality The collegial nature of the church means that both the bishop of Rome and the college of bishops united with him have full, universal, and supreme power over the whole church.[70] With regard to a particular diocese, the bishop is its head, representing

the disputed question among theologians over whether the jurisdictional power of a bishop derives from the pope, who has its fullness, or whether the pope simply coordinates and determines its concrete form and limits. The former was a widely held opinion in the Western church, an opinion with roots back to the patristic age; the latter, however, better harmonizes with the teaching of LG. The Western patristic tradition speaks about the fullness of the episcopal office first being given to Peter and to all bishops in Peter to ensure the unity of all the churches.

68. This consideration concerns the validity of a pontifical act without the college rather than its moral qualification. A papal act that goes against the majority opinion of bishops may be providentially right and beneficial (cf. the popes' refusal to consent to a conciliar constitution of the church in the fifteenth century), or imprudent or even gravely immoral.

69. LG 22.

70. I avoid here a theoretical discussion of whether there are two inadequately distinguished subjects of supreme power in the church or only one. Those who believe in two distinguish the pope as head of the church and the pope along with the college of bishops. Others say there is only one subject of supreme power in the church: the pope along with the college of bishops. But even those who believe only in one subject of supreme power admit that the pope may act alone, e.g., he may make an *ex cathedra* statement, but even then he acts as head of the college and defines the faith of the whole college after having consulted with them. Practically, there is a wide range of possibilities between two limited cases: from the pope acting alone after little consultation, through acting alone but after a substantial consultation to simply accepting the deliberations of an ecumenical council.

Christ directly, yet the pope also has immediate and full jurisdiction in any diocese of any bishop, and every bishop must remain subject to the pope. This structure of twofold authority is based on the relationship between the local (particular) church and the church universal. If the local churches were mere administrative units of the universal church (like local branches of a centralized corporation), the bishops would merely represent the pope and would be simply his delegates. In fact, however, the universal church manifests itself in the local church since Christ himself is present in his eucharistic body and in his Word in every local church. At the same time, the integrity of the local church requires its insertion into the communion of the universal church. Thus, insofar as the universal church manifests itself in the local church, the local bishop directly represents Christ. But, insofar as the local church must insert herself into the one communion of all local churches, the local bishop is also subject to the bishop of Rome, whose charism is to assure and safeguard the universal communion of local churches.

The pope's supreme and universal jurisdiction, as Tillard points out, should assure that each and every local church is indeed an authentic manifestation of the church universal; that the local church's sacraments, church order, teaching, and moral life make present the Catholic Church of Jesus Christ.[71]

In communion with, but at the same time in subjection to, the bishop of Rome, the role of the local bishop is to listen to "what the Spirit says to the Churches" (Rv 3:6, etc.) and apply the teachings of Christ to local situations, providing new impetus, new inspiration, new styles of Christian life adapted to the situation of Christians in his diocese. He cannot be merely a spokesman for the pope, but must teach in the name of Christ and take the initiative when necessary. This will certainly create tensions, but tensions are a necessary consequence of life and growth.

The collegial structure of the church manifests the church as communion. Any authority in the church is given within the communion of brothers and sisters and for the sake of fostering this communion. The pope is both brother to his fellow bishops and head of the college of bishops. As head, his role is to promote the communion of all the bishops. The bishop

71. See J.-M. R Tillard, *Church of Churches: The Ecclesiology of Communion* (Wilmington, De.: Michael Glazier, 1992), 287–306.

is both brother and father to his priests. His role as father is to promote a communion of brotherhood among his priests. The pastor is both father and brother to his people. His fatherhood is to promote a real communion of brothers and sisters in his parish.

These levels of collegiality reveal the eschatological orientation of the church. All authority will have achieved its goal and will no longer be needed when the communion of saints is consummated in heaven.[72]

The Church's Charism of Infallibility

The development of Christian doctrine does not take place in a historical vacuum, nor is it only the result of the Christian people's piety or theological reflection.[73] The challenges of a changing cultural environment and the errors that derive from it are often the stimulant for seeking greater clarity and conceptual articulation of a truth of revelation. A milestone in the development and formulation of the dogma of the church's infallibility and in particular the pope's participation in it took place in response to the Enlightenment, which attempted to enthrone human reason as the ultimate authority.

Neither patristic nor medieval theology makes mention of the church's infallibility. Before the modern age, theologians saw the incorruptible permanence of the church in divine truth as a consequence of the church's virginal and, ultimately, Marian nature. Jesus Christ is the only bridegroom,

72. In this section on collegiality I follow to a large extent Joseph Ratzinger, *Das neue Volk Gottes: Entwürfe zur Ekklesiologie* (Düsseldorf: Patmos Verlag, 1969), 171–97. Ratzinger claims that his insight on collegiality serving the communion of the church on different levels originates from the tradition. He points out that in the first centuries Christians of every rank called each other "brothers and sisters." In the third century a new usage begins: Cyprian calls his faithful "beloved brothers," but he uses "brother" in the singular for his fellow bishops. At the same time his faithful and priests address him as *papa*, "father." In the fourth and fifth centuries the address "brother" is replaced by the more formal *collega* and the fraternity of bishops by *collegium* (208–10). Thus the "brotherhood" of all members in the church is a more fundamental notion of the tradition than *collegium*, and the activities of the latter serve the actualization of the former.

73. Roch Kereszty, "The Infallibility of the Church: A Marian Mystery," *Communio* 38, no. 3 (2011): 374–390; Vinzenz Gasser, *The Gift of Infallibility: The official Relatio on Infallibility of Bishop Vincent Gasser at Vatican Council I*, trans. with commentary and a theological synthesis on infallibility by James T. O'Connor. (Boston: St. Paul Editions, 1986); Francis A. Sullivan, *Creative Fidelity: Weighing and Interpreting Documents of the Magisterium* (Eugene, Ore.: Wipf and Stock, 1996); Avery Dulles, *Magisterium: Teacher and Guardian of the Faith* (Washington, D.C.: Sapientia Press, 2007). Some recent discussions on Petrine primacy between Catholics and Protestants: Wolfhart Pannenberg, "A Lutheran's Reflections on the Petrine Ministry of the Bishop of Rome," *Communio* 25, no. 4 (1998): 604–18; Roch Kereszty, "A Catholic Response to W. Pannenberg Regarding the Petrine Ministry of the Bishop of Rome," *Communio* 25, no. 4 (1998): 619–629; Sara Butler, "Authority in the Church: Lessons from the Anglican–Roman Catholic Dialogue," *Theology Digest* 45, no. 4 (1998): 337–53.

and the church is the one bride. Whoever knowingly and stubbornly denies or distorts any truth of God's revelation sins against the bride's virginal integrity and her total dedication to the bridegroom. Just as in the Old Testament, where idol worship was considered adultery against the bridal relationship of Israel to God, any heresy is judged to be adultery by the fathers of the church.[74] As St. Cyprian declares: "Whoever separates himself from the Church, unites himself with an adulteress."[75] Origen complains that the heretics, by being heretics, build a brothel.[76] Augustine expresses the mind of all the Fathers by explaining that what corrupts the chastity of the virgin spouse is the violation of the church's faith.[77] For Hildegard of Bingen, the most wicked corrupting agents are the errors of the heretics, "who attack her by trying to corrupt her virginity which is the catholic faith; she, however, strongly resists them lest she be corrupted for she has always been and is and will remain a virgin."[78]

The church remains a virgin even while "she gives birth to her sons without any opposing error remaining in the integrity of faith."[79] Particular local churches may develop heresies and thus they may change from virgin to adulteress, just as, according Hegesippos, the church in Jerusalem lost her virginity after the death of her bishop Simeon.[80] However, the bishops of Rome have been aware that, due to the Lord's promise to Peter, "in the Apostolic See the Catholic religion has always been preserved without any stain."[81]

Before a systematic consideration of the charism of infallibility, we should first explain why it is necessary for the church.

1. God intends to reveal himself effectively. Even human communicators want to make sure that what they say or write is correctly understood. How much more effective God must be when he reveals himself and our ultimate destiny to us.

74. Cf. Clement of Alexandria, *Stromata* 3.12.
75. Cyprian, *De unitate Ecclesiae* 6.
76. Origen, *Homiliae in Ezechielem* 2.
77. Augustine, *In Evangelium Johannis tractatus* 8.5.
78. Hildegard of Bingen, *Scivias* 2.3.
79. Hildegard of Bingen, *Scivias* 2.3.
80. See Hegesippos in Eusebius, *Hist. eccl.* 4.22.4.
81. DS 363: "in Sede Apostolica immaculata est semper catholica servata religio" (363). See the so-called *Decretum Gelasianum*: "Est ergo prima Petri Apostoli sedes Romanae Ecclesiae, non habens maculam neque rugam nec aliquid eiusmodi [Therefore the first see is that of the apostle Peter's Roman church which has no stain or wrinkle or anything of this kind]" (DS 351). This was repeated by the First Vatican Council (DS 3066).

2. Revelation, which centers on the person of Jesus Christ, by whom the mystery of the Triune God and our assumption into that mystery are revealed, infinitely exceeds yet includes propositional truths, such as those found in Romans 1:2–4, 1 Corinthians 15:3–8, and Philippians 2:6–11. Even one's understanding of another human person transcends all propositional truths about that person because it involves a direct experience based on empathy. Yet without propositions, we cannot claim the truth of the experience.[82] We cannot claim the truth of God's revelation without making affirmative or negative statements.

3. A true proposition is not a subjective construct of the mind, but it always refers to some kind of reality. The logical copula "is," which connects subject and predicate, participates in the reality of what it affirms and denies the reality of what it negates.

4. God himself must guarantee the truth of his revelation since mere human authority is insufficient to ensure the absolute certainty of the truth of faith. Without divine guarantee, the object of faith could not demand unconditional adhesion of our mind and will, even at the risk of losing our lives. With a mere human warranty, we run the risk of believing an erroneous human opinion to be part of God's revelation.[83]

82. Lovers know that no word can express their experience of love adequately, yet they communicate their experience to their friends by words, which, even in their most poetic forms, include statements. Verbal expression makes the experience itself more perfect and more articulate.

83. The Protestant objection to this reasoning often goes like this: Catholics think that they believe what the church teaches not by the private judgment of their conscience but by the divine guarantee of the magisterium. Yet they too ultimately act by their own private judgment, since it is the conscience that commands them to believe the church's magisterium and that chooses one of the many interpretations of a dogma that are based on private judgment. Indeed, we accept the authority of the magisterium based on Scripture to inform the most personal act of our own conscience. We also interpret the dogmas (truths of revelation defined as such by the church) by choosing through private judgment what appears to us the best. Yet the dogmatic definitions exclude false ways of interpretation, point us in the right direction, and provide a partial, imperfect, but nonetheless true contemplation of the mystery. At the same time every dogma is an invitation and signpost to call us to search further for understanding the mystery that will always remain above our minds in this life. But while the interpretation of the teachings of Scripture by private judgment has led to many contradictory positions and constant splintering of the church, the dogmatic definitions have strengthened the church's unity of faith. Thus Catholics and Protestants agree that we need private judgment to embrace God's truth, and for that embrace we need the grace of the Holy Spirit. Catholics claim to need both private judgment *and* the teaching of the magisterium. For a better understanding of the context of this dispute, see the Mark E. Powell, "The 'Patient and Fraternal Dialogue' on Papal Infallibility: Contributions of a Free-Church Theologian," *Theological Studies* 74, no. 1 (2013): 105–18; John T. Ford, Infallibility—Terminology, Textual Analysis, and Theological Interpretation: A Response to Mark Powell," *Theological Studies* 74, no. 1 (2013): 119–28; Gerard Kelly, "The Roman Catholic Doctrine of Papal Infallibility: A Response to Mark Powell," *Theological Studies* 74, no. 1 (2013): 129–37.

How Has God Provided His Own Guarantee for the Truth of His Revelation?

Since the Bible is a collection of books written by different authors who were separated by time and culture, it cannot effectively teach us without a divinely guaranteed interpretive agency. In theory, this agency could be any one of the following alternatives.

1. Individual interpretation of Scripture guided by human reason and confirmed by the inspiration of the Holy Spirit. The history of the church, however, displays a chaos of conflicting interpretations. The Holy Spirit cannot be the author of chaos and contradictory teachings.

2. Consensus of the faithful or of the bishops. However, history shows that this consensus never lasts long and an effective criterion of truth is needed precisely when contrary teachings are threatening the unity of faith. Both a majority and minority of bishops and faithful have demonstrably erred in matters of faith and morals. Without a further criterion, deciding which group(s) was or is right would be impossible.

3. The bishop of Rome. Throughout history, only the bishop of Rome has a credible claim for possessing an effective criterion of infallible magisterium. This claim is supported both *negatively*: there is no evidence of a doctrinal error on the part of the bishop of Rome when he has solemnly taught a doctrine of faith; and *positively*: there is strong scriptural evidence for the decisive role of Peter the rock who shares through Christ's empowerment in Christ's divine authority to preserve and confirm the faith of the church. Arguing from mere historical evidence, it can be shown with a high degree of probability that the church of Rome has preserved the "substance of Christian faith." Even Paul Tillich, the famous Protestant theologian of the twentieth century, has cautiously allowed its possibility.[84]

Thus we have to conclude that either there is no infallible teaching authority in the church or it resides in a special way in the bishop of Rome.

84. See Gustave Weigel, "Contemporary Protestantism and Paul Tillich," *Theological Studies* 11, no. 2 (1950): 194. For the papacy in other Christian denominations, see Joseph Famerée, "Le ministère du pape selon l'orthodoxie" [The ministry of the pope according to the Orthodox churches], *Revue théologique de Louvain* 37, no. 1 (2006): 26–43; Butler, "Authority in the Church," 337–53; Harding Meyer, "Das Papstamt—ein mögliches Thema evangelischer Theologie?" [Is the papal office a possible theme of evangelical theology?], *Freiburger Zeitschrift für Philosophie und Theologie* (2005): 42–56, condensed in *Theology Digest* 52 (2005): 225–30.

Forms of the Magisterium (See LG 12)

1. Ordinary:

a. Universal: all bishops in communion with the bishop of Rome teaching with moral unanimity a truth of faith and morals

b. Particular: teaching authority of a single bishop, or a regional or national conference of bishops

c. Magisterium of the bishop of Rome

2. Extraordinary:

a. Teachings of ecumenical councils

b. *Ex cathedra* pronouncements of the bishop of Rome

The universal ordinary magisterium teaches infallibly when all the bishops in communion with each other and the bishop of Rome, although residing in their own sees all over the world, teach with moral unanimity a truth to be held definitively in matters of faith and morals. The definitions, but not all of the texts, of ecumenical councils and the *ex cathedra* pronouncements of the bishops of Rome are also infallible. *Lumen Gentium* has declared that infallible teaching "extends just as far as the deposit of divine revelation."[85] According to the Catechism of the Catholic Church, infallibility "also extends to all those elements of doctrine, including morals, without which the saving truths of the faith cannot be preserved, explained, or observed."[86] The teachings of the (non-infallible) ordinary magisterium of the bishop of Rome call for a religious assent of mind and will, but not for an act of the divine virtue of faith.[87] The latter is due to the infallible teachings of the church regarding divine revelation. The faithful also receive the "anointing of the Holy Spirit," in whose power they believe infallibly under the guidance of the magisterium.[88]

Conclusions

There is an intrinsic unity among the four marks of the church. We might say that the unity of the church is holy, catholic, and apostolic. The church

85. *LG* 25.

86. *Catechism of the Catholic Church* (New York: Doubleday, 1995), 2035; cf. Congregation for the Doctrine of the Faith, *Mysterium Ecclesiae* (June 24, 1973), 3.

87. *LG* 25.

88. *LG* 12.

unites us in the Holy Spirit to the one holy Christ. This unity of the church is catholic in that it offers us the fullness of divine life, which transforms all human faculties as well as their whole being, and it extends to all races and cultures. This unity of the church is apostolic in the sense that the churches of all times and places are one with the church of the apostles.

The four marks of the church are always both an existing gift and a task or challenge to work for throughout the entire course of human history.

CHAPTER 13

The People of God Shares in the Priestly, Prophetic, and Kingly Role of Christ

Before explaining the hierarchical ministries of the church, *Lumen Gentium*—following the works of contemporary theologians, especially Yves Congar—describes the whole people of God as participating in the threefold office of Christ as Priest, Prophet, and King.[1] This threefold articulation of Christ's redemptive work goes back to John Calvin, even though the elements of this doctrine derive from Scripture and from patristic tradition. While basing this summary on the doctrine of *Lumen Gentium*, I will try to systematize it in the light of the New Testament and patristic theology.

The People of God Participates in the Priesthood of Christ

The Sacrifice of Jesus

Offering sacrifice is an archetypical human gesture as old as humankind itself.[2] Analogous to it and shedding light on it is another primordial human act, the offering of a gift in various forms, such as from one individual to another, from one individual to a community, from a community to an individual, or an exchange of gifts between communities. The motives for

1. LG 10–12, 34–36. Yves Congar, *Lay People in the Church* (London: Geoffrey Chapman; Westminster, Md.: Christian Classics, 1985).

2. Jean Marie Henneau, "Le rapport intrinsèque du sacerdoce ministériel et du sacerdoce commun de fidèles: Pour une symbolique du sacerdoce" [The intrinsic connection between the ministerial priesthood and the common priesthood of the faithful: The symbolic meaning of the priesthood], *Nouvelle revue théologique* 131, no. 2 (2009): 211–24.

a gift are also quite varied: in thanks for a service, an attempt to win over the goodwill of a person or community, making up for a willful or inadvertent offense committed by the gift giver or someone else, or in hope of establishing a closer relationship. The material gift is the external, tangible sign of these inner motives, feelings, and attitudes. The above motives are also present in the act of sacrifice, but no one has ever offered sacrifice to anyone believed to be a "mere man." (The sacrifices offered to kings and emperors implied their divine status.)

What is, then, the distinctive feature of sacrifice? I will attempt an answer by reviewing its main forms. By giving to God (or a god) a material object as a thanksgiving sacrifice, a certain gratitude is implied, a gratitude that no human being is ever justified expressing for another human being. That is, a gratitude for *all* that the person has and *is*. Humankind owes its very being to God. When asking for a favor through sacrifice, humans are ultimately asking for life, a favor only God can bestow. When trying to "make up for an offense" in a sacrifice of atonement or expiation, humans acknowledge that through their sin they have forfeited their life. They deserve to die and through the sacrifice they are asking God to forgive them and restore them to life. Individuals who represent a community can also offer atoning sacrifice vicariously for the whole community. In communion sacrifice, humans are yearning for communion with God (and at times through God with their fellow humans). Such communion with God could not be achieved through mere human mediation. Underlying all these particular forms of sacrifice is a motive toward adoration. Sacrifice is a tangible external sign of acknowledging God as God, as the absolute source and Lord of one's life. To him I owe everything; to him I want freely to return myself as a gift. Only God has the right to this total self-giving of humankind, since he alone gives to humankind all that they are and he alone is absolute goodness and holiness.

Of all creatures on earth, only humans are capable of offering sacrifice, since they alone have reason and free will. As rational beings, humans alone truly "possesses themselves" and by their free decisions they give shape and direction to their lives. By freely choosing to surrender in love to God's will in everything, they can in some real sense give themselves to God. On the other hand, by freely choosing to disobey God, they can refuse themselves to God (although his refusal would not be possible without God allowing his sin for a greater good).

Through the body, humans are part of the material universe. Through their activity, they are called to realize God's plan for the material universe by understanding, enjoying, preserving, and perfecting it. In this way, humankind offers a "cosmic sacrifice" to God insofar as they carry out God's will not only for themselves but also for the universe.

However, his human situation disqualifies humanity from offering God an acceptable sacrifice. Because of original sin and personal sins, the human will is more inclined to prefer itself to God instead of serving God in love. Humanity's lower faculties often oppose, weaken, and enslave the decisions of its will. Humans are not whole; so they cannot wholly give themselves to God on their own. Moreover, through sin, human beings have separated themselves from God and thereby made themselves incapable of offering God an acceptable sacrifice. But even if humans had not sinned, they could not offer God a perfect sacrifice because they are creatures that cannot fully know God's holiness and goodness, nor can they love, praise, and give thanks to God as he deserves to be loved, praised, and thanked. To put it briefly, being a finite creature, humans cannot give God a gift worthy of God himself.

Only against this background can we appreciate the significance of Christ's sacrifice. Fully integrated in himself because sin and concupiscence have not infected him, Jesus subjects himself to God with an undivided heart. His love for God is not weakened by the disorder in his personality. His giving of self extends to every moment of his life and is consummated on the cross, where it becomes complete and irrevocable. The sign in which this sacrificial attitude is expressed is not an object distinct from himself (such as an animal or the firstfruits of the crops), but his own body. An "object-sacrifice," even though it may symbolize the giving of the self, has only a tenuous, extrinsic relationship to the self. Jesus gave his physical life, his body, which is not just linked to his self, but is its concrete tangible expression. By freely giving up his body, he gives his whole humanity, and by giving his humanity—because of the hypostatic union—he gives his whole divine self in a human way to God. This is, then, the other reason why Jesus gave God *the* one perfect sacrifice. Through the man Jesus, through his human freedom, love, and obedience, the eternal Son himself loves, obeys, and worships the Father. Humankind has finally achieved what it has been unable to achieve by the unending repetition of object-sacrifices: in the God-man, man has fully given himself to God and, through himself, the God-man returned also the material universe to its Creator.

In a sinless world the offering of sacrifice would have been a joyful act without suffering and death. In a fallen world, however, which lies within the power of the Evil One, the sinless and All-Holy One has no choice but to encounter opposition, suffering, and ultimately death. Even more so since his death is a vicarious self-sacrifice for all sin-laden human beings.

Participation in the Priesthood of Christ (LG 10, 11, 34)

As there is only one perfect sacrifice, there is only one perfect priesthood, that of Jesus Christ. The unique value of the sacrifice and the priesthood of the church consists, then, in participating in the one priesthood and in the one once-for-all perfect sacrifice of Christ.

All Christians participate in the priesthood of Jesus Christ in the following sense: They offer themselves in the Spirit through Christ as one body to the Father. They do this in the sacraments, but especially in the Eucharist, by which they are empowered to carry out this offering in their daily life and consummate it in their death (1 Pt 2:4–10; Rom 12:1).[3] This sacrifice of the Christians, which participates in that of Christ through the Holy Spirit, is called in the New Testament the "spiritual sacrifice" or "spiritual worship" (*thysia pneumatikē, logikē latreia*).

The offering of self through Christ in the Spirit includes also a horizontal dimension of brotherly love. At least implicitly, a Christian may offer themselves to God in the communion of the body of Christ. St. Augustine emphasizes this so much that he defines the sacrifice of Christians in the following way: "This is the sacrifice of Christians, the many, making up one body in Christ."[4] Hebrews 13:16 warns the Christians: "Do not neglect good deeds and be in communion with one another [*koinōnia*], for God is pleased by sacrifices of that kind" (see also Phil 4:18). *Lumen Gentium* also explains that the people of God exercises its priesthood not only by receiving the sacraments, by praying and in acts of self-denial, but also "by active charity."[5]

Note that only in Christianity does the sacrifice, which by definition is directed to God, include acts of love for the neighbor. In fact, the guarantee

3. LG 10, 34.
4. Augustine, *City of God* 10.6.
5. LG 10.

of our sincerity in offering our lives to God is our readiness to offer it for our neighbor for God's sake. The unity of the act of love directed to both God and neighbor is based on the reality of the incarnation: Christ, the Son of God, has identified himself with every human being.

The common priesthood of all the faithful (*sacerdotium commune*) differs not simply by degree, but also in nature from the ministerial priesthood.[6] The ministerial priest, the bishop, and the presbyter, express sacramentally the dependence of the church on her head, Jesus Christ. Since the ministerial priest acts "in the person of Christ the Head" when he builds up the priestly people by administering the sacraments and by preaching the Word of God,[7] he shows forth in a tangible, sacramental way the truth of Jesus' saying: "Apart from me you can do nothing" (Jn 15:5).

The relationship between the ministerial priesthood and the priesthood of all the faithful becomes evident in the celebration of the Eucharist. The ministerial priest alone has the power from Christ by the Holy Spirit to make present the one sacrifice of Christ in a given place for a given community. But the purpose of the consecration is that all the faithful may join their self-offering to that of Christ and may join the priest in offering Christ and themselves in, with, and through Christ to the Father.[8]

The celebration of the Eucharist, then, makes clear that the ministerial priesthood and the common priesthood of all the faithful relate to each other as means and goal. The ministerial priesthood is at the service of the priesthood of all the faithful and not the other way around. It is a service in a twofold way: It serves Christ in whose name the priest acts, and it serves the faithful so that they may actualize their priesthood. The words of Paul summarize beautifully the twofold service of the apostle: "It is not ourselves we preach, but Christ Jesus as Lord, and ourselves as your servants for Jesus' sake" (2 Cor 4:5).[9]

6. LG 10.

7. PO 2.3; 6.1.

8. LG 10, 11.

9. For the details of how this common priesthood of all the faithful is exercised in the sacraments and in daily life, see LG 10, 11, 34.

The People of God Participates in the Prophetic Role of Christ (LG 12, 35)

Christ as Prophet

In the Gospels, Jesus is often proclaimed prophet by the people, but he refers to himself as prophet only implicitly (Mt 13:57; Lk 13:33). According to Jesus, even John the Baptist is greater than a prophet since he was directly connected with the mission of Jesus (Lk 7:26–28). Many just people and prophets desired to see what Jesus' contemporaries see (Mt 13:16–17). Jesus fulfills all that the prophets have written. Thus, in the Synoptics, and especially in Luke, Jesus considers himself as the one whose coming every other prophet foretold and John the Baptist prepared the people for in a special way. The earliest catechesis of the church calls Christ the prophet about whom Moses wrote in Deuteronomy (Dt 18:15–19). Yet the title will soon be forgotten because it falls short of expressing who Jesus really was. That the Gospel of John called Jesus the Word made flesh showed more clearly in what sense Jesus transcended the prophets. He did not merely transmit some words of God, but he himself is *the Word*, the perfect revelation of God in Jesus' concrete bodily reality, in all that he says, does, and suffers, in all that he is (see also Heb 1:1–2).

Another unique feature of Christ, the Word of God, is—as Calvin believed—his twofold role for us: he speaks to us in the gospel from outside us, but as the risen Lord he teaches us directly in our hearts (see Jn 16:12–15; 1 Jn 2:20–27).[10]

The Participation of the Whole People of God in the Prophetic Office of Christ

Scripture and *Lumen Gentium* (12, 35) All Christians are called to the prophetic office of Christ in order to bear witness to their faith in words and especially through their lives (see 1 Cor 1:5–6) as well as by praising God for his mighty deeds (Acts 2:11, 17–18; Heb 13:15). Before we can bear witness to the Word of God, however, we must accept it in faith and be transformed by it. Thus the prophetic role of all Christians presupposes a knowledge of the faith that LG 12 calls "a supernatural sense of faith." Its author and

10. John Calvin, *Institutes of Christian Religion* 2.15, trans. Henry Beveridge, 1559 ed. (Grand Rapids: Eerdmans, 1983), 425–32.

sustainer is the Holy Spirit himself, by whom Christians are "anointed" (see 1 Jn 2:20, 27).

As a result of this "anointing," the people of God accomplish the following: (1) perceives in the gospel not human words but the Word of God itself (see 1 Thes 2:13); (2) adheres to the apostolic faith "once delivered to the saints" (Jude 3); (3) is infallible in her faith under the guidance of the magisterium and through the "supernatural sense of faith"; (4) this infallibility manifests itself in the consensus of all the faithful concerning matters of faith and morals; (5) moreover, by this "supernatural sense of faith" that comes from the Holy Spirit the faithful can more deeply understand the mysteries of faith and apply the principles of faith to their lives.

Explanation of the "Supernatural Sense of Faith" The teaching of LG 12 and 35 requires some further elucidation.

1. The supernatural sense of faith is a direct experiential knowledge of the mysteries of faith, achieved not through conceptual knowledge but through the direct presence of the Holy Spirit in the believer. In Thomistic thought this is known as *cognitio per connaturalitatem*. This presence transforms the nature of believers so that they develop a real "connaturality" or kinship to the supernatural reality of the Holy Spirit; the Holy Spirit then configures us to Christ and thus makes us children of the Father.

2. Yet this *cognitio per connaturalitatem*, this "faith instinct" or intuitive knowledge of the mysteries of faith, needs explicit teaching for its clarification and articulation. Those who possess this "faith instinct" receive the teachings of the church not as completely unknown, new information, such as reading about a new country that has never been heard of or visited before, but rather as a confirmation and elucidation of the intuitive vision of a reality present and active in us. Even without elaborate conceptual knowledge, the faithful who live their faith can instinctively distinguish the voice of the true Shepherd from the voice of a false teacher, the stranger (Jn 10:4–5). The history of the church shows that the simple faithful have often clung to the truth, while sophisticated theologians, without a strong life of grace, have gone astray.

3. From this perspective, the apparent contradiction in 1 John 2:20–27 can be resolved. On the one hand, the author insists that his readers do not need to be taught about anything, because they have in themselves

the anointing from the Holy One that teaches them about everything. On the other hand, the purpose of John's letter is to teach them to distinguish between false and true teachings. His readers recognize that the letter speaks the truth because it agrees with their "sense of faith" received by the anointing of the Holy Spirit (2:21).

The Distinction and Correlation between the Prophetic Office of the Hierarchy (Magisterium) and the Prophetic Gift Received by the Laity (LG 35) The hierarchy teaches in the name of Christ and with his authority, while the laity receives the teaching from them. Yet, as we have seen, the laity is also taught directly by the Holy Spirit, just as the magisterium receives the Holy Spirit's special assistance in teaching the truth of the gospel. As seen above, the laity can perceive the Word of God in the teachings of the magisterium only to the extent that they remain open to the direct teaching of the Spirit in their hearts. In parallel with the priestly office of Christ, the two ways for the people of God to share in Christ's prophetic office are related as means and goal. In other words, the teaching of the magisterium serves the people of God by encouraging a growth in knowledge and a deeper penetration of this knowledge through its application in new situations. The rapid development of technological knowledge, especially in the field of biochemical engineering, requires of the church a certain expertise and Christian common sense in its competent laypeople.

The Charismatic Structure of the Church

Lumen Gentium 12 speaks about the charismatic gifts of the church in connection with the prophetic role of the people of God. A charism is a gift of the Holy Spirit given for the building up of the church. Charisms are not only such extraordinary gifts as the charism of healing, but also simple and ordinary ones like the gift of service, wisdom, strong faith that provides encouragement, and so on (see 1 Cor 12:4–11; 27–30). Since *Lumen Gentium* only deals with the charismatic structure of the church as an appendix to the prophetic role of the people of God, its doctrine remains underdeveloped. Therefore, while *Lumen Gentium* can provide a starting point, it needs to be expanded.

1. The Holy Spirit distributes charisms to the faithful of every rank for

the various tasks and offices which serve the renewal and building up of the church.

2. In fact, if the life of grace reaches a certain intensity in anyone, grace will result in a charism that will contribute to the common good of the church. In other words, holiness will always bear fruit in some charism. This becomes obvious if we read 1 Corinthians 12 and 13. For St. Paul, the highest of all charisms is love. In fact, what could serve more effectively for the building up of the church community than love? Thus charisms in the Pauline sense of the word are not something rare and extraordinary, but a normal part of the life of the church. Every Christian should reach that level of spiritual development in which he or she can contribute in one way or another with his charism to the life of the church. Note that many if not all charisms are based on some natural ability (good administrator, good speaker, etc.), which the Holy Spirit transforms and uses for his purpose.

3. However, while true holiness will necessarily overflow into some charism, not every charism implies holiness (Mt 7:21–23). If someone is a powerful prophet, healer, or miracle worker, they still might be in the state of sin. The charism they have received for the sake of others does not necessarily indicate personal holiness. The scholastic distinction concerning charisms is still valid: they are a *gratia gratis data*, a gift freely given for the good of others, but they are not a *gratia gratum faciens*, a grace that makes its recipient pleasing in God's sight.[11]

4. The role of the hierarchy is not to suppress the charisms but to test, encourage, and coordinate them.[12] In cases of conflict, the ultimate judgment remains with the hierarchy.[13] In fact, if a so-called charismatic does not acknowledge this right of the church, they should not be acknowledged as a true charismatic.

11. Yet the above scholastic distinction, as seen before, has its limits. All gifts of God, especially sanctifying grace ("*gratia gratum faciens*"), are given in view of the community and not just for the sake of one individual. Thus one cannot live, let alone develop, the life of grace in oneself without, in one way or another, building up the church.

12. Note that in the usage of the NT there is no terminological distinction between charismatic gifts and hierarchical gifts. Both kinds of gifts are called *charisma*, and the lines of distinction often remain blurred. In every Pauline list of charisms, the gift of apostleship comes first. For example, Timothy receives a permanent *charisma* of apostolic leadership by the imposition of hands (2 Tm 1:6). Yet already in the NT the distinction becomes evident. The role of the apostle, the apostolic delegate (Timothy), and the *episkopos* and *presbyteros* is to ensure the link between the crucified and risen Christ and the church. In contrast, the charismatic charisms are given to ensure the flourishing of the life of a local community.

13. See 1 Cor 14:37–38; LG 12.

5. A tension necessarily arises between true charismatics and the hierarchy since their respective roles are different and complementary. The hierarchical gift is to assure that the church of a given time and place remains in continuity, that is, basically identical with the church of the apostles. The role of the charismatic is to make that concrete church flourish and adapt to a given historical situation. Such tension, however, is a sign of life and could be suppressed only at the expense of the health of the church.

6. In spite of the tensions, in principle there can be no opposition between the hierarchical and charismatic elements in the church since both gifts spring from the same Holy Spirit. The church has flourished when both hierarchy and the charismatics were open to the Holy Spirit. Many are the examples from the history of the church of a pope or bishop who has recognized the providential appearance of a charismatic person or movement in the church and integrated these initiatives into the life of the church, which was renewed by them.

7. One of the important charisms in the New Testament is prophecy (see especially 1 Cor 14). Prophecy is here understood not in the general sense in which every Christian is called to testify to his faith, but as a special charism given only to some members in the church. This gift did not necessarily imply the prediction of future events; it seems that prophecy in the New Testament had a much broader meaning of revealing God's will for a given individual or community and thereby providing criticism, encouragement, and direction. The word "prophet," while often used in the New Testament and by the apostolic fathers, fell into desuetude after the New Testament canon was closed and Montanism was rejected by the church. The Montanist prophets claimed a new and superior revelation by the Holy Spirit, a revelation not contained in the sacred Scriptures.

Thus, after the closure of the canon it became clear that authentic prophecy cannot exist in the sense that some new or even superior revelation cannot be added to what has been revealed in Jesus Christ. Therefore, the use of the terms "prophecy" or "prophet" were no longer applied to messages and persons in the postapostolic church.

Yet the gift of prophecy has remained throughout the history of the church. It does not imply new revelations, but the application of the revelation of Christ through the inspiration of the Spirit to new situations, persons, and communities. Even though certain saints may have criticized the hierarchs and renewed the ecclesial institutions, they were not called prophets.

The People of God Participates in the Kingship of Christ (LG 36)

The Kingship of Christ

Jesus fulfilled what the kings of the Old Testament foreshadowed but failed to realize: God rules through him. Originally, Israel had only God for King. When Samuel yielded to the pressure of the people by anointing Saul king for them, it was made clear that the Old Testament kings would not rule in their own name and should not follow their own will. Instead, they were supposed to be God's representatives and fulfill his will. But even their "ideal king," David, failed to live up to the ideal.

Jesus does not claim to be the messianic king. In fact, he first refuses kingship as a diabolic temptation and then later Pilate finds him innocent of the charge of conspiring to become a political king. Jesus claims for himself the role of the Suffering Servant and that of the Son of Man. By his suffering and death, he will be exalted to become the transcendent Son of Man, to whom all power and dominion is given in heaven and on earth. According to John, his royal enthronement and exaltation as King of the Jews and king of the universe (his kingly title is written in Aramaic, Greek, and Latin so that the whole world may understand) takes place when he is lifted up on the cross (Jn 18:33–19:22; esp. 19:21–22).

Christ's kingship (of course, we speak here of the eternal Son within the context of the incarnation; the Son has always ruled with his Father and the Holy Spirit) is brought to fulfillment when he accomplishes his work of obedience by completely subjecting his whole existence to God's will with his last breath on the cross. By allowing his fleshly humanity to be destroyed by the power of death, his risen humanity is fashioned anew by the Holy Spirit, and it is this humanity through which God now rules universally, but in a particular way in the church, to which the risen Christ bestows the Holy Spirit. This is the paradox of Christ's kingship: he rules so that all things can be subjected to God because he has subjected himself in perfect obedience to God the Father so that God's rule is perfectly carried out in him and through him.

To the Extent That Christians Are United to Christ in Obedience, They Share in His Kingly Rule

To the extent that Christians subject themselves to Christ and participate in his death and resurrection, they restore dominion over themselves because they are no longer enslaved by sin. They also restore communion with their brothers and sisters by serving them in love. Moreover, they become free to appreciate the true value of the goods of the world, participate in building up a more just order in society, and promote cultural and technological development in the right direction. By doing so, they carry out the command they received at the dawn of creation: "subdue the earth." Thus, paradoxically, only those Christians who die to the world can really help the world by building up a "civilization of love."

Even so, this subduing of the earth by using the goods of this world to develop the potential of the material universe for the service of humanity remains a precarious endeavor this side of the consummation of history. We can only prepare for the "new heaven and new earth." No matter how far scientific and technological development carries us, the powers of the material universe that we discover, such as nuclear power and genetic engineering, will remain open to abuse that can threaten us with destruction.

Nevertheless, in spite of earth quakes, famines, possible nuclear catastrophes, and terminal illnesses, Christians share in the kingship of Christ already in this world because, to the extent that we are conformed to Christ, all things "recognize" us as their master and serve our good. St. Bernard clarifies any possible misunderstanding. This does not mean that everything serves our pleasure and whim, but that everything cooperates for our good, provided that we love God.[14]

The Special Participation of the Hierarchy in the Kingship of Christ

In an additional way, the hierarchy shares the kingship of Christ in that they possess a pastoral authority to shape and form the Christian community and thereby (especially through the preaching of the Word and through administering the sacraments) to build up the kingly people of God. Just as

14. See Bernard, "*Sermones de Diversis*" 1.6, in S. *Bernardi Opera*, vol. 6/1, *Sermones*. III, ed. J. Leclercq et al. (Rome: Editiones Cistercienses, 1957–1977), 77; for the whole tradition, 1 Cor 3:22–23 is of utmost importance.

the priestly and prophetic role of the hierarchy is a means, or rather a service, that would actualize the priestly and prophetic vocation of the people of God, so does the pastoral office promote their royal dignity and their task of building up—with the help of all well-intentioned human beings—a universal civilization of love. While ultimate responsibility for shaping and forming the kingly people of God rests with the hierarchy, the building of a more just society and the "consecration of the world," which means the conservation, right use, or ultimately the perfection of creation for the good of humankind and the glory of God is specifically the task of the laity.[15]

Concluding Remarks on the Threefold Role of Christ

We have seen that the threefold office or role of Christ and the Christian are not separate from each other, but three distinct yet interpenetrating aspects of one saving mission for the world. Without faith in God's Word (prophetic role) no spiritual sacrifice (priestly role) is possible. In fact, faith in the biblical sense means surrender to God, which is nothing else but the Christian's spiritual sacrifice. Moreover, if one surrenders to God in sacramental actions and in daily life (priestly role), they will bear witness to Christ by their daily life (prophetic role). Furthermore, only the one who has surrendered to God in faith and love shares in the kingship of Christ.[16]

Beyond a common participation in Christ's threefold office by the whole people of God, the hierarchy has an additional and different way of participating. Although the hierarchy's task is to preach and administer the sacraments, in grave necessity, members of the laity also may administer baptism, teach in the name of the church under a special mandate, and they always administer to each other the sacrament of matrimony. Furthermore, the whole people of God as a community of faith, hope, and love, as well as the individual members or smaller communities, serve as powerful means of grace to each other and to outsiders in ways other than preaching and sacraments.

15. Perhaps this special role of the laity in the world is the reason why the kingly role of the people of God is treated only in chapter 4 of *LG* and not in chapter 2 along with the priestly and prophetic role of the whole people of God. In some sense, however, the share in the kingship of Christ precedes any distinction between laity and hierarchy. The priest and bishop are also called to a royal freedom from sin and to become masters of themselves and have all things serve their good, etc.

16. These three roles correspond to three fundamental desires in humankind: to offer a gift (ultimately himself) to God, to be inspired by God (prophets and poets in all religions and cultures), and to restore harmony in themselves and in the world.

CHAPTER 14

Comprehensive Notions of the Church

The Church as Sacrament

The sacramental notion of the church, which is implicit in the New Testament, has developed further throughout her history. It views her every aspect as consisting of a sensible sign and a hidden spiritual reality. The sacramental structure reveals the transitional, interim character of the present age. The signs still belong to the first creation insofar as they are perceptible by the senses, yet they express and communicate through different modes and to varying degrees of efficacy the eschatological reality of Christ's active presence, perceptible only by the eyes of faith.

During the renewal of ecclesiology that has taken place in the twentieth century, many important theologians such as Otto Semmelroth, Henri de Lubac, Karl Rahner, and Edward Schillebeeckx have articulated the church's sacramental nature.[1] *Lumen Gentium* refers to the church as sacrament several times in a twofold sense: the sacrament of union with God and the sacrament of the unity of all humankind.[2] We will examine the meaning and the implications of both aspects.

1. Otto Semmelroth in the Theological Commission of the Second Vatican Council has greatly contributed to the inclusion of the sacramental view of the church in *Lumen Gentium*. His major work has never been translated into English: *Die Kirche als Ursakrament* [The Church as the primordial sacrament] (Frankfurt: Joseph Knecht, 1953). Cf. Dennis M. Doyle, "Otto Semmelroth and the Advance of the Church as Sacrament at Vatican II," *Theological Studies* 76, no. 1 (2015), 65–86.

2. LG 1, 9, 48.

The Church Is the Sacrament of Jesus Christ in an Analogous Sense as Jesus Christ Is the Sacrament of God

As mentioned above, we understand "sacrament" in a broad sense as an outward sign that points beyond itself to a divine reality that it expresses and communicates effectively. In his actions and sufferings; in his life, death, and resurrection; and ultimately in his very being, the man Jesus Christ reveals and communicates God. He is the eternal Son, the perfect image of the Father. In spite of the sinfulness of her members, the church in her institutions (sacraments, teaching, and hierarchical office), in her community life, and in her individual saintly members reveals and communicates Christ to her members and to the world.

In reflecting on the sacramental nature of the church, the following truths become evident. First, the church on earth has a twofold structure: it is both a complexus of signs, which, working in a variety of ways, effects the sanctification of the church community; and the church community, once established and sanctified, becomes herself an effective sign of the active presence of Christ.

Second, therefore, none of the sacramental signs, including the church herself, exists for its own sake. Each points beyond itself to Christ, whom it reveals and communicates. The more perfectly a local community becomes church, the more transparent she becomes to Christ. As the editorial change in the final text of *Lumen Gentium*'s first sentence demonstrates: "*Lumen gentium cum sit Ecclesia*" was emended to "*Lumen gentium cum sit Christus.*"[3] The true light of the nations is Christ and, according to the patristic image of the church as moon, the church is light only to the extent that it mirrors the light of the sun, who is Christ. Conversions to the Catholic faith happen when someone discovers Christ in a liturgical service, in a Catholic community, or in a personal friend who is a member of the Catholic Church.

Third, this sacramental dynamism is threatened by two diametrically opposed deviations: Either the visible elements are cultivated in a manner that obstructs access to the spiritual reality signified, or the visible structures are rejected or truncated. Some examples of the former are ritualism,

3. "Since the light of the nations is the Church" was changed to "since the light of the nations is Christ" (LG 1).

legalism, clericalism, "papolatry," or the reduction of the Eucharist to "a community experience."

The ritualist mentality is so preoccupied with the outward signs of the liturgy, such as vestments, incense, the choreography, and the music of the celebration, that scant attention remains for genuine "worship in spirit and in truth." A legalist concentrates on the exact and minute observance of every prescription of the law at the expense of paying attention to the purpose of canon law, the good of souls. Clericalism is excessive concern for the real or imagined privileges of the clergy, and for lording it over the laity instead of serving them as servants of Christ. Papolatry is literally the worship of the pope in contrast to sincere reverence. The danger of such an exaggeration has increased during the rule of the great and saintly popes in the last 150 years, beginning with blessed Pius IX's election in 1846. Awe and the joy of greeting the bishop of Rome, the apostle Peter, who, according to the words of ancient popes, "carries in him the solicitude for all the churches," is quite natural for a Catholic. Papolatry, however, means that we accept every word of a pope as the infallible word of God, every action he takes as the action of Christ, and no circumstance could justify any criticism of the pope.

One of the widespread dangers in today's church is to seek in the eucharistic celebration first and foremost a satisfying community experience. Many, perhaps most, Catholics today would answer the question, "Why do you go to church?" by saying they like community worship. And if they do not go, they excuse themselves by listing all the reasons why the community of their parish, including the priest, is too annoying for them. Only a small fraction would declare that they go to church because they want to meet Christ and unite with him.

And fourth, in contrast to an extreme emphasis on ritualistic externals is the tendency to partially or completely reject external ritual by those who would rather worship in a "spiritual church." The temptation to "purify" the church from what is not spiritual has affected some groups in the church almost from her beginnings. The Montanist movement in the third and fourth centuries set above the church hierarchy the charismatic "prophets" who claimed to possess higher spiritual power than bishops and priests. To varying degrees, many of the different denominations born of the Reformation in the sixteenth century have discarded many external elements that are important and even essential to the structure of the Catholic Church, such as Petrine and episcopal succession, the sacraments of confirmation, penance, anointing of the sick, matrimony, and holy orders. Besides such fundamentals, pictures of Christ and the saints were also eliminated as leading to idolatry. The most radical of the Protestant ecclesial communities has been the Quakers, who intended to purify their worship from almost every external element and concentrate on silent prayer even in community. Their underlying assumption was that a worship pure in spirit and truth should eliminate all but the most necessary material elements. This is quite different from the Catholic Church, which built up from her New Testament beginnings a sacramental structure, an extension of Christ's active presence into the church community and her signs.

Those who reject the sacraments of the church although they know they are instituted by Christ cannot possess the Spirit of Christ. In this sense, Origen's saying is true: *extra Ecclesiam non est salus*: "there is no salvation outside the church." Augustine expresses the inseparable connection between love of Christ and love of the church with lapidary precision: "*Quantum quisque amat Ecclesiam Christi, tantum habet Spiritum Sanctum*": "One possesses the Holy Spirit to the extent that one loves the church of Christ."[4] But even if one acts on good faith, the more the sacramental structures are reduced, the greater the danger for confusing the Holy Spirit with one's own spirit, where the Holy Spirit is either replaced by one's own rationalism or by an irrational emotional enthusiasm. The material element and spiritual reality must be closely linked because of the human being's twofold nature of body and soul. External, sensible elements anchor the soul outside of itself in objective reality. Left on its own, the human soul's gravitational center turns into itself, seeking security in abstract intellectual principles or reassurance in fickle emotions.[5]

The Church Is the Sacrament of Unity for Humankind

Since the church is the sacrament of Christ, who, through his Spirit, unites to himself and to each other all who enter the church, she is also the effective sign of humankind's unity. In other words, the Holy Spirit in the church extends the forgiving and sanctifying presence of Christ to every

4. Augustine, *In Evangelium Johannis tractatus* 32.8.

5. See Henri de Lubac, *The Splendor of the Church*, trans. Michael Martin (San Francisco: Ignatius, 1986), 84–125.

human being who is open to him. The Spirit then draws them to Christ, the Center, as well as transforms them into Christ's likeness while connecting them with each other as members of the same body. In this way the church represents and effects the communion of all peoples, races, and cultures, and brings about their unity in such a unique way that every human being's personal uniqueness as well as every culture's riches can flourish in her. Every major Catholic international event such as World Youth Day, International Eucharistic Congress, and even a canonization Mass are empirical demonstrations of this constantly expanding and mutually enriching communion. This brings to light the following truths.

First, the more the church is conformed to Christ, who lived and died for the world, the more she lives not for herself but for the world. An ecclesial existence then is a twofold service: serving Christ and serving the world. More precisely, the church serves the world by letting Christ become visible and active in her for the world. Second, the church is missionary in its very nature. A local church that turns on itself and cares only about its own members and its own self-preservation betrays its mission.[6]

This sacramental notion of the church leaves several aspects of her mystery unexplained. It doesn't bring to light the historical character of the church as a community of human beings who share in the threefold office of Christ, and it does nothing to illuminate the sinfulness of her members and the effects of this sinfulness on the church.

The Church as the People of God Becoming the Body of Christ

The above notion sheds light on some other aspects of the church's mystery, aspects that have remained unmentioned in the sacramental approach. One such aspect is the church as the people of God constituted by the Word and the eucharistic body of Christ to become his mystical body. This quasi-definition, which was favored by the early Joseph Ratzinger,[7] elucidates and synthesizes several truths discussed in the historical section, such as the following.

6. See Dietrich Bonhoeffer, *Letters and Papers from Prison*, ed. Eberhard Bethge (New York: Macmillan, 1967).

7. See Joseph Ratzinger, *Das neue Volk Gottes: Entwürfe zur Ekklesiologie* (Düsseldorf: Patmos Verlag, 1969).

1. It places in relief the continuity of the New Testament church with the people of the old covenant, since God's election of Israel is irrevocable and the gentile church has been inserted into the believing remnant of Israel as wild olive branches are grafted onto a noble olive tree. As we have seen in our historical survey, St. Thomas, mindful of the patristic tradition, explains that the object of the faith of Israel and of the church are ultimately identical since Israel has believed in the coming Messiah and the church in the Messiah who has come. The identity of faith establishes a certain identity between the two peoples.

2. It highlights also the specific difference between historic Israel and the church. The latter has transcended the division between Jew and gentile through a common faith and baptism, and both Jew and gentile are united and formed into the one body of Christ by the Eucharist. As a union this surpasses any natural union since the principle of unity that is actively present in both members and in Christ is the one and the same Holy Spirit, who conforms the members of the church to Christ and enables them to live and love as Christ does.

3. The history of the ecclesial body of Christ is a dynamic process in two ways. No member of the church on earth is fully a member of Christ since the Holy Spirit has not penetrated and transformed all of his or her being. To varying degrees, everyone on earth is still simultaneously spiritual *and* carnal; that is, humans are at times inspired by the Spirit and at other times by earthly desires. Most Christians in the state of grace are still not fully penetrated by grace. Rahner and others have insisted that this sense of the body of Christ is essentially a Catholic understanding of the Lutheran thesis *simul iustus et peccator*: "simultaneously sinful and just." To use a simile, the light of Christ is more or less obscured in every earthly member and fully extinguished by those in the state of mortal sin. The proportion of light and darkness increases and diminishes throughout history. The light can never be fully defeated, nor become fully victorious, until the last judgment and the resurrection of the body.

4. As discussed above, the history of the church as body of Christ is marked by constant change; bright and dark spots alternate in different regions or ages. In her members who strive to progress in spiritual life, the Paschal mystery of Christ is at work. The more they allow Christ to be shaped and formed in them, the more radically they share in his dying and rising

in their earthly lives. Earlier, the historical section of this work showed how keenly aware Paul was of this process. He constantly carries about in his body the dying of Christ so that the life of Christ may also be revealed in his mortal body. In other words, the trials and sufferings of Paul's apostolic life dispose him to share more abundantly in the energies of the new creation, in invincible courage, unshakeable trust, and all-embracing love.

5. The church as body of Christ shows her intrinsic connection with the earthly Jesus of Nazareth, his death and resurrection. Without the historical body of Jesus, his glorified body would not exist, that body which, through faith and the Eucharist, joins to itself and enlivens all the bodies of the faithful.

6. Since it is a people, the church must also have an institutional structure with leadership and within which each member has a unique function to fulfill for the good of the whole body.

7. Since the church is a people on the march toward the heavenly homeland and under constant attack by hostile forces, the sinfulness of her members is understandable. Their sins may oppose, to varying degrees and in different modes, in certain places and times, the sacramental function of the church, but they cannot destroy it. Christ himself has guaranteed that his church will never lose the gospel, and in her sacraments he will continue to forgive sins and sanctify those who receive them with the right disposition. Moreover, after a period of decline, the Holy Spirit always raises up saints and saintly leaders who renew the church.

The Church as the Virginal Bride of Christ

The meaning of the church as spouse of Christ becomes clearer when seen in relationship with that of the body of Christ.[8] As discussed in the historical section, God has lavished his love on Israel, who, except for a remnant, has become a harlot by pursuing foreign gods. Her entire history may be viewed as God's repeated attempts to cherish, threaten, punish, and forgive his bride time and again, but without long-term success. Nonetheless, the prophets proclaim that, at the end of times, God will purify Israel and betroth her in a splendid wedding feast.

8. Even today, the best classical works on the church as virginal spouse and mother are Louis Bouyer, *The Seat of Wisdom* (Chicago: Henry Regnery, 1960), and de Lubac, *Splendor of the Church*.

From this perspective, the good news of the New Testament is that God sends his own Son to find and transform the filthy harlot into a beautiful bride, faithful, glorious, and pure. On the cross, Christ purifies the harlot from her sins by taking them upon himself out of love. And through the gushing forth of water and blood from his side—baptism and the Eucharist—he creates anew and incorporates in his bride all those who desire to follow him in faith and love.

The bestowal of his sacrificial love upon the bride is in no way an imposition. Christ's prevenient grace enkindles the church's desire to unite herself with him. She draws Christ to herself; she longs to decrease and let him increase. In this way, the church becomes the body of Christ, conformed to him, living by his life and expressing his traits.

However, Christ's love for uniting himself with her goes in the other direction as well. While the church wants to be ruled, overwhelmed, and conformed to him, the bridegroom's love intends the bride to become fully herself, the perfect and "immaculate dove" of the Song of Songs. He makes her a queen adorned with jewels, the *aurora rutilans*, the rising dawn, which radiates splendor and beauty.

In the church's mystery, then, the images "body of Christ" and "spouse of Christ" express the dynamics or "playfulness" of divine-human love. On the one hand, the church's ambition is to let Christ be everything in her and thus to become his body, filled with Christ and communicating Christ to others. On the other hand, Christ's love does not allow the church to disappear in him, but instead to become his loveable, attractive bride, the queen of creation. Their mutual desire for each other creates a quasi-equality between the Lover and the beloved, Christ and the church. Their union is infinitely more perfect than the union of spouses in a sacramental marriage, so much so, that St. Augustine calls the *totus Christus*, Christ and the church, *una quaedam persona*, and Aquinas, *una mystica persona*.[9] But the more united they are, the more the church becomes her own self. Christ's love does not absorb her, but creates her beauty.

Their wedding feast was anticipated sacramentally by the first Eucharist at the Last Supper, and fulfilled by Christ's sacrificial death on the cross and by his resurrection. As some of the Fathers wrote: it is on the cross that

9. Augustine, *Enarrationes in Psalmos* 30, *Enarr.* 2, *Sermo* 1.4: "Fit ergo tanquam ex duobus una quaedam persona, ex capite et corpore, ex sponso et sponsa." Aquinas, ST 3, q. 48, a. 2; Aquinas, *De veritate* q. 29, a. 7.

God formed the second Eve out of the side of the second Adam. Through her full, existential identification with the sacrifice of her Son, the first perfect individual realization of the new Eve was the virginal mother of Jesus at the foot of the cross.

Although on an ontological level all believers are inserted into the spousal relationship between Christ and the church as well as simultaneously incorporated into his body through their faith and the sacraments of Christian initiation, the actual unfolding of the spousal relationship and the intensity of a believer's union with Christ depend on the dynamics of the encounter between divine and human freedoms. Depending on God's generosity and the individual's free cooperation with grace, this union increases or decreases in perfection. Many saints affirm emphatically the potential for every human being to become spouse of the Word. All human beings are created in the image of the Image of God, the Word himself. Even though a soul has been tarnished and distorted by sin, she should not give up hope. St. Bernard of Clairvaux solemnly teaches that "every soul, even if burdened with sins, enmeshed in vice, ensnared by pleasure, captive in exile, imprisoned in the body, caught in mud, fixed in mire," should dare to aspire not only to mercy, but also to becoming the bride of the Word.[10] There are two reasons for this hope. In spite of sin's distortions, the soul's nature retains the ability to be re-formed by the Word so that she may be again con-formed to her archetypal image. Second, the Son, who for our sake became flesh, was crucified, and was raised from the dead, searches for the sinner with an infinite love and calls her not only to repentance but also, through an arduous process of purification, to a spiritual marriage with him.

Even though, beginning with Hippolytus and Origen, the Fathers applied the spousal terminology, borrowed primarily from the Song of Songs, to both the relationship between the church and Christ, and to that of the perfect individual soul to Christ. They insist at the same time that Christ has only one unique spouse, the church, and that the many spouses are in fact one spouse. Thus the individual soul cannot be saved and united with the Word as an individual separate from the church. Her spiritual development depends on her progress in actualizing in herself the church's relationship to Christ. The more she participates in the mystery of the church,

10. Bernard, *Super Cant.* 83.1: 2:298.

the more she is united to Christ and simultaneously becomes more perfectly her unique individual self.[11]

The Church as Mother

The church as spouse makes it clear that her oneness with Christ is not based on the sameness of nature, but on a union of love. She shares in the life of Christ because she surrenders to him in love as a spouse to her husband. Her union with him is life-giving. As explained in detail in the historical section of this book, the virginal bride of Christ becomes mother and remains fertile throughout history.[12]

This fact casts into relief an essential aspect of Catholic soteriology. Being a mother does not mean that the church is merely a passive recipient of the gift of redemption, "not an empty bomb crater of grace" (as the early Karl Barth said about the human subject) but that she actively cooperates with Christ in bringing to life the children of God. While this active cooperation itself is received from Christ, it is nonetheless a real mediation of divine life. It takes place not only in baptism (the baptismal pool was called by the Fathers the womb of the church) and in preaching, but every Christian, by her faith and love, is called to become a "mother of souls." Such a motherhood does not necessarily mean active evangelizing, even though it is essential for those who are called to it. For example, Pope Pius XI declared St. Thérèse of Lisieux a co-patroness of Catholic missions even though her illness prevented her from transferring to a mission convent in Vietnam. Thérèse was aware that the offering of her sufferings and dying would be a source of grace for the missions.

St. Bernard distinguishes two different kinds of birth. A soul who has reached the stage of spouse will first give birth to Christ in herself, and second, if she progresses further in spiritual life, she will be able to form Christ in other souls who, in a way, will be born of her:

11. Note that that the spousal imagery is never applied by Bernard to the soul's relationship with the earthly Jesus, but describes her relationship with the risen Christ, whose body is fully transparent to his divine glory. Only those who cannot fathom intimate union except for that of a sexual nature suspect that such a spiritual union is actually a symptom of repressed sexuality.

12. The image of "mother" is not very popular in today's church. Various reasons may account for this. In the ecclesiastical jargon of the preconciliar church, the phrase "Holy Mother Church" was used to justify the authoritarian style of teaching and shepherding. Another reason could be our all-pervasive individualism. We find it difficult to think of the church as—in some real but analogous sense—one subject.

Let us stand before the Lord and praise him that, sanctified and prepared, we may merit to see the Lord as he is being born within us. If, however, a soul has progressed to the point—which is indeed too much for us—that she becomes a fecund virgin, a star of the sea, full of grace and overshadowed by the Holy Spirit, I believe that she would not disdain both to be born in her and also from her. No one, of course, should presume to attribute this to oneself; only those [can do it] whom he [Jesus] has designated in a special way, by pointing them out with his hand, as it were: "Behold my mother and my brothers." Listen to one of these [mothers]: "My little children, to whom I am giving birth again until Christ is formed in you" [Gal 4:19].

The church's activity is analogous to Mary's. What Mary did in both flesh and Spirit by giving birth to the head of the church, the church does every day by giving birth by the Spirit to the members of Christ's body. Mary conceived Jesus first by faith and only later in her womb.[13] Due to her Son's sacrifice, she was conceived without original sin and full of grace in order to become the perfect virginal spouse of the eternal Son and the mother of the incarnate Son.[14] Under the cross, her motherhood has been extended to embrace the whole church by accepting in faith the words of her dying son: "Woman, behold your son" (Jn 19:26). Yet Mary is not outside the church. In fact, Mary is the church's "most excellent member," her perfect beginning and perfect consummation.[15] The radiance of her love and purity shines on the entire church, because, as our generous mother, she wants to share all her graces with all of us. Thus Mary's virginity is fertile, beyond the birth of Jesus. She cooperates with the rest of the church in bringing about the birth of all believers in faith and baptism.

The motherhood of Mary and that of the church mutually contain one another. Matthias Scheeben calls the relationship between Mary and the church a kind of *perichoresis*: Mary is within the church and the church is within Mary. This undifferentiated view persists in the Fathers, but its meaning begs clarification. As we have seen above, the entire work of redemption is conditioned by Mary's Fiat, her free acceptance in faith of God's Son and his work.[16] Acceptance of the redemptive grace by each in-

13. See Augustine, *Sermo* 215.4.

14. This medieval view may raise some eyebrows among Freudians who cannot see the virginal-spiritual nature of the spousal relationship.

15. See *LG* 53.

16. See Joseph Ratzinger and Hans Urs von Balthasar, *Mary, the Church at the Source* (San Francisco: Ignatius, 2005); Hugo Rahner, *Our Lady and the Church* (San Francisco: Ignatius, 2005).

dividual also requires faith. This act is an individual's most personal act, yet it shares in and is helped by the faith of all the members of the church. Thus the faith of the church is not simply the sum total of the faith of all its members.[17] This faith is specifically one and the same act in each person since it is inspired by the same Spirit and directed to the same Redeemer, yet at the same time it is different since it is profoundly personal and enacted in the very center of each person's being. Infant baptism reveals an extreme case of how the faith of the church, through the faith of those who offer the child for baptism, operates as the child's own faith in receiving the grace of new birth from above.

The motherhood of Mary and of the other members of the church is exercised also by their prayers.[18] When we say that "the church prays" we mean that Mary and the saints pray with Christ.

Just as Mary completed the birth of the Messiah under the cross as she accompanied her Son up to his final handing over of the spirit (Jn 19:30), her motherly role for a member of Christ is completed when this member dies and is born to eternal life in heaven. For this reason, we recite in the Hail Mary: "Pray for us sinners now and at the hour of our death."[19]

People outside the church often see in her nothing but an ancient institution, one of the oldest forms of "organized religion." Even Catholics have a tendency to reduce the church's reality to an institution, although they may defend its necessity and usefulness. With such a view in mind, frustrations over the church's rules and bureaucracy, even more the sins of her members, may easily lead some to abandon her. Of course, one may easily be disillusioned with any institution. But if we discover behind the institutional aspect of the church the very person of the crucified and risen Lord as he pours his life into us from his opened side; if we believe that

17. Balthasar calls our attention to the fact that St. Paul says not only that love "remains," but also about faith and hope (1 Cor 13:13). Faith in heaven can be faith only in an analogous sense insofar as an essential ingredient of faith is the willing acceptance of someone else's knowledge. In heaven, this knowledge is the increasing participation in the incarnate Son's vision.

18. I mean here the saints in heaven and on earth, even those members of the church who are not yet fully purified.

19. From this perspective, we begin to appreciate the truth of Ratzinger's and Balthasar's insight: the ecclesiology of the ancient church is Mariology without the name of Mary. The early Fathers most often spoke of the church as *ecclesia virgo*, *ecclesia immaculata*, *ecclesia mater* without further explanation. They had an intuition that, in spite of the presence of sinners within the church, in some real sense one must call the church an immaculate virgin and mother. Only later could the church articulate the reason for these terms: it is Mary's immaculate virginal motherhood along with the holiness of the saints that shines through and is active in the church's virginal motherhood.

Mary herself, along with the saints, prays for us and embraces us in the sacraments and in the prayer of the church; then for a loving person it would be impossible to abandon the church. Our love for her, the immaculate virgin mother in heaven, will grow even greater if we have to face from time to time the filth and rot that disfigure her face here on earth.[20]

The Church as an Independent Metaphysical Subject

The images of virginal bride and mother suggest that the church is, in some analogous sense, one subject, one "person."[21] But what is the possible metaphysical foundation for such personalist language? The following discussion in greater detail of the definition of the church in *Lumen Gentium* 8 will begin to answer this question.

Following a heated discussion within the Theological Commission of the council on how to articulate the unique character of the Catholic Church vis-à-vis other Christian churches, Fr. Sebastian Tromp proposed the crucial verb *subsistit* to articulate the relationship of the church established by Christ to the Catholic Church, a suggestion that was quickly and unanimously accepted.[22] The members of the commission and the vast majority of bishops were sufficiently versed in scholastic theology to know that *subsistit* means the mode of being of a subject, and they also must have been aware of the dogmatic tradition that holds that the hypostasis of the Son "subsists" as the one subject of both human and divine natures.[23]

In order to clarify further the meaning of the church as an ontological

20. Some readers will prefer the treatment of the title "Mary, the Mediatrix of All Graces." In my opinion the title "Mary, Mother of the Church" contains all that is true and positive in the former. Moreover, "Mary, Mother of the Church" has a strong foundation in Scripture while the title "Mediatrix of All Graces" is more abstract, nonbiblical, and prone to serious misunderstandings.

21. See Stephan Ackermann, "The Church as Person in the Theology of Hans Urs von Balthasar," *Communio* 29, no. 2 (2002): 238–49; Jean-Noel Dol, "Qui est l'Église? Hans Urs von Balthasar et la personnalité de l'Église" [Who is the church? Hans Urs von Balthasar and the personality of the church], *Nouvelle revue théologique* 117, no. 3 (1995): 376–95.

22. See Maximilian Heinrich Heim, *Joseph Ratzinger: Life in the Church and Living Theology; Fundamentals of Ecclesiology with Reference to Lumen Gentium* (San Francisco: Ignatius, 2007), 74–75.

23. The Congregation for the Doctrine of the Faith clarified the meaning of *subsistit* without further articulating its metaphysical base: Christ "established here on earth" only one Church and instituted it as a "visible and spiritual community," that from its beginning and throughout the centuries has always existed and will always exist, and in which alone are found all the elements that Christ himself instituted. "This one Church of Christ, which we confess in the Creed as one, holy, catholic and apostolic.... This Church, constituted and organized in this world as a society, subsists in the Catholic Church, governed by the successor of Peter and the Bishops in communion with him" (*Responses to Some Questions regarding Certain Aspects of the Doctrine on the Church* [June 29, 2007]).

subject, we must start with the notion of a juridical subject, a notion ultimately based on the unity of human nature. The concept of a juridical person involves the association of natural persons (in companies, sovereign states, international organizations) for a definite purpose, with collective duties and privileges, and acknowledged as such by a competent legal authority. Such a person is recognized in law as one subject of action and responsibilities. Its legally designated representatives are entitled to represent the juridical subject, with consequences for its representative actions or omissions for the whole community. Such legal-speak would be artificial and absurd without a shared rationale and free human nature. Those who share this nature are capable of setting common goals, engaging in common activities, and designating one individual to justifiably represent the entire association.

In many countries, the church and its organizations enjoy the status of legal persons. Yet as subject, the church universal expresses a transcendent, qualitatively higher unity, even though her unity includes also the qualities of a juridical person. The basis for the unity of the church is not merely human nature, but the indwelling of the Holy Spirit in different ways and to different degrees in each of her members, as discussed above. The role of the Holy Spirit in the church (or his "mission," in traditional terminology) is to extend within the church his intratrinitarian role as the bond that unites Father and Son in their mutual difference. The Holy Spirit is also the bond that unites every member of the church to the one spouse of Christ, and unites the spouse to Christ as one body and one Spirit. The encyclical *Mystici Corporis* of Pius XII speaks more extensively than *Lumen Gentium* about the role of the Spirit in the mystical body of Christ:

> [The Holy Spirit] is entire in the Head, entire in the Body, and entire in each of the members. To the members He is present and assists them in proportion to their various duties and offices, and the greater or lesser degree of spiritual health which they enjoy. Through His heavenly grace, He is the principle of every supernatural act in all parts of the Body. It is He who, while personally present and divinely active in all the members, nevertheless in the inferior members acts also through the ministry of the higher members. Finally, while by His grace He provides for the continual growth of the Church, He yet refuses to dwell through sanctifying grace in those members that are wholly severed from the Body.[24]

24. Pius XII, Encyclical Letter *Mystici Corporis* (June 29, 1943), 57; see DS 3808.

Thus, the encyclical continues, the principle that the unity of the church is "something not of the natural, but of the supernatural order; rather it is something in itself infinite, uncreated: the Spirit of God, who, as we quoted the Angelic Doctor above, 'is numerically one and the same, fills and unifies the whole Church.'"[25]

While *Mystici Corporis* does not hesitate to quote Pope Leo XIII's statement in "Divinum illud" that "as Christ is the Head of the Church, the Holy Spirit is her soul,"[26] *Lumen Gentium*, realizing the difference between the function of the soul of a human being and the role of the Holy Spirit in the church, transforms the plain identification of *Mystici Corporis* into a comparison:

> In order that we might be unceasingly renewed in Him, He has shared with us His Spirit who, existing as one and the same being in the Head and in the members, gives life to, unifies and moves through the whole body. This He does in such a way that His work could be compared by the holy Fathers with the function which the principle of life, that is, the soul, fulfills in the human body.[27]

Human persons are singular entities of the same human nature, and unions based on the commonality of this nature are therefore limited forms of unity. In a family, city, nation, or international organization, individuals can be united in their shared goals. The members strive with the same means to realize their goals, and some may also develop a certain empathy for each other, but they cannot exist within each other. However, in the church of Christ, as stated above, the numerically identical Holy Spirit is present in each living member as well as in Christ, the head of the members. Christ extends to us the Spirit, and within us the Spirit acts as the principle of our transformation into Christ. Thus, since the one transcendent principle of unity is being given by Christ and is working in each member, we become united with Christ and also with one another at the deepest level of our unique subjectivities so that we become one ontological subject—analogically speaking—the spouse and mother of Christ.

The church, then, can be thought of as a "supra-personal person" in whom the one and the same principle of life and action, the Holy Spirit, does not replace the individual person, but by uniting each one he actualizes and perfects each individual subjectivity.

25. MC 62; see DS 3811; Aquinas, *De veritate*, q. 29, a. 4.
26. Leo XIII, "Divinum illud," *Acta Apostolicae Sedis* 29 (1896/97): 650.
27. MC 7.

The Holy Spirit, however, is not the hypostasis of the church. We cannot say that the church is the incarnation of the Holy Spirit. If she were, the Spirit should appear as the (ultimate) subject of all ecclesial actions. According to the Scriptures and the Fathers, however, the Holy Spirit has a different role in the church. He joins her liturgical actions to Christ, assists the teaching and preaching of her ministers, and distributes charisms to whom he wills. The role of the Holy Spirit has a unique efficacy in the sacraments. That is, he joins Christ's historical actions of worship and sanctification to the church's sacramental actions in such an intimate union that the ultimate subject of the latter is Christ himself. In the Holy Spirit, Jesus Christ wants to reach every human being in all places and all times.[28] In the liturgical prayers and sacramentals, the Holy Spirit inspires the prayers and those who pray them, but in these cases the ultimate subject remains the church, the bride of Christ who cannot do anything without the support of her bridegroom.

Those members of the church who surrender to the sanctifying action of the Holy Spirit are transformed, depending on the extent that they have surrendered, by the Spirit into the image of Christ. All become images of Christ, but not carbon copies of him since they together display a dazzling variety of individual differences. The same Spirit who carves out in them the image of Christ also actualizes each unique personhood. In fact, their resemblance to Christ coincides with what is their own unique personal self. Each loves the Father and human beings with the very love of Christ, but each in his or her own way. Since the same Spirit dwells in each of them, the members are both in God and in each other, and they share in each other's experience. All this begins in this life on earth, but it is completed and manifested in the world to come.

Since the Holy Spirit is present and active whole and entire in each member and, in the same way, in the whole, the mystery of the church is realized in each (spiritually) living member and in the whole church. Thus every member is not just a member, but becomes the body of Christ (in whom Christ is present and active through the Holy Spirit) and becomes bride and mother as well. Those who "allow" this mystery to unfold in them, become in the Origenian tradition *homo ecclesiasticus*, which might

28. This is the christological foundation of the *ex opere operato* principle: the sacraments offer grace to the recipient by the performance of the rite itself. They do so because Christ himself acts through the ecclesial rite.

be freely translated as an ecclesial existence. This realization helps our understanding of the mystery of Mary. She is not merely the perfect image of the church within the church, but she is *the* church in her full eschatological perfection because she alone has fully surrendered to the action of the Holy Spirit. Her body is the very body of Christ, not just biologically, but also spiritually, as she is "full of grace"; she is also *the* bride since she alone consented fully to the sacrifice of Christ; she is *the* mother who conceived the Word of God first in her mind and then also in her womb. Her motherly role for us, then, consists in sharing with us what she has—without any merit of her own—received from God.

The images of bride and mother characterize throughout history the unique kind of subject that is the church. If we reduce them to mere extrinsic metaphors, the very mystery of the church becomes a very flat image indeed. The church as bride and mother expresses a true analogy that sheds light on the church's inmost mystery.

What, then, is the similarity between the two *analogata* in spite of their greater dissimilarity, that is, between the literal bride and mother and their archetypes in the church? The church and the Christian become bride not because fleshly love joins them to Christ, but because of an entirely spiritual love that loves Christ for his own sake. The spousal union in marriage is initiated by the bridegroom and so is the spiritual union between Christ and the church. Just as marital union is by its very nature ordained toward offspring, so is spiritual union. As the earthly spouse, then, becomes mother, so too is the church or the mature member of the church. Just as the former is a partner with her husband in giving natural life, so is the spiritual mother instrumental in mediating divine life, not by physical activity, but by cooperating with God and bringing into this world children of God, children in whom Christ is present and active.

As previously stated, Christ's love for the bride creates her in her distinct spousal beauty, while the church's love flowing back to the groom wants to abolish all difference and be one with her bridegroom as intimately as possible. Thus they become two in one, a dual subject, head and body in one.

Isaac of Stella summarizes the entire tradition about the joint activity of this dual subject: the bridegroom never acts without his bride.[29]

29. Isaac of Stella, *Sermo* 11.14.

These reflections I hope have identified one of the most intriguing challenges of ecclesiology after Vatican II. *Lumen Gentium* speaks about the church as spouse and mother and implies her subsistence as one independent subject, but deeper penetration and articulation of these relationships remain the task for future ecclesiology.

CHAPTER 15

Renewal and Reformation in the Church

After reviewing the history of the church's self-understanding and describing the different aspects of her mystery, we are in a better position to look at the question of renewal and reformation in the church.[1] In the Old Testament God preserved the existence of a faithful remnant through great crises and tragedies not by the institutions of a theocratic kingdom and the official temple cult—both of which God allowed to be destroyed in punishment—but rather through a series of prophets. Unexpectedly and without any institutional guarantee, inspired individuals arose to chastise and reform God's people as well as to keep alive the hope of a glorious messianic future.[2]

In the new covenant, Jesus Christ has bound himself definitively and unconditionally to his bride and promised to remain with and within her until the end of history. Thus, in addition to inspiring free charismatic initiatives among his people, God has been present in the church's institutions, her sacraments, teaching, and leadership in order to establish and nourish his presence within the faithful. Individual church members have fallen away from Christ, but the church as such cannot, since she is Christ's own bride and body. The body cannot be severed from the head, nor the bride from her groom. As the famous patristic statement puts it: Peter's boat *tunditur, non submergitur*: it is "tossed about but does not submerge." Yet

1. Although synonyms, we use the term "renewal" to refer to spiritual and doctrinal renewal, and "reform" to the changes in the liturgy and in the church's institutions

2. He still upholds Israel until the end of history, when "all Israel will be saved" (Rom 11:26).

Christ's permanent presence also assures that he constantly purifies and renews the church by the power of the Holy Spirit.

We can summarize the most important effects of Christ's guaranteed presence in the church under five headings: (1) She will not lose the gospel of her Lord; (2) her sacraments will always be the Lord's forgiving and sanctifying actions; (3) In the Eucharist the Lord himself, the crucified and risen Lamb, will always remain with her as her Priest, King, sacrifice, and nourishment; (4) by feeding the members with himself, he builds them into his mystical body; and (5) through the Holy Spirit he unceasingly inspires the renewal and reform of his church.

Nonetheless, the church has gone through periods of time when decline and even wide-scale corruption have prevailed, but also times that were characterized mainly by renewal and reform. However, these two contrary tendencies, decline and renewal, can never be adequately separated in time and place. Even in a period of decline, saints and vibrant church communities have risen in various places; and inversely, during epochs of renewal we find sick or lukewarm local churches, even entire countries, untouched by renewal and reform.[3]

This chapter inquires into the various aspects of authentic reform at the most important junctures of church history in order to reach some general conclusions. First, the theological dimensions of true reform and renewal are examined; second, those areas where reforms have taken place; third, who and/or what were the decisive forces of reform; and fourth, the conditions of successful reforms in history.

The Theological Dimensions of True Renewal

Every genuine church renewal in history is two-dimensional in that it has both a horizontal and a vertical coordinate. A deeper and more complete understanding of a mystery always reaches back to the origins of the church, to the time of the apostles, who were eyewitnesses of the earthly and risen Christ. Nothing essential should be missing or compromised

3. For the work of reform and renewal of the Second Vatican Council and afterward, there was no more influential book than Yves Congar, *Vrai et fausse réform dans l'Église* (Paris: Cerf, 1950). This happened despite the Holy Office forbidding the reprinting and translation of the first edition into other languages. Abbreviated and translated by Paul Philibert: *True and False Reform in the Church* (Collegeville, Minn.: Liturgical Press, 2011).

from what Jesus Christ has entrusted to the apostles and what the apostles with their cooperators and first and second generations of disciples have put down in writing under the inspiration of the Holy Spirit; nothing essential should perish from the liturgy and from the way of life of the apostolic community to whom Christ has entrusted not only his personal presence, his way of living and teaching, but also the task of constructing the normative structures of his church.[4]

Humans, however, even in the church, are subject to the law of forgetfulness and of changing their past memories. When a church community becomes aware of her forgetfulness and the danger of losing her entrusted treasures, she must refresh her memory, restudy her Scriptures and traditions, reform her way of life, and replenish her liturgy from what has happened "once and for all" and "in the beginning."

To remember and reappropriate the constitutive beginnings of her history, not only does the church rely on the work of theologians, historians, and magisterium, but her renewal also includes a vertical dimension. She relies on the Holy Spirit, whose presence assures the fundamental identity of the church of all times with the church of the apostolic beginnings. If every return to the sources were restricted to the research of the church's beginnings and to those epochs when she flourished, the church would become nothing more than a giant museum. A return to the sources rejuvenates the present church only if, in addition to the experts and competent church leaders, the Holy Spirit himself is involved. He cleanses, renews, and applies the recovered treasures to current situations. By using the felicitous terms of Yves Congar, we must say that true *ressourcement* is successful only if it is combined with *aggiornamento*, and true *aggiornamento* is a homogeneous unfolding of the seeds that the apostolic church has already possessed. The same gospel, the same original sacraments, the same personal presence of Jesus Christ crucified and risen, the same lifestyle of the apostolic church, all of these and more need to become enculturated into every new historical situation, so that the church may find a way to speak to human beings of every age in their own language.

As this outline of the tasks of *ressourcement* and *aggiornamento* suggests, there is—as there is with every aspect of the church—a trinitarian foun-

4. See Karl Rahner, *Über die Schriftinspiration* [On the inspiration of the Scriptures] (Freiburg: Herder, 1958).

dation. True *ressourcement* rediscovers some of the "inscrutable riches of Christ" (Eph 3:8), and authentic *aggiornamento* is inspired or assisted by the Holy Spirit.[5] The goal of all renewal and reform is to reflect on earth more perfectly the *vera Ecclesia* of heaven, the "family" of the Father, so that the church on earth may become more authentically a holy people of priests, prophets, and kings insofar as they are united in the body of Christ and shine forth more brightly with the beauty of bride and mother.

Areas of Renewal and Reform

Following Congar's lead, three major areas of renewal can be distinguished: doctrine, liturgy, and community life.

Doctrine

The important factors that stimulate doctrinal development are heresies, cultural influences, theological reflections, and popular or liturgical piety. Here are a few examples.

In the fourth century, the Arian heresy almost eliminated the Catholic faith. Arius and his adherents quoted Scripture (Pr 8:22 and Jn 14:28) to prove their orthodoxy, while the Council of Nicaea inserted a nonbiblical, vaguely philosophical term, *homoousios*, "consubstantial," into the creed. Paradoxically, this latter term expressed the biblical faith that the eternal Son, the Logos, is of the same substance as the Father; therefore, he is truly God, equal in divinity to the Father. But the biblical formulas of Arianism, on the other hand, contained the Neoplatonic, Hellenistic conviction that the transcendent God needs a middle being, neither fully god nor fully human, in order to bridge the infinite abyss between God and humankind.

During the twentieth century, religious indifferentism has prevailed; that is, each religion is equally true, or, according to some, equally unreasonable. Therefore, the state should not privilege one religion over others, but assure full religious freedom to all. Traditional Catholics countered this trend by rejecting religious freedom altogether, quoting documents of the nineteenth-century popes who claimed that error has no right what-

5. As we have explained before, in both dimensions, renewal and reform, human expertise and human common sense enlightened by faith are indispensable. In fact, solving merely technical issues regarding reform obviously does not need faith and can be carried out by technical experts.

soever to spread and corrupt society.[6] Admittedly, it has been a long inner struggle for the Catholic Church to accept the decree *Dignitatis Humanae* of the Second Vatican Council, which declared the right for all to freely choose and exercise their religion without compulsion from the state. This right is based on the dignity of the human person, who has been created free. And furthermore, the freedom of the act of faith has been confirmed by divine revelation. Jesus Christ himself always called for such a free decision. At the same time, *Dignitatis Humanae* upheld the truth of the Catholic faith and humanity's obligation to seek the truth, while rejecting religious indifferentism, the chief target of Popes Gregory XVI's and Pius IX's encyclicals. The issue of religious liberty has shown that, through dialogue with the post-Christian zeitgeist, the church has been able to return to her original tradition while differentiating and better articulating her past declarations.[7]

Liturgical Life

Since the liturgy is the extension in time and space of the prayer and sanctifying activity of the incarnate Son of God with his bride the church, it must necessarily be enculturated always and everywhere. The success of any specific enculturation, though, depends on how authentically a certain language and culture is used and transformed to express the faith and worship of the church of the apostles. Liturgical forms have become obsolete when and where they became so fossilized or overdecorated that the forms could hardly express the inward worship of a congregation, or the meaning of the liturgical actions was no longer clear. A more dangerous development often moves in the opposite direction. Instead of using and transforming the values of a culture for an authentic communication of the Christian faith, a hybrid liturgy, a mixture of pagan and Christian elements, is simply juxtaposed (for example, sacred texts of another religion introduced into the ritual itself of the Eucharist).

From the late sixteenth century through the late twentieth century, the Latin church carefully preserved the forms of the Latin liturgy, which had been codified by St. Pius V after the Council of Trent. While this strict policy successfully protected the expressions of the authentic Catholic faith,

6. Gregory XVI, *Mirari vos* (August 15, 1832); Pius IX, *Syllabus of Errors* (December 8, 1864).

7. Note that according to the generally known criteria, the above-mentioned papal documents and others with similar conclusions do not qualify as infallible teaching.

it severely limited the active vocal participation of the faithful. This long stagnation of liturgical development explains, at least in part, the explosive force of the twentieth-century liturgical renewal which swept through the entire Latin church after the Second Vatican Council.

No other issue has caused so much bitter controversy after Vatican II as the reform of the liturgy. Archbishop Lefebvre's traditionalists claim, quite ironically, that they defend tradition from the "innovation" of what they call "Pope Paul's Mass." However, they actually cling to the less-than-five-hundred-year-old Tridentine rite over and against the fourteen-hundred-year-old Mass of Gregory the Great. They do not see, nor do they want to see, that the *Novus Ordo*, the so-called Mass of Paul VI, is fundamentally the Mass of Leo the Great and Gregory the Great.[8] The *Novus Ordo*, then, is much more "traditional" than the Tridentine Mass, since its application to the needs of the contemporary church has resulted only in nonessential modifications while retaining, or even restoring, previous elements of the liturgy. Nevertheless, in comparison to the long and quiet stability of the Tridentine Mass, the introduction of the changes appeared abrupt, radical, and inorganic. In the majority of places, an unprepared clergy carried out the reforms for an unprepared congregation.

Especially at the beginning, the experimentation with popular music, "creative," improvised prayers and symbols, as well as the omission of some gestures of reverence, introduced a forced lightheartedness into the eucharistic celebration. The first English translation of the prayers of the Mass at times simplified their meaning to the point of distorting them. In summary, I see two major problems, not with the *Novus Ordo* itself, which has now become widely accepted, but with the spirit of its celebration: (1) No sufficient awareness exists that the celebrant has no right to "create the liturgy." The liturgy is a gift from Christ through the church; our duty is to celebrate it simply and worthily. (2) In many places, the focus of the eucharistic celebration has become the community, rather than Christ crucified and risen, to whose sacrifice we unite our gift of self to the Father. As a result, active participation has been reduced, in varying degrees, to external gestures such as singing, reading, and responding to prayers. In fact, active participation means primarily the union of minds and hearts with Christ and with each

8. See Joseph Jungmann, *The Early Liturgy to the Time of Gregory the Great* (Notre Dame: University of Notre Dame Press, 1959). For the later additions see Denis Cruan, *The History and the Future of the Liturgy* (San Francisco: Ignatius, 2005), 58–66.

other, as well as understanding what is unfolding at each liturgy; the external participation is only its expression.[9]

In spite of all these problems and difficulties, wherever the spirit of the liturgical reform was understood by clergy and people, in my opinion the reform bore positive fruits, and vibrant parish congregations and religious communities, and it facilitates a more effective evangelization.[10]

Community Life

The discussion above touched on the unique character of church community, namely, that the same (*numerice idem*) Holy Spirit is present in each member, that the Spirit joins to Christ and to each other the local communities. As a fruit of the activity of the Spirit, the members of the church are conformed to Christ and thus become children of the heavenly Father, brothers and sisters in the one family of God. All the activities of the local and universal church, (shepherding, teaching, liturgy, practices of charity, evangelizing the world, promoting universal peace, and the improvement of the spirit and structures of society) aim at bringing about and strengthening the universal communion of worship and brotherhood. In human history, this communion has never been and never will be perfect, it but needs to be renewed and deepened every day. The health of a local church can be gauged by watching the authenticity of its community life: Are the members united in their faith, values, and ideals; and do they obey the injunction of Paul: *to auto phronein*, "think the same"? Is the center of their liturgy Christ in the Eucharist? Do they share their hearts and material resources with each other and with the poor according to their abilities? Are they an open circle, attracting outsiders? Does the parish priest, the bishop, and the pope promote this kind of community on their level? From this outline of the criteria of genuine Christian community it becomes obvious what would constitute true reform and what would weaken or compromise true communion.

9. Joseph Ratzinger, *Spirit of the Liturgy* (San Francisco: Ignatius, 2005) offers, in my opinion, the best guide for understanding the true spirit of the liturgy and the problems with its postconciliar reform. That being said, I am more optimistic than he is about its positive fruits.

10. My evaluation may appear unrealistically optimistic even in the eyes of some nontraditionalist theologians. They refer to the data of the Pew Institute and the yearly CARA reports (Center for Applied Research in the Apostolate) as evidence that the liturgical reforms resulted in lower Mass attendance and the departure of millions of Catholics from the church. I don't think there has been reliable research about the causes of lower levels of practice and departures from the church. Perhaps the dissolution of the so-called Catholic ghetto, with its parish-centeredness and the absorption of the Catholic masses into the mainstream of American life and culture is a more powerful factor.

A few examples of weakening tendencies should suffice: Tyrannical or predominantly bureaucratic, impersonal or passive, disengaged or laissez-faire leadership seriously damages communion at any level. Brotherhood without authentic liturgical life tends to degenerate into an emphasis on "feelings" and socializing. Liturgical life without community building and evangelizing leads to sterile *l'art pour l'art* aestheticism. On one hand, a pastor who tries to do everything by himself and distrusts the charisms of the laity, and, on the other hand, a pastor who lets all the charisms pullulate without coordinating and testing them—both of these would harm the local community.

Often intractable tribal or national prejudices overpower the sense of Christian communion, possibly ending in violence and war between Christian tribes or nations. The hierarchies of Europe in the two World Wars were unable and sometimes unwilling to stop these fratricidal wars.[11]

The unity of the local churches in the one Christ is expressed and protected by the one bishop of Rome, Christ's vicar in whom "Blessed Peter carries solicitude for all the churches." We have seen that the minimum requirement for accepting the Petrine ministry is twofold: communion with him is the criterion for individuals and local churches to belong or not belong to the universal church of Christ; and, in controversial doctrinal and disciplinary matters he is the judge of last appeal.

These basic requirements, in conjunction with the divine institution of the bishops in the local churches, admit a wide range of different ecclesial structures, which take into account different historical and cultural contexts. The Latin rite Catholic Church developed a strongly centralized system. The Eastern churches emphasized the importance of local churches around their bishop and their communion of faith; in the East, sacraments and church order have not been supported by strong juridical ties. Their reunion with the see of Peter obviously will not require their acceptance of the same legal structures as exist in the Latin church.[12]

An irreconcilable diversity of opinions concerning church constitutions is quite legitimate. Disagreements have always existed and will exist in the church regarding what the best church structure is for any point in time. One example will show the difficulty of establishing the right balance and

11. Fortunately, the popes in both wars unequivocally opposed the hostilities and worked for peace.

12. As is well known, even now the Eastern-rite churches that have already reunited with Rome have their own special canon law.

relationship between the center and the peripheries. By implementing the decrees of Vatican II, Pope Paul VI has strengthened the autonomy of the local bishops. At the same time, and especially under Pope John Paul II, the media, even the Catholic media, routinely criticized the pope for granting only limited autonomy to local bishops and to national bishops' conferences. But when individual bishops mishandled or concealed cases of sexual abuse or financial mismanagement, the same media condemned the Holy See for not preventing or for not quickly handling the crimes. They did not realize that the newly granted greater autonomy of the local bishops made the Holy See's intervention much more difficult. I mention this not to justify manifest wrongdoing, but to point out that every reform of a juridical kind, centralized or decentralized, remains imperfect, and each is vulnerable to a different set of abuses.

CHAPTER 16

The Eschatological Consummation of the Church

The Eschatological Perfection of Humankind

The book of Revelation, which seals the canon of the entire Bible, describes the vision of "a new heaven and a new earth," where the heavenly church, the new Jerusalem, descends from heaven (21:1–27). St. Thomas sums up in these words this scriptural and patristic theme with his usual lapidary simplicity: "The true Church which is our mother and toward which we strain and which is the exemplar of our Church militant" exists in heaven.[1] *Lumen Gentium* also declares that "the church ... will reach its completion only in the glory of heaven."[2] In fact, every comprehensive notion we have reviewed has a built-in dynamism toward an eschatological fulfillment.

Through the remainder of this chapter, as I attempt to outline in greater detail the church in her definitive perfection, I will revisit one by one the comprehensive notions that have been treated to the extent revelation and theological reflection will allow me.

The Sacrament Unveiled

The sacramental notion of the church looks beyond the signs (the human words and rituals, and the assembly of people) to what the signs effect in various ways. The scholastic theologians called this *res sacramenti*, the eschatological reality. In that light, the church on earth can be seen as the sacrament of the eschatological reality, that is, already present and opera-

1. Thomas Aquinas, *Commentary on Ephesians* 31.3.
2. LG 48.

tive, but still veiled under the signs of this world. Its very center is the risen and glorified Jesus Christ, who has already arrived at the end of history and entered God's eternal realm, but who still exists at the same time in our midst. He draws us in every moment into his eucharistic sacrifice, heals and sanctifies every stage of our lives through the sacraments, and speaks to us in his Word. All this takes place so that everyone who responds to Christ's love may reach the fullness of salvation in the heavenly church. Thus, in the Catholic perspective individual salvation and the church's eschatological consummation are inseparable; they are two sides of the same event. But on one hand, no one is saved individually. We are only saved within the church; or better still, only the church is saved. On the other hand, the heavenly church will coincide with the whole of redeemed humankind in which every individual will have reached their unique individual perfection, the effect of their insertion into ecclesial communion.

The Pilgrim Church Arriving in the Promised Land

The long pilgrimage of God's people in the desert of this world will come to an end. No more temptations, no more falling away through lack of faith and love, those who have persevered arrive in the heavenly homeland, which coincides with the heavenly sanctuary. Not only shall we have free access to the holy of holies (we've had access since the Last Supper through the flesh and blood of the Lord in the Eucharist) but we will abide in the heavenly sanctuary, where we will share for eternity with and through Jesus, our firstborn brother, the face-to-face vision of the Father. Seeing the face of the Father will not be a mere intellectual operation, but simultaneously a union of love. According to Gregory of Nyssa and other Fathers, it will be a constant movement and delightful rest in God. The more delight we find in God, the more we hunger for a deeper union and vision. Thus, with Gregory's words, it will be an eternal dialectic of *stasis* and *kinesis*, rest and movement, satiety and hunger, each soul according to his or her capacity as each acquired here on earth.

The activity of ministerial priests will come to an end since the sacramental signs will then have been unveiled in the active presence of Christ. The universal priesthood of the faithful will activate its full potential. The spiritual sacrifice of the faithful, the giving of their selves, will coincide with their entire lives; their prophetic office will be fulfilled in unceasing praise and thanksgiving to the Lord. They will be seated on royal thrones and share with Jesus the governance of the entire universe.

The Body of Christ Perfected

According to Paul and expanded in the patristic tradition, the goal of history is the *totus Christus*: the whole Christ, head and members, the incarnate Son extending his life into all members of redeemed humanity. We are to "form that perfect man who is Christ come to full stature" (Eph 4:13). God will bring "all things in the heavens and on earth into one under Christ's headship" (Eph 1:10).

Here on earth, no one is fully a member of the body of Christ. Even if we are in the state of sanctifying grace, we still pose many obstacles to the inspirations of the Holy Spirit, and as a result the life of Christ is not allowed to be fully present, manifest and active within us. Apart from the saints, who can honestly say with Paul even while still living their earthly lives, "I am living now, yet not I, but rather Christ is living in me" (Gal 2:20), we do not reveal him to the world with our whole life, and with all of our words and actions, but only sporadically. Once we enter the heavenly Jerusalem, Christ will be able to take possession of our entire being, remove all the obstacles to his presence, and enable the free activity of every saved member. Through his Spirit, he will transform our lowly bodies into the likeness of his glorified body (Phil 3:21). We will then be only "light in the Lord," because our glorified bodies will become fully translucent to his light. Each of us will screen it through the prism of our unique individuality, so that the one light will be at the same time a rich harmony of all.[3]

In the heavenly church, then, each of the redeemed and the whole of redeemed humankind will receive as its own the filial consciousness of Jesus and share in his activity. We will see the Father face-to-face as the Son does, will love the Father and all the redeemed as the Son loves them, will worship the Father with the same dedication and reverence as the Son. We will be given as our own the very heart, mind, and body of Christ. In the words of St. Cyril of Alexandria, all that Christ has and is will be truly offered to

3. The following sections through the end of the "redemption" of the material world has been derived, with some changes, from my work: *Jesus Christ: The Fundamentals of Christology*, 3rd ed. (New York: Alba House, 2002), 435–42. In the eschatological order the full realization of the *totus Christus* requires a synthesis of Christology and ecclesiology.

us as our gift and we will participate in him to varying degrees, according to the potential we have developed in our earthly life.

The Family of the Father

Yet this centering on the role of Christ serves only to underline the absolute primacy of the Father. The entire economy of salvation has its origin in the Father's generosity and returns to the Father. He wanted to extend his eternal Son's filiality to an innumerable multitude of sons and daughters. Thus he handed over his Son in order to redeem us, the slaves. Through his perfect sacrifice we have been made ready to enter "in the blood of Jesus" and "through . . . his flesh" to the heavenly sanctuary (Heb 10:19–20), where the Father receives us, his dear children, adopted not through a legal act but by receiving a share in the generation of the eternal Son. We will then "attain to the fullness of God himself" (Eph 3:19) so that in the end, "God will be all in all" (1 Cor 15:28).[4]

As explained earlier, the special characteristic of the Holy Spirit is that he unites persons as persons rather than fusing them into some sort of an impersonal amalgam. He does this with the Father and Son within the Trinity, and also with the members of the church. As the Spirit unites the Father and the Son in their unique personhood, so does he join every member of the church and the whole church to Christ while preserving the personal identity of each.

So distant from abolishing personal distinctions in the *totus Christus*, the Holy Spirit actualizes our unique personalities by transforming us into Christ, the transcendent archetype of every human being. Instead of becoming carbon copies, the more we participate in Christ, the more we become ourselves.

Virgin, Bride, and Mother

An ecclesiology that reduces the traditional images of the church as virginal bride and mother to mere metaphor could devolve in two opposite distortions. It might either emphasize the unity of the church with Christ to the point of risking a pantheistic unity, a "christological monism." Or it could reduce the church as body of Christ to a metaphor, resulting in a

4. In the NT the term "God" without further qualifications means, as a rule, not the Son or God the Holy Trinity, but the Father.

unilateral emphasis on the church as an institution, a mere social body. However, the previous chapter showed that Scripture and tradition often describe the church as virginal spouse and mother, alluding to her analogous supra-personal personhood vis-à-vis Christ. In this way, the Pauline and traditional understanding has been preserved regarding the image of the church as the body of Christ; it expresses a real union of life and activity rather than just a social body. But the union is the result of a personal relationship of love, a transcendent virginal union between bride and groom, church and Christ, rather than a unity based on an identity of their natures. In this perspective, then, the eschatological church is both ontologically united with Christ, yet simultaneously an autonomous ontological subject. Better, it is precisely the perfection of the union of love that results in the perfect autonomy of the church.

As seen above, the church as the virginal bride and mother applies not only to the church as a whole but to every (spiritually) living member to varying degrees, which depend on the level of each person's spiritual maturity. Mary the mother of the Lord is the most perfect member to the extent that she is *the* church in her full perfection. Her free acceptance of the incarnation and her consent to the sacrifice of her Son have established her universal motherhood over every member of the church. She shares with God in giving birth to every child of God. At the end of history, with her motherly intercession completed, her role in the salvation of her children will come to light and be forever enjoyed by her and every saved member of the church. However, every saved person must have helped others in a limited way on their way to salvation, and thus can justly be called their mother also in heaven.[5]

This leads to the conclusion that the church—and, in the full sense, the heavenly church—is not only the body of the *totus Christus*, the Christ come to full stature, but also virgin and mother.

The creation of this woman, in union with Christ, is the final goal of all of God's works. Since the creation of this woman exceeds creation's own capabilities, it is achieved through the Holy Spirit through whom humankind, uniting to itself the entire cosmos, becomes the beautiful, highly de-

5. There are weighty theological arguments for the opinion that no one is saved or damned alone. We necessarily influence others positively or negatively. But even those who will eventually be saved may have, at certain times in their lives, exerted some negative influence on their neighbors. At the last judgment, the operation of God's justice and mercy will be made manifest within, and by means of, the intricate web of contrary and ambiguous human relationships.

sirable, and beloved partner of the Son. But even more so, in this woman the creature is in some sense raised by God's free mercy to a quasi-equality with God himself, because in Mary, and analogously in the whole church, the woman becomes the mother of God: Mary brings forth the Son of God in her own flesh and heart, and she brings him forth in the hearts of all redeemed men and women. The eschatological woman, then, reveals what is most divine in God, his infinite humility and gratuitous love. Through this love and humility, God elevates creation out of nothing to the status of a worthy partner for himself (as bride) and he becomes dependent on her as son upon her mother.

This, then, is the final goal of history, expressed in three complementary ways: the family of God the Father, Christ in his body the church, and the woman, the virginal spouse and mother of the Son.[6]

Following this discussion of the church's final shape in relation to the Trinity, it would be appropriate to speculate somewhat concerning the humanity of the individual eschatological man and woman. A useful analogy is gained by looking first at the mature, integrated man and woman during their earthly lives. The male actualizes his full humanity only if he liberates in himself the feminine dimension; the woman, only by actualizing in herself the masculine dimension; both become in the process a more mature man or woman.[7]

This seems to be only a prefiguration of our final reality. If we are to perfect rather than lose our humanity, as God's revelation assures us, everyone would preserve his or her personal identity as male and female. Nevertheless, both man and woman will become united with and transformed by the risen body of the man, Christ. Yet, at the same time, both men and women will also embody in themselves the eschatological woman, the bride and mother of Christ. Likewise, regardless of their genders, men and women will share in the attitude and activity of the Son, loving and worshiping the Father by "breathing back" the Holy Spirit to him and breathing him forth into all the redeemed. But they will also share in the

6. The reader may wonder why I have not synthesized ecclesiology around the notion of communion. I believe my approach includes all the positive elements of communion ecclesiology, but is also more comprehensive by centering on participation in the Trinity and on the resulting trinitarian anthropology.

7. The ideal is obviously not a bisexual or hermaphrodite human being, but the fully human male and the fully human female. On this point, both Jungian psychology and the Chinese wisdom on the harmony of yin and yang agree.

attitude and activity of the woman (Mary and the church) in that they surrender themselves to Christ their bridegroom in pure love and become nurturing "mothers" for all the redeemed, who cherish the continued growth of divine life in them.[8]

Here an excursus seems warranted on what might be called *eschatological humanism*, meaning that only eschatological salvation achieves our perfection *as human beings*. Our full potential is realized not only through our union with Christ, but, through Christ, with every member of redeemed humankind. Individuals cannot unfold in themselves all the perfections of human nature. "The idea of the human being" in its full richness, as conceived by God from all eternity and realized gradually in history, can be actualized in each individual only in a limited and one-sided fashion. For instance, it is just as difficult to simultaneously develop gifts as diverse as poetic creativity and mathematical talent as it is to combine the self-giving love of a mother with the single-hearted devotion of a virgin. Each individual is only one variation of the potentially limitless ways of being human. Thus the individual will become perfect as a human being only if, in some way, he or she can appropriate all human perfections. This he or she cannot do unless he or she enters into communion with all men and women, past, present, and future, who have developed and preserved their humanity for eternal life. Thus the only one through whom we can reach all men and women of all ages is the one in whom all men and women are alive and who keeps them all united, the risen Christ who is present in them through the Holy Spirit. Through the Spirit of Christ, we will participate in each other's perfections. Of course, such mutual possession of one another's perfections will not lead to the extinction of the unique beauty of each individual. The poet will still be very different from the mathematician, the mother with a large family will still be easily distinguishable from the twelve-year-old St. Agnes, virgin and martyr. Yet, by loving the special beauty of the other, and by rejoicing that the other is so beautiful, each will in some real way share in the perfections of all. Thus will the love that unites all in the redeemed Christ result in the enrichment of each individual by the riches of all. A radical humanism, the full actualization of the human potential, is possible only in the eschatological Christ.

8. See Louis Bouyer, *The Seat of Wisdom* (Chicago: Henry Regnery, 1960); Hans Urs von Balthasar, *Theodramatik*, vol. II/2, *Die Personen in Christus* (Einsiedeln: Johannes, 1978), 260–330.

The Eschatological State of the Material World

Revelation does not say much about the shape and role of the material world in the final age.[9] Only a few texts refer to this issue: "What we await are new heavens and a new earth where, according to his promise, the justice of God will reside" (2 Pt 3:13; see also Acts 3:21; Rom 8:19–25; Rv 21:1 and Is 66:22). The image "new heavens and a new earth" does not designate primarily the material world, but symbolizes the kingdom of God realized in its fullness, to which the new shape of the material universe serves only as a "cosmic habitat." The New Testament, following the prophetic tradition, cannot envision the final state without a new material creation. Humankind is to rise in a new spiritualized body that is nonetheless a true body and, therefore, in need of a corresponding material environment: "The former heavens and the former earth had passed away" (Rv 21:1). This statement underlines the difference between the old and new creation. Yet the discontinuity cannot mean a complete destruction of our world and a *creatio ex nihilo*, an emergence out of nothing, of a new universe. The risen body of Christ and the glorified body of Mary guarantee that the material elements of our universe will be assumed into the new world. The spiritualized bodies of the new Adam and the new Eve are the foundation and the pattern of the new creation to be completed at the end of times.

Beyond this, there is very little evidence in Scripture and tradition about the shape and function of the new material world. However, by reflecting on the available data in the light of the totality of the Christian mystery, some further insights may be gained.

Humankind is the climax of the evolution of the material world; in our spiritual reality, we transcend the whole of matter, but through our bodies we belong to the world of matter as its integral part. Thus we cannot be perfected without the redemption of our bodies, and our bodies require a corresponding material environment. But what could "redemption" mean for matter?

As a consequence of our sins, a conflict arose between humankind and nature. Instead of developing the full potential of the material world, we have abused it for our sinful purposes (Rom 8:19–25). Beginning with the

9. See Stanislas Lyonnet, "The Redemption of the Universe," in *Contemporary New Testament Studies*, ed. M. Rosalie Ryan (Collegeville, Minn.: Liturgical Press, 1966), 423–36; Pierre Teilhard de Chardin, *Hymn of the Universe* (New York: Harper and Row, 1965).

first stone hurled at an innocent victim and continuing through the destruction of Hiroshima and Nagasaki by nuclear bombs and the present destruction of the environment, we have regularly harnessed nature's powers to harmful ends. The progress of civilization, while it has admittedly accomplished many worthwhile goals, has become inextricably linked with an increasing abuse of nature. However, as the material world became a tool for our sins, so did it also become an instrument of punishment for our sins. Ever since the fall, nature has not simply served us; we have had to subdue nature through constant struggle, and it has repeatedly threatened our happiness as well as our very existence.[10]

The fall has also affected our view of nature as revelation. Instead of serving as a sign through which God shows us his power, wisdom, and glory, the universe has become a trap for the sinner. We are easily overwhelmed by its power and charm. We have, in fact, worshiped the sun, the moon, the stars, and mother earth, and later, at a more sophisticated stage, we have endowed nature as a whole with the attributes of divinity. Pantheism and nature worship in various forms seem as widespread today as they were in ancient times.

In the eschatological state, we expect that, just as the Spirit of Christ will transform our mortal bodies into the likeness of Christ's glorified body, so will he change our material world into a "worthy habitat" for risen humankind. Nature will no longer be abused by man and woman for sinful purposes, nor will it threaten their life and happiness. Peace between humankind and nature, as it existed in paradise, will be restored. The material world will serve us, and through us it will be integrated into Christ.

Nor will nature, through its beauty and mystery, impede or distract our vision of the Creator. Instead, through the Spirit it will become fully transparent to the Son, through whom it has been created, and to the Father, who is its primordial source and final goal. Two analogies will shed additional light on the role of the new cosmos.

The first analogy comes from the union of body and soul in human beings. Already in our earthly life, the body is the expression of our soul. Yet the body's substantial unity with the soul does not diminish its material reality; on the contrary, matter reaches its highest form of organization and

10. This does not mean that had we not sinned we would not have earthquakes, droughts, and other natural disasters. But their impact on human existence would not lead to tragedy and loss of happiness.

complexity precisely as the expression of the human spirit. If the finite human spirit can raise matter to a higher level of being without suppressing its material nature, how much more will God's Spirit be able to unite the material world to Christ through humankind in such a manner as to actualize it in its highest possible perfection?

The sacraments provide an even more apt analogy, since they foreshadow the function of material elements in the eschatological state. In the sacraments, material elements (water, oil, bread, and wine) become part of a symbolic act, and as such they communicate and manifest (to those who have faith) the sanctifying and worshiping activity of Christ. This happens most radically in the Eucharist. The bread and wine in the Eucharist become not merely the carriers of Christ's action (as, for instance, water is in baptism), but are changed into his body and blood. In this transformation, the material world reaches its highest perfection. The material reality of eucharistic bread and wine is not annihilated by the consecration to be replaced by the presence of Christ, but their empirical reality becomes the effective sign of Christ's real personal presence. This raises the question of the meaning of the substantial transformation of the eucharistic elements. Their whole material reality is exhausted by becoming effective signs of Christ, in pointing to Christ, and in communicating him to us as sacrificial food. For this reason, the Eucharist is indeed the best analogy for the world to come, because it is its initial realization. The new universe in which Christ will be all in all (Col 3:11, to transpose Paul's statement from the present situation to eschatology, where it will be fully realized) may be conceived (as Teilhard de Chardin does) as the cosmic extension of an unveiled eucharistic presence. At the present stage of salvation history, "the species" of the consecrated bread and wine point to but also veil the presence of Christ. At the end of times, when the whole material universe will be transformed by Christ as an (attenuated) extension of his glorified body, the universe will no longer hide his glory from us. We will see his presence manifested in the whole cosmos, which will radiate him to all of us. In this act of manifesting and communicating Christ, and through Christ, the Father himself, the material world will transcend itself and reach the final perfection God has intended for it from eternity. Then, indeed, not only the heavens but also the earth will be filled with God's glory.

Review Questions to Parts 1 and 2

Chapter 1

1. Who belonged to the *Ecclesia ab Abel* according to the Fathers? In other words, what were the condition(s) for belonging to this "church"?
2. How could those living before Christ share in Christ's redemption?
3. On what basis did St. Thomas declare that the "ancient fathers [in Israel] belonged to the same body of the Church to which we belong"?
4. Explain the goal and method of God's *paidagogia* in Israel's history.
5. Why and how is Abraham's faith a prototype of the faith of Israel and of the church?
6. Concerning the relationship of Israel's kings to God, why does the institution of royalty in Israel become a disaster?
7. Explain the meaning and significance of *qəhāl YHWH* for Israel and for the church.
8. How did the Torah serve to lead Israel to Christ?
9. Illustrate the filial and bridal relationship between Israel and YHWH with some important Old Testament texts.

Chapter 2

1. In what ways did the Jews expect the coming of the kingdom of the Messiah?
2. Characterize Jesus' proclamation of the kingdom. How does its coming differ from the expectations? Who are invited, who can enter, and what are its central images?

3. What was Jesus' original plan and how was it frustrated?
4. What does the election of "the Twelve" reveal about the intentions of Jesus?
5. Why can we say that the church is constituted by the first Eucharist at the Last Supper?
6. Why can we call Matthew's Gospel the "ecclesial" Gospel par excellence?
7. Show that, according to Matthew, Jesus did not definitively give up on Israel.
8. Explain the significance and the mode of the speaking of languages at Pentecost by the apostles.
9. Characterize the life of the church in Jerusalem according to Luke.
10. Describe the significance of the division of Acts in two connected parts (1:1–12:19; 12:20–28:31).
11. How does Acts express hope about the eschatological future of Israel?
12. Why does the arrival of the captive Paul in Rome mark a new stage in the history of the church?
13. Why did many Fathers call John the "spiritual Gospel"?
14. What do we man by the statement that in John Jesus' activity, passion, and resurrection are contemporaneous to the church?
15. How the words of the risen Christ in John 20 sum up the entire mission of the disciples?
16. What is the ecclesiological significance of the relationship between "those who have seen and believed" and "those who have not seen yet believed" (cf. Jn 20:29 with 1 Jn 1:1–4)?
17. What does the book of Revelation teach about the history of the church?
18. Who is the woman with a crown of twelve stars in Revelation 12?
19. Summarize Romans 11 on the relationship between Israel and the church.
20. Explain the meaning of the *ekklēsia tou theou* in Paul.
21. Explain the twofold meaning of Paul's understanding of the church as the body of Christ.
22. What is the role of the Holy Spirit in the body of Christ?
23. What is the meaning of the Pauline notion of "head" to the body of Christ? Where in the Epistles of Paul is this term found?
24. How does the bridegroom-bride image qualify the relationship between Christ's personal body and his ecclesial body?

25. Explain in what sense the body of Christ is a dynamic reality.
26. Show that Paul's ecclesiology exhibits the characteristics of "early Catholicism."

Chapter 3

1. List and explain briefly each of the characteristics of patristic ecclesiology.
2. Explain at length the trinitarian aspect of Irenaeus's ecclesiology.
3. Characterize briefly the close relationship, bordering on identity, between the mystery of Mary and that of the church in the Fathers.
4. Comment on the relationship between the local church and its bishop in the theology of the Fathers.

Chapter 4

1. Explain briefly the positive and negative results of the Constantinian and medieval symbiosis between the church and the empire.
2. Explain the "investiture controversy" between the empire and the papacy (causes, outcome, positive and negative effects).
3. Characterize the curial ecclesiology.
4. Explain the image of bride and groom in St. Bernard and the relationship of the many brides to the one bride.
5. Explain the relationship between the personal body of Christ and his ecclesial body.
6. What does Bernard say about the radical centralization of power in the hands of the Roman pontiff, and how does he say it?
7. Who is the symbol of the ministerial priesthood for Bernard, and why did Bernard choose this figure?
8. What does Thomas Aquinas say about the just men and women of the Old Testament regarding the church?
9. Why is the "true church" the heavenly church according to St. Thomas?
10. What is the most preponderant factor in the law of the New Testament according to St. Thomas? Why? What is the role of the other elements of the church?
11. What does St. Thomas mean by "one mystical person"?

Chapter 5

1. Without elaboration, list the causes of corruption in the church of the sixteenth century.
2. What was Luther's great discovery in the tower?
3. How did this discovery facilitate for Luther his abandonment of the magisterium?
4. What essential truths of revelation did Luther reject?
5. Why is the true church "hidden" for Luther?
6. How does Luther justify infant baptism?
7. What does Luther say about the priesthood?
8. Evaluate the article of the Augsburg Confession of Faith on the church from a Catholic perspective.
9. Show the inconsistency of Calvin regarding the visible church.
10. How did the Council of Trent respond to the Lutheran notion of the church?
11. Study and comment on Bellarmine's definition of the church.
12. In comparison with patristic ecclesiology, what is missing in this definition?

Chapter 6

1. Why did Vatican I deal only with the papacy and not treat the role of the bishops?
2. Why were Vatican I's definitions of the two dogmas on the papacy opportune for that time?
3. Explain the dogma on papal jurisdiction.
4. If every bishop has ordinary jurisdiction in his own diocese, what is the rationale for the pope's ordinary jurisdiction in each diocese of the church?
5. Explain the dogma on infallibility in opposition to the ultramontanist position.
6. How and why did Britain and Germany misinterpret the dogmas on the papacy?
7. Characterize briefly the various aspects of what Romano Guardini called "the awakening of the Church in the souls" of the twentieth century.

8. Explain the reaction of Pius XII in *Mystici Corporis* to the ecclesiological renewal. What are its well-developed themes and what was treated only in *Lumen Gentium*?

Chapter 7

1. How did John XXIII and Paul VI articulate the goals of Vatican II?
2. Compare the first draft and the final text of the Dogmatic Constitution on the Church and explain the salient points of the latter.

Chapter 8

1. What were the causes of the so-called postconciliar crisis in ecclesiology?
2. Draw up a "balance sheet" showing the positive developments and distortions of the postconciliar period in ecclesiology.
3. What are the achievements of the ecumenical movement? Why did it stall?

Chapter 9

1. Why do we need the church?
2. Explain the significance of Paul's handshake of communion with the three pillars (James, Peter, and John) for understanding the unity of the apostolic church.
3. Explain the trinitarian and anthropological bases for the unity of the church.
4. Explain the purpose of the essential external structures of the church.
5. How does Vatican II articulate the relationship of the Catholic Church to the church Christ has founded and to the other Christian denominations? Explain the Catholic view on the Orthodox churches.
6. How does the theory of "analogous participation" explain the above relationships.
7. Outline the controversies of the council around the verb *subsistit* and the reason why the council fathers chose this verb.
8. How would you translate the title of the Decree on Ecumenism (*Unitatis Redintegratio*)? Why so?

9. Outline the major achievements and major obstacles of the ecumenical movement beginning with the pontificate of St. John XXIII.

Chapter 10

1. Describe the different meanings of holiness in the Old Testament (ontological and ethical) and how the understanding of holiness developed.
2. How does Christ reveal his holiness before and after his resurrection?
3. How do you reconcile the Fathers' conviction that the church is a *columba sine macula* and yet consists of sinful members?
4. Give examples of the heresies that wanted to reduce the church to those who are "pure." Why has the Catholic Church always rejected such a trend? Explain Joseph Ratzinger's statement: "Is it not appropriate that the Church appear in inseparable communion with sin and with the sinners?"
5. What is preserved holy in the church regardless of the personal sins of the hierarchy and laity?
6. Why is holiness impossible outside the church, that is, without any link to the church?
7. In what sense can we say that the church will always remain holy, and in what sense can we say that the church is sinful?
8. Why is the holiness of the Christian(s) the most effective "weapon" of evangelization?

Chapter 11

1. Explain the meaning of catholicity according to Augustine, Cyril of Jerusalem, and St. Thomas.
2. Explain the foundations of catholicity in the Triune God and human nature.
3. If one can be saved outside the visible boundaries of the Catholic Church, what motivation remains for missionary activity?
4. Explain the polarities in the church's relationship to the world in Scripture and in church history, including Vatican II.

Chapter 12

1. Explain the apostolic mission in the New Testament and in the early history of the church (Clement of Rome, Ignatius of Antioch, Irenaeus, Tertullian).
2. Explain the theology of apostolicity relying mainly on Yves Congar's insights.
3. How is the Protestant understanding of apostolicity different from that of Catholic theology?
4. Narrate the many general indications in the Gospels of Peter's leadership role in the church.
5. Analyze in detail Matthew 16:13–23, Luke 22:24–34, and John 21:1–19.
6. Highlight the features from Galatians that show Paul knew the tradition of Matthew 16:16–19.
7. Characterize the relationship of Peter and Paul on the basis of Paul's Letters.
8. Characterize the relationship of Peter and Paul on the basis of the New Testament canon. Focus on 2 Peter.
9. Illustrate by mentioning several examples the emerging leadership role of the bishop of Rome in the early church. What were two ways that the bishop of Rome's primacy was exercised in the first four to six centuries?
10. Show evidence from the beginning of church history of the episcopal college.
11. What does Vatican II (including its "prefatory note") teach about the episcopal college?
12. Explain the collegial structure of the church on every level (pope-bishops, bishop-priests, pastor-parish). What is the purpose of this collegial structure?
13. Deduce from the nature of revelation and faith the need for the charism of infallibility in the church.
14. How can you show that the final criterion of revealed truth rests with the bishop of Rome along with the bishops in communion with him?
15. Explain the different branches of the magisterium and how we are expected to respond to each.

Chapter 13

1. Why is the sacrifice of Jesus the perfect sacrifice?
2. How does every baptized person practice their priesthood?
3. What is the special role of the ministerial priesthood and its relationship to the priesthood of all the faithful, in particular in the eucharistic celebration?
4. In what sense is Jesus *the* Prophet?
5. How do all of the people of God participate in the prophetic office of Christ?
6. Explain the *sensus fidei* of the people of God.
7. How does the above relate to the conceptually formulated truths of faith?
8. Comment on the role of the charisms in the life of the church.
9. Comment on the relationship of the charismatic and hierarchical structures of the church. Provide some examples from history.
10. Explain the relationship between earthly "progress" and the kingdom of God on the basis of magisterial documents (*Gaudium et Spes*, the encyclicals of popes, and the instructions of the Congregation for the Doctrine of the Faith).
11. Explain the role of the special charism of prophecy in the church. How is it practiced today?
12. Why is the enthronement of Jesus enacted by the crucifixion?
13. How do the people of God share in the royal dignity of Christ?
14. How does everything cooperate unto the good of Christians?

Chapter 14

1. Explain the twofold meaning of sacrament as applied to the church.
2. What happens to a community that rejects or neglects one of the two essential aspects of the church as sacrament?
3. Explain the relationship between the bridal aspect of the church and the mystical body.
4. What is the motherly role of the church and of each member of the church?
5. Show the parallelism between Mary's motherhood and the motherhood of the church.

6. In what sense is the church an ontological subject? How does it differ from a legal subject or a pantheistic union?
7. What basis do you find for the notion of the church as ontological subject in the Catholic tradition?
8. Show why the heavenly church is the *vera Ecclesia*, the "true church," and how does it differ from the earthly church?

Chapter 15

1. Explain the criteria of an authentic renewal in the church.
2. Show how *ressourcement* and *aggiornamento* complement each other.
3. Provide some examples of dogmatic development promoted by popular piety.
4. Explain the difference between legitimate enculturation and harmful adaptations in the liturgy.

Chapter 16

1. How is the ecclesial body of Christ perfected in the eschatological state?
2. Comment on the church's relationship to the Father in the eschatological state.
3. How do the images of the church as body of Christ, virgin, and mother complement and balance out the other in the eschatological state?
4. What guarantees a certain continuity between the present universe and the "new heaven and new earth"?
5. What purpose(s) will the material universe have in the eschatological state?

PART 3

Particular Themes in Ecclesiology

CHAPTER 17

The Unity of the Church in the Theology of Irenaeus

Unity, in its various forms and applications, is a central concern in Irenaeus's theology. This is only partly explained by his anti-Gnostic polemics. More fundamentally, it derives from the inner dynamism of his faith and theology. Over and against the various divine beings of the Gnostic systems and the two gods of Marcion, he emphasizes again and again that there is only one God, the Father of the one Jesus Christ. This one and the same God created humankind and planned our redemption from the very beginning. He revealed himself through his Word from the beginning of history, thereby preparing the coming of his Word in the flesh. Jesus Christ is truly one; he is both God and man. Contrary to the basic antiflesh thrust of Gnostic thought, Irenaeus stressed that the Word became flesh so that he might communicate his Spirit to our flesh. Thus, progressively transformed by the Spirit into the likeness of the Son, our humanity will be admitted to personal communion with the Father and filled with his life. In this way, the beginning is joined to the end, the first Adam is redeemed in the second, and God's creation is fully recapitulated through the Spirit in the Son and introduced into the Father's presence.

Where does the concept of the church fit into the Irenaean synthesis? He uses the term *ekklēsia* only for the central phase of salvation history; it is the community in and through which the Spirit communicates Christ to all humankind and transforms humankind into the body of Christ. Yet everything in the Old Testament prepares for the church, the people of Israel even anticipate it, and the church itself is the beginning and anticipation of the final consummation, the heavenly Jerusalem.

Irenaeus often uses the word in the singular, meaning the universal church scattered all over the world to its farthest ends. He also uses the same term about the church at a given place (*hē ekklēsia kata ton topon*); for instance, "the church in Rome" or the "church in Smyrna." By using the same term about the universal church and the local church without any further modification, he indicates that he considers these two things in some sense identical. The local church is the church at a given place, but only in communion with all the local churches.

The following discussion attempts to substantiate this tentative thesis: first by surveying the various forms and structures that show a basic identity of the church in both space and time and its intimate link with the people of Israel; then second, by exploring the ultimate foundations of the unity of the church in the Triune God and in human nature. Finally, the attitude and activity of Irenaeus with regard to the Paschal controversy under Pope Victor are outlined. This should provide some insights into how Irenaeus applied his theology of unity to church politics.

Forms and Structures of Church Unity

Irenaeus personally knew the church of Asia Minor, Rome, and Gaul, and he was acquainted with many of the heretical currents of his time. Thus he speaks about the unity of the "church everywhere," of "the church throughout the whole world," with a conviction that comes from personal experience.

According to Irenaeus, unity on various levels distinguishes the church from all the heresies that differ from each other and whose doctrines constantly change and fluctuate. But more than a distinctive mark that sets the church apart from heresies, unity reveals something so essential in the church that Irenaeus can hardly speak about the church without also elaborating on its unity. The same church organization appears everywhere: "the same shape of Church order";[1] "the ancient structure of the Church throughout the whole world."[2]

The unity of the church manifests itself not only in the same basic or-

1. Irenaeus, *Against Heresies* 5.20.1: "eandem figuram quae est erga Ecclesiam ordinationis." For the Latin and Greek texts of *Adversus Haereses*, I used the critical edition of Adelin Rousseau, Louis Doutreleau, and C. Mercier in Sources Chrétiennes 34, 100, 152–53, 210–11, 263–64 (Paris: Cerf, 1965–1979). For the English texts I used Alexander Roberts, James Donaldson, and A. Cleveland Cox, eds., *The Ante-Nicene Fathers* (1885–1887; repr., Peabody, Mass.: Hendrickson, 1994), vol. 1, with some corrections.

2. Irenaeus, *Against Heresies* 5.33.8: *to archaion tēs ekklēsias systēma kata pantos tou kosmou.*

ganization. A more fundamental unity orders the church everywhere in the world. Even though scattered and isolated like islands in the midst of a turbulent sea and suffering under the storm of blasphemies, the church is, as it were, one subject of action:

She . . . believes these points [the faith received from the apostles] just as if she had but one soul, and one and the same heart, and she proclaims them, and teaches them, and hands them down, with perfect harmony, as if she possessed only one mouth. For although the languages of the world are dissimilar, yet the import of the tradition is one and the same. For the Churches which have been planted in Germany do not believe or hand down anything different, nor do those in Spain, nor those in Gaul, nor those in the East, nor those in Egypt, nor those in Libya, nor those which have been established in the central regions of the world. But as the sun . . . is one and the same throughout the whole world, so also the preaching of the truth shines everywhere and enlightens all men that are willing to come to a knowledge of the truth.[3]

Only after discussing the foundations of the unity of the church in the Spirit and in Christ does Irenaeus clarify whether figures of speech such as "she [the church] had but one soul and one and the same heart" and "as if she possessed one mouth" are mere poetic images or, in fact, the church—in some real sense—must be seen as one personal subject.

Not only does the church appear as one agent in preserving and proclaiming the faith she has received, but it is also one subject in offering a pure sacrifice to God. Irenaeus, pointing to Malachi 1:10–11, stresses that a universal sacrifice is offered throughout the world. Yet in all the different places it is one and the same agent—the church—that offers it everywhere.[4]

The church is also viewed as one under the image of a mother. Those who separate themselves from the church are not nourished to life by her breasts.[5] The church appears most strikingly one in a text that describes the incarnation of the Son of God in the Virgin: "The pure One opening purely that pure womb, which regenerates men unto God and which He Himself made pure."[6]

The pure womb whom the Pure One purely opens is both the womb of Mary and the church. The womb of Mary gives birth to Jesus and continues

3. Irenaeus, *Against Heresies* 1.10.2.
4. Irenaeus, *Against Heresies* 4.17.6; 4.18.1; 4.18.4.
5. Irenaeus, *Against Heresies* 3.24.1; see also 3.25.7; *Apostolic Preaching* 94.
6. Irenaeus, *Against Heresies* 4.33.2; cf. also 4.33.4.

to give birth to the members of the church, but also the womb of the church gave birth in Mary to the firstborn of many brothers. The figures of Mary and the church interpenetrate and mutually contain one another.

The unity of the church implies that the church acts as one subject, but it also implies that the church has the same object of faith. The expressions that Irenaeus never tires of repeating manifest this: "one and the same faith," "one and the same doctrine," "one and the same way of salvation." Everyone in the church believes in one and the same God the Father; in one and the same plan of salvation leading to the incarnation of the Son of God. Everyone acknowledges the same gift of the Spirit, expects the same coming of the Lord, and waits for the same salvation of the whole person, body and soul.[7] However, this one and the same faith is not to be reduced to one verbally fixed creed or to a set number of propositions that would definitively and exhaustively summarize it. In *Against Heresies*, Irenaeus has various formulations of what the Christian faith or "the rule of truth" entails.[8] All of these, of course, display a basic conceptual unity. Yet the identity of Christian faith in every member of the church lies deeper than the convergence of slightly different conceptual formulations (even though these formulations are necessary to safeguard it). It seems that precisely the one reality of the object of faith gives rise to various conceptual formulations, depending on what heresies Irenaeus is combating in a given part of *Against Heresies*. That the oneness of faith transcends any fixed formula is most clearly articulated in 1.10.2:

> Nor will anyone of the superiors in the Churches, however powerful he may be in speech, say something different from these [truths of faith], for no one is greater than the Master; nor, on the other hand, will he who is deficient in power of speech diminish the tradition. For the faith being ever one and the same, neither does one who is able at great length to discourse regarding it, amplify it, nor does one, who can say but little, diminish it.

This one and the same faith, however, does not make further inquiry into the mysteries of faith superfluous. Some may know more, some less about these mysteries according to the wisdom (*synesis*) that comes from God. Irenaeus even presents a random list of questions that would warrant

7. Irenaeus, *Against Heresies* 5.20.1.

8. The main texts in which Irenaeus explains the rule of truth are: *Against Heresies* 1.10.1; 1.22.1; 2.11.1; 2.28.1; 2.30.9; 3.3.3; 3.4.2; 3.11.7; 3.15.3; 3.16.6; 4. 35.4.

further theological investigation, such as: to elucidate the meaning of the "parables" (the stories and images in the Scriptures) that require a spiritual interpretation; and to explain God's economy of salvation of humankind (mainly the "why" and the "how" of God's past, present, and future work in salvation history). Yet in all this, the theologians should not change the *hypothesis*, the groundwork of faith, which is centered on the one Triune God and his one economy of salvation for the sake of humanity. Nor can the Christian theologian dissolve the mystery into a conceptual system; his final act is not an act of knowing the truth (in the sense of Gnostic speculation), but of praise for God's unsearchable wisdom and impenetrable mystery.[9]

Besides the unity of faith, another distinctive mark for the church is its unity in morals. All members keep in mind the same precepts (*eadem meditantibus praecepta*). These precepts, given by the Word already in the Old Testament and fulfilled and extended by Christ, have as their goal the establishment of friendship between God and humankind, and also communion and concord based on justice and generous love among human beings. This is a morality of freedom. The Christians are, as it were, freed people. They no longer need the servitude of the ritual observances given by Moses that, through the body, induced the soul to obedience. The soul now moves freely, by itself, to purify the body. Just as a freed person has more devotion to their master than the slave, so has the Christian for God. They abstain now not only from evil acts, which the slave has done also, but also from evil words and desires;[10] in fact, they love and fear God now as their Father.[11]

The Identity of the Contemporary Church with the Church of the Apostles

So far, this work has surveyed the various forms, structures, and images that disclose the unity of the church as it is extended throughout the whole

9. Irenaeus, *Against Heresies* 1.10.2–3. For more on this digression about possible topics for theologizing, see W. C. Van Unnik, "An Interesting Document of Second Century Theological Discussion (Irenaeus, *Adv. Haer.* I.10.3)," *Vigiliae Christianae* 31 (1977):196–228. See also W. R. Schoedel, "Theological Method in Irenaeus," *Journal of Theological Studies*, (1984) 35:31–49.

10. Irenaeus, *Against Heresies* 4.13.1–2.

11. Irenaeus, *Against Heresies* 4.16.4. Of course, this morality is presented as an ideal. Irenaeus is aware that not every Christian lives it sincerely. Some of them are wolves disguised in sheep's clothing (4.15.2).

world. This unity extended in space is inseparably linked to the unity extended in time: the present church is the same everywhere because she is everywhere identical with the church of the apostles. In other words, the unity of the churches scattered throughout the world presupposes their identity with their beginnings. The unity of the church in space and her unity in time are correlative. As Irenaeus has concisely put it: Contrary to the heretics, "the Church throughout all the world, having its origin firm from the apostles, perseveres in one and the same doctrine with regard to God and His Son."[12]

According to Irenaeus, the apostles founded the churches or, in a stronger sense of the words, they laid down their foundations.[13] Then they handed over "the church at every place" to the bishops: "*quibus* [to the bishops] *illi* [the apostles] *eam quae in unoquoque loco est Ecclesiam tradiderunt.*"[14] Note that in Irenaeus's mind, they handed over not only the faith or doctrine, but the *church itself*; in other words, all those elements that make up the church. This is why Irenaeus believes that, at his time, not only the doctrine of the apostles, but also "the original structure of the church" exists everywhere in the world.[15]

There are certain essential elements that Irenaeus believed assured the identity of the church of his day with that of the apostles. Besides the apostolic preaching and the sacraments of baptism and the Eucharist, Irenaeus attributes great importance to the continuation of charisms. Both the church of the apostles and the church at the time of Irenaeus displayed an abundance of charisms, such as speaking in all the languages, revealing the secrets of humans for their benefit, explaining the mysteries of God,[16] healing the blind and the lame, and even raising the dead to life.[17] But more important than any other charism for Irenaeus is the gift of love. This had been present in the church from the beginning: "[Love] is more precious than knowledge (*gnosis*), more glorious than prophecy, and excels over all the other gifts. Wherefore the Church does in every place because

12. Irenaeus, *Against Heresies* 3.2.7.

13. Irenaeus, *Against Heresies* 3.3.1; 3.3.3–4. The term used to describe the founding of a church by an apostle is *themelioō* (laying down a foundation), whereas for founding churches in general, Irenaeus uses the verb *hidruō* (1.10.2).

14. Irenaeus, *Against Heresies* 4.33.8; see also 3.1.1; 3.1.19; 3.3.1; 3.4.1: 3.9.9.

15. Irenaeus, *Against Heresies* 4.33.8.

16. Irenaeus, *Against Heresies* 5.6.1.

17. Irenaeus, *Against Heresies* 2.31.1.

of that love which she cherishes towards God, send forward, throughout all time, a multitude of martyrs to the Father."[18] Again, the church is described here as one subject possessing the love of God and displaying this love in a multitude of martyrs. It is one and the same church who loves God in the martyrs throughout the ages and everywhere in the world.

Thus the church of Irenaeus's day did not possess only certain charisms of the church of the apostles. For Irenaeus, the church of the apostles is identical with that of his age because *all* of the gifts of the former are available in the church of his time. A telling image of the church is the wife of Lot turned into a pillar of salt that endures forever: "The Church also, which is the salt of the earth, has been left behind within the confines of the earth, and subject to human sufferings. And while entire members are again and again taken away from it, the pillar of salt still endures, which is the foundation of faith, strengthening and sending forward children to their Father."[19]

What assures this identity throughout time is the historic continuity of all the churches with the churches founded by the apostles in Asia Minor, Greece, and especially with the church in Rome, which was founded and built up by Peter and Paul, who suffered martyrdom there as well.[20]

The guarantee against any distortion of the apostolic doctrine is the charism of truth, which has been preserved in the church by the presbyter-bishops, to whom the apostles handed over their mission of teaching: "*suum ipsorum locum magisterii tradentes*."[21] Yet from another viewpoint, the groundwork and foundation of the church are the four written forms of the Gospel that support the church throughout the ages. The presbyters do not teach something else that is not to be found in the Scriptures, but rather explain and confirm it.[22]

18. Irenaeus, *Against Heresies* 4.33.8–9.

19. Irenaeus, *Against Heresies* 4.31.3.

20. Irenaeus, *Against Heresies* 3.3.2. See Gustave Brady, *La Théologie de l'Église de saint Clement de Rome à saint Irénée* [The Theology of the Church from St. Clement of Rome to St. Irenaeus] (Paris: Cerf, 1945), 198–200, 204–10; K. Baus, *From the Apostolic Community to Constantine*, Handbook of Church History 1 edited by Hubert Jedin and John Dolan (New York: Herder & Herder, 1965): 356–357; also Emmanuel Lanne, "L'Église de Rome 'a gloriosissimis duobus apostolis Petro et Paulo Romae fundatae et constitutae ecciesiae' (Adv. Haer. 3.3.2)," *Irénikon* 49 (1976): 275–322.

21. Irenaeus, *Against Heresies* 3.3.1; 4.26.5. The succession of presbyter-bishops is intimately connected in Irenaeus's mind not only with the uncorrupted purity of the word but also with an irreproachable integrity of life (4.26.5). The presbyters within the Catholic Church have higher moral standards than those of the heretics and schismatics. According to him, the leaders of the latter "who pass for presbyters in the eyes of many" are enslaved by their passions, conceited because of their first place in the assembly and do evil in secret (4.26.3).

22. Cf. J. R. Geiselmann, *Die heilige Schrift und die Tradition* [Holy Scripture and Tradition] (Freiburg:

Irenaeus insists that the Word gave us a "fourfold Gospel bound together by one Spirit."[23] The Gospel is one, just as the person and the activity of the Word through salvation history is one and the same. Yet there are four written Gospels, each with a distinct form or character (*species*, *persona*, or *charaktēr*) manifesting a particular aspect of the personality and activity of the Word.[24]

That Irenaeus accepts all four Gospels as the columns on which the church is built shows the breadth of his vision of unity.[25] He is the first church father who clearly makes use of all four Gospels that emerged from and were first used in different milieus of the early church. He consciously accepts that they diverge, rather than opting for one version against the other. This broad "ecumenical" basis of Irenaeus's Christianity is in sharp contrast with Marcion's exclusive use of Luke as *the* one Gospel in his canon of sacred books.

The Two Peoples

As mentioned earlier, Irenaeus uses the term *ekklēsia* only for the people of the new covenant before its final consummation in the heavenly Jerusalem. Yet the whole of humankind from the beginnings of history is related to the church. Abel, the symbol of the just man murdered unjustly, anticipates the harvest of the church.[26]

There is a particularly close link and correspondence between the Israel of the Old Testament and the church. Their unity and sameness are expressed by these terms: "prophets and apostles," "the older and the younger people," and "the two assemblies" (*synagogae*). However, when he wants to show that they are different, they are opposed to each other as "the people" and "the church."[27]

Herder, 1962), 222: "Die heilige Schrift . . . ist der nachfolgende schriftliche Niederschlag des vorausgehenden mündlich verkündeten Evangeliums, Fundament und Säule unseres Glaubens. Die heiligen Schriften . . . sind volkomrnen, weil vom Worte Gottes und seinerm Geiste diktiert. Irenaeus beruft sich zwar des öfteren auch auf das Zeugnis der Presbyteroi . . . Allein, ihr Zeugnis ist nicht eine Ergänzung der Heiligen Schrift, sondern ihre Bestätigung." See also Douglas Powell, "Ordo Presbyterii," *Journal of Theological Studies* 26, no. 2 (1975): 290–328.

23. Irenaeus, *Against Heresies* 3.11.8: *tetramorphon to euangēlion heni de pneumati synechomenon*; cf. also 3.1.1.

24. Irenaeus, *Against Heresies* 3.11.8–9. For more on the unity and diversity of the four Gospels, see Denis Farkasfalvy, "Theology of Scripture in St. Irenaeus," *Revue Bénédictine* 78, vols. 3–4 (1968): 329–30.

25. Irenaeus, *Against Heresies* 3.11.8.

26. Irenaeus, *Against Heresies* 4.34.4.

27. Irenaeus, *Against Heresies* 4.28.1.

The prophets proclaim the same message as the apostles. In fact, Irenaeus calls the prophets "the members of Christ," because each shows in himself or prophesies some aspect of Christ in some aspect of his work. Taken together as a whole, they sketch out in advance (*praeformantes*) the *whole* Christ and *all* his work.[28] This "sketching out in advance" (*praefiguratio, praeformatio*) of the whole mystery of Christ in the Old Testament through the life and words of the prophets is so complete that if one compares the gospel given by the apostles and the prophets, "you will find the whole activity, the whole doctrine, and the whole passion of our Lord predicted in them [the books of the Old Testament]."[29]

Just as Christ is prefigured in the prophets, so is the church: "Just as in the first [economy of God] we were prefigured and announced beforehand, so do they [the patriarchs and prophets] receive their perfect form in us; that is, in the Church and receive the reward for their labors."[30] Both peoples issued from Abraham, but only the church, the object of God's promises to him, is his true seed.[31] Abraham is not only a prophet for the church but also the father of all who believe.[32]

The two peoples, the older being Israel of the Old Testament and the younger being the church of the New Testament, are prefigured in the twin brothers Esau and Jacob, Perez and Zerah of Tamar, the two wives of Jacob, and the two daughters of Lot.[33] The older people were subjected to servitude through the law so they could be prepared for the coming of Christ; the younger enjoyed the freedom of friendship with God. The older people sowed, the younger reaped the harvest; the older people announced and prefigured Christ, while the younger were gathered together by Christ in person. Yet both peoples were made fertile by Christ. Both synagogues gave birth to living sons for the living God by receiving "the vital seed of the Spirit" from Christ in his passion and death.[34]

When the Son came in the flesh, the older people (prefigured by Esau) rejected him, but the younger one (prefigured by Jacob) accepted him and inherited all the blessings of the older one.[35] While now all the pagan na-

28. Irenaeus, *Against Heresies* 4.33.10.
29. Irenaeus, *Against Heresies* 4.34.1.
30. Irenaeus, *Against Heresies* 4.22.2.
31. Irenaeus, *Against Heresies* 4.7.1; 4.8.1.
32. Irenaeus, *Against Heresies* 4.20.12.
33. Irenaeus, *Against Heresies* 4.21.2; 4.24.2; 4.21.2; 4.31.2.
34. Irenaeus, *Against Heresies* 4.21.3; 4.31.2.
35. Irenaeus, *Against Heresies* 4.21. 2; see also 3.21.1.

tions participate in God's life, fleshly Israel is excluded from inheriting the grace of God and no longer possesses the Spirit.[36]

Yet the church remains a union of those who were far off and those who were close, of pagans and Jews. The two arms of Christ extended on the cross symbolize the two peoples dispersed to the ends of the world. By extending his arms, Christ, who is the head of both, unites them to one God through himself.[37]

The church is then the goal and fulfillment of the economy of the Old Testament: the seed promised to Abraham, the harvest grown out of what the patriarchs and prophets have sown, the manifestation in herself of the reality of Christ whom the prophets announced and prefigured. But in her turn, the church also moves toward fulfillment, the realization of the promises of Christ in the heavenly Jerusalem.

The Relationship between the Unity of the Church and the Unity of the Father, Son, and Holy Spirit

The church, as a complexus of distinct structures, is not in the center of Irenaeus's theology. His main concern is to show the unity of the Triune God and to present a unified history of salvation constituted by the one God. This history consists of several stages, but every stage leads toward a recapitulation of all creation in heaven and on earth in Christ, the Word made flesh. In him humankind reaches its full growth when, by participating in the sonship of the Son, it is introduced into the Father's presence.

This ascent begins and is "propelled," so to speak, by the Spirit who is most directly and inseparably linked with the church since this is the sphere where he is present and active: "where the Church is, there is the Spirit."[38] The gift of the Holy Spirit includes all the charisms, but in particular those of prophecy, by which the church teaches the truth and, the highest gift of all, the love of God by which the martyrs of the church bear witness to the truth.[39]

The Holy Spirit, who gives life to the whole church and every member in the church, is the ultimate reason why the church believes everywhere

36. Irenaeus, *Against Heresies* 3.21.1; 3.17.2.
37. Irenaeus, *Against Heresies* 3.5.3.
38. Irenaeus, *Against Heresies* 3.24.1.
39. Irenaeus, *Against Heresies* 3.24.1.

in the same way, teaches everywhere one and the same faith, practices everywhere the same morality and loves God to the point of martyrdom. Nor are expressions that refer to the church as teaching everywhere "as it were with one mouth" or possessing everywhere "one soul and one and the same heart" mere poetic hyperbole. And neither is speaking of the church as one subject a mere legal fiction. The same transcendent principle operates in each and every member of the church so that in some very real sense the church is indeed one and is one subject of action. Moreover, since the same Holy Spirit is present in every local church and in the whole church, then indeed the whole church is truly present in every local church.

The Spirit is ultimately also responsible for the unity of the four Gospels: "The Word ... gave us a fourfold gospel which is bound together by one Spirit."[40] The inspiration of the Spirit also explains why the object of the messages of both the prophets and the apostles is identical. Both groups proclaim Christ.[41]

The Spirit is the ultimate basis for the identity between the churches founded by the apostles and the churches at the time of Irenaeus: He, the Spirit, constantly rejuvenates the faith of the church and "its container," the structures of the church.[42]

Yet the church is not a "magic container" of the Spirit. One can be in the church and not be vivified by the Spirit. As discussed previously, some Christians live a Christian life only outwardly. Those who fear God and trust him "make the Spirit of God dwell in their hearts through faith."[43]

When Irenaeus views the incarnation from a universal perspective as uniting all humankind to the Word, recapitulating everything in him, he speaks about the union or communion (*tēn henosin kai koinōnian*) of flesh and Spirit or man and Spirit.[44] The concrete way of achieving this intimate bond between flesh (weak, mortal humanity devoid of divine life) and the Spirit is the Eucharist. In the Eucharist, Christians proclaim the "union and communion of flesh and spirit."[45] By these terms Irenaeus does not mean a personal relationship of communication and partnership between the

40. Irenaeus, *Against Heresies* 3.11.8.

41. See Farkasfalvy, "Theology of Scripture," 331–32.

42. Irenaeus, *Against Heresies* 3.24.1: "quam [fidem] perceptam ab Ecclesia custodimus, et quae semper a Spiritu Dei quasi in vaso bono eximium quoddam depositum iuvenescens et iuvenescere faciens ipsum vas in quo est."

43. Irenaeus, *Against Heresies* 5.9.2.

44. Irenaeus, *Against Heresies* 5.9.4; 5.9.2; 5.11.1.

45. Irenaeus, *Against Heresies* 4.18.5.

Holy Spirit and humankind. In the words of Stuart Dickson Curie: "What is meant is that sort of permeation by which, for example, heat penetrates, diffuses throughout, and becomes mingled with an object so that a common unity is formed."[46]

The Spirit becomes the immanent principle of divine life within the human being. He penetrates and transforms the flesh "so that the flesh forgets itself and assumes the quality of the Spirit."[47] Participation in the Spirit is so real that the Holy Spirit in fact does become our spirit, completes our humanity and leads us to full maturity through the vision of God. Already in the here and now "we see, hear, and speak" through him; that is, we know the Father, hear the voice of the Son, and bear witness to our faith.[48] Even now, the Spirit, who is divine life itself, is already making our flesh capable of incorruption and immortality.[49] Already in our earthly life we can "mix" the power of the Spirit with the weakness of the flesh so that our weakness is absorbed by his power. Thus "spiritualized," the Christian becomes capable of martyrdom. The weakness of the flesh overcome shows forth the power of the Spirit.[50] Yet this most intimate union does not abolish the distinction between the creature and God, between humankind and the Spirit. Even the "spiritual person" transformed by the Spirit remains a creature of God, who through the good pleasure of the Father participates in divine life.[51] The Spirit, however, is strictly divine and not a creature. Rather, together with the Word, the Spirit is the "offspring" (*progenies*) of the Father.[52] Thus, while being totally immanent to humankind, the Spirit is also totally above humankind: He is humanity's "head."[53] Humankind cannot lay any claim on him; he is essentially a "gift of God."[54] He is both inside and outside humanity: *circumdans intus et foris hominem.*[55]

Does the Spirit show himself as a person in this communion? Sometimes Irenaeus does attribute personal acts to him: He compares the Spirit

46. Stuart Dickson Curie, "Koinonia in Christian Literature to 200 AD" (Ph.D. diss, Emory University, 1962), 219.

47. Irenaeus, *Against Heresies* 5.9.3.

48. Irenaeus, *Against Heresies* 5.20.2.

49. Irenaeus, *Against Heresies* 5.12.1; 4.18.5.

50. Irenaeus, *Against Heresies* 5.9.2.

51. Irenaeus, *Against Heresies* 5.3.5.

52. Irenaeus, *Against Heresies* 4.7.4.

53. Irenaeus, *Against Heresies* 5.20.2.

54. Irenaeus, *Against Heresies* 3.24.1: *Dei munus*.

55. Irenaeus, *Against Heresies* 5.12.2.

to a bridegroom who takes delight in his bride, assumes and possesses his bride. He is the Living One par excellence who inherits the corruptible members of humankind in order to transfer them into the kingdom of heaven.[56] We might say that in Irenaeus's mind the Holy Spirit has some personal qualities, but unlike the Father and the Son he lacks, so to speak, a distinct "personal character." He does not imprint his own image on us, but leads us to the Son.

Briefly, communion with the Spirit is *communicatio Christi*: an imparting of communion with Christ.[57] This means both personal communion with him and being conformed to his image. The Spirit is the agent who brings about the process of conformation to Christ.[58] However, he does not work on isolated individuals, but rather on the whole church, which is being "configured to the image of the Son"[59] and participates in his sonship as adopted sons.[60] This conformation to Christ is as real and as radical in Irenaeus as it is in St. Paul. Through the Holy Spirit we become members of the body of Christ in the sense that Christ truly identifies himself with us. He dwells in us; expresses his traits in us. And our mortal, frail, and earthly body—in a word, our flesh—becomes members of Christ.[61]

Christ is also the head of his body, the church. This means not only the rule of Christ over his church, but also that the body must follow the head; it must share in his passion, death, and resurrection.[62]

The identification of the church with Christ as his body never blurs the distinction between Christ and the church. The types of the church in the Old Testament show that the union between the church and Christ should be understood as analogous to the union of husband and wife. For example, the wedding between Moses and the Ethiopian woman prefigured the wedding between Christ and the church gathered together from the gentiles.[63] Jacob's enduring many years of labor for the beautiful Rachel prefigures Christ, who endured the cross for his bride, the church.[64] Hosea's taking a prostitute for his wife and sanctifying her by this union is an image

56. Irenaeus, *Against Heresies* 5.9.4.
57. Irenaeus, *Against Heresies* 3.24.1.
58. Irenaeus, *Against Heresies* 5.9.1.
59. Irenaeus, *Against Heresies* 4.37.7.
60. Irenaeus, *Against Heresies* 3.18.7.
61. Irenaeus, *Against Heresies* 5.6.2; cf. 3.25.7.
62. Irenaeus, *Against Heresies* 4.24.4; 3.19.3.
63. Irenaeus, *Against Heresies* 4.20.12.
64. Irenaeus, *Against Heresies* 4.21.3.

of Christ, who, by uniting himself to the church of sinners, sanctifies her by this communion.[65] The spiritual union between Christ and the church is fertile. As explained above, on the cross, Christ communicates the vital seed of the Spirit to his bride, thereby enabling the church to engender children for God.[66] Thus the church, through her union with Christ, gains, as it were, a distinct "personal" identity vis-à-vis Christ as a loving spouse and fertile mother. Because of her union with Christ through the Holy Spirit, the church truly mediates salvation to the world.[67]

The dynamism of ascent to God does not stop at union with the Son. Its final goal is personal communion with the Father. The new person perfected by the Spirit, conformed to the image of the Son, ascends to the Father, becomes filled with his vision and life, and begins an eternally new dialogue of friendship with him: *novus homo . . . semper nove confabulans Deo.*[68]

The whole human race is called into this communion with the Father through the one Spirit and through the one Son in the church. Irenaeus's perspective is so universal and so much centered on the Trinity that we may formulate the center of his ecclesiology in anthropological and trinitarian terms: the church is nothing else but humanity renewed by the Spirit, regaining the lost likeness of the Son and reaching full perfection and maturity in communion with the Father.

The union of all humankind with the Triune God is possible only because the human race is one: *unum genus humanum in quo perficiuntur mysteria Dei.*[69] Irenaeus must stress the unity of humankind, over against the Gnostic division of humankind into various groups descending from various divine beings.[70] The one and the same common nature in every person enables Irenaeus to extend the saving activity of the Word to all humankind.

The Son, being present to his own handiwork from the beginning, reveals the Father to all; to whom he wills, and when he wills, and as the Father wills. Wherefore, then, in all things, and through all things, there is one God, the Father, and one Word, and one Son, and one Spirit, and one salvation to all who believe in him.[71]

65. Irenaeus, *Against Heresies* 4.20.12.

66. Irenaeus, *Against Heresies* 4.31.2; 3.25.7.

67. On the theology of the church as mother, see Karl Delahaye, *Ekklesia Mater chez les Pères des trois premiers siècles* (Paris: Cerf, 1964), 46.

68. Irenaeus, *Against Heresies* 5.36.1; cf. 3.18.7; 5.36.2.

69. Irenaeus, *Against Heresies* 5.26.3.

70. See for instance Irenaeus, *Against Heresies* 3.15.2. On the various types of men in Gnosticism, see A. Orbe, "La definicion del hombre en la teologia del s. II," *Gregorianum* 48 (1967): 522–76.

71. Irenaeus, *Against Heresies* 4.6.7.

Having surveyed Irenaeus's conception of the unity of the church, his severe judgment on heresies and schisms is not surprising. Those who refuse the faith of the church, who do not participate in her life, cannot participate in the Spirit, since "the Spirit is where the Church is"; they cannot have the truth since the Spirit is truth; they cannot have eternal life since the Spirit alone gives life.[72]

Irenaeus and the Paschal Controversy

Irenaeus has harsh words for those who cause schisms in the Church:

> [The spiritual man] will judge those who give rise to schisms, who are destitute of the love of God, and who look to their own special advantage rather than to the unity of the Church; and who for trifling reasons, or any kind of reason which occurs to them, cut in pieces and divide the great and glorious body of Christ, and so far as in them lies, destroy it—men who prate of peace while they give rise to war, and do in truth strain out a gnat, but swallow a camel. For no reform of so great importance can come from them as will compensate for the damage arising from the schism.[73]

He must be referring here to one or several people who, for the sake of a reform, caused divisions in the universal church. ("The great and glorious body of Christ" manifestly denotes the whole church rather than a local assembly.) B. Reynders and, following him, Emmanuel Lanne think that the above text refers to the decision of Pope Victor to excommunicate all the churches that did not accept the Roman tradition of celebrating Easter on the Sunday following the Jewish Passover.[74] At the time, Eusebius showed that Victor's imposition of the Roman custom (which had been adopted by a majority of the churches already) on those that celebrated Easter according to what they claimed was the apostolic tradition of the fourteenth of Nisan did not please all the bishops: "They replied with a request that he [Victor] would turn his mind to the things that make for peace and for unity and love towards his neighbors. We still possess the words of these

72. Irenaeus, *Against Heresies* 3.24.1.

73. Irenaeus, *Against Heresies* 4.33.7.

74. See Emmanuel Lanne, "L'Église de Rome 'a gloriosissimis duobus apostolis Petro et Paulo Romae fundatae et constitutae ecciesiae.' Adv. Haer. III.3.2," *Irénikon* 49 (1976): 309–11; and B. Reynders, "Premières réactions de l'Église devant les falsifications du dépot apostolique: Saint Irénée: L'infaillibilité de LÉglise," in *Journées oecuméniques de Chevetogne, 25–29 septembre 1961*, ed. O. Rousseau et al. (Chevetogne, 1962), 48–50.

men who very sternly rebuked Victor."[75] From among these letters, Eusebius mentions only those of Irenaeus. Irenaeus agrees with Victor that one should indeed celebrate the mystery of the resurrection on Sunday, but he disagrees with Victor's policy of excommunicating the dissenters. As Eusebius summarizes it: "[Irenaeus] gave Victor a great deal of excellent advice, in particular that he should not cut off entire churches of God because they observed the unbroken tradition of their predecessors."[76]

Irenaeus also reminded Victor of the tolerant practice of his predecessors who all lived in peace with the churches that celebrated Easter differently from them. He describes in detail the visit of Polycarp to Anicetus. Eusebius quotes verbatim this part of Irenaeus's letter to Victor:

> When blessed Polycarp paid a visit to Rome in Anicetus' time, though they had minor differences on other matters too, they at once made peace, having no desire to quarrel on this point—Anicetus could not persuade Polycarp not to keep the day since he had always kept it with John the disciple of our Lord and the other apostles with whom he had been familiar; nor did Polycarp persuade Anicetus to keep it: Anicetus said that he must stick to the practice of the presbyters before him. Though the position was such, they remained in communion with each other, and in church Anicetus made way for Polycarp to celebrate the Eucharist—out of respect obviously. They parted company in peace, and the whole Church was at peace, both those who kept the day and those who did not.[77]

Seemingly, Irenaeus's letter was effective. The churches of Asia Minor celebrated Easter according to the quartodeciman tradition for more than a century longer, and they remained in communion with Rome.

Thus, Irenaeus's attitude on church unity is nuanced. He insists unceasingly on unity in the essentials, but he also insists on tolerating differences in traditions that do not concern the "one and the same faith." He testifies to the unique authority of the church of Rome, with whom every church must agree in matters of faith, but at the same time he opposes and (if the passage in *Against Heresies* is indeed directed against Pope Victor) condemns vigorously the attempt of Rome to impose her discipline on the universal church. It seems that precisely his theology of a unity based on

75. Eusebius of Caesarea, *Hist. eccl.* 5.24.10. For the Eusebius texts I have quoted from the translation of G. A. Williamson: Eusebius, *The History of the Church: From Christ to Constantine* (Baltimore: Penguin, 1965).

76. Eusebius of Caesarea, *Hist. eccl.* 5.24.11.

77. Eusebius of Caesarea, *Hist. eccl.* 5.24.16–17.

the transcendent unity of God lets him tolerate and accept different customs where there was no danger to the unity of faith. As he himself put it with admirable precision: "the divergency in the fast emphasizes the unanimity of our faith."[78]

Conclusions

Irenaeus is keenly aware of the unity of the church. He emphasizes it in contrast to the multiplicity and diversity of heretical groups. Yet, rather than simply an apologetical concern, his understanding of the unity of the church derives from the central tenet of his theology: humankind is recapitulated by the Spirit into Christ so that humankind may come to maturity and have communion and friendship with the Father.

From Irenaeus's perspective, the one universal church does not consist of local churches in the way that a whole consists of its parts. He does not envision the universal church (as later Western ecclesiology will) as one universal social body whose members are the local churches and whose head is the pope.[79] For him the church is primarily not a social body, but the body of Christ identified in some real sense with the personal reality of Christ crucified and risen. The members of the body are individual Christians in whose physical bodies Christ dwells through his Spirit. The head of the body is always Christ.

Irenaeus uses the same term for the universal church and the local church because, in some sense, the two are identical. A survey of the most important ecclesiological texts of Irenaeus shows that to him *the* church with all its essential elements is present in every local church. Each and every local church possesses the same ecclesial reality, the same faith, the same church order, the same Eucharist. But above all, each and every local church possesses the fullness of the Holy Spirit with all his gifts; each and every local church is the body of Christ, displays the traits of the Son, and is on the way toward the Father. The sameness of this full ecclesial reality and,

78. Eusebius of Caesarea, *Hist. eccl.* 5.24.13.

79. A typical text of Johannes Andreae is quoted by Yves Congar: "Ecclesia universalis est unum Christi corpus . . . cuius caput est Romana ecclesia: inferiorae [*sic*] ecclesiae sunt hujus capitis membra, quae sunt vel membra ex capite, vel membra ex membris ("Autonomie et pouvoir central dans l'Église vus par la théologie catholique" [Autonomy and central power in the church as viewed by Catholic theology], *Irénikon* 53 [1980]: 291–313).

in particular, the presence of the Holy Spirit (whose role is to make one out of the many) in each local church demands an intimate union among the local churches and proscribes any attempt to break up their communion for "a trifling reason."

The church is one and the same not only everywhere in space but also throughout history. The guarantee of this identity in time is twofold. On one hand is the tangible historical guarantee of the succession of presbyter-bishops from the apostles, and the agreement in essentials of all the local churches with the churches founded by the apostles and, in particular, with the church of Rome. On the other hand, the ultimate guarantor is the Holy Spirit who abides in the church.

Even though Irenaeus does not use the term, his conception of the church is clearly sacramental. The tangible, visible structures are the locus and the means in and through which the Holy Spirit furthers communion through the Son with the Father. This communion begins here on earth, but the same structures, such as the harmony of many in the one faith, the Eucharist, and the love of God expressing itself in brotherly love, are also the initial expressions and the beginning of the realization of the eternal communion in the heavenly Jerusalem.

Irenaeus is the first church father who possesses most elements for a future ecclesiological synthesis. His insistence on preserving, balancing, and unifying so many diverse elements is of great ecumenical significance today. Many aspects of his ecclesiology were further developed and differentiated in later ages, but more often than not this happened at the expense of *the whole*. For instance, Western Latin ecclesiology developed a concern that the faith of all the churches must agree with the faith of the church of Rome, while neglecting Irenaeus's collegial rebuke of Victor for *imposing* a uniform discipline on all the churches. The Eastern Orthodox churches elaborated on Irenaeus's assumption that the universal church is present in every local church, but rejected his insistence on a normative center for all the local churches. Catholic ecclesiology further refined Irenaeus's doctrine on the importance of apostolic succession, but for many years his emphasis on the variety of charisms in the church was passed over in silence. On the other end of the spectrum, Protestant churches retained the importance of charisms, but deemphasized the apostolic succession of office. Congregational churches stressed the primacy of the local assembly versus universal church structures, while forgetting that a local church is not only a gathering of people, but truly one subject in preaching the Word and in offering the Eucharist to God.

That Irenaeus was capable of holding on to all these elements without sacrificing one at the expense of the others remains a challenge for the contemporary Christian theologian, who today faces a similar ecumenical task of integrating all the aspects of the church of Christ.

CHAPTER 18

A Catholic Perspective on the Mission of Israel

In the second volume of his book *Jesus of Nazareth*, Joseph Ratzinger, writing not as pope but as a theologian, makes the rather startling statement that in the present time, until the fullness of the gentiles enters the church, "Israel retains its mission," and that "Israel is in the hands of God who will save it as 'a whole' at a proper time when the number of the Gentiles is complete."[1] Ratzinger bases his statement on the Pauline view of the history of salvation as sketched out in Romans 9–11. What is new in his position is the positive affirmation, only implicit in Paul, that during the time of the gentiles "Israel retains its mission." In the context of Ratzinger's theology of history, this cannot mean two parallel covenants, whereby Israel has a special way of salvation apart from Christ. Ratzinger has always maintained the universal salvific role of Christ for all human beings. There is only one covenant, he states,[2] but it has several stages in history, each directed toward Christ, fulfilled in him and made effective by him. The Mosaic covenant, then, was and is salvific for the Jews in good faith who express their trust in God's promise of redemption by their obedience to the Mosaic law. To clarify this topic, consider this quotation from Ratzinger's book mentioned above, which explains his statement on the interim mission of Israel: "[The] question of Israel's mission has always been present in the

1. Joseph Ratzinger (Pope Benedict XVI), *Jesus of Nazareth*, vol. 2, *Holy Week: From the Entrance into Jerusalem to the Resurrection* (San Francisco: Ignatius, 2011), 44, 46. The pope does not imply here that individual conversions from Judaism are to be discouraged. In his writings he emphasizes the church's universal mandate of evangelization.

2. See Joseph Ratzinger, *Many Religions, One Covenant* (San Francisco: Ignatius, 1999).

background [of Catholic theology]. We realize today with horror how many misunderstandings with grave consequences have weighed down our history. Yet a new reflection can acknowledge that the beginnings of a correct understanding have always been there, waiting to be discovered, however deep the shadows."[3]

What follows is an exploration of some of the "deep shadows" as well as the "beginnings of a correct understanding" of the past two millennia. In addition, a tentative and partial outline is proposed of a reflection on "what waits to be discovered" regarding the mission of Israel.[4]

The View of Israel's Mission in the New Testament

For those familiar with St. Paul's explanation of Israel's role in God's plan of salvation, Ratzinger's position may not be too surprising. In Romans 9–11, Paul outlines the complex relationship between Israel and the church, as well as Israel's past, present, and future in the light of his christocentric view of history. Even though "a hardening has come upon Israel in part" on account of its unbelief, this will last only "until the full number of the Gentiles comes in, and thus all Israel will be saved" (11:25–26). In the meantime, Israel is both an enemy of the Christians with respect to the gospel and "beloved" by God "because of the patriarchs" (11:28). The Israel of the Old Testament is the "noble olive tree," and the gentile Christians are the "wild olive shoots" who are grafted onto it, nourished by the rich sap of the root that supports them (11:17–24). Even the branches that were broken off on account of their unbelief may be grafted on again if they do not remain in unbelief (11:20, 23). Paul seals his affirmation of God's enduring love for Israel by stating that "the gifts and the call of God are irrevocable" (11:29).

Paul is not alone in the New Testament in his showing forth of the enduring importance and final "acceptance" and salvation of "all Israel" (Rom 11:15, 26).[5] Each of the four Gospels, in its own way, affirms or at least implies the enduring presence of Israel and its salvation at the end

3. Ratzinger, *Many Religions, One Covenant*, 44.

4. In this chapter, I use the term "Israel" in the sense of religious Jews, faithful to the first covenant, rather than the state of Israel. I also talk about "Catholic" rather than "Christian" attitudes toward Israel since in Protestant Christianity there is a widely divergent range of views on the relationship between Judaism and Christianity.

5. It is not clear what "acceptance" (*proslēmpsis*) means in the text: acceptance into the kingdom of God, into the church, or Israel's acceptance of the gospel?

of history. Matthew, written for Jewish Christians, draws a stark picture of Israel's unbelieving *elite* by presenting the parable of the wicked tenants of the vineyard. He also denounces the sins of the scribes and Pharisees in a passionate discourse on the terrible judgment awaiting them and the temple. Yet after his sevenfold woe of condemnation, he finishes his address by announcing, "I tell you, you will not see me again until you say: Blessed is he who comes in the name of the Lord" (Mt 23:39). In Matthew, unlike in Luke, this prophecy cannot refer to his triumphant entry into Jerusalem (21:9), since he has already entered the city. Being placed before the eschatological discourse, it must mean his coming at the end of this age.

Moreover, the angel's message to Joseph before the birth of Jesus, "You are to name him Jesus because he will save his people from their sins" (1:21) is a divine promise that must ultimately be fulfilled. God's design to save Israel is irrevocable. In fact, his saving plan for Israel is revealed paradoxically by the shouting of the "whole people" before Pilate: "His blood is on us and on our children" (Mt 27:25). The bloodthirsty crowd, of course, is unaware that Jesus' blood cries out not for vengeance, but for mercy and forgiveness. The saving power of his blood had been already manifested by Jesus to the disciples at the Last Supper, when he pronounced the words over the chalice: "For this is my blood of the covenant, which is to be poured out for many unto the remission of sins" (26:28). In the "for many," all humankind is included and yet, before the gentiles, Jesus' saving blood is offered to, and falls upon, Israel.[6]

As seen above, Jesus in Matthew's Gospel predicts that Jerusalem will accept him as her Messiah at the end. The evangelist, however, goes on to suggest even more. In harmony with the early kerygma, the evangelist sees in Jesus the embodiment of the final, eschatological Israel. This needs some explanation. The Servant in the four Songs of Isaiah refers to both an individual and also to Israel in a collective sense (Is 49:3). The Son of Man in Daniel 7 also designates both an individual heavenly being who accedes to the throne of the Ancient of Days (7:13–14) and the "holy ones of the Most High" (7:18, 21–22), the collective Israel of the end times. This does not create any confusion in Hebrew thought, since those who represent the

6. Paul also respects this *Heilsgeschichtliche* priority, which follows from God's plan: "[The gospel] is the power of God for the salvation of everyone who believes: for Jew first, and then the Greek" (Rom 1:16). The same priority of Israel is expressed by Paul's way of acting in Acts. He first visits the synagogue in every city and only goes over to the gentiles after the Jews refuse to listen to him.

people, such as ancestors, kings, and prophets, can naturally be identified with the people; they embody, as it were, Israel in themselves. If, then, Jesus is the Servant who through his suffering has become the glorious Son of Man, he is not merely one of the Israelites, but the new, eschatological Israel. Hence, this new perspective clarifies that, through being called back from Egypt (Hos 11:1 as interpreted by Mt 2:15), through his temptations and also through his public ministry, Jesus relives the historic experience of Israel. This identification of Jesus with Israel is already prepared in the ancient kerygma, quoted by Paul in 1 Corinthians 15:3–7. In this perspective, far from being contrived, the application of Hosea 6:1–3 to the resurrection of Jesus on the third day (v. 4) sheds light on the mysterious link between the destiny of Israel and that of Jesus: God becomes man as the eschatological Israel and the resurrection of Christ is the resurrection of Israel, which the prophet Hosea recounted.[7]

Even though addressed to a Hellenistic audience, the first two chapters of Luke's Gospel represent a traditional Jewish perspective. Mary's son will sit on the throne of his father David and rule in the house of Jacob forever (1:32–33).[8] Only the prophecy of Simeon opens up a universal perspective. The child is destined to be revealed to the gentiles, but he remains the glory of God's people, Israel (2:32).

Although by the end of Luke-Acts, the center of the church has been transferred from Jerusalem to Rome (after the persecutions in Jerusalem caused Peter's departure and Paul's imprisonment), the divine promise by Gabriel and Simeon's prophecy was never revoked. In fact, when the apostles ask Jesus before his ascension, "Lord, is it this time that you are going to restore the kingship to Israel?" Jesus does not reprimand them for this narrow nationalistic perspective, but simply refuses to reveal the time of this *apokatastasis* (restoration): "It is not for you to know the time or seasons that the Father has established by his own authority" (Acts 1:6–7). Thus not even the universalistic Jesus of Luke excludes the kingship of Israel from the end stage of salvation history.

The Fourth Gospel has long been the target of accusations on account

7. C. H. Dodd, *According to the Scriptures: The Substructure of New Testament Theology* (New York: Fontana, 1965), 103. Above the text of Dodd, I included a modified quote from my *Jesus Christ: The Fundamentals of Christology*, 3rd ed. (New York: Alba House, 2002), 157–58.

8. Marcion was so disturbed by the Jewish character of the infancy narratives that he cut out the first two chapters of Luke's Gospel.

of its alleged anti-Jewish tendency, as it frequently equates the enemies of Jesus with the "Jews." This assertion is indeed factual because it reflects the situation around the end of the first century, when Christians everywhere were excommunicated from the synagogues and treated as dangerous heretics. Nevertheless, the Gospel of John, like all the New Testament documents (and even more forcefully than some of them), insists that all that Jesus did and suffered fulfills the Scriptures and rituals of Israel: Abraham rejoiced when he saw the day of Christ, Moses wrote about him, and Isaiah saw his glory. Christ's last word on the cross, *tetelestai*, "it has been completed" or "achieved," means in context that he fulfilled not only the will of his Father but also the Scriptures.[9] Even though the Jews are often characterized as enemies, Jesus expresses the greatest praise for a Jew in any of the four Gospels when he calls Nathanael "the true Israelite in whom there is no guile" (1:47). Moreover, Jesus counts himself among the Jews when he tells the Samaritan woman, "You worship what you do not understand; we worship what we understand," and he gives the cause of this knowledge by saying what no other Gospel does, "because salvation is from the Jews" (4:22).

A most surprising but often overlooked feature of this Gospel concerns the kingship of Jesus. At a superficial glance, it appears that Jesus' kingdom is completely different from the Davidic kingship because it is not of this world. In fact, Jesus is not labeled anywhere "son of David" in John, nor is his kingdom that of David. Yet the evangelist uses the device of inclusion to emphasize that Jesus, as the Son of God and the Son of Man, is the messianic king of Israel. The exclamation of Nathanael in 1:49, "Rabbi, you are the Son of God, you are the King of Israel," is echoed and intensified by the shouts of a "big crowd," which greets Jesus when he solemnly enters Jerusalem as the king prophesied by Zechariah: "Hosanna! Blessed is he who comes in the name of the Lord, the king of Israel" (Jn 12:13; Zec 2:14–17). Of course, Nathanael and the crowd do not understand the nature of Jesus' kingship, which is gradually revealed during Jesus' trial, passion, and resurrection. The hearing before Pilate centers on the question, "Are you the king of the Jews?" Aware that Jesus has no political ambition, Pilate and the soldiers nonetheless mock the kingly claim of Jesus,

9. Recall 19:28, which interprets the last cry: "after this, aware that all has been fulfilled [*tetelestai*], so that the Scripture may be fulfilled [*teleiothe*], Jesus said: 'I thirst.'"

not only when they dress him in a purple cloak and place a crown of thorns on his head, which is also described in the Synoptics, but also when Pilate seats Jesus on his own bench of judgment and declares, "Behold your king!"[10] The title fixed above his head on the cross and written in Hebrew, Latin, and Greek read: "Jesus the Nazorean, the king of the Jews." When the chief priests protest the wording, Pilate remains firm: "What I have written, I have written" (19:19–22). This presentation is a fascinating example of what the exegetes call "Johannine irony." On the level of what this world can understand, Jesus is enthroned on the cross out of mockery. Those who contemplate the scene with the eyes of faith, however, know that, unaware and unwilling, Pilate and the soldiers are carrying out God's design. Jesus is truly enthroned on the cross as the King of Israel. At the same time, the inscription in three languages, which from a contemporary Jewish viewpoint encompassed the entire world, proclaimed to all peoples the universal kingship of Jesus. But he is made universal king *as* king of Israel. Having fulfilled God's will to the end, he enthrones him on the cross to rule over all creation. In a similar way as in Matthew, the universal king of Israel embodies in himself the eschatological Israel; he is the mysterious Son of Man in Daniel who represents "the saints of the most high." Thus also in the Gospel of John, the mission of Israel is fulfilled in Jesus the messianic King, the Son of Man, to whom is given "dominion, glory, and kingship; nations and peoples of every language serve him" (Dn 7:14, 18).

Regarding the New Testament's appraisal of Israel, one might conclude that her mission culminated in Jesus. The unbelief of the "official" Israel is experienced as a "great sorrow and constant anguish" (Rom 9:2), yet none of the New Testament texts consider her unbelief definitive. Moreover, her survival to the end of times is not just one of many possible historical scenarios; it becomes, rather, a necessary part of God's providential plan of mercy. In this sense, then, and according to the New Testament, Israel has a mission. God wills its existence so that after the fullness of the gentiles enters the church, all Israel may be saved.

10. The Jerusalem Bible and the New American Bible translate *ekathisen* as transitive, since the seating of Jesus on the bench of judgment marks the climax of Johannine irony.

The View of Israel's Mission in the History of the Church

Most Jewish and Christian theologians hold a one-sided and negative appraisal of historic Christianity's view on Israel's mission. For example, a recent study by a Jesuit scholar quotes approvingly the phrase coined by the Jewish French historian Jules Isaac, who characterized Catholic teaching on Jews throughout the centuries as "un enseignement du mépris" (a teaching of contempt).[11] Therefore, most historians regard the document *Nostra Aetate* of Vatican II and the subsequent actions and speeches of Popes John Paul II and Benedict XVI as causes of a revolutionary turn in Jewish-Christian relations. While no one can deny the momentous change that occurred after the council, the history of the relationship is far more complex than an unambiguously negative critique suggests.[12]

Like the New Testament, later Catholic tradition has never ceased to consider the (temporary) unbelief, and the existence and destiny of Israel as intrinsic to the existence and destiny of the church. For the fathers of the church, Israel is both the mother of Jesus and the mother of the church. However, many added that Israel acted more like a cruel stepmother who persecuted her son, crowned her son with thorns, and killed him.[13] Yet as the mother of Jesus and of the church, she belongs to their very mystery. When, in the second century, Marcion removed the Old Testament from his Bible, the church removed Marcion from the body of the church and continued to consider herself the legitimate heir of the Jewish Scriptures. Furthermore, she asserted that the Jewish Scriptures are an integral part of the inspired Word of God without which the New Testament becomes incomprehensible. Whenever pogroms and persecutions threatened the survival of the Jewish people, the official church, especially the popes, condemned it. According to rabbi and professor David Dalin, the

11. David Neuhaus, "Engaging the Jewish People: Forty Years since *Nostra Aetate*," in *Catholic Engagement with World Religions: A Comprehensive Study*, ed. Karl J. Becker and Ilaria Morali (Maryknoll, N.Y.: Orbis, 2010), 395.

12. A notable exception to the wholesale negative appraisal is the book by David Dalin, *The Myth of Hitler's Pope: Pope Pius XII and His Secret War against Nazi Germany* (Washington, D.C.: Regnery, 2001), which shows the popes' consistent policy of protecting the Jews from persecution throughout the centuries.

13. See, for example, Petrus Chrysologus, *Collectio sermonum, sermo* 164: Cetedoc Library of Christian Latin Texts 0227; Eusebius Gallicanus, *Collectio Homiliarum* 49: Cl 0966; Apponius, *In Canticum Canticorum expositio* 5: Cl 0194.

only state that never expelled the Jews in history was the papal states.[14] Pope Gregory X officially states that he offers the Jews "the shield of his protection," following, as he writes, "in the footsteps of our predecessors . . . Callixtus, Eugene, Alexander, Clement, Celestine, Innocent and Honorius." Gregory also condemns those Christians "who falsely claim that Jews have secretly and furtively carried away [Christian] children and killed them."[15] St. Bernard of Clairvaux severely reprimands the monk Rudolph who incited a pogrom in the Rhine valley. If the Jews were exterminated, he asks,

> where does that saying come in, "not for their destruction I pray" and "When the fullness of the Gentiles shall have come in, then all Israel will be saved," and "the Lord is rebuilding Jerusalem, calling the banished sons of Israel home"? Who is this man that he should make out the Prophet to be a liar and render void the treasures of Christ's love and pity? This doctrine is not his own, but his father's. But I believe it is good enough for him, since he is like his father who was, we know, "from the first a murderer, a liar and the father of lies." What horrid learning, what hellish wisdom is his! A learning and wisdom contrary to the prophets, hostile to the apostles, and subversive of piety and grace. It is a foul heresy, a sacrilegious prostitution "pregnant with malice."[16]

Note that according to Bernard, Satan himself instigated the monk to persecute the Jews.

In sermon 79 of his *Sermones super Cantica Canticorum*, Bernard explains the relationship between synagogue and church as root to branch, mother and daughter: "The branches should not be ungrateful to the root, nor daughters to their mother. The branches should not envy the root since they have drawn (the sap) from the root, nor daughters be envious toward their mother since they sucked her breast."

Bernard interprets the words of the bride in Songs of Songs 3:4 as the words of the church bride to her bridegroom, Christ: "I have held on to him and will not let him go until I introduce him into my mother's house and into the bedroom of the one who bore me." Thus, according to Bernard,

14. Dalin, *The Myth of Hitler's Pope*, 18–19.

15. Letter of Gregory X, October 7, 1272. Even though the popes consistently defended the Jews from persecution, they did insist on discriminatory measures: the Jews had to live in a ghetto, wear special clothing, and were barred from public office and the military. They were free, however, to engage in trade, banking, and medicine.

16. Bernard, *Letter* 393, in *The Letters of St. Bernard*, trans. and ed. Bruno Scott James (Chicago: Regnery, 1953), 466.

the church bride is not at all envious of her estranged mother, the synagogue, but wants to introduce her bridegroom to her:

How could this be that she yields her spouse, or rather desires her spouse for another? No, this is not the case. Indeed, as a good daughter she desires Him for her mother but this is not the same as yielding Him to her, but rather to share Him. One (Groom) suffices for both; they, however, will no longer be two but one in Him. He is our peace who makes the two into one, so that there will be one bride and one Bridegroom who is Jesus Christ our Lord.[17]

Bernard here (and elsewhere) expresses in a new and passionate way a general patristic belief: Israel is the object of a special providence and will exist until the end of history, when all Israel will be saved. Moreover, Bernard advises Pope Eugene III that it was an inopportune time to convert the Jews: "For them a determined time has been fixed which cannot be anticipated."[18]

On the other hand, at the same time that the church hierarchy protected the Jews, they also supported repressive measures. For example, the Fourth Lateran Council ruled that Jews may not hold public office, must wear distinctive dress, and may not appear among Christians during the Easter holidays.[19] Thus, according to Jewish scholar Robert Chazan, the official policy of the Catholic Church was "moderate toleration."[20] Three false beliefs justified the church's approval and even promotion of unjust laws against the Jewish people. Throughout the centuries, the church acted of the conviction that the Jews were collectively responsible for the execution of Jesus, since the Jews of any particular time in history were the descendants of those who condemned the Son of God. Thus they share in their forefathers' guilt. The second misunderstanding was the belief that

17. Bernard, *Super Cant.* 79.5–6. It should be acknowledged that there has been much friendly contact between certain Christians and Jews throughout ancient and medieval history. Many popes had Jewish physicians as their personal doctors. St. Jerome learned Hebrew from Jewish rabbis, and in his Bible translation he consulted the Hebrew text of the books of the Old Testament. In the Middle Ages, Blessed Stephen Harding, one of the founding abbots of the Cistercian order, amended the Vulgate translation of his Bible by asking for the help of Jewish rabbis. St. Thomas studied and used the works of the great Jewish philosopher Maimonides. Thomas himself teaches that after all the pagans chosen for salvation have embraced the faith, all Jews in general (not every individual) will be saved (see *Super Epistolam ad Romanos* 2.2).

18. Quoted from *De consideratione* 3.1.2 in Ratzinger, *Holy Week*, 44.

19. Fourth Lateran Council, constitutions 68–69: Norman P. Tanner, ed., *Decrees of the Ecumenical Councils* (Washington, D.C.: Georgetown University Press, 1990), 1:266–67.

20. Robert Chazan, "Christian-Jewish Interactions over the Ages," in *Christianity in Jewish Terms*, ed. Tikva Frymer-Kensy et al. (Boulder, Colo.: Westview Press, 2000), 7–24.

the truth of Christianity is so evident to everybody that the Jews' refusal to believe in Christ manifests their bad faith and, therefore, makes their rejection inexcusable. The third reason was fear: the pastors of souls were afraid that "Jewish error" might compromise the faith of their flock.

A more balanced picture of the relationship between Jews and the Catholic Church is found in the official declaration of the church in the sixteenth century regarding Jewish guilt. This statement was included in the Roman catechism composed after the Council of Trent: "The guilt in us seems more enormous than in the Jews, since, according to the testimony of the same Apostle, 'If they had known it, they would never have crucified the Lord of glory' (1 Cor 2:8); while we, on the contrary, professing to know him, yet denying him by our actions, seem in some sort to lay violent hands on him."[21]

In light of this history, *Nostra Aetate* of Vatican II and the words and actions of Popes John Paul II and Benedict XVI do not appear completely new or contrary to Catholic thought throughout history. Even though supersessionism, which definitively rejects Israel and replaces it with the gentile church of the new covenant, has been the prevailing belief of Catholics at large, the Fathers and the best theologians of the church as well as the popes have never succumbed to it. They could not do so, since they have read and accepted the teachings of the Letter to the Romans, which excludes such a position.

In spite of the Jewish opposition to the gospel, the official church remained convinced on theological grounds that the Jews had to be preserved and protected against the violent outbursts of popular anti-Judaism. If Israel were wiped out, God's promise, made known through Jesus and Paul, would prove false. Moreover, if the church were to participate in the destruction of Israel, she would be guilty of matricide, the murder of her own mother.

Before Benedict XVI, the awareness of the church's duty to preserve Israel admittedly did not include the explicit recognition of her mission. It was implied, however, in the belief that the actual survival of Israel in spite of so many adversities bears witness to God's absolute fidelity before the world.

21. *Catechism of the Council of Trent for Parish Priests* (New York: J. F. Wagner, 1923), 50–61, 362–65.

The Present and Future Mission of Israel from a Christian Perspective

On the heels of the above historical overview, the following is an attempt to start a "new reflection" on what Benedict calls "the beginnings of a correct understanding" of the mission of Israel during the time of the gentiles, which "has always been there, waiting to be discovered."

According to David Novak, the renowned professor of Jewish studies at the University of Toronto, the most important contribution Judaism has made to the world is its teaching on the natural moral law, which derives from what he calls a general revelation to all humankind.[22] If both Jews and Christians proclaim together the principles and demands of the natural moral law, the secular world cannot ascribe this position to a particular religious belief, which more readily leads to a recognition that the natural law is universally valid and inscribed in the very nature of humanity. This is a welcome recommendation, and it is worth noting that a united witness in certain moral matters (such as the protection and promotion of the dignity and rights of persons, the struggle against any sort of discrimination, poverty, disease, and oppression) has already begun in some regions of the world. However, in addition to proposing the natural moral law to all humankind, believing Jews have a much more specific mission in the world, which derives from their irrevocable election as the people of the first covenant. This mission has been expressed with great depth in a short story by Franz Werfel, a famous German-Jewish novelist. The story is based on real events. The following excerpt is taken from a scene in an Austrian village where a Catholic priest and a Jewish rabbi have become good friends. One day the rabbi asks this question of his Catholic companion:

"What would happen if one day all Jews in the world became Christians? Israel would disappear. But with Israel, the only real witness of God's revelation would also disappear. In that case, the Bible would no longer be documented by our own existence; it would become an empty and lifeless saga, just like the Greek myths are. Does the church not see this danger?... Reverend Father, we belong to each other but we are not ONE. In the Letter to the Romans it is said that the church is built on Israel. My conviction is that as long as the church exists, so also will Israel, but if Israel were to fall, so must the church, too." "Why do you think this is true?"

22. See David Novak, *The Natural Law in Judaism* (New York: Cambridge University Press, 2008).

asked the priest. "On account of our sufferings that last up to this very day," replied the rabbi. "Do you think that God allowed us for no reason to endure what we have endured and to survive what we have survived for two millennia?"[23]

We Catholics can only hope that Jewish readers will not hold it against us that we can only partly agree with this profound statement. We cannot be expected to give up our hope that in the end Israel will recognize her Messiah in Jesus of Nazareth. For us, a full agreement would be tantamount to disregarding the love that animated the soul of Jesus, whose direct mission was to gather the lost sheep of Israel. Moreover, as a Catholic theologian, I believe that even after "all Israel" recognizes her Messiah in Jesus, Israel will not disappear within the church, but will always retain its special identity and mission within it as the "noble olive tree" onto which the gentile "branches" have been grafted.

At the same time, we must all acknowledge the rabbi's admirable insight into the inseparable connection of Israel and the church: "As the church exists, so will Israel. But if Israel were to fall, so must the church too." Martin Buber expresses a similar awareness of mutual belonging to one another: "Only we two, the church and Israel, know what Israel really means."[24] John Paul II also describes the intrinsic bond that unites the church to Judaism:

The church of Christ discovers her "bond" with Judaism by "searching into her own mystery." The Jewish religion is not "extrinsic" to us, but in a certain way is "intrinsic" to our own religion. With Judaism, therefore, we have a relationship which we do not have with any other religion. You are our dearly beloved brothers and, in a certain way, it could be said that you are our elder brothers.[25]

It would be appropriate at this point to examine the different aspects of the church's and Israel's mutual belonging to each other and, in particular, the mission of Israel from a Catholic perspective.

1. Along with Werfel's rabbi, we must acknowledge that Israel in its very existence witnesses to the reality of God; not simply to the ultimate cause

23. Franz Werfel, *Die wahre Geschichte vom geschändeten und wiederhergestellten Kreuz* [The true story of the twisted and restored cross] (Berlin: Verlag Haude/Spener, 1965).

24. Martin Buber, *Die Stunde und die Erkenntnis: Reden und Aufsätze* [The hour and the knowledge]. Berlin: Schocken, 1936), 148.

25. In the pope's original Italian: "Il primo è che la Chiesa di Cristo scopre il suo 'legame' con l'Ebraismo 'scrutando il suo proprio mistero.' La religione ebraica non ci è 'estrinseca,' ma in un certo qual modo, è 'intrinseca' alla nostra religione. Abbiamo quindi verso di essa dei rapporti che non abbiamo con nessun'altra religione. Siete i nostri fratelli prediletti e, in un certo modo, si potrebbe dire i nostri fratelli maggiori" (John Paul II, *Acta Apostolicae Sedis* 78 [1986]: 1120).

of the cosmos and the ultimate foundation of morality, but to the living God of the covenant, who cares about us, speaks to us, and freely binds himself to us by covenant. He chose Abraham, Isaac, and Jacob, and promised that the entire world would be blessed by their offspring. In spite of the multiple infidelities of his people, he remains unshakable in his faithfulness. With the rabbi, we must also include the sufferings of Israel throughout history in this witness. In fact, we should consider these sufferings a sign of Israel's election. As the rabbi said: "Do you think that God allowed us for no reason to endure what we have endured and to survive what we have survived for two millennia?" In 2006, Pope Benedict confirmed this aspect of Israel's mission during his visit to Auschwitz:

> The rulers of the Third Reich wanted to crush the entire Jewish people, to cancel it from the register of the peoples of the earth. Thus the words of the Psalm: "We are being killed, accounted as sheep for the slaughter" were fulfilled in a terrifying way. Deep down, those vicious criminals, by wiping out this people, wanted to kill the God who called Abraham, who spoke on Sinai and laid down principles to serve as a guide for mankind, principles that are eternally valid. If this people, by its very existence, was a witness to the God who spoke to humanity and took us to himself, then that God finally had to die and power had to belong to man alone—to those men, who thought that by force they had made themselves masters of the world. By destroying Israel, by the *Shoah*, they ultimately wanted to tear up the taproot of the Christian faith and to replace it with a faith of their own invention: faith in the rule of man, the rule of the powerful.[26]

2. In his deeply emotional speech, Pope Benedict points not only to the vocation of Israel as the living witness of the living God, but also to the patrimony of her faith as a taproot of our Christian faith. He has evoked this Pauline metaphor of Israel's heritage as "taproot" many times, and has shown concretely in his speeches and writings how Israel's faith serves him personally to enrich and deepen his own insights.

Pope Benedict almost always begins his theological writings with an explanation of what the Old Testament (and, often, what Jewish tradition) says about his topic. In this way he shows the direction and consistency of God's revelation, the gradual process by which God educated his people and, through them, the church as well. But, in contrast with our Jewish interlocutors, who often note that the sacred books are only a preparation

26. Benedict XVI, *Address by the Holy Father: Visit to the Auschwitz Camp* (May 28, 2006).

in the eyes of Christians, most of these texts are considered by the Catholic Church to be essentially more than mere preparation. Through the Old Testament we understand better not only the background and preparation for the realities of the New Testament but also its full meaning. For instance, Jon D. Levenson has gathered much convincing evidence that the entire Jewish sacrificial system, including the Passover Lamb, was understood during the Second Temple period as patterned and inspired by the Akedah, the sacrifice (the binding) of Isaac by Abraham.[27] This conclusion implicitly questions the theories of a number of Christian exegetes who claim that Jesus could not have understood his death as sacrifice and that this interpretation was developed only at a later stage of the New Testament. From Levenson's book, one can plausibly come to the conclusion that Jesus and his immediate disciples had at hand the conceptual tools to interpret his death as the fulfillment of all previous Jewish sacrifices.

In addition to being a preparation, the sacrifice of Isaac by Abraham helps us enter more deeply into the mystery of Jesus' sacrifice. It reveals the depth of God the Father's love for humankind: he did not let Abraham sacrifice his beloved Son, but allowed the sacrifice of his own beloved Son. As the hymn of the Paschal candle goes, "In order to redeem the slave, you handed over your Son." The examples of the deepening of our faith by relating the New Testament fulfillment to the type in the Old could go on indefinitely. The type is not simply a stepping stone to be left behind once we come to know its fulfillment in Christ; rather, it continues always to shed light and provide a deeper understanding of the Christian mystery. This awareness is expressed in the liturgy by proclaiming the texts of the Old Testament without which our understanding of our feasts and of the Eucharist would be flat and distorted.

3. Israel's faith also belongs to her mission before the end of history. On the level of its explicit, propositional content of the true faith, a Christian must see Israel's as incomplete.[28] Yet if we consider not what scholas-

27. See Jon D. Levenson, *The Death and Resurrection of the Beloved Son: The Transformation of Child Sacrifice in Judaism and Christianity* (New Haven: Yale University Press, 1993).

28. Our Jewish friends at times express regret and incomprehension about the fact that Christians consider the Jewish faith incomplete in comparison to the fullness of the Catholic faith. Even Buber thinks that we look at their Bible as a forecourt while for them it is the sanctuary itself. In fact, if we consider the conceptually formulated content of what we believe, he is right. We hold that the Catholic Christian faith is the fulfillment of the Old Testament but still awaiting a final consummation. Obviously, this position is not inspired by arrogance, but rather by the desire to remain faithful to Christ.

tic theology calls *fides quae* but *fides qua*, namely, the grace-bestowed act of faith by which we reach out to God himself, adhere to him, and build our existence on him beyond concepts and propositions, this aspect of faith depends ultimately on the strength and depth of our love for God. On this intuitive or mystical level, a Jew who loves God with all their heart, mind, and strength grasps the mystery of God more deeply and more fully even today during the "time of the gentiles" than a Christian with a mediocre love but sophisticated theological knowledge could.[29] Gregory the Great and the medieval monastic tradition knew that *amor ipse notitia est* (love itself is knowledge), a knowledge based on God's indwelling in the soul and the purity and depth of the love that flows from this indwelling.

4. Regarding the existential application of the biblical texts to the life of the individual and community, Christians can learn much from our "older brothers." In fact, every Christian must go through the "school" of the Old Testament. We need to experience slavery to sin and our hopeless inability to break this imprisonment. In this way, we learn to cry out to God and put all our hope in him. In this way, we also experience the miracle of Exodus. He will liberate us from our sins so that we may become part of his people, a "a kingdom of priests, a holy nation (Ex 19:6). We need to go through some desert places in our lives and experience God's providential care that keeps us alive materially and spiritually. And we must also, like Israel, go through situations when we become either materially or spiritually poor, so that we can learn how poverty can liberate us from the dangers of earthly riches and find our true riches in God.

When we Christians see Jews who are alive to the covenant of Sinai and fulfilling the law with zest and joy, we discover in them the foretaste of the new covenant in which God implants his law into our hearts. But observant Jews, like observant Christians, may become pharisaic if they boast of their moral performance. Those Jews who obey the Law in order to sanctify the divine Name and consider their whole life a sacred worship provide a shining example for those Christians who complain about their observance of

29. Thus, on the level of intuitive grasping, even the *fides quae* (the content of faith) of the loving Jew may "fairly compete" with a Christian's faith. Nevertheless, by acknowledging the value of this intuitive, love-inspired knowledge, we should not diminish the importance of knowing the propositional truths of the Catholic faith and the reception of the sacraments. The explicit knowledge of the Christian mysteries (such as God as trinitarian communion, the incarnation and redemption, the mystery of the Eucharist) and Christian sacramental practice have a built-in dynamism that increase our love for God and thus intensify his presence in us.

some minimal obligations. Indeed, Pharisaic Christians should venerate in these Jews the anticipated eschatological gift of the Holy Spirit.[30]

Of course, Catholics cannot agree with the Jewish denial of the christological meaning of the entire Old Testament. The Catholic position, namely, that all of the Old Testament points to Christ and finds its full meaning in Christ, is, according to Jewish scholars, arbitrary and untenable. Yet many believing Jews still have hope in the messianic promises of the prophets, and this hope remains an essential dimension of their lives. These Jews, whose faith has been nourished by the Jewish Bible, know that "the world to come" cannot result from the civilizational and moral efforts of humankind alone. They learned from the Holocaust that God calls for constant and maximum engagement from us in the battle against moral and physical evil, but they also know that the new heaven and new earth of which Isaiah dreamed can only be the final redemptive work of God. Our eschatological faith is strengthened by the presence of these Jews, who read with faith the prophetic texts of their Bible and thus share in the experience of the prophets; that is, in some real sense they also see and taste in the Spirit the eschatological reality, the salvation promised to Israel and the world.[31] This partial unity by sharing in and testifying to our converging eschatological expectations does confirm our mission, but it does not eliminate our division regarding the person and role of Jesus Christ. Yet even in this fundamental opposition, Israel provides Christians with a great service. Our faith in the incarnation is enriched by a new, concrete dimension as we discover that God became not some generic human being, but he has become man by becoming a Jew; in fact, more than *a* Jew. Jesus of Nazareth is *the Jew*, the embodiment of the new eschatological Israel. This is so because he fulfills both the Suffering Servant prophecies of Deutero-Isaiah and the Son of Man vision of Daniel. And as the historical sections of this work have shown, these two figures represent both an individual and the

30. Neighborly love as the sum total of the law is not an exclusively Christian insight. In the Talmud Rabbi Akiba declared: "This is the most fundamental principle enunciated in the Torah: 'Love thy neighbor as thyself'" (*The Talmud: Selected Writings*, trans. Ben Zion Bokser, introduced by Ben Zion Bokser and Baruch M. Bokser [Mahwah, N.J.: Paulist Press, 1989], 28).

31. This renewed emphasis on the prophets would counter the tendency of rabbinic Judaism that focuses on the Torah. Yet the secular eschatology of "enlightened Judaism" has been crushed by the experience of the Holocaust. There is a new openness even in Reform Judaism to hope in a transcendent "world to come," an act of divine redemption. On traditional Jewish eschatology see Menachem Kellner, "How Ought a Jew View Christian Beliefs about Redemption?," in Frymer-Kensy et al., *Christianity in Jewish Terms*, 269–75.

eschatological Israel. In this way, paradoxically, we are united with believing Israel even in the sharpest difference between us. Jesus of Nazareth is our unbreakable bond with Israel. For us too, Israel is a holy nation. Once the fullness of the gentiles enters the church,[32] the separate yet temporary mission of Israel will come to an end as she discovers in the face of Jesus her own deepest mystery, the face of the eternal Israel of God.

32. We do not know what in God's plan this "fullness of the gentiles" means in relation to world population.

CHAPTER 19

"Bride" and "Mother" in the *Super Cantica* of St. Bernard

An Ecclesiology for Our Time?

While the controversy around feminist theology is becoming more intense, it is surprising to note that one of the most fundamental biblical and patristic images of the church, woman as virginal bride and mother, has nearly vanished from today's ecclesial consciousness.[1] Even though some groundbreaking works had been written on this topic before Vatican II, after the council it has never become the center of theological inquiry.[2]

Yet a rediscovery of the church as bride and mother could lead to new

1. The only exception to this universal forgetfulness is the insistence of some conservative Catholics on obedience to "Holy Mother Church." A call to obedience is certainly justified, but in the tradition the image of the church as mother does not refer to a disciplinarian. To highlight the prevailing notions of Catholic ecclesiology over the past hundred years, this simplified sequence could provide some help: The end of the nineteenth century was still dominated by the notion of the church as a perfect, hierarchically organized, supernatural society. As a result of the works of Emile Meersch (*The Theology of the Mystical Body*, trans. Cyril Vollert [St. Louis: Herder, 1952]) and Pius XII's Encyclical *Mystici Corporis*, the first half of the twentieth century saw the ascendancy of an ecclesiology that centered on the church as the mystical body of Christ. While Vatican II provided a rich repertoire of notions and images for the church, mainstream postconciliar ecclesiology chose the people of God theme as its favorite. In recent times a fourth notion has been gaining ground, that of communion. Each of these views expresses a permanent truth about the church. She is indeed a visible supernatural institution in which everyone receives a gift that imposes a task; she is the body of Christ in that Christ communicates and manifests his life as well as performs his various functions in and through the members of the church. She is also communion, that is, a unique community since it shares in the perfect unity of the Holy Trinity and every local church is called to manifest the mystery of the universal church.

2. At the council this image provided the theological rationale to insert the mariological document of the council into *Lumen Gentium*, the Dogmatic Constitution on the Church. After the council, Henri de Lubac, Hans Urs von Balthasar, and Louis Bouyer never stopped calling attention to the centrality of the image of virgin, bride, and mother in ecclesiology; their contributions, however, have been by and large ignored up to the present day.

insights uniquely suited to answer a threefold question that today concerns not only professional theologians but also the Christian public at large. (1) Why does one need a church instead of or in addition to a direct personal relationship to Christ? (2) What is the role of the ministerial priest, and how could one work out an effective priestly spirituality? (3) What is the theological relevance of the "feminine"? I believe that St. Bernard, "the last of the Fathers" and a precursor of modern sensitivity, can provide some surprising contributions to our quest.

While occasionally completing Bernard's thoughts from other works of his, I will concentrate on his *Homilies on the Song of Songs*,[3] which contain the principal texts on the church as bride and mother. The literary genre of this work is an exegesis in the patristic and medieval sense.[4] Beginning with Origen's homilies and commentary, the Song of Songs has been viewed by tradition as a divine-human drama,[5] the chief protagonists of which are the bride (church and the individual soul) and the bridegroom (Christ). St. Bernard's interpretation is heavily indebted to the works of Origen, Ambrose, and Gregory the Great; yet, out of traditional elements, Bernard has created a uniquely personal drama, interspersed with "lyrical inserts" of high poetic quality.

The action moves on two levels. The background story line is that of salvation history, involving not only the church but also the angels, the material universe, and the former bride, Israel, in a universal drama of redemption. It begins with the yearning of the saints before the incarnation for the kiss of the bridegroom; it culminates in the piercing of the Son's heart on the cross. The open heart of the bridegroom reveals the Father's heart and the Son's death creates his new bride, the church. The disfiguration of the groom in his passion brings about the beauty of the bride,

3. *Sermones super Cantica Canticorum*, in its abbreviated form, *Super Cant.* Other abbreviations in this article follow, by and large, those used in the critical edition. *Ben.*: *Sermon on the Feast of St. Benedict*; *Circ.*: *Sermon on the Feast of the Circumcision of the Lord*; *Ep.*: *Letter*; *Miss.*: *Homilies on the Annunciation*; *Nat.*: *Sermon on the Feast of Christmas*; *Nat. Bapt.*: *Sermon on the Feast of John the Baptist*; *Par.*: *Parables*; *QH*: *Sermons on Psalm 90*; *Sent.*: *Sentences*; *V HM*: *Sermon on Holy Thursday*. My English text of the excerpts from *Super Cant.* is based on the translation in the series Cistercian Fathers 4, 7, 31, 40 (Kalamazoo, Mich.: Cistercian Publications, 1971–80), but it often changes that translation substantially. In my references, the volume and page numbers following citations of Bernard's works refer to the critical edition: *Sancti Bernardi Opera*, vols. 1–8, ed. J. Leclercq, C. H. Talbot, and H. M. Rochais (Rome: Editiones Cistercienses, 1957–1977).

4. See Denis Farkasfalvy, *L'inspiration de l'Écriture sainte dans la théologie de saint Bernard*, Studia Anselmiana 53 (Rome: Herder, 1964).

5. This shows how deeply the conception of Balthasar on salvation history as *Theodramatik* is rooted in patristic and medieval tradition.

his ascension and the period of waiting afterwards prepare the bride for a new relationship with the risen Christ, a new intimacy made possible by the outpouring of the Holy Spirit. salvation history will be consummated when the church unites with the synagogue (the former spouse temporarily rejected) and with the angels into one bride, the final goal and crown of all God's works, the supreme delight prepared by the Father for his Son.

The second level of dramatic action, "the love story" of the individual soul with Christ, is not merely a parallel line with structural similarities. The challenge for the individual is to become the one unique spouse of Christ by going through the stages of the drama of the church and by participating in the being, attitude and actions of the church-bride. In Bernard's work the story of the individual soul occupies the central stage, that of the church remains in the background. Yet the space and objective structure for the individual soul's development is provided by the events of salvation history. Moreover, the soul on her way to becoming bride is much more than an abstraction. Her figure comes alive as the embodiment of Bernard's personal experience. Even though Bernard alternately distances himself from the bride only to again identify himself with her, most incidents bear the mark of Bernard's personal experience, including the bride's longing for the groom, her reprimand by him, the process of her purification, the adventures of mystical experience, and the description of spiritual marriage at the end.

Thus the theology of the bride and mother has to be gleaned from meditating on the vicissitudes of the individual soul's love story with her groom, Christ, while not forgetting the key to its interpretation, the universal drama of salvation history.

All Humankind Is Called to Become Bride

For Bernard, to become the bride of Christ is not an extraordinary privilege, reserved only for a few selected individuals. All human beings are created in the image of the Image of God, the Word himself. In spite of the fact that our soul, the image of the Image, has been tarnished and distorted by sin, she should not give up hope. It is Bernard's solemn teaching that "every soul, even if burdened with sins, enmeshed in vice, ensnared by pleasure, captive in exile, imprisoned in the body, caught in mud, fixed in mire," should dare to aspire not only to mercy but also to becoming the bride of the Word.[6] There are two reasons for her hope. In spite of the distortions caused by sin, the soul's nature retains the ability to be re-formed by the Word so that she may be again conformed to her archetypal image. Second, the Son, who for our sake became flesh, was crucified, raised from the dead, and glorified, searches for the sinner with an infinite love and calls her not only to repentance but also to a spiritual marriage with him. Of course, the sinner must complete an arduous process of purification, the stages of which are described from various perspectives in Bernard's works.

The Rebuke of the Bride: Know Nothing but Jesus Crucified

"If you, the fairest of women, do not know yourself, leave." These words of the Song of Songs in the Vulgate introduce one of the severe crises in the bride and groom relationship. Prior to this stern warning of the groom, the bride wanted to know where the groom lies down at noon. In other words, she wanted to contemplate the Word in his divine glory, the full-noon splendor of the divine light. No longer enslaved by the desires of the flesh and rediscovering her own spiritual identity, the soul became all aflame by the desire for a direct, intimate union with God, who is pure, infinite spirit. She disdains the obstacle of her own flesh that pulls her down toward the many concerns, needs, and distractions of this world. Impatient with the mediating and tempering role of a sacramental economy in which one can know God only through signs and one's own imagination, she is craving for the full, unscreened light of the Word. This daring boldness, which ignores the bride's own nature, her earthly body, calls forth the terrible thundering of the groom: "if you do not know yourself, leave." Even the pains of hell would be more tolerable for someone who tasted divine wisdom than to leave the groom's sight and be again enslaved by the insatiable desires of the flesh. Yet the harsh words of the groom do not express anger at his bride; he simply intends to frighten her "so that, frightened, she may be purified, and purified, she may become ready for the vision she longs for."[7] This vision is reserved for the end of times:

6. Bernard, *Super Cant.* 83.1: 2:298.
7. Bernard, *Super Cant.* 38.3: 2:16.

It will happen at the time of my appearance that your beauty will be complete just as my beauty is complete; and you will be so perfectly like me that you will see me as I am. Then you will hear: You are all beautiful, my love, there is no stain in you. But for now, you are partly like me but partly unlike me; so be content with a partial knowledge. Be aware of what you are and do not search for things that are above you.[8]

Thus a rash attempt at a pure spiritual union in this life shows that the individual has not as yet accepted their own nature, namely, that they are not only spirit but also a corruptible body that pulls down the spirit. If one ignored their own fleshly nature out of pride, they would relapse into the dreadful condition of fleshly existence from which they had yearned so much to escape.[9]

The groom's stern reproof obtained its purpose. It made the bride humbler, bade her accept her own nature and called her back to God's economy of salvation, the center of which is the incarnate and crucified Christ. Of course, the bride was not motivated by pride and so she did not commit any sin in desiring to see the splendor of the bridegroom. In fact, such a desire was in itself praiseworthy. "Yet, reprimanded, she repented and said, 'My beloved is for me a bundle of myrrh that will rest between my breasts' [Song 1:12]. She means: 'This is enough for me; I no longer want to know anything but Jesus and him crucified' [1 Cor 2:2]."[10]

If the bride did not share and imitate the humility of the crucified Christ, not only would she disown her own nature but she could also not grasp the nature of the groom's divine splendor. It is only by contemplating the pierced side of Christ, where God's love has been revealed to the fullest, that the bride is prepared for contemplating his glory. In projecting his own mentality onto God, the sinner interprets God's majesty as the jealously guarded privilege of a divine autocrat. God's glory appears in its true nature as the splendor of love itself only to the one who shares and imitates God's attitude of self-emptying poverty. Only to the extent that

8. Bernard, *Super Cant.* 38.5: 2:17.

9. It seems likely that Bernard speaks here of his own temptation to pursue too early a purely spiritual life in opposition to the requirements of his own bodily existence. According to the *Vita prima*, written by his friend William of St. Thierry, the young founding abbot of Clairvaux created a real crisis for his monks. He was so vehemently attracted to an angelic life of contemplating spiritual realities that he could hardly comprehend the down-to-earth, fleshly temptations of his subjects. Yet the deep humility that his monks revealed in confessing Bernard their temptations was a strong lesson of humility for Bernard himself. He began to admire their humility and doubt his own (William of St. Thierry, *Vita prima Sancti Bernardi* 7.28–29: PL 185:243–44).

10. Bernard, *Super Cant.* 45.3: 2:51.

one is conformed to God's love can one enjoy God's truth, which is the truth of his love. For this reason, the individual bride, as long as she lives in this body, cannot break out of the church's sacramental economy, where she finds the *memoria*, the recalling and celebration of the incarnation and passion. She must be satisfied "with the husk, as it were, of the sacrament, with the bran of the flesh, with the chaff of the [Bible's] letter, with the veil of faith." Nevertheless, through all this she receives already the first fruits of the Spirit.[11]

As soon as the bride accepts correction and humbles herself to know the crucified Christ and nothing else, the reward follows: Christ is present again as the bride's beloved, rather than as a teacher and king in solemn dignity. "And just as once Moses spoke to God as a friend to his friend and God replied in kind, so now the Word and the soul converse as intimate friends. And no wonder: their mutual love and cherishing flows from the same source."[12]

The Bride Found by the Teachers of the Church

Bernard finds it most unusual that according to the Song of Songs the church was neither founded nor built nor gathered together by the apostles as is stated elsewhere in the Scriptures. According to Song of Songs 3:3 ("The watchmen found me, those who are guarding the city"), the bride, already predestined by God from all eternity and inspired by God in the opportune time (after the resurrection, ascension, and outpouring of the Holy Spirit) to search for her groom, was merely found rather than established by the watchmen, the apostles, and the preachers of the gospel. Just as Mary the mother of the Lord was found with child in her womb by the Holy Spirit, so also was the bride of the Lord. Led by the Spirit of the bridegroom, she addresses the apostles and preachers as one who already knows them well: "Have you not seen the Beloved of my soul?" It was easy for the apostles to convert so many people in such a short time. The bride had already been visited and prepared for their teaching by the Holy Spirit.[13] It is indeed providential that the bride "did not find the one she was search-

11. Bernard, *Super Cant.* 33.3: 1:235.
12. Bernard, *Super Cant.* 45.1: 2:50.
13. Bernard, *Super Cant.* 78.5: 2:269; 78.8: 2:271.

ing for but was found by those for whom she was not searching at all."[14] This disappointing adventure of the primitive church serves as a paradigm for everyone at every time who wants to find the groom. Those who begin a spiritual quest must accept the teaching of the church, or else they will fall into the trap of the flesh: "Anyone who does not give his allegiance to a teacher, will give it to a seducer."[15] Before the bride can find her groom, she must be instructed in all the truth about her beloved.[16]

Yet the teachers of the church are still in this world, while the groom has already ascended into heaven. Thus, even though the former are indispensable for the formation of the bride's faith, the bride must pass beyond them in order to reach the groom directly through faith. As long as the bride searches for the risen groom in this world as if he could be reached by sense experience, she cannot find him. As the bride says in the Song of Songs: "When I passed a little beyond them, I found the Beloved of my soul" (Song 3:4). This is, then, the paradox of the church: "[The church] has passed beyond herself, standing in faith where she has not yet arrived in reality."[17] Without the apostles and their successors, the bride could not have found her groom. Yet the hierarchy does not stand between the bride and Christ as a middleman or mailman carrying messages from one to the other. Rather, through her faith, shaped and formed by the hierarchical church, the church-bride transcends any hierarchical mediation and directly touches with the "finger of faith" her groom who has already ascended into heaven. Bernard cannot stress enough the infinite power and extension of faith:

What are you going to do, O Bride? Do you think you can follow him there [to heaven]? Dare you, can you penetrate that sacred secret, that secret sanctuary in order to contemplate the Son in the Father and the Father in the Son? Certainly not. Where he is, you cannot go now; but you will go afterwards. Still, even now, get moving, follow, and seek him; do not let that unapproachable grandeur and splendor deter you from searching for him or make you despair of finding him. "If you can believe, all things are possible to him who believes." The Word is in your mouth—as he himself says—and in your heart." Believe and you have found him. To believe is to have found him. The faithful know that Christ dwells in their hearts by faith. What could be nearer?...

14. Bernard, *Super Cant.* 77.6: 2:265.
15. Bernard, *Super Cant.* 77.6: 2:265.
16. Bernard, *Super Cant.* 77.5: 2:264.
17. Bernard, *Super Cant.* 79.3: 2:274.

What is it that faith would not find? It reaches what has not been reached, grasps what has not been known, encompasses what is beyond measure and lays hold of the end of all things; in a way faith envelopes eternity itself in its wide embrace. I speak with assurance: I believe the eternal and blessed Trinity that I do not understand; I hold by faith what I cannot comprehend with my mind.[18]

While every soul who is conforming herself to Christ experiences his presence and receives his unique self-revelation, the growth and variety of individual experiences never measures up to the infinitely vast embrace of faith. Faith always envelopes the whole mystery while experience is always limited by the individual's capacity and the free initiative of the groom.

The above adventures of the bride show that whoever sets out on a spiritual quest faces a twofold danger. They either want to reach God directly while ignoring their fallen fleshly nature, or continue to seek Jesus in the flesh, unaware of the need to transcend the realm of the flesh so that they may find the risen Christ. For the first danger, Bernard's remedy is to lead the person to a deeper self-knowledge and thereby to a deeper appreciation of the church's sacramental economy. It is by studying the Scriptures of the church that the bride learns to contemplate the Son of God in the humility of his incarnation and passion.[19] Also the second danger, that of remaining fixated on a fleshly love for Christ, can only be overcome by the church. Whoever seeks the risen Christ must be formed by the teachers of the church, but once their faith has been formed, they should go beyond their teachers so that by faith they can directly reach Christ and the infinite plenitude of his mystery. The hierarchy, then, is essential for Bernard, but only to prepare for the direct encounter between the bride and the groom, the soul and Christ.

The Individual Soul and the Church-Bride

As has already been pointed out, the *Super Cantica* concentrates on the vicissitudes of the individual soul-bride's relationship to Christ. However, the individual grows in proportion to his or her becoming the one church-bride. The one groom has only one "dove," one bride, rather than many individual ones. Each soul becomes bride only to the extent that he or she

18. Bernard, *Super Cant.* 76.6: 2:257–58.

19. While acknowledging their importance, Bernard cannot find a vital role for the individual sacraments of the church in spiritual life. This is certainly a limitation of his spiritual theology.

appropriates the loving surrender of the one unique church-bride. Bernard respects to the utmost the individual differences and gifts of each member of the church, the variety of lifestyles (laity and several religious orders), which all together make up the many-colored cloak of the queen. But at the same time, each person flourishes to the extent that he or she becomes integrated into the suprapersonal "personality" of the one bride.

Note that the one bride for Bernard is not simply a metaphor for a moral unity, for one and the same attitude of love toward the groom. Rather, the *unanimitas* of the many is based on an ontological reality.[20] Each and every individual soul participates in the one kiss between the Father and the Son, this one kiss symbolizing the person of the Holy Spirit.[21] The Holy Spirit is the plenitude of mutual love and knowledge between the Father and the Son. Yet the one bride (the church, the synagogue at the end of times, and the angels) also possesses a certain fullness. She is not the kiss itself but receives a kiss from the kiss, a participated fullness, in which the individual souls share only to the extent that they become bride: "There is no contradiction to say that what we all together possess fully in its entirety [*plene et integre*], each single one of us possesses by participation."[22] Thus there are two levels of participation in the plenitude of love and knowledge that exists as the person of the Holy Spirit. The one bride possesses the participated plenitude "fully and in its entirety," while the individual souls only share in the church's plenitude.

The Bride Becomes Mother and Friend of the Bridegroom: Contemplation and Apostolate

The more the bride progresses in her loving union with the groom, the more she can help the "young maidens" (*adolescentulae*), the souls, who are only at the beginning of the spiritual quest. All that the bride does she does for their sake:

> She should say to them [the young maidens, her companions]: "Rejoice and be confident: 'The King has brought me into his bedroom (of contemplation).' Consider yourselves as introduced too. I alone seem to have been introduced, but it is not

20. Bernard, *Super Cant.* 61.2: 2:149; see also 27.6: 1:185–86.
21. Bernard, *Super Cant.* 8.2: 1:37.
22. Bernard, *Super Cant.* 12.11: 1:67; see also *Super Cant.* 8.8: 1:41.

only for my advantage. All my progress is yours. I advance for your sake, and I will share with you whatever more merit I may gain."[23]

Whoever has not reached the stage of becoming bride should not dare to assume ecclesiastical office. If he has not experienced the love of the groom, if he has not "seen" him in faith, how can he bear witness to him? "Why do they speak about what they do not see? 'We speak about what we know and bear witness to what we have seen' (Jn 3,11). Go, then, and dare to bear witness to what you have not seen and speak about what you do not know."[24]

However, the bride's role for others includes more than witnessing. The spiritual union between the bride and the groom is "fruitful." The bride "conceives by the Word"[25] and becomes mother in that she carries Christ in herself in order to give birth to him for others; or rather, she gives birth to others for Christ.[26] She also conceives images, similitudes, and spiritual interpretations of scriptural texts in order to provide food for her offspring.[27] The price to become mother is to leave everything, spurn everything as refuse, so that such a soul can say with Paul, "for me to live is Christ and to die is gain."[28] Paul is Bernard's favorite example of spiritual motherhood: "You make yourself everything for everyone and become like a vessel discarded to the point that you may be always and everywhere ready to help; you become dead for yourself so that you may live for all."[29] Then, like Paul, who was in labor again and again while Christ was being formed in his faithful (Gal 4:19), the soul becomes a mother and her breasts are filled with milk.[30] The milk means either spiritual nourishment or compassion with those who are in crisis, and rejoicing with those who are progressing.[31] The empathizing love of the mother should know no limits, but embrace all humankind just as the mercy of her groom, Christ, is universal and all-encompassing. Insofar as the church lives this universal love, extending to all the ends of the earth, the whole church can be compared to an immense sky. At the same time, she has in herself many "skies," those perfect souls, whose love has grown into the universal dimensions of

23. Bernard, *Super Cant.* 23.2: 1:139.
24. Bernard, *Super Cant.* 62.8: 2:160.
25. Bernard, *Super Cant.* 85.12: 2:315.
26. Bernard, *Div.* 51: 6/1:273.
27. Bernard, *Super Cant.* 85.13: 2:315–16.
28. Phil 1:21 in Bernard, *Super Cant.* 85.12: 2:315.
29. Bernard, *Super Cant.* 12.1: 1:61.
30. Bernard, *Super Cant.* 12.2: 1:61.
31. Bernard, *Super Cant.* 10.1–3: 1:48–50.

the church's love so as to include all human beings, even their enemies.[32]

The bride-mother then is torn between two desires. She yearns to be united in chaste love with her groom, but also to gain souls for him—souls who would glow with the same fire of love by which she is being consumed. The result is a constant tension. "When resting in prayer, I accuse myself of neglecting my work; when at work, of disturbing my prayer." The holy man is "violently tossed between the fruit of action and the quiet of contemplation." This being torn apart, this restless burning, is not an unhealthy state but rather the wellspring of spiritual strength. The two occupations energize each other. The more fruitful the soul is in apostolic work, the more she yearns to return to contemplation. When refreshed by the taste of contemplation, she runs back with new vigor to gain souls for Christ. She can never become complacent, lest in this dangerous balancing act she may lose sight of God's will. Therefore, prayer becomes her only refuge and medicine. Groaning and sighing every moment, she beseeches God "to show us always what he wishes us to do, and at what time, and in what measure."[33]

The minister of the church, then, must realize in himself, above all else, a spiritual motherhood before he may safely accept and fruitfully carry out his ministry. Yet, for Bernard, feminine qualities are not sufficient for the ministry. He excuses himself for not accepting a public ministry in the church by claiming to be a weak woman, like the one who anointed Jesus before his death. He makes Jesus himself come to his defense and assure that he may continue in penance and prayer:

> Why are you bothering this woman? . . . This is not a man as you think, who can handle difficult matters, but a woman. Why then try to impose on him a yoke that I do not think he can bear? He is performing a good work for me. Let him stay in this good work until he gains strength to do better. If he eventually progresses from woman to man, in fact, if he turns into the perfect man, he may then engage in the work of perfection.[34]

However, the main reason why Bernard often characterizes the minister as a man is not this widely shared prejudice of his age that women by nature are weak and soft.[35] It is the analogy between the work of the Son of

32. Bernard, *Super Cant.* 27.11–12: 1:189–91.

33. Bernard, *Super Cant.* 57.9: 2:124–25.

34. Bernard, *Super Cant.* 12.8: 1:65–66. The phrase "perfect man" (*in virum perfectum*) is a reference to Christ come to full stature in the growth of his church according to Eph 4:13.

35. See also Bernard, *Super Cant.* 38.4: 2:16, in which Bernard characterizes as *virile* (manly) the

God, who came out from the Father "to sow his seed," and the work of the preacher, apostle, bishop, and abbot, who are also sent to sow their seed, which is ultimately not their own, but the divine Word-seed of the Son.[36] Yet Bernard never pushes the similarity between the minister and Christ so far as to speak about the priest or bishop as an *alter Christus*, "another Christ."[37] His favorite image for the role of bishop and pope is "the friend of the bridegroom." They have authority over the church, but they do not possess her. The church does not belong to them but to her groom. The authority of the hierarchy consists in the service of leading the church as a chaste bride to her one husband, Christ, and to mediate their immediate encounter. Thus the role of the groom's friend is to decrease in stature, and to share the groom's joy in finding his bride.[38]

The above texts make clear that Bernard's appeal to church leaders to combine in themselves the best qualities of mother and father is far more than moral exhortation. It derives from a consistent theology and psychology of spiritual life and church office:

> Realize that you ought to be mothers for your subjects, not masters. Strive to be loved rather than to be feared. If at times severity is needed, be severe as a father, not as a tyrant. Show yourselves mothers in loving, fathers in correcting. Act gently, avoid cruelty. Stop the blows, bring forth breasts. Let your bosoms expand with milk, not swell with arrogance.[39]

The Triumph of Love: The "Equality" between Bride and Groom

Here we come to the boldest aspect of Bernard's thought, the final denouement of the drama of the divine love that guides both salvation history

spiritually mature soul and calls *femineum* (womanly) the fleshly and worldly soul whose life and actions are still sluggish and soft.

36. Bernard, *Ep.* 129: 7:323; see also *Super Cant.* 51.3: 2:86; *Vit. Mal.* 32: 3:340; *Ben.* 8, 10: 5:7, 9.

37. It would be interesting to research the origin of the later formula *sacerdos–alter Christus*. It certainly supposes an emphasis on the priest's sacramental ministry, an emphasis foreign to Bernard.

38. Bernard, *Nat. Bapt.* 12: 5:184; *Ep.* 191.2: 8:43; *Ep.* 238.2: 8:116–17. As in many other instances, Bernard combines here Pauline and Johannine texts so that Jn 3:29 and 2 Cor 11:2 become the foundation for his theology of church office. For more on this, see Yves Congar, "L'ecclésiologie de saint Bernard": *Saint Bernard théologien: Actes du Congrès de Dijon 15–19 sept 1953 = Analecta Sacri Ordinis Cisterciensis* 9 (1953): 136–90. This article remains the best treatise on Bernard's ecclesiology up to the present day. On the role of the hierarchy as "friend of the groom," see 171–75. Congar's work was my most important source for this chapter.

39. Bernard, *Super Cant.* 23.2: 1:140.

and the individual history of human souls. The end is already anticipated and prepared for in the beginning. God, who cannot transcend himself in greatness and majesty, transcends himself in humility by becoming not just equal to us, human beings, but truly one of us:

> Is it true that the highest of all has become one of us all? Who has brought this about? Love itself, unaware of its own dignity, rich in mercy, powerful in affection, effective in persuasion. What could be more violent? Love triumphs even over God.... He has emptied himself so that you might know that out of love fullness has been poured out, highness made equal to us, and his unique dignity associated with us.[40]

While the language seems to be that of the new courtly love, the passion of love triumphing over all rational considerations expresses a theological truth that is central to Bernard's thought. The law of God's being is love itself so that love triumphing over God simply means that God freely forgets his own transcendent majesty in order to descend even lower than humanity, accepting the consequences of all human sins. The self-forgetting love of the groom does not retain anything for himself, shares all that he has with his bride. They share everything with one another, "the same inheritance, the same table, the same home, the same marriage bed." They are one flesh in the sense that the groom shares in the bodily nature of his bride.[41] But their union is purely spiritual. The soul becomes "one spirit" with the Lord in the sense that the bride subjects her will to that of the groom by the love that comes from the Holy Spirit. The result is "a communion of wills," an agreement in charity.[42]

The bride's love flowing from the same source as that of the groom is so pure that it seeks nothing but love, nothing but the person of the groom. Since she no longer seeks her own glory, she is no longer rebuked when she asks admission to the wine cellar of contemplation. Her love is so vehement that, forgetting all rational limits, all inhibition of respect, it seeks a direct spiritual union with her beloved.

At this point, rather than reprimanding the bride, the groom encourages her boldness and inspires the pure flame of her passion. The bride can now enjoy God, who is love itself, in his own nature. In this state

40. Bernard, *Super Cant.* 64.10: 2:171.
41. Bernard, *Super Cant.* 7.1: 1:31–32.
42. Bernard, *Super Cant.* 71.10: 2:221.

even majesty yields to love. Yes, my brothers, love neither looks up nor looks down on anyone. It regards as equal all who love one another perfectly and joins together in itself the lofty and the lowly. In fact, it makes them not only equal but one. You may have thought up to now that God should be an exception to this law of love. However, he who clings to the Lord, becomes one spirit with him (1 Cor 6:17).[43]

Not only does love create a certain equality between the bride and the groom (presupposing rather than abolishing the essential difference between divine and human natures),[44] it also provides a mutual delight for both of them. St. Bernard expresses this mystery by the images of the bride and groom mutually "eating one another." The groom feeds us with himself while at the same time he is fed by our progress in virtues. He refreshes us with his spiritual joy while equally rejoicing in our progress. The result is that bride and groom are mutually living in one another.[45] Their mutual delight is perfected in heaven, where the groom will not eat, but rather drink our virtues. Our joy will also be perfected by the groom's intense and irrevocable presence. But the fulfillment of our joy in heaven will be like oil poured out on flames. It will not quench but rather increase our desire to search for him even more, without end.[46]

The consummation of all predestined human beings into the one bride in heaven (composed of angels, the saints of the Old Testament, the church, the converted synagogue, and the pagans who had a faith in the coming Savior) is the final goal of all creation in God's eternal plan.[47] She is that one perfect bride whom "the Father has predestined before all ages and prepared for his beloved Son. She is to be an everlasting delight for him throughout eternity so that she may become holy and immaculate in his sight, growing like a lily and flourishing forever before the Lord, the Father of my Lord Jesus Christ, the Bridegroom of the Church."[48]

43. Bernard, *Super Cant.* 59.2: 2:136.

44. Bernard, *Super Cant.* 71.7–9: 2:218–21.

45. Bernard, *Super Cant.* 71.4–5: 2:217.

46. Bernard, *Super Cant.* 84.1: 2:303.

47. Note that the church is of central importance among the various "components" of the one bride. The number of the angels and their joy will not be complete, nor will the patriarchs and the prophets be consummated without the church. Thus at times "the church" designates not only the historical Catholic Church, but all those who are destined for eternal life. In fact, the perfection of the whole of creation, including the material universe, depends on the church. See, for instance, Bernard, *Super Cant.* 68.4: 2:199.

48. Bernard, *Super Cant.* 78.8: 2:271.

A Theology of Gender in St. Bernard?

Evidently, Bernard has not faced the challenge of the feminist critique of the Bible. Yet his use of sexual and gender-related terms about God, church, soul, and church leaders—consistent with the usage of the whole patristic and medieval tradition—is guided by a theological understanding that is quite relevant for some of our contemporary questions. However, to perceive the theological significance of this usage, first we need to understand what the sexual and gender-related terms do not mean in Bernard's works. For him God alone is pure spirit so much so that the phrase "God is spirit" from John 4:24 becomes a quasi-definition of God, a definition Bernard uses much more frequently than his other favorite Johannine statement, "God is love" (1 Jn 4:8).[49] Of course, the more frequent use of John 4:24 does not diminish the centrality of love in Bernard's thought but rather specifies its nature. Precisely because God is infinite, pure spirit, he is capable of a transcendent and direct intimacy. He infuses himself into the soul directly, without any material means. He penetrates to her very core and achieves a union that is infinitely more intimate than any sexual encounter could bring about. God's presence in the soul calls forth an incomparably more passionate desire for love than any romantic love could enkindle. Thus, in Bernard's mind the most perfect and most powerful intimacy is the spiritual intimacy between the Word-spirit and the human soul.[50] In comparison, everything else fades. Yet, paradoxically, this spiritual union with God leads Bernard to use uninhibitedly a concrete imagery of romantic love in order to provide metaphors for what cannot be properly described.[51] Thus marital union, marriage bed, breasts, embrace, and other images such as these must be understood in a transcendent sense that attempts to adumbrate what is in itself inexpressible.

It is in this context that we should try to perceive the meaning of masculine and feminine qualities and images applied to God, the soul, and to the church. The church grows into the perfect man, Christ, and constitutes

49. Jn 4:24 occurs eighteen times, while 1 Jn 4:8 only twelve times.

50. Bernard, *Super Cant.* 5.4–8: 1:23–25.

51. It is remarkable that the bride-bridegroom and marital-union imagery are never used about the relationship between the Christian and the man Jesus. The *Verbum spiritus* always refers to Christ in his glorified state, including his humanity. The divine glory shines through his glorified humanity undimmed and unscreened so that the soul is united to the divine Word.

the body of Christ insofar as she manifests him and is animated by his life. But insofar as she is in a loving partnership with him, giving herself over in a free, loving surrender to the groom, she is called bride, and Christ is called bridegroom. If you look at an individual soul as one with Christ, she is a member of his body. If you see her as sharing in the loving partnership of the church-bride, she is also bride, loved by Christ as if she alone were the sole object of Christ's love and concern.

The church is mother insofar as she gives birth to children or rather gives birth to Christ in her children. Yet she is not the source of the life she gives. The Father, as ultimate source, and the Word-seed of the Son make her fertile. It is also for this reason that the second person of the Trinity is called by masculine names, Son and Bridegroom. He is the immediate cause of the church's spiritual fecundity.

Here, I cannot even provide an outline for Bernard's Mariology.[52] For our topic it should suffice to say that humankind reaches its highest dignity, as well as the summit of its own autonomy and free cooperation with God, in the form of a woman, "a virgin whose name was Mary" (Lk 1:27). In God's eternal plan the world's salvation has depended on Mary's "yes," by which she first received the Word into her mind and then into her womb.[53] Precisely in her femininity as virgin and mother, Mary is the most perfect actualization of human freedom expressing itself in a loving surrender to God the Father.

Mary reaches higher in faith than does any other human being, up to the very heart of the Father, from where she receives the Word into her womb. She obtains the plenitude of grace that has been in the Father from all eternity not only for herself but for the salvation of all. Thus she not only shares in the grace of her Son as other members of the church do, but through her, the fullness of all grace flows to each one of us.[54] In response to her faith, God's favor raises Mary in some sense above God himself: "Admire then both mysteries and choose which one you admire more, the most gracious favor of the Son or the highest dignity of the Mother. Both are stunning miracles. That God would submit to a woman, it is unprece-

52. The best treatment of Bernard's Mariology is H. Barré, "Saint Bernard, docteur mariale," in *Saint Bernard théologien*, 92–113.

53. Bernard, *Miss.* 4.8: 4:53–54.

54. Bernard, *Nat. BM* 11–12: 5:283; *Super Cant.* 29.8: 1:208.

dented humility. That a woman rule over God, it is unparalleled dignity."[55]

Thus the symbol of the woman, virgin, bride, and mother stands primarily for the highest perfection of creation in distinction to God and for creation's free, loving partnership with God. Yet, even before creation, in some sense the bride has already been present in the divine groom. She was also manifested to us through Christ, for "we have seen the Bride in the Groom, admiring one and the same Lord of glory both as Bridegroom decked with a crown and as Bride adorned with her jewels."[56] God the Son provided for us in himself a "preview" of his own beautiful bride, and thereby revealed the bride's divine origin.

As we have seen above, the masculine names for God, Father and Son, express primarily intra and extratrinitarian relationships, and only secondarily, qualities connected with those relationships. God's fatherly quality consists in his mercy.[57] He is the father of love, the father of mercies insofar as he is Father of his Son.[58] The masculine quality of the Son consists in his role of taking and keeping the initiative in the groom-bride relationship, while at the same time he also emboldens his bride to search for him, to forget about the distance of reverence and to desire the kiss of his mouth, which is a share in the Holy Spirit, the mutual love between Father and Son.

Yet Bernard also applies feminine images both to Father and Son. This apparent contradiction enhances our sense of transcendence. It convinces us that any univocal application of sexual and gender-related terms to God would completely distort the mysteries of faith. The first person of the Trinity is the ultimate source of the Son's life, and in that sense he must be called Father. But he is unlike any human father and in a transcendent sense unites in himself the role of both father and mother. He is the one and only principle not only begetting the Son but also giving birth to him. Using the Vulgate translation of Psalm 109:3, according to Bernard the Father gives birth to the Son from his womb, from all eternity. Moreover, the Father's mercy is also that of a mother. One of Bernard's favorite quotations to describe the Father's love toward us (and the spiritual person's love patterned on that of the Father) is Isaiah 49:15: "Can a woman forget her baby

55. Bernard, *Miss.* 1.7: 4:19.
56. Bernard, *Super Cant.* 27.7: 1:186.
57. Bernard, *Super Cant.* 66.9: 2:184.
58. Bernard, *Nat.* 5.3: 4:268.

so that she would have no mercy on the son of her womb? But even if she forgets her baby, I will not forget you."[59] Twice he transforms the quotation in an astonishing way: "Can the Father forget the son of his womb?"[60] Such a strange mixture of masculine and feminine characteristics to describe the Father's fatherhood prevents any literal, univocal interpretation. Moreover, it suggests a transcendent meaning for divine fatherhood, a meaning that also includes motherhood by raising both to a spiritual level, where their different functions and traits are integrated.

Since the risen Christ is Wisdom made manifest and the Latin word for wisdom, *sapientia*, is feminine, references to Wisdom occur in the feminine forms of various pronouns. But Bernard goes beyond merely applying a grammatical rule. At times he personifies Wisdom as "mother Wisdom" insofar as wisdom dwelling in the soul is the origin of wise counsel.[61] Moreover, following the commentary of Gregory the Great, Bernard also speaks about the bridegroom's breasts that provide sweet milk for the soul.[62] Even though the bridegroom of the church is the risen Christ rather than the preexistent Word, in describing the divine nuptials Bernard still prefers to speak about the union of *Verbum* and *anima*, Word and soul.[63] In this way, since *Verbum* is a neutral noun and transparently symbolic of a spiritual reality, the sexual connotations of nuptial terms are negated. The result of this conjunction of feminine and masculine images with the term "Word" is similar to what happens in the case of the Father. Even though Christ is termed predominantly Son of the Father and bridegroom of the church, the feminine images of mother Wisdom and the feeding breasts of the bridegroom, combined with the designation of the groom as Word, enrich the meaning and raise it to the level of transcendent mystery.

Outside of a trinitarian context, where the feminine is complementary but subordinate to masculine imagery, divine love is expressed equally by the image of a loving father and mother. In fact, Bernard uses the allegory *mater caritas*, "mother charity."[64] It is "mother charity" that reconciles God

59. Bernard, *Super Cant.* 68.3: 2:198. Bernard applies this quotation in various forms ten times in his works.

60. Bernard, *Circ.* 3.3: 4:284; *Par.* 1.3: 6/2:262.

61. See, for instance, Bernard, *V HM* 1: 5:68; *Ep.* 42.3: 7:103.

62. Bernard, *Super Cant.* 9.4–6: 1:44–46.

63. He calls the bridegroom by his proper name, Jesus Christ, routinely at the end of each *Sermo super Cantica* when speaking not about the union of the individual soul with her groom, but about the marital union of Christ and the church.

64. Bernard, *Ep.* 7.1: 7:32.

to man and man to God.[65] Bernard also loves the biblical image of God or Wisdom as a mother bird hiding her little ones under her wings and warming them with her body heat.[66]

Conclusions

I hope the above summary has shown how stimulating Bernard's thought is for contemporary theology. Here I select only three insights, relating to ecclesiology, ministry, and "the theology of gender."

1. Bernard's ecclesiology, intellectually and existentially appropriated, would prove a powerful antidote to the widespread allergy to and resentment against the institutional model of the church. Indeed, if one loses oneself in an institution to the point of identifying one's personal life with its activities and concerns, it will damage or even destroy one's humanity. How many zealous church leaders became victims of a "burnout," feeling that they have to quit before they "die" emotionally?

Bernard dedicates his whole life to the institutional church, to his monastery, to the Cistercian order, and allows himself to be snatched away regularly from his community for the crisis management of the church universal. While complaining constantly about being torn apart by conflicting demands, he thrives and grows spiritually under the pressure. The secret of his spiritual sanity in the midst of constant turmoil lies in the fact that he identifies with the church not so much as an institution, but rather as bride and mother. His personal life grows increasingly into the universal dimensions of the church as one bride and mother, who is pure love for the groom and filled with compassion for all humankind. This is, then, the *anima ecclesiastica* of St. Bernard, "the churchly soul" in the sense of Origen. His ideal is not the church lackey who always and everywhere zealously and uncritically champions the latest "party line" of the papacy or a national episcopacy.[67] In this way Bernard unites in himself the greatest personal freedom with the greatest identification with the church. The growth of his personal life and freedom actually derive from this identification.

2. Bernard's theology of apostolic ministry does not furnish any argu-

65. Bernard, *Ep.* 2.1: 7:13.

66. For instance, Bernard, *QH* 5.4: 4:400–401; *Sent.* 2.47: 6/2:35.

67. He shows immense respect for the institution of the papacy but unrestrained freedom to criticize its abuses and deformations. See Congar, "L'ecclésiologie de saint Bernard," 157–75.

ment in favor of women's ordination. In fact, his understanding of the minister's role as the sower of the Word in continuity with Jesus and the apostles, his favorite image of the shepherd of souls as "the friend of the bridegroom," speaks against such a change. Nevertheless, his thought and practice profoundly challenge the prevailing priestly ideals of formation both on the "neoconservative" and "liberal" end of the spectrum.[68]

To the neoconservatives who push too far the dictum *sacerdos alter Christus* (the priest is another Christ) he would counsel caution. One should not fall into the trap of identifying himself with his priestly or episcopal dignity. In fact, the priest's role is to arrange for a direct meeting of the bride and the groom. His function is indeed necessary; without him the soul would not be prepared for Christ. But he must be surpassed so that the bride may find her beloved. Moreover, before anyone can safely (that is, without jeopardizing his own salvation) become a church leader, he himself must become bride, be introduced into the bridal chamber of contemplative love, and become a mother anxious to feed her little ones with milk, who cannot yet endure the solid food of contemplation. Thus, for Bernard the male priesthood lacks any male "mystique." The ideal bishop is not an authoritarian, aggressive male who orders around his flock as if it were his own possession. He is to embody the qualities of both mother and father, and in this order. Bernard cannot stress enough the motherly images of tender love, feeding, giving birth again and again until Christ is formed in those entrusted to the shepherd's care.[69]

To those on the liberal end of the spectrum, whose priestly ideal is the community organizer for improving social conditions, Bernard would indeed stress Christ's solidarity with the poor. But he would also emphasize that both poor and rich, great and small sinner, are equally called to a spiritual marriage with Christ, and that the final goal of all priestly activity is to lead all men and women to this chaste and eternal union. So that his preaching be fruitful, the priest must testify to his flock about his own experience of loving union with Christ. He must be able to speak of what he

68. We must admit that, while possessing a deep theology of the sacramental economy of salvation, Bernard has never developed a theology of sacramental ministry. The administration of the sacraments is essential for him, but he prefers to speak about the ministry of preaching.

69. Beyond the theology of spiritual motherhood based on both Scripture and patristic tradition, the prevalence of motherly images could also be explained by Bernard's concern for "taming" the "mordax increpatio praelatorum" (*Super Cant.* 9.6: 1:46), "the biting preaching style of the church leaders" of his time, as well as his own fierce temperament.

himself has seen and heard. Thus only contemplatives ought to be entrusted with the pastoral ministry.

3. As we have seen above, Bernard uses both masculine and feminine images for God. He employs the former to express the mutual relationships of Father and Son and their relationship to the world, while complementary but subordinate feminine images assure the transcendent meaning of divine fatherhood and sonship. At the same time, when describing God's love as the very law of his being, Bernard uses both masculine and feminine terms with fairly equal emphasis.

However, the privileged locus for feminine imagery is the church as the focal point of God's eternal plan on which the consummation of all creation hinges. God's final goal is the one perfect bride, prepared by the Father for the Son from all eternity. Thus, in spite of occasional concessions to male prejudice, the "feminine" in Bernard's theology represents precisely the opposite of forced subjection, servitude, and dehumanization that was, according to the feminist critique, the actual state of women in a patriarchal society.[70] The woman as virgin, bride, and mother represents redeemed humankind in union with the angels at its highest, transcendent perfection. The Christian vision of Bernard turns upside down the customary values of his and our own environment. In medieval society it was the male who represented autonomy and freedom. In salvation history it is the woman who symbolizes a free, autonomous partnership of creation with God. As the one bride, she is made out of pure grace so perfect that God the Son desires her beauty and finds eternal delight in her. Ultimately, the exaltation of the woman reveals something unfathomable in God himself, his divine humility, which raises his creation, that which is different from God, symbolized through what is most frail in human eyes,[71] to a relationship of mutuality with God.

70. I am convinced that a more detailed study would prove that Bernard follows here the best elements of a consistent patristic and medieval tradition.

71. Here creation is not just dialectically opposed to God as in Hegel, but it is ontologically and definitively other than God.

CHAPTER 20

A Catholic Response to W. Pannenberg, "Evangelische Überlegungen zum Petrusdienst des Römischen Bischofs"

Professor Wolfhart Pannenberg's reflections are an important Lutheran contribution to the "patient and fraternal dialogue" on the Petrine ministry to which, in his encyclical *Ut Unum Sint*, John Paul II invited church leaders and theologians who are not in full communion with the church of Rome.[1] The goal of this dialogue, as John Paul envisioned it, was to find a way for the bishop of Rome to become an effective servant for the unity of all Christians, a way that, while respecting what is essential for the Petrine office, "is nonetheless open to a new situation."[2] The following highlights what seems to be the most important theses in Pannenberg's article, followed by an invitation for him to reflect further on the biblical, historical, and theological issues that still separate us.

1. Pannenberg's conclusions move considerably beyond the statement of the "Malta Report" of the Joint Commission of the Lutheran World Council and the Roman Catholic Church, in which the Lutheran side acknowledges that "the office of the papacy as a visible sign of the unity of the church is not excluded, provided that, through a theological re-interpretation and practical restructuring, this office is subjected to the primacy of

1. John Paul II, Encyclical Letter *Ut Unum Sint* (May 25, 1995), 96.
2. John Paul II, *Ut Unum Sint*, 95.

the Gospel."[3] In his article, Pannenberg proposes exactly such a "theological re-interpretation and practical re-structuring," but he views a reformed Petrine office not only not excludable on the basis of the gospel but also "basically desirable, an office which the church could hardly do without" ("*nur schwer entbehrlich*").[4]

2. On obvious historical grounds, a reformed Petrine office to guard and articulate the faith of the universal church would belong to the church and bishop of Rome. In spite of the chronic power politics and abuse of authority on the part of Rome, an abuse that has tragically hurt Rome's task of serving the unity of the church's faith, "there is no realistic alternative" to the bishop of Rome.

3. While not accepting the succession of the Roman bishops to Peter as a succession "by divine right," Pannenberg sees the emergence as early as the second century of a certain primacy of Rome ("*Vorrang*") as "the effect of God's providential guidance in the course of history."

4. The theological reinterpretation of the Petrine ministry must include a clear subordination of this ministry to the gospel. Pannenberg notices that *Dei Verbum* of the Second Vatican Council subordinates the magisterium to the Word of God. However, he considers the conciliar formulation ambiguous since *Dei Verbum* sees the magisterium not merely at the service of the Bible but also at service of the Word of God as it has been handed down through the living tradition of the church.[5]

5. Pannenberg proposes the natural role model for the bishop of Rome in the figure of Peter as it emerges from the whole of the New Testament, but he does not see in any Petrine office in the New Testament an office that could be inherited by the bishops of Rome.

6. According to Pannenberg, Peter renounced his official leadership ("*Leitungsamt*") when he left Jerusalem, but he maintained until the end of his life an *auctoritas*, a moral authority. The bishop of Rome may use a similar *auctoritas*, but should not exercise a formal leadership over the universal church. Pannenberg seems to admit the right of the bishop of Rome as

3. Lutheran–Roman Catholic Study Commission, *The Gospel and the Church—The Malta Report* (February 9, 1972), 66 (http://www.prounione.urbe.it/dia-int/l-rc/doc/e_l-rc_malta.html).

4. In pointing out the desirability of a reformed Petrine ministry, the American Lutheran-Catholic dialogue came to a similar conclusion. See Paul C. Empie and T. Austin Murph, eds., *Lutherans and Catholics in Dialogue*, vol. 5, *Papal Primacy and the Universal Church* (Minneapolis: Augsburg, 1974), part 1, nos. 32, 22–23.

5. DV 10.

the patriarch of the West to exert jurisdictional powers over the Western church, but (rightly) distinguishes from his patriarchal role his Petrine service for the unity of all the churches. In the service of the universal church, the pope should abstain from issuing orders that require obedience. "The less the bishop of Rome demands obedience, the more effective his utterances will be in this regard (of furthering unity)."

7. Pannenberg acknowledges that, to the extent the pope articulates the faith of the universal church, his utterances must be true (just like any true proposition) in virtue of itself (*ex sese* of Vatican I), rather than because of a second instance, its reception by the church. When expressing the faith of the universal church, the pope's teaching, as Vatican I said, participates in the infallibility of the church. Nevertheless, the pope must first ascertain through consultation and through the study of the gospel that indeed he is to express the faith of the universal church. The mere intention to do so does not assure that the pope in fact has issued an infallible statement. Only the reception of the papal teaching by the universal church (the *Gesamtkirche* to which also the Orthodox and Protestant churches belong) will show that the pope has truly exercised the Petrine ministry and thus expressed the faith of the universal church.

Pannenberg's theses provide hope that the dialogue on this highly divisive issue can actually move forward; at the same time, his reflections challenge Catholic theologians to rethink the meaning and practice of the Petrine ministry within a theology of the Word of God, which will, we hope, prove congenial to Lutheran Christians. Obviously, only some select, initial considerations can be proposed here in response.

1. Catholic theology will always consider the Petrine office not only "desirable and hard to do without" but also an indispensable safeguard for the unity of the church. This conclusion arises not from one isolated text in Scripture, such as Matthew 16:13–28, but from the lived and defined faith of the Catholic Church, a faith that finds ample justification in the converging evidence of the many Petrine texts of the New Testament and in the structure of the New Testament canon.

True, the primacy of the bishop of Rome did not emerge as a result of exegetical arguments from the Petrine texts of the Bible; it was initially derived from the joint presence, teaching, and martyrdom of the chief apostles Peter and Paul in the church of Rome. But many other doctrines of the church were first practiced and lived before the church found the scriptural foundations for their confirmation.[6] In fact, a large number of individual texts in the four Gospels indicate the leadership role of Peter.[7] In fact, this Peter's leadership is explicitly stated in two independently formulated traditions, Matthew 16:13–19 and Luke 22:30–33. Why was an appendix added to the Fourth Gospel in which the "competition" between the beloved disciple and Peter is clearly decided in favor of Peter, the universal shepherd? The author of the Second Letter of Peter, written in the first decades of the second century, clearly attributes to Peter the role of the authentic interpreter of all the letters of his "beloved brother Paul." Why were all these traditions that extol the primacy of Peter as the rock on which the (universal) church is built, the holder of the keys of the kingdom, the universal shepherd, the authentic interpreter of the Letters of Paul preserved and made part of New Testament documents after the martyr death of Peter? Franz Mussner rightly points out that these texts had to have a relevance for the subapostolic church.[8] The authors of these New Testament documents must have assumed that Peter continues his ministry, his universal shepherding and his strengthening of the faith of the church after his martyr death. In fact, they imply that Peter becomes most effective in the church because of and after his martyrdom.[9] Thus the early bishops of Rome, who claimed that the blessed Peter channels through them his "concern for all the churches," expressed a view rooted in the Petrine texts of the New Testament: Peter (and Paul in union with Peter) exercise his leadership role through the bishop of Rome.[10] The earliest theology of primacy, then, is not of succession, but of representation. The bishop of Rome is the visible representative of the living and reigning martyr Peter,

6. For instance, before quoting Rom 5 in support of original sin, infant baptism was practiced. Before finding out that the permanent seal of baptism in Scripture implies an indelible character, the Roman church did abide by the practice of never repeating the sacrament of baptism.

7. Cf. the fact that he is always first in the list of the Twelve, that he serves as spokesman for the apostles, that Jesus pays the temple tax for himself and for Peter together.

8. See Franz Mussner, "Petrusgestalt und Petrusdienst in der Sicht der späten Urkirche: Redaktionsgeschichtliche Überlegungen," in *Dienst an der Einheit. Zum Wesen und Auftrag des Petrusamts*, ed. Joseph Ratzinger (Düsseldorf: Patmos, 1978), 27–45.

9. According to Mt 16:13–28 Peter receives the promise to become the rock on which the church will be built, but soon afterward Jesus reprimands him as Satan, as being a stumbling block (*skandalon*) to him for opposing his suffering. Only the Peter who accepted taking up his cross will be able to fulfill his mission.

10. The pope describes his Petrine ministry by quoting a text from Paul: 2 Cor 11:28. See more on this topic in William R. Farmer and Roch Kereszty, *Peter and Paul in the Church of Rome: The Ecumenical Potential of a Forgotten Perspective* (Mahwah, N.J.: Paulist Press, 1990), 92–95.

who works through him,[11] and simultaneously also of the martyr apostle Paul. The bishop of Rome, then, performs his ministry by making visible the *martyria*, the witnessing of Peter and Paul and by his readiness to share in their destiny of martyrdom.[12]

2. The distinction of Pannenberg between *potestas* and *auctoritas* seems to be a retrojection of Roman concepts into biblical usage. According to Matthew, the eleven disciples-apostles received a share in the *exousia*, the full power of the Son (28:18–20). Paul is aware that, as an apostle of Jesus Christ, he was given *exousia*, which can be used both for "building up" and "tearing down" (2 Cor 10:8). Analogously to the *exousia* of Jesus Christ, which Jesus uses only in absolute dependence on the Father, the apostle uses the participated *exousia* in absolute dependence on the person and gospel of Jesus Christ for the sake of the faithful. He acts both as a father and mother, pleading, entreating, and persuading his faithful with tender affection whenever he can. But he does not hesitate "to make the full weight of his apostolic *exousia* felt when setting out norms for the eucharistic life (1 Cor 10–11), marriages (1 Cor 7), lawsuits in the church in Corinth (1 Cor 6), and excommunication of an incestuous man "in the name of our Lord Jesus Christ" and with his "power" (1 Cor 5:4).[13] Paul's apostolic authority goes well beyond simple moral persuasion.

The bishops of Rome at their best used all these Pauline (and Petrine) ways of exercising their authority. Clearly, gentle persuasion and sympathetic listening are preferable to disciplinary measures. But on what biblical grounds could we deny the right and the duty of the bishop of Rome to demand obedience, to use severe reprimand and even excommunication, when the gospel of Jesus Christ is at stake and all other means have already been exhausted? Of course, the pope may discipline only those who freely acknowledge him as the representative of Peter. Regarding the churches not in full communion with the church of Rome, he should never use au-

11. Until Innocent III, the bishop of Rome claimed to *bevicarius Petri*, not *vicarius Christi*. The First and Second Letters of Peter were both written from Rome; the second certainly, the first possibly, is pseudepigraphic. Their attribution to Peter may be explained by the same belief: Peter the martyr apostle continues to teach from Rome even after his death.

12. See in detail, J.-M. R. Tillard, *L'évêque de Rome* (Paris: Cerf, 1982). English translation: *The Bishop of Rome* (Wilmington, De.: Michael Glazier, 1983).

13. Farmer and Kereszty, *Peter and Paul in the Church of Rome*, 128. His instructions regarding the charismatics in Corinth are equally enlightening. He encourages the well-ordered use of all charisms, but he also warns the Corinthians: "If anyone seems to be a prophet or a spiritual man, he should recognize that what I am writing to you is a commandment of the Lord. If anyone ignores this, he is ignored" (1 Cor 14:37–38).

thoritative language, but as their brother, he should present them with his witness to the gospel. Such brotherly treatment is not a diplomatic ruse, but the honest recognition of the freedom of faith.

3. Pannenberg rightly calls attention to the frequent abuse of power by the bishops of Rome.[14] But Catholic theology has always maintained the right of bishops and faithful to protest such abuse. Contrary to widespread public opinion, the power of the pope is limited. His teaching is limited to proclaiming the Word of God; he may not abolish the episcopal structure of the church, and he is under grave moral obligation not to intervene in the affairs of a local church unless the good of the local church requires it. The purpose of his universal and immediate jurisdiction over all churches serves only to assure that all the essential qualities of the church of Christ are safeguarded in the local churches.

Regarding a future church in which Orthodox and Protestants would be in full communion with Rome, it seems obvious that the pope should not consider these churches as part of the patriarchate of the West; he should respect their autonomy, their proper laws and liturgies, as long as they do not oppose the one faith of the church.

4. Not only Pannenberg but some Catholic theologians have also proposed the assent of the church to an infallible statement of the pope as a sign which indicates that it was indeed an infallible pronouncement. Conversely, if the assent fails to occur, it suggests that one of the conditions for an infallible statement did not materialize.

Indeed, Vatican II teaches that the assent of the church to infallible papal teaching cannot fail to occur. However, the assent of the universal church can often not be verified by sociological methods. In our society, the influence of mass media can easily distort the *sensus fidei*, the Spirit-inspired faith instinct of the believers, so that a church teaching may appear to them outdated or even absurd. Another question that cannot be precisely an-

14. Whether or not this abuse has indeed been "chronic," as Pannenberg claims, would require much further discussion. The secular power of the popes over the papal states led indeed to tragic consequences from time to time, especially at the end of the Middle Ages. But being the only remaining institution with public authority, did Leo the Great and Gregory the Great have a choice not to defend Italy against the barbarian hordes in the power vacuum of late antiquity? Moreover, how could the freedom of action of the pope have been assured throughout history if the pope had been the subject of a state? We need to think only of the disastrous consequences of the popes' "Babylonian captivity" in Avignon and keep in mind the history of the Greek Orthodox Church under the Byzantine emperors, that of the Russian Orthodox Church under the czars and communism, and the subjugation of the Protestant churches of Eastern Europe under socialist regimes.

swered concerns the time of the assent. Must the assent occur immediately? If not, within how many years? This complex state of affairs shows that no theological argument for the non-infallibility of an *ex cathedra* statement (which the pope intended to define as such) may be made on the basis of a sociologically verified dissent within the church.

But the decisive argument against the necessity of a sociologically verifiable and timely assent of the universal church as sign of the infallibility of a prior papal statement is this: If before or soon after an infallible pronouncement, universal assent to a papal teaching were required as a criterion of validity, the infallible magisterium of the pope could not effectively function precisely in that situation where it would be most needed, in the conflicts of opposing views. Throughout history, papal interventions were most helpful (often though not always) exactly when divided churches struggled to reestablish the unity of faith. In fact, subsequent consent of a large part of the church (never the whole sociological unit that had called itself Catholic before the teaching was defined) occurred in these instances, but hardly ever immediately.[15]

This issue of the division in matters of faith and morals leads us to the heart of the matter: Why does the church of Christ need an infallible magisterium? Or, to use Pannenberg's words and those of the encyclical *Ut Unum Sint*, why does she need "an ultimately binding" magisterium, which, in some way or another, must always include the bishop of Rome?[16]

5. If God's Word is an effective divine self-communication not only on the level of experience but also on the level of communicating propositional truths,[17] divine providence must have created an effective instance that, with God's help, assures the infallible reception of that revelation, especially when the meaning of God's Word is controverted. Otherwise, the Word of God would remain ineffective. To put it simply, God's Word, if it is indeed God's Word, does assure its own infallible understanding. Without an ultimately binding magisterium, the faithful would have only more or

15. See, for instance, the interventions of the bishops of Rome in the Nestorian, monophysite, and monothelite crises, in the controversy about the rebaptism of heretics between Stephen and Cyprian, and in the Jansenist controversy. See more details in W. de Vries, "Das Mühen des Papsttums um die Einheit der Kirche," in Ratzinger, *Dienst an der Einheit*, 66–80.

16. Remarkably, the often misunderstood word "infallible" does not occur in the encyclical *Ut Unum Sint*. The pope seems quite satisfied in expressing the truth of the dogma of infallibility by using the language preferred by his Protestant interlocutors.

17. The Bible teaches in propositional truths most frequently. The oldest Christian confession of faith says: "Jesus is Lord."

less certain personal conclusions to rely on in the midst of any serious controversy touching on the heart of Christian faith. They would be strongly tempted to put their private judgment above the Word of God and "pick and choose" according to each one's personal taste.[18] In other words, while it is true that indefectibility and infallibility belong to the whole church, the magisterium is the Christ-given means to maintain the church's universal infallibility in faith and oppose the general human tendency of distorting God's Word to fit one's personal preferences.

The next question that arises naturally leads us from the theoretical to the historical: Where can one find this ultimately binding magisterium that enjoys the divine guarantee of truth?

6. If we review the history of Christianity, at times the majority of the church, or at least a large part of the faithful and of the bishops, was in error (for instance, the Arian crisis and the "Robber Synod" in Ephesus in 449 and others). Even in the present, one cannot assert with any certainty that the majority of Christians believe in the real presence of Christ in the Eucharist, according to the official creeds of the Roman Catholic and Lutheran churches. Thus, neither a majority of the faithful, nor of the bishops, provide a reliable criterium for infallibility. However, the bishops of Rome have claimed throughout history and with increasing frequency that, due to the special assistance of Christ in the Holy Spirit, when they have engaged their full Petrine authority, they and the bishops in communion with them did not err in matters of faith and morals. Their claim—to say the least—cannot be disproved historically. In fact, if we investigate the history of church councils in the first millennium, the only formal criterion that distinguishes the ecumenical councils (whose decrees have been accepted as true and binding both by both the Catholic and Orthodox Churches) from the nonrepresentative gatherings of bishops (which were rejected by both Catholics and Orthodox) is their acceptance or rejection by the bishop of Rome.[19]

18. Think of such central truths of faith as the bodily resurrection of Christ, the mystery of the Trinity, and the real presence of Christ in the Eucharist, doctrines on which Catholics and traditional Lutheran confessions of faith basically agree but that were and are controverted and distorted by many Christian theologians. Of course, even without a magisterium there remains the experiential certainty of the believer, a certainty that derives from the inspiration of the Holy Spirit. Without this inner testimony of the Spirit there can be no certainty of faith even in the case of a functioning magisterium. However, without the ultimately binding teaching of the magisterium there is no objective, communicable criterion of truth for distinguishing between the false and true articulation of experience.

19. For instance, if we look at the number of bishops at the Ecumenical Council of Ephesus (431)

If the above line of reasoning is correct, the only conclusion is that either there is no ultimately binding magisterium in the church or it rests with those bishops who are in communion with the bishop of Rome. Of course, at the same time we must acknowledge that from the first claim of binding authority by a Roman bishop, who tried to set a universal date for Easter in the second century, until this very day even Catholics have a natural repugnance against a binding magisterium. In this "anti-Roman resentment," as Hans Urs von Balthasar calls it, there is a legitimate reaction against the past abuses of Roman authority.[20] But beyond that, we face in the person of the pope the perennial stumbling block of the incarnation: How can a sinful man or rather the sinful head of a sinful group of bishops mediate for us God's Word and call for our "obedience of faith" to his teaching? It would certainly be easier to follow in everything our personal interpretation of the Bible. But if this were the case, our encounter with the absolute authority of God's own Word would indeed become more difficult because of our propensity to distort the meaning of the written word of God.

7. Once the scandal of the papacy as a consequence of the authority of God's Word versus individual human preferences has been stated as sharply as possible, we must begin to search together with Pannenberg and with all Protestant and Orthodox Christians for a way that would reduce the possible abuses of papal power in the future and would do full justice to the collegial nature of authority in the church. In this short response, I can only briefly point to the way that, according to my reading of the encyclical *Ut Unum Sint*, was suggested by John Paul II himself. (1) When speaking of his role as the "first servant of unity," the pope does not present himself as a "superbishop," a notion that had been associated by many Catholics and non-Catholics with the title "pope." Instead, he consistently refers to himself as the bishop of Rome. (2) John Paul II seems to propose as a starting point for discussion the practice of the first millennium, during which time the bishop of Rome was not the head of a centralized bureaucracy, but his role was, in cooperation with his brother bishops, to ensure the communion of all the churches. "If disagreements in belief and practice arose among them [the local churches], the Roman see acted by common con-

---

and the "Robber Synod" in Ephesus (449), the difference in the number of bishops is negligible; nor do any of the early ecumenical councils consist of a representative majority of the world's Catholic bishops.

20. See Hans Urs von Balthasar, *Der antirömische Affekt: Wie lässt sich das Papstum in die Gesamtkirche integrieren?* (Freiburg: Herder, 1974).

sent as moderator."[21] Thus, in spite of his own towering personality and inclination to lead, I see in this encyclical a humble recognition that the pope should not impose centralization on those Christian churches that might enter into full communion with the church of Rome in the future.

We should indeed hope and work for a future model of Petrine ministry that, while maintaining its full authority, will use this authority by respecting and promoting the full development and the legitimate autonomy, as well as the rich diversity, of the local churches in the one faith, one church polity, and one way of Christian life.

21. John Paul II, Ut Unum Sint, 95.

CHAPTER 21

The Infallibility of the Church and the Mystery of Mary

The development of Christian doctrine does not take place in a historical vacuum, nor is it only the result of the Christian people's piety or theological reflection. The challenges of the changing cultural environment and the errors deriving from it are often stimulants for seeking greater clarity and conceptual articulation of a truth of revelation. A milestone in the development and formulation of the dogma of the church's infallibility and, in particular, that of the pope's participation in it took place in response to the Enlightenment, which attempted to enthrone human reason as the only authority. As a result, theologians, and finally the First Vatican Council, formulated the church's teaching on the role and limits of human reason in matters of divine revelation and asserted the final authority of Peter's successors in defining, with the assistance of the Holy Spirit, what is and what is not revealed doctrine. While formulating the doctrine of infallibility, Vatican I concentrated only on this disputed issue and provided proof of the doctrine of infallibility from the scriptural deposit of divine revelation and the immemorial tradition of the church. In our age, however, theology and church praxis alike have turned from investigating individual dogmas in themselves toward focusing on the whole of the Christian mystery; from further differentiation of doctrine toward rediscovering the original comprehensive vision of Christian faith. This dialectic of contrary movements, from further differentiation back to the undifferentiated whole, and vice versa, provides an antidote to theological "forgetfulness" and enriches our understanding of the Christian faith.

Such rerooting of the dogma of infallibility in the totality of revelation has achieved notable success in Karl Rahner's theology. He has argued convincingly that infallibility is ultimately a necessary, a priori condition of effective divine revelation.[1] Unless there is an infallible criterion for us to judge what is and what is not divine revelation, we cannot accept God's Word the way it ought to be accepted, with the absolute surrender of our intellect and will. Without such an ultimate criterion, faith can only mean—as Paul Tillich has logically deduced—a state of ultimate concern without any definite object. The traditional objection to an infallible magisterium has been the claim that it "divinizes" the church and, in particular, the papacy, since God alone is infallible. Rahner, however, has shown that the Catholic dogma does exactly the opposite. It safeguards the divine efficacy of God's self-communication. Without an agency that can interpret with certainty what God has revealed and explain its meaning, God would have proved to be a woefully ineffective communicator. Thus the Catholic dogma safeguards God's transcendent power rather than idolizes human beings.

A few theologians, however, discovered not only the roots of infallibility in the biblical doctrine of apostolicity and Petrine ministry but also its link to the Marian mystery of the church. In other words, whereas most of contemporary theology treats the church's infallibility as required by the effectiveness of God's revelation, patristic and medieval theology sees the incorruptible permanence of the church in the divine truth as a requirement of the church's virginal and, ultimately, Marian nature. What follows is a summary of this nearly forgotten tradition and an exploration of its implications for a deeper understanding of the doctrine of infallibility. In addition, the mystery of Mary is shown as the "Catholic dogma"—to use in a positive sense Barth's disparaging statement—that assures the orthodoxy of the main doctrines of Christianity.[2]

1. Of course, under the condition that this divine revelation is addressed also to the human intellect, which, for the sake of deeper and more precise understanding, must formulate revealed truths.

2. On Barth's comments see Henri de Lubac, *The Splendor of the Church*, trans. Michael Mason (New York: Paulist Press, 1963), 198–200. Next to the invaluable studies of Hugo Rahner, *Symbole der Kirche: Die Ekklesiologie der Väter* (Salzburg: Otto Mülle Verlag, 1964), and Rahner, *Our Lady and the Church* (Chicago: Regnery, 1965), I relied mostly on de Lubac's *Splendor of the Church* for his insights and for his rich collection of patristic texts.

Mary and the Church

As early as the book of Revelation (12:1–18), the mystery of Mary and that of the church appear so closely linked as to imply a certain identity. The vision of the woman clothed with the sun, resting her feet on the moon and giving birth amid loud wailing, and under attack by the dragon, the ancient serpent, is a complex symbol. The twelve-star crown on her head symbolizing the twelve tribes presents her as Israel; and her struggle with the ancient serpent indicates that she is the new Eve who will not be conquered by Satan. Her giving birth in pain, however, cannot refer to the happy birth of Jesus in Bethlehem. In the light of John 16:21 and 19:25–27, she is also Mary, the virgin daughter Zion, who completes giving birth to the Messiah when she suffers the sword piercing her heart (Lk 2:35) as she witnesses Jesus enthroned on the cross and taken up to heaven in the resurrection. Finally, Mary, the new Eve and the virgin daughter of Israel, is also the church, the mother of those who bear witness to Jesus (Rv 12:17). In the same perspective, Irenaeus presents the symbol of the womb as both the womb of Mary and the church: "The pure One [Christ] opens purely that pure womb, which regenerates men unto God and which He Himself has made pure."[3]

There is a plethora of patristic texts in which Mary and the church interpenetrate each other and are seen, as it were, in a *perichoresis*. The Marian church is a spotless, immaculate virgin, the spouse of Christ, the mother who bears children configured to Christ, the firstborn of many brothers, or—what is equivalent to the latter—she gives birth to Christ unceasingly by regenerating people through baptism and by preaching to them the word of Christ. In the *Letter of the Martyrs of Lyons and Vienne*, written probably by Irenaeus, the church is described as virgin and mother who rejoices over those Christians who had first denied the faith under torture but, with the help of their martyr brothers and sisters, were "conceived" again and "reanimated and thus made ready for martyrdom." Watching the revived Christians being torn to pieces by the wild beasts in the arena, Alexander, a Christian physician, acted out in pantomime the pangs of labor. By acting out Mother Church's childbearing, he was interpreting to the martyrs

3. Irenaeus, *Against Heresies* 4.33.2; see also 4.33.4.

what was happening to them in the arena.[4] Not only the church, local or universal, is spouse and mother, but so also are individual Christians who, having an intact faith, firm hope, and genuine charity, realize in themselves the church's spousal mystery. And as the fruit of their virginal love they give birth to Christ in themselves, meaning that they are transformed unto the image and likeness of Christ. At a higher state of perfection, they give birth to Christ in others, in those who are entrusted to their care. This insight also derives from Paul, who addresses his "foolish" Galatians in these terms: "My children, for whom I am again in labor until Christ be formed in you!" (Gal 4:19). From an early time, the baptismal pool was also called the *uterus Ecclesiae*, womb of the church, from which the catechumens arose reborn to a new life in Christ.

Blessed Isaac of Stella, a twelfth-century Cistercian abbot, formulated the terminology to legitimately speak about these three interpenetrating realities: Mary, church, and the individual soul.

> In the divinely inspired Scriptures, what we say about the virgin mother Church in a universal sense we understand in a singular sense about the virgin mother Mary, and what we say about the virgin mother Mary in a special sense, we rightly understand in a general sense about the virgin mother Church. And when a text speaks about one or the other, its meaning applies almost without distinction to both. In addition, each faithful soul may be considered in its own way as the spouse of the Word of God, as the mother, daughter and sister of Christ and as virgin and fecund.[5]

But beyond the terminological distinctions, how can these relationships themselves be clarified? In promulgating the Dogmatic Constitution on the Church of the Second Vatican Council in 1964, Pope Paul VI solemnly declared that the Virgin Mary is the mother of the church. The beginnings of this teaching are present in the early Fathers' identification of Mary with the new Eve, the "mother of all the living." This view was further developed by the contemporary exegesis of John 19:25–27. In the Fourth Gospel most events and utterances of Jesus have a deeper meaning beyond the obvious. Thus, in Jesus' last words to his mother and to the beloved disciple ("Woman, behold your Son ... Behold your mother") the ecclesial dimension of Mary's motherhood is disclosed to us. The beloved disciple represents all

4. Letter quoted by Eusebius of Caesarea, Hist. *eccl.* 5.1.45–46.
5. Isaac of Stella, *Sermo* 51 *in Assumptione* 8.

the disciples of Jesus, and thus Mary's motherhood is stretched by Jesus so wide as to embrace all of them. At the foot of the cross, "wailing aloud in pain" (Rv 12:2),[6] she completed, by her consent to the self-offering of her Son, the birth of Jesus into being the enthroned Messiah, the king of Israel and the world. Thus Mary's (existential) consummation of giving birth to the Son of God coincides with receiving her universal vocation as the mother of all believers, the mother of the church.

The meaning of the title (mother of the church) clarifies Mary's relationship to the church. She gave birth bodily to the head of the church, Christ, and spiritually to the members of the body of Christ. As Augustine said, "She contributed by her charity so that the faithful might be born in the Church."[7] Relying on Origen's insight, Blessed Guerric explains that Mary has the desire to form her only begotten Son in all her adopted sons: "Even though they were already conceived by the word of truth, she still gives birth to them every day by her desire and tender care until they reach the state of the perfect man to the extent of the full stature of her Son."[8]

The Faith of Mary and the Faith of the Church

In this context, then, the church as mother appears not as a vague poetic hyperbole, but as a concrete personal reality; she is Mary, the mother of all believers and, along with her, all faithful and loving members of the church who have become particular mothers of souls. Thus, when we speak about the "faith of the church," without which the sacraments could not be validly administered and the church could not have existentially fully appropriated the sacrifice of Jesus in the offering of the Eucharist, we mean the perfect faith of Mary and secondarily the faith of all the believers in heaven and on earth in whom the Holy Spirit is actively present. The role of Mary in the

6. Only later reflection, by interpreting Rv 12:1–18; Jn 16:21; 19:25–27 as belonging together, grasped the full meaning of Jesus' last words to his mother and the beloved disciple. See André Feuillet, "L'heure de la femme (Jn 16,21) et l'heure de la Mère de Jésus (Jn 19,25–27)," *Biblica* 47 (1966): 169–84, 361–80, 557–73.

7. Augustine, *De sancta virginitate* 1.6.

8. Guerric, *Sermo II in Nativitatem Mariae* 3.84–87. According to Origen, Mary has only one son, Jesus. When hanging on the cross, "Jesus tells her, mother, 'behold your son,' not 'behold, this also is your son.' What he meant is: 'behold this is Jesus to whom you have given birth.' For everyone who is perfected no longer lives, but Christ lives in him. Since Christ lives in him, Mary was told: 'behold your son the Christ'" (*Commentarii in evangelium Joannis* 1.4(6).7–11.

communion of the saints, however, is unique. Had she not been immaculately conceived and full of grace, her Fiat, that is, her response to God accepting the Son and his redemptive work, could not have been complete. The work of redemption could not have been fully accomplished without an adequate human response. Mary's motherly role, then, is to include us in her acceptance, in her full yes to God's entire plan of salvation.

A false way to imagine Mary's motherly role would be to assume that it merely parallels the role of the Holy Spirit and the sacraments. Obviously, the activities of Mary and the saints, let alone the sovereign work of the Holy Spirit, cannot be limited to the sacraments and other official ecclesial acts. The Holy Spirit blows where he wills; and Mary and the saints always freely communicate with us and pray for us as they carry out God's plan. Outside the church's liturgy we cannot predict when and how Mary and the saints intercede for us. However, in the sacraments and in the official prayers of the church, we know that the faith and prayers of Mary and the saints are always active. When we pray to Christ during Mass that he should not look at our sins but "at the faith of your church," when we offer in the Mass "this holy and perfect sacrifice" to the Father, when in the priest's absolution the forgiving grace of Jesus Christ is offered to the penitent, during all of these activities, we always share—whether we know it or not—in "the faith and prayers of the church," which is the faith and prayers of Mary and the saints. Thus, when we say "the church prays" we mean not a mere literary device or a legal person. It is the prayer of Mary and the other living members of the church in heaven and on earth, united with the prayers of Christ and effective with, and pleasing to, the Father.

Just as Mary completed the birth of the Messiah under the cross by identifying with her Son until his final handing over the spirit (Jn 19:30), her motherly role for the members of Christ is completed when members die and are born to eternal life in heaven. This is the reason we recite in the Hail Mary, "Pray for us sinners now and at the hour of our death."

Hans Urs von Balthasar remarks that it took the church about a millennium to discover the identity of the *ecclesia immaculata*, the *ecclesia sine macula et ruga* in Ephesians 5:27, and the *columba immaculata* in the theology of the Fathers, that is, the immaculate church without stain and wrinkle, the immaculate dove of the Song of Songs who absolves the sinner from excommunication through the bishop. The church has known from its beginning that these terms cannot mean the empirical church as she appears to believers and unbelievers alike, full of the stain and filth of her members. Eventually, the church fathers realized that she is the immaculately conceived, full of grace mother of God in communion with all the saints, who as the *ecclesia immaculata* is at work in the church's perfect response to the Son's gift of self.[9]

Infallibility in the Context of the Mystery of Mary

Even a brief outline such as this of the Marian mystery of the church can be the basis for an exploration of how the Marian context enriches and deepens the meaning of the dogma of infallibility. There is only one bridegroom, Jesus Christ, and one bride, the church. Whoever knowingly denies or distorts any truth of God's revelation sins against the pure virginal dedication of the bride to the bridegroom. Just as in the Old Testament idol worship was considered adultery against the bridal relationship of Israel and God, the fathers of the church judged any heresy to be adultery.[10] As St. Cyprian declared: "Whoever separates himself from the Church, unites himself with an adulteress."[11] Origen complains that the heretics, by being heretics, build a brothel.[12] Augustine expresses the mind of all the Fathers by explaining that what corrupts the chastity of the virgin spouse is the violation of the church's faith.[13] For Hildegard of Bingen, the most wicked corrupting agents are the errors of the heretics, "who attack her by trying to corrupt her virginity which is the Catholic faith; she, however, strongly resists them lest she be corrupted for she has always been and is and will remain a virgin."[14]

The church remains a virgin even while "she gives birth to her sons without any opposing error remaining in the integrity of faith."[15] Particular local churches may develop heresies, and thus they may change from virgin

9. See Hans Urs von Balthasar, *The Office of Peter and the Structure of the Church*, 2nd ed. (San Francisco: Ignatius, 2007), 226–29.

10. See Clement of Alexandria, *Stromata* 3.12.

11. Cyprian, *De unitate Ecclesiae* 6.146.

12. Origen, *Homilia in Ezechielem* 2.

13. Augustine, *In Evangelium Johannis tractatus* 8.5.

14. Hildegard of Bingen, *Scivias* 2.3.

15. Hildegard of Bingen, *Scivias* 2.3.

to adulteress, just as according to Hegesippos the church in Jerusalem lost her virginity after the death of her bishop Simeon.[16] The bishops of Rome, however, have been aware that, due to the Lord's promise to Peter, "in the Apostolic See the Catholic religion has always been preserved without any stain."[17] Long before the Lord called the apostles and after his resurrection charged them to go and teach all the nations, Mary had already accepted becoming the mother of the Son of God and, thereby, accepted the fullness of redemption for the human race. Thus the primary ecclesial reality is the Marian church, namely, the church as virgin, spouse, and mother in which Mary (with the growing number of the saints joining her) is active by her motherly intercession. The apostolic ministry, including the Petrine office, is posterior to this Marian aspect. Moreover, the apostolic ministry including the Petrine office has been established for the sake of guarding and guiding the virginal bride-church to full eschatological union with her divine bridegroom. The apostolic church structure exists for and because of the Marian church. Moreover, without her immaculate conception, Mary would not be full of grace and thus the church could not have fully embraced God's gift in the Son, which would have meant that there would not have been an immaculate spouse to be guarded and led to final union with God. Thus we can confidently say with Balthasar that the immaculate Marian church is prior to the apostolic mission, which includes the infallibility of its magisterium.[18]

As long as the virgin church lives her life of dedication and love, her ministers do not need to judge and condemn, but only nourish the faithful by preaching and by administering the sacraments. Only when a false doctrine threatens the community do the ministers intervene by denouncing the error and warning the church. Thus Paul protects the Corinthian church with these words: "I am jealous of you with the jealousy of God, since I betrothed you to one husband to present you as a chaste virgin to Christ. But I am afraid that, as the serpent deceived Eve by his cunning,

16. See Hegesippos in Eusebius, *Hist. eccl.* 4.22.4.

17. DS 363: "in Sede Apostolica immaculata est semper catholica servata religio." See the so-called *Decretum Gelasianum*: "Est ergo prima Petri Apostoli sedes Romanae Ecclesiae, non habens maculam neque rugam nec aliquid eiusmodi [Therefore, the first see is that of the apostle Peter's Roman church, which has no stain or wrinkle or anything of this kind]" (DS 351). This was repeated by the First Vatican Council (DS 3066).

18. See Hans Urs von Balthasar, *Theological Explorations*, vol. 3, *Creator Spirit*, trans. Brian McNeil, CRV (San Francisco: Ignatius 1991), 239–40.

your thoughts may be corrupted from a sincere and pure commitment to Christ" (2 Cor 11:2–3).

In the twenty-first century, the attitude of the apostles and their patristic and medieval successors appears strange and unduly harsh. We would prefer a more irenic approach, which allows for the good faith and good intentions of the heretic. Certainly, the apostolic, patristic, and medieval church had not developed sufficient sensitivity to consider the heretic's subjective state of mind. However, by adopting the attitude of the early church fathers, which perceived heresy to be not simply a theoretical error, but the corruption of the virginal bride of the Lord, and if we consider ourselves to be the father and mother of this virgin bride, then we can more easily empathize with the fierce reaction of the apostles and their successors.

The Marian context of the church's infallibility also sheds light on the epistemological structure of the church's object of faith. The deposit of faith has not begun as one global idea, which, with the passing of time and through encounters with different cultures, gradually develops into a list of increasingly more differentiated propositions. If we reflect on the remarkable fact that the early Fathers recorded rules of faith (*regulae fidei*) of different length and content, varying according to the nature of the heresy, then we see more clearly that behind the different sets of propositions is a more fundamental reality that evokes different propositional truths in response to different situations in the world. This fundamental reality is Christ present "in the womb of the church's faith" and, as a result, in the hearts of believers to varying extents. Thus the genesis and growth of faith in the believer is not only an intellectual process but also a giving birth to Christ in the believers' hearts. Similarly, as seen above, the work of evangelizing is characterized by enduring labor pains until Christ is shaped and formed in the evangelized. These images evidently need conceptual articulation. We may explain them as the process of the increasing intensity of Christ's indwelling in the soul and the conforming of the soul to Christ by the Holy Spirit. In the light of the Marian mystery, then, the primary object of faith is not assent to a set of propositional truths, but the person of Christ himself in his transforming presence within the church. St. Thomas's view can be interpreted as leading in the same direction. He explains that "the act of the believer terminates not in what can be enunciated, but in the reality [of what is believed]."[19] And this reality—Christ crucified and risen—is present within us.[20]

Following the patristic tradition, Aquinas also asserts the necessity of enunciating propositional truths concerning the object of our faith: "We do enunciate propositions in order to know about the realities both in science and in faith."[21] This, then, is the paradoxical character of the object of faith, which is disclosed in the perspective of the Marian mystery. Faith embraces the living reality of Christ himself by one global act, but this faith cannot say anything true and definite about his reality and its implications without formulating true propositions. Through particular propositions, each of which is incomparably less comprehensive than our intuitive grasp of the whole reality present within us, we have slowly and in piecemeal fashion over the centuries shed light on this one reality. Without this painstakingly long and never-ending process by which the magisterium formulates the mysteries of faith, our faith cannot be explained to ourselves or to others, it cannot be distinguished from errors, and, above all else, it cannot be confessed by the martyrs as truths more important and more valuable than their own lives. However, each particular truth of faith has its full truth and full value in its relationship to the one reality of Jesus Christ through his relationship to the Trinity and the history of salvation. And, in the light of the Marian mystery, we begin to see that all these propositional truths relate to the person of Christ as the church's bridegroom. They shed light on his person, on his Father and mother, on his Holy Spirit, and on his work in creation and in history. Therefore, as mentioned earlier, no heresy is seen to be only about truth or error in itself. Spreading a false teaching is the betrayal of the divine bridegroom and an attempt to corrupt his bride. Viewed from this perspective, the otherwise strange phrase used by the Fathers and medieval theologians to describe the faith of the church becomes intelligible: *fides incorrupta* (uncorrupted faith). This term expresses the faith of the church insofar as it is modeled after the faith of Mary. More than assent to the fullness of God's revelation, as preserved by the church in its integrity, it is the total surrender of the church's mind and heart to

19. Thomas Aquinas, ST II-II, q. 1, a. 2, ad 2.

20. See, among many other texts, Thomas Aquinas, *Commentarium in Johannem* 6, l. 6: "It is evident that he who believes in Christ takes him into himself according to Eph 3:17, namely, Christ dwells through faith in our hearts."

21. ST II-II, q. 1, a. 2, ad 2.

her bridegroom and for which the possession of the truth of the gospel is an essential part.

The church is striving with her *fides incorrupta* toward full union with the bridegroom, expressed in the kiss of the bride and groom in the Song of Songs; and, as the fruit of this union, she bears children to God.[22] This is a theme that runs from Origen through the later Fathers to the medieval monastic writers. For the church, just as for the perfected soul, the mediated knowledge of the bridegroom received from angels and prophets is not enough. The church as one person and each holy soul in the church begs the Father that the bridegroom himself "may come in person and that he may kiss her with the kisses of her mouth; that is, that he may pour into my mouth the words of his mouth, that I may hear himself speaking, that I may see himself teaching me."[23]

Vatican I's definition of the pope's decisive participation in the magisterium's infallibility concerns only the intellectual aspect of faith. It defined that, under definite conditions, the bishop of Rome shares in the infallibility of the church in such a way as to exclude error in defining matters of faith and morals.[24] This indeed is the minimum necessary for the church's faith to be preserved from corruption. Yet the Marian dogmas of the immaculate conception and bodily assumption of the Virgin Mary reveal and assure us that this faith, guarded by the magisterium, remains faith informed by charity, a faith aiming at the eschatological union of the immaculate church with her divine bridegroom.

"You Vanquished All the Heresies"

The preceding sections inquired into what light the Marian mystery sheds on the doctrine of the church's infallibility. The following is a brief reflection on how the acceptance of the Marian doctrine assures orthodoxy in other key areas of Catholic teaching. For this reason, a quotation from an ancient antiphon has been chosen as the title of this subsection: "You vanquished all the heresies." It is well known that the title *theotokos*, God-

22. The symbol of the kiss comes from Song 1:2 and, beginning with Origen, the Christian tradition saw in it both the intimate union between the Word and human nature in the incarnation, and/or the eschatological union of the church with Christ anticipated in the saints' mystical union.

23. Origen, *Commentaria in Cantica* 1.1.10.

24. DS 3065–75.

bearer or mother of God, as defined by the Council of Ephesus in 431, became the battle cry of orthodoxy against all forms of Nestorianist reduction of the incarnation to a mere indwelling of God in Jesus. The Marian dogmas reveal also God's transcendent *eros* towards his creation, his respect toward human freedom and the guarantee of a final consummation of the church and all creation.

Here, however, I would like to concentrate only on one issue: if understood in its ecclesial dimension, the mystery of Mary provides the orthodox antidote to the feminist crisis. Evidently, the feminist movement would have arisen in the world and in Christianity even if Marian doctrine and piety had not been at a very low ebb after Vatican II. I am convinced, however, that it would not have struck such a responsive chord in many Catholics had they not forgotten Mary's role in the church. There appears to be a close link between the crisis in Marian piety and the feminist outcry against the male hierarchy of the church. I hope I can clarify that an integral and catholic view of the church understands the Marian principle to be prior to, and more fundamental, than the Petrine ministry. The immaculate conception stands at the very beginning of the church; and at its consummation, the assumption of Mary invites the entire church to join her. The Petrine ministry, including the episcopal college, exists only to preserve the virginal Marian church and assure her safe arrival in heaven for the wedding feast of the Lamb.

Moreover, the Marian mystery clarifies the relationship between the priestly ministry and the universal priesthood of all the faithful by disclosing the latter's full realization in Mary. The universal priesthood's fundamental activity is to consent to the Son's perfect self-offering to the Father and unite with that offering. But how could a church full of sinners—asks Balthasar—consent perfectly to Christ's sacrifice of infinite love and purity? "The assent of the *Ekklesia* to the sacrifice of the Son must press on until it reaches Mary's perfect selflessness, so that this agreement may not retain any stain of the egotism that allows Jesus the Paschal Lamb to be slain for one's own redemption and perfection."[25]

Thus, only in union with Mary can the rest of the church exercise her priesthood, which is the final goal of the church's existence. The result of

25. Balthasar, *Creator Spirit*, 239–40.

the church's sacrifice (in the Eucharist and in its existential realization in our living and dying) is the union of the bride and groom from which the mystical body of Christ is daily being built up and nourished as Christ is being shaped and formed in every member. This, then, is the most sublime task of all members of the church, whether they belong to the hierarchy or not. The role of the hierarchy serves the church's universal priesthood; that role is to make present Christ sacrificed as head of the church so as to enable the entire body of the church to participate in the Son's self-donation to the Father. Thus the two priesthoods compare as means to goal. The role of the ministerial priest is to provide a twofold service: he is a servant of Christ for the service of the faithful to enable them to offer Christ's perfect sacrifice, and themselves with him. In the words of Augustine, they offer themselves as *multi unum corpus in Christo*, "the many forming one body in Christ."[26] The priesthood of all the faithful in union with Mary is permanent. It will be fulfilled in heaven and become the saints' eternal joy and honor. But the ministerial priesthood is temporary. It will cease upon achieving its goal at the end of history.

Thus, if the radical feminists were willing to consider the issue of ordination of women not in terms of demanding equal rights and equal power sharing in the church (a battle Jesus consistently reproved of in his disciples), but in terms of the nature and function of the two priesthoods, they might appreciate more what the female gender can best live and express: the ecclesial role of Mary, virgin, bride, and mother. Of course, men are also called in the church to become bride, virgin, and mother, but women are, by their very nature, even more suitable to express and fulfill this eschatological vocation.

In the figure of the eschatological woman fully realized in Mary and glorified in her soul and body as well as, albeit to a lesser degree, in the saints in heaven, "the eternal feminine," the new and eternal Eve, obtains its full realization, which has always been the final goal of all of God's works. This final perfection of creation is achieved through the Holy Spirit, through whom redeemed humankind, uniting to itself the whole cosmos, becomes the beautiful, highly desirable, and beloved spouse of the Son. More than that, in this woman the creature is in some sense raised by God's free mercy above God himself, because in Mary and, analogously, in the

26. Augustine, *De civitate Dei* 10.6.

whole church, the woman becomes the mother of God. She brings forth the Son of God in the flesh and in the hearts of all redeemed men and women. The eschatological woman, then, reveals what is most divine in God: his infinite humility and gratuitous love. Through this love and humility, God elevates creation out of nothing to the status of a worthy partner for himself (as bride) and even above himself (as mother). The woman remains a creature, but she is endowed by God's grace with such beauty that God himself finds in her his joy and delight.[27]

Conclusions

Our age is thirsty for spiritual, even mystical, experiences, but it ignores or rejects as useless squabble any discussion over "doctrine." Indeed, how could it believe that the human mind can attain to supernatural truths when our post-Enlightenment age questions its competence even within the realm of nature? The very word "dogmatic" has gained a pejorative meaning of mindless intellectual rigidity. Consequently, the church's magisterium appears a priori as an odd remnant of a defunct culture. The present essay does not claim to overturn this mindset, but I hope it has helped to clarify a number of points.

1. The church's charism of infallibility follows not only from the efficacy of divine communication but also from the church's virginal Marian nature. For the Fathers, heresy meant adultery, the corruption of the virginal union between Christ and the church. Individual local churches may be corrupted, but the church of Rome has always preserved the virginal integrity of her faith.

2. Even in the patristic age, however, the sins of the church's members, including her bishops and even the bishops of Rome, clearly stained the church on earth. The virginity of the church of Rome, which God has preserved intact, guarantees only the integrity of her faith.

3. Yet, on account of Mary, the integrity of the church's faith can never be fully separated from her immaculate, spotless holiness. Beginning from her immaculate conception up to her glorious bodily assumption, she realizes and reveals in herself the immaculate church, the wholly beautiful

27. The last paragraph has been taken, with some modifications, from my *Jesus Christ: Fundamentals of Christology*, 3rd ed. (New York: Alba House, 2002), 423.

bride of Christ, and, as the church's mother, she shares by her intercession her holiness with all her children, the brothers and sisters of Christ.

4. This chapter, I hope, has also shed some light on the nature of the church's faith. The primary object of her faith is Christ himself, and in Christ the totality of the Triune God. Her secondary object, the creeds and dogmatic definitions, however, are necessary on earth for articulating and communicating—though partially and as in a mirror—the reality of Christ. Thus the Marian mysteries bring to light the final intentionality of all the theoretical truths of revelation. Dogma and spiritual/mystical experience are not only not in conflict, but the former should lead to the latter. Moreover, while poetic language may intimate much more than proper theological discourse can, the latter still has an indispensable task of clarifying and distinguishing genuine spiritual experience from its counterfeits.

5. Thus, viewed from the perspective of the patristic tradition, the church's authority, which includes her magisterium, is an indispensable but not central truth of Catholic ecclesiology. It only serves as a necessary, temporary means to protect and safeguard the virgin church for her eschatological nuptials and to help anticipate this consummation in the holy souls' mystical kiss of the divine bridegroom. In heaven, the church as virginal spouse and mother will forever display her full beauty primarily in Mary and to varying degrees in all her holy members; in heaven, having completed its duty, the authority and teaching office of the church will disappear.

6. After describing how the Marian context illumines the charism of infallibility, its role as a safeguard of the Catholic faith in many areas was briefly explained. In addition, greater detail was offered on this charism's great potential for positively channeling the energies of the feminist movement. Without the human race's redemption through the incarnation, which was made possible by a woman, the church's role of giving birth to Christ in innumerable human beings would have been impossible.

St. Francis of Assisi's jubilant greeting of Mary and the church is an appropriate way to conclude. Francis sees Mary and the church existing not only in parallel to each other but also *within* one another. Just as the woman was clothed with the sun in the book of Revelation, and just as Irenaeus identified the womb of Mary and the womb of the church, Francis addresses Mary and the virgin church in one enthusiastic exclamation:

Hail holy Mistress and Queen, O Mary, the holy mother of God who has been made and chosen by the most holy Father in heaven to be the virgin church, whom the Father, with his most holy and beloved Son and the Holy Spirit, the Paraclete, has consecrated; you Mary in whom was and is all the fullness of grace and all good.[28]

28. Francis of Assisi, *Salutatio Beatae Mariae Virginis* 1.

Conclusions

At the end of this inquiry, I would like to sketch out the close connection between ecclesiology and anthropology, showing briefly how the multifaceted mystery of the church fulfills, purifies, and transcends the conflicting desires of the human mind and heart. Human beings desire unlimited space for developing their unique individualities, but they also want to belong to a community for mutual support and protection. In reality, however, human history shifts back and forth between extreme collectivism and unabashed individualism. Its latest fluctuation took place between the socialist-communist model and unbridled capitalism.

There is another pair of conflicting tendencies within the human heart: passion for material things and passion for spiritual things. In the modern age, we have subjugated and utilized the material world to the point of neglecting or denying spiritual realities altogether. The temptation is to believe that material, technological progress equals the progress of human civilization. But the dehumanizing effects of our idolization of technology have created a powerful hunger for Eastern spirituality. So the pendulum subtly shifts to the opposite extreme: Hindu and Buddhist theories and practices claim to actualize the human spiritual potential of humankind, but to the point of divinizing the soul and devaluing the body.

Christians know that our original fall from grace has brought about the mutually destructive conflict between our basic aspirations. To the extent that we cooperate with the redemptive work of Christ that reaches us through the church, our inner conflicts begin to heal, and our relationships to people and to the material universe can be restored. What had appeared contradictory can indeed become complementary.

By sanctifying the relationship of husband and wife and uniting children to himself through water and the Holy Spirit, thus making them children of the Father, Christ establishes the family as the basic cell of the church, the *ecclesia domestica*. To the extent that we cooperate with him, he not only orders our conflicting desires and heals our relationships but also inserts us into the life and love of the trinitarian God.

The church is the one unique bride of Christ, and yet simultaneously each and every member may become one unique bride whom Christ embraces with his fullness of love. The more the individual soul allows herself to be molded by the church into the pattern of the one bride, the more her individual beauty shines forth.

The loving virginal union between the church-bride and Christ results in the one mystical body of Christ in which every member fulfills a unique role. The more intimately members are united to the one body of Christ, the more fruitfully they fulfill their unique personal vocation. This one body of Christ and its spiritually mature members may also be called mother, since the church as a whole and each mature member participate in Christ's life-giving and nourishing activity.

Instead of disdaining matter over the spirit or vice versa, the church reconciles the two while acknowledging a hierarchy between them. In the risen, glorified human being, the Holy Spirit transforms the human spirit that elevates matter to the status of a portal through which the spiritual is conveyed, thus lending a special beauty to our transformed spirit that shines through our body. *Caro salutis cardo*, wrote Tertullian: salvation hinges on the flesh. The Word became flesh in order to become one of us and die for us, so that our reunited risen body and spirit may reflect the splendor of Christ. However, as long as human history goes on, material means, such as water, bread and wine, ointment and words join us in the sacraments to the risen Lord and thereby foreshadow the eschatological form of the entire universe, where heaven and earth will be filled with the glory of God.

SELECTED BIBLIOGRAPHY

Ancient, Medieval, and Papal Sources

All Latin texts have been taken from the Patrologia Latina online and translated by author unless indicated otherwise. Unless otherwise indicated, all Greek patristic texts are from standard modern translations.

Ambrose. *Commentary on Luke.*

———. *De paenitentia.*

———. *Hexamaeron.*

The Ante-Nicene Fathers. Edited by Alexander Roberts and James Donaldson. 1885–1887. 10 vols. Repr., Peabody, MA: Hendrickson, 1994.

Apponius. *In Canticum Canticorum expositio.*

Augustine. *City of God.*

———. *De baptismo.*

———. *De catechizandis rudibus.*

———. *De civitate Dei.*

———. *De sancta virginitate.*

———. *De unitate ecclesiae.*

———. *Enarrationes in Psalmos.*

———. *Epistula.*

———. *In Evangelium Johannis tractatus.*

———. *Sermones.*

Baltimore Catechism. From the Third Plenary Assembly of Baltimore, 1891. Available online.

Bellarmine, Robert. *De controversiis.* Naples: Giuliano, 1857.

Benedict XVI. *Address by the Holy Father: Visit to the Auschwitz Camp.* May 28, 2006.

———. *Anglicanorum Coetibus.* Apostolic Constitution. November 4, 2009.

———. *Address to the Clergy of Rome.* February 14, 2013.

Bernard of Clairvaux. *De consideratione.*

———. *The Letters of St. Bernard.* Translated and edited by Bruno Scott James. Chicago: Regnery, 1953.

———. *Sancti Bernardi Opera.* Vols. 1–8. Edited by J. Leclercq, C. H. Talbot, and H. M. Rochais. Rome: Editiones Cistercienses, 1957–1977.

———. *Second Sermon on First Sunday after the Octave of Epiphany.*

———. *Sermones de Diversis.* In *S. Bernardi Opera.* Vol. 6/1, *Sermones. III.* Edited by Jean Leclercq et al. Rome: Editiones Cistercienses, 1970.

———. *Sermon on the First Sunday after the Octave of Epiphany.*
———. *Sermons on the Song of Songs.* Cistercian Fathers 4, 7, 31, 40. Kalamazoo, Mich.: Cistercian Publications, 1971–80.
———. *Sermon 3 on All Saints Day.*
———. *Super Cantica.*
Bettenson, Henry, ed. *Documents of the Christian Church.* London: Oxford University Press, 1963.
Boniface VIII. Bull *Unam Sanctam.*
Cajetan. *Opuscula.* Lyons, 1562.
Catechism of the Catholic Church
Catechism of the Council of Trent for Parish Priests. New York: J. F. Wagner, 1923.
1 Clement.
Congregation for the Doctrine of the Faith. *Mysterium Ecclesiae.* June 24, 1973.
———. *Libertatis nuntius: Instruction on Certain Aspects of the Theology of Liberation.* August 6, 1984.
———. *Instruction on Christian Freedom and Liberation.* March 22, 1986.
———. *Letter to the Bishops of the Catholic Church on Some Aspects of the Church Understood as Communion.* May 28, 1992.
———. *Dominus Iesus.* August 6, 2000.
———. *Responses to Some Questions regarding Certain Aspects of the Doctrine on the Church.* June 29, 2007.
Clement of Alexandria. *Stromata.*
Cyprian. *De lapsis.*
———. *De unitate ecclesiae.*
———. *Epistula.*
Cyril of Jerusalem. *Catechetical LecturesCatechetical Lectures.*
Denzinger, Heinrich, and Adolf Schönmetzer, eds. *Enchiridion Symbolorum, Definitionum et Declarationum de Rebus Fidei et Morum.* 36th ed. Freiburg: Herder, 1976.
Eusebius Gallicanus. *Collectio Homiliarum.*
Eusebius of Caesarea. *Historia ecclesiastica.*
———. *The History of the Church: From Christ to Constantine.* Translated by G. A. Williamson. Baltimore: Penguin, 1965.
Francis. *Evangelii Gaudium.* Apostolic Exhortation. November 24, 2013.
———. *Laudato si'.* Encyclical Letter. May 24, 2015.
Francis of Assisi. *Salutatio Beatae Mariae Virginis.*
———. *The Testament.* In *Francis and Clare: The Complete Works.* Classics of Western Spirituality. New York: Paulist Press, 1982.
Gelasius. *Letter to Emperor Anastasius.*
Gregory X. Letter. October 7, 1272.
Gregory XVI. *Mirari vos.* August 15, 1832.
Gregory of Nazianzus. *Theological Orations.*
Gregory the Great. *Forty Homilies.*
Guerric. *Sermo II in Nativitatem Mariae.*
Hermas. *Shepherd.*
Hildegard of Bingen. *Scivias.*

Ignatius of Antioch. *Letter to the Romans.*
———. *Letter to the Smyrneans.*
Irenaeus. *Adversus haereses.* Edited by Adelin Rousseau, Louis Doutreleau, and C. Mercier. Sources Chrétiennes 34, 100, 152–53, 210–11, 263–64. Paris: Cerf, 1952–1979.
Isaac of Stella. *Sermo 51 in Assumptione.*
John of Damascus. *Against the Iconoclasts.*
John of Ragusa. *Tractatus de ecclesia.*
John Paul II. *Acta Apostolicae Sedis* 78. 1986.
———. *Sollicitudo Rei Socialis.* Encyclical Letter. December 30, 1987.
———. *Redemptoris Missio.* Encyclical Letter. December 7, 1990
———. *Centesimus Annus.* Encyclical Letter. May 1, 1991.
———. *Ut Unum Sint.* Encyclical Letter. May 25, 1995.
John XXIII. *Radio Message to all the Christian Faithful One Month before the Opening of the Second Vatican Ecumenical Council.* September 11, 1962.
———. *Address on the Occasion of the Solemn Opening of the Most Holy Council.* October 11, 1962.
Juan de Torquemada. *Summa de Ecclesia.*
Justin Martyr, *Dialogue with Trypho.*
———. *First Apology.*
Leo XIII. "Divinum illud." *Acta Apostolicae Sedis* 29. 1896/97.
Marsilius of Padua. *Defensor civitatis.*
The Martyrdom of Polycarp.
Origen. *Against Celsus.*
———. *Commentarii in evangelium Joannis.*
———. *Commentary on the Canticle of Canticles.*
———. *Homiliae in Ezechielem.*
———. *Homilies on the Song of Songs.*
Paul VI. Apostolic Exhortation *Evangelii Nuntiandi.* December 8, 1975.
Paulinus. *The Life of St. Ambrose.*
Peter Damian. *Dominus vobiscum.*
Petrus Chrysologus. *Collectio sermonum.*
Pius IX. *Syllabus of Errors.* December 8, 1864.
Pius XII. *Mystici Corporis.* Encyclical Letter. June 29, 1943.
Synodal Letter of the Council of Chalcedon to Leo the Great.
Tanner, Norman P., ed. *Decrees of the Ecumenical Councils.* 2 vols. Washington, D.C.: Georgetown University Press, 1990.
Tertullian. *Adversus Marcionem.* Corpus Scriptorum Ecclesiasticorum Latinorum vol. 47.
———. *Contra Praxean.* Corpus Scriptorum Ecclesiasticorum Latinorum vol. 47.
———. *On the Soul.* Corpus Scriptorum Ecclesiasticorum Latinorum vol. 47.
———. *Prescription against Heretics.* Corpus Scriptorum Ecclesiasticorum Latinorum vol. 47.
Thomas Aquinas. *Commentarium in Johannem.* Index thomisticus online.
———. *Commentarium super Epistolam ad Ephesios.* Index thomisticus online.
———. *De veritate.* Index thomisticus online.
———. *In Boethium.* Index thomisticus online.

———. *Opusculum*. Index thomisticus online.
———. *Summa theologiae*. Index thomisticus online.
———. *Super Epistolam ad Romanos*. Index thomisticus online.
———. *Super Sententias Lombardi*. Index thomisticus online.
Vatican Council II. Decree on Ecumenism *Nostra Aetate*. October 28, 1965.
———. Decree on Missionary Activity *Ad Gentes*. December 7, 1965.
William of St. Thierry. *Vita prima Sancti Bernardi*. PL 185:222–466.

Modern Sources

Ackermann, Stephan. "The Church as Person in the Theology of Hans Urs von Balthasar." *Communio* 29, no. 2 (2002): 238–49.
Akiba, Talmud R. *The Talmud: Selected Writings*. Translated by Ben Zion Bokser. Introduced by Ben Zion Bokser and Baruch M. Bokser. Classics of Western Spirituality. Mahwah, N.J.: Paulist Press, 1989.
Alberigo, Giuseppe, and Joseph A. Komonchak, eds. *The History of Vatican II*. 5 vols. Marynkoll, N.Y.: Orbis; Louvain: Peeters, 1998–2006.
Allen, John L., Jr. *The Global War on Christians: Dispatches from the Front Lines of Anti-Christian Persecution*. New York: Image, 2013.
Avis, Paul D. L. *The Church in the Theology of the Reformers*. London: Marshall, Morgan and Scott, 1982. Reprint, Eugene, Ore.: Wipf and Stock, 1982.
Balthasar, Hans Urs von. *Schleifung der Bastionen*. Einsiedeln: Benziger, 1952.
———. *Der antirömische Affekt: Wie lässt sich das Papstum in die Gesamtkirche integrieren?* Freiburg: Herder, 1974.
———. *Theodramatik*. Vol. II/2, *Die Personen in Christus*. Einsiedeln: Johannes, 1978.
———. *Theological Explorations*. Vol. 3, *Creator Spirit*. Translated by Brian McNeil, CRV. San Francisco: Ignatius 1991.
———. *Theo-drama: Theological Dramatic Theory*. Vol. 5, *The Last Act*. Translated by Graham Harrison. San Francisco: Ignatius, 1998.
Baptism, Eucharist, and Ministry. Faith and Order Paper 111. Geneva: World Council of Churches, 1982.
Barré, H. "Saint Bernard, docteur mariale." In *Saint Bernard théologien: Actes du Congrès de Dijon 15–19 sept 1953 = Analecta Sacri Ordinis Cisterciensis* 9 (1953): 92–113.
Baus, Karl. *From the Apostolic Community to Constantine*. Handbook of Church History 1. New York: Herder & Herder, 1965.
Beal, Rose. *Mystery of the Church, People of God: Yves Congar's Total Ecclesiology as a Path to Vatican II*. Washington, D.C.: The Catholic University of America Press, 2014.
Bonhoeffer, Dietrich. *Letters and Papers from Prison*. Edited by Eberhard Bethge. New York: Macmillan, 1967.
Bouyer, Louis. *The Seat of Wisdom*. Chicago: Henry Regnery, 1960.
Brady, Gustave. *La Théologie de l'Église de saint Clément de Rome à saint Irénée* [The theology of the church from St. Clement of Rome to St. Irenaeus]. Paris: Cerf, 1945.
Brown, Peter. *The Cult of the Saints*. Chicago: University of Chicago Press, 1981.
Brown, Raymond E., and John P. Meier. *Antioch and Rome: New Testament Cradles of Catholic Christianity*. New York: Paulist, 1983.

Buber, Martin. *Die Stunde und die Erkenntnis: Reden und Aufsätze* [The hour and the knowledge]. Berlin: Schocken Verlag, 1936.

Butler, Sara. "Authority in the Church: Lessons from the Anglican–Roman Catholic Dialogue." *Theology Digest* 45, no. 4 (1998): 337–53.

Calvin, John. "Catechism of the Church of Geneva." In *John Calvin: Selections from His Writings*. Edited by John Dillenberger. Garden City, N.Y.: Doubleday, 1971.

———. "The Institutes of the Christian Religion—1536 [Selections]." In *John Calvin: Selections from His Writings*. Edited by John Dillenberger. Garden City, N.Y.: Doubleday, 1971.

———. *The Institutes of the Christian Religion*. Translated by Henry Beveridge. Grand Rapids: Eerdmans, 1983.

Chazan, Robert. "Christian-Jewish Interactions over the Ages." In *Christianity in Jewish Terms*, edited by Tikva Frymer-Kensy, David Novak, Peter Ochs, David Fox Sandmel, and Michael A. Signer, 7–24. Boulder, Colo.: Westview Press, 2000.

Clue, Richard de. "Primacy and Collegiality in the Works of Joseph Ratzinger." *Communio* 35, no. 4 (2008): 642–70.

Codex of Canon Law of 1917.

Colson, Jean. *Tradition Paulinienne et tradition Johannique de l'épiscopat des origines à saint Irénée* [The Pauline and Johannine tradition on the episcopacy from the beginnings to Irenaeus]. Paris: Cerf, 1951.

Congar, Yves. *True and False Reform in the Church*. Abbreviated and translated by Paul Philibert. Collegeville, Minn.: Liturgical Press, 2011. Originally published as *Vraie et fausse réforme dans l'Église*. Paris: Cerf, 1950.

———. "L'ecclésiologie de saint Bernard." In *Saint Bernard théologien: Actes du Congrès de Dijon 15–19 sept 1953 = Analecta Sacri Ordinis Cisterciensis* 9 (1953): 136–90.

———. *Power and Poverty in the Church*. Baltimore: Helicon, 1965.

———. "Die Ekklesiologie der Gegenreformation." In *Handbuch der Dogmengeschichte*. Vol. III/3d, *Die Lehre von der Kirche vom Abendländischen Schisma bis zur Gegenwart*, edited by Michael Schmaus, 52–65. Freiburg: Herder, 1971.

———. *Handbuch der Dogmengeschichte*. Vol. III/3c, *Die Lehre von der Kirche: Von Augustinus bis zum Abendländischen Schisma*. Freiburg: Herder, 1971.

———. *Handbuch der Dogmengeschichte*. Vol. III/3d, *Die Lehre von der Kirche: Von Augustinus bis zum Gegenwart*. Freiburg: Herder, 1971.

———. "Die apostolische Kirche" [The apostolic church]. *Mysterium Salutis*. Vol. 4/1, *Das Heilsgeschehen in der Gemeinde*, edited by Wolfgang Beinert et al., 535–600. Einsiedeln: Benziger, 1972.

———. "Die Wesenseigenschaften der Kirche" [The essential marks of the church]. *Mysterium Salutis*. Vol. 4/1, *Das Heilsgeschehen in der Gemeinde*, edited by Wolfgang Beinert et al., 357–600. Einsiedeln: Benziger, 1972.

———. "Autonomie et pouvoir central dans l'Eglise vus par la théologie catholique" [Autonomy and central power in the Church as viewed by Catholic theology]. *Irénicon* 53 [1980]: 291–313.

———. *Thomas d'Aquin, Sa vision de théologie et de l'Église*. London: Variorum Reprints, 1984.

———. *Lay People in the Church*. London: Geoffrey Chapman; Westminster, Md.: Christian Classics, 1985.

———. *After Nine Hundred Years: The Background of the Schism between the Eastern and Western Churches*. New York: Fordham University Press, 1998.
———. *I Believe in the Holy Spirit*. 3 vols. New York: Crossroad-Herder, 2000.
———. *Eglise et papauté: Regards historiques* [The church and the papacy: historical aspects]. Paris: Cerf, 2002.
Crouzel, Henri. "Témoignages de l'Eglise ancienne" [Testimonies from the church of the Fathers]. *Nouvelle revue théologique* 104, no. 5 (1982): 723–48.
Cruan, Denis. *The History and the Future of the Liturgy*. San Francisco: Ignatius, 2005.
Cullmann, Oscar. *Christ and Time: The Primitive Christian Conception of Time*. Translated by Floyd V. Filson. Philadelphia: Westminster, 1950.
Curie, Stuart Dickson. "Koinonia in Christian Literature to 200 AD." Ph.D. diss., Emory University, 1962.
Dalin, David. *The Myth of Hitler's Pope: Pope Pius XII and His Secret War against Nazi Germany*. Washington, D.C.: Regnery, 2001.
Davies, W. D., and Dale C. Allison. *The Gospel according to St. Matthew*. 3 vols. International Critical Commentary. Edinburgh: T&T Clark, 1988–1997.
Delahaye, Karl. *Ekklesia Mater chez les Pères des trois premiers siècles*. Paris: Cerf, 1964.
Dodd, C. H. *According to the Scriptures: The Substructure of New Testament Theology*. New York: Fontana, 1965.
Dol, Jean-Noel. "Qui est l'Église? Hans Urs von Balthasar et la personnalité de l'Église" [Who is the church? Hans Urs von Balthasar and the personality of the church]. *Nouvelle revue théologique* 117, no. 3 (1995): 376–95.
Dominique de la Soujeole, Benoit. "The Economy of Salvation: Entitative Sacramentality and Operative Sacramentality." *The Thomist* 75, no. 4 (2011): 537–53.
Doyle, Dennis M. "Otto Semmelroth and the Advance of the Church as Sacrament at Vatican II." *Theological Studies* 76, no. 1 (2015): 65–86.
Dulles, Avery. "The Church according to Thomas Aquinas." In *A Church To Believe In: Discipleship and the Dynamics of Freedom*, 149–70. New York: Crossroad, 1982.
———. *The Catholicity of the Church*. Oxford: Clarendon, 1985.
———. *Magisterium: Teacher and Guardian of the Faith*. Washington, D.C.: Sapientia Press, 2007.
———. *My Journal of the Council*. Adelaide: ATF Theology, 2012.
Ehrman, Bart. *The Orthodox Corruption of Scripture: The Effect of Early Christological Controversies on the Text of the New Testament*. Oxford: Oxford University Press, 2011.
Empie, Paul C., and T. Austin Murphy, eds. *Lutherans and Catholics in Dialogue*. Vol. 5, *Papal Primacy and the Universal Church*. Minneapolis: Augsburg, 1974.
Fameree, Joseph. "L'ecclésiologie du Père Yves Congar: Essai de synthèse critique." *Revue de sciences philosophiques et théologiques* 76, no. 3 (1992): 377–419.
———. "Le ministère du pape selon l' Orthodoxie" [The ministry of the pope according to the Orthodox churches]. *Revue théologique de Louvain* 37, no. 1 (2006): 26–43.
Farkasfalvy, Denis. *L'inspiration de l'Écriture sainte dans la théologie de saint Bernard*. Studia Anselmiana 53. Rome: Herder, 1964.
———. "Theology of Scripture in St. Irenaeus." *Revue Bénédictine* 78, vols. 3–4 (1968): 319–33.
———. "The Ecclesial Setting of Pseudepigraphy in Second Peter and Its Role in the Formation of the Canon." *Second Century* 5, no. 1 (1985–86): 3–29.

Farmer, William R., and Roch Kereszty. *Peter and Paul in the Church of Rome: The Ecumenical Potential of a Forgotten Perspective*. Mahwah, N.J.: Paulist, 1990.

Feuillet, André. "L'heure de la femme. Jn 16,21. et l'heure de la Mère de Jésus. Jn 19,25–27." *Biblica* 47 (1966): 169–84, 361–80, 557–73.

Ford, John T. "Infallibility—Terminology, Textual Analysis, and Theological Interpretation: A Response to Mark Powell." *Theological Studies* 74, no. 1 (2013): 119–28.

Füglister, Notker. "Strukturen der alttestamentlichen Ekklesiologie: Das Heilsgeschehen in der Gemeinde Jesu Christi." In *Mysterium Salutis*. Vol. 4/2, *Das Heilsgeschehen in der Gemeinde: Gottes Gnadenhandeln*, edited by Johannes Betz et al., 23–100. Einsiedeln: Benziger, 1972.

Gasser, Vinzenz. *The Gift of Infallibility: The official Relatio on Infallibility of Bishop Vincent Gasser at Vatican Council I*. Translated with commentary and a theological synthesis on infallibility by James T. O'Connor. Boston: St. Paul Editions, 1986.

Geiselmann, J. R. *Die heilige Schrift und die Tradition* [Holy Scripture and Tradition]. Freiburg: Herder, 1962.

Gnilka, Joachim, ed. *Neues Testament und Kirche: [Festschrift] für Rudolf Schnackenburg*. Freiburg: Herder, 1974.

———. *Wie das Christentum enstand* [How Christianity came into being]. Freiburg: Herder, 2004.

Guardini, Romano. *Vom Sinn der Kirche*. Mainz: Matthias-Grünewald, 1922.

Gutiérrez, Gustavo. *Taking the Side of the Poor: Liberation Theology*. Maryknoll, N.Y.: Orbis, 2015.

Halton, Thomas. *The Church*. Message of the Fathers of the Church 4. Wilmington, De.: Michael Glazier, 1985.

Heim, Maximilian Heinrich. *Joseph Ratzinger: Life in the Church and Living Theology; Fundamentals of Ecclesiology with Reference to Lumen Gentium*. San Francisco: Ignatius, 2007.

Henneau, Jean Marie. "Le rapport intrinsèque du sacerdoce ministériel et du sacerdoce commun de fidèles: Pour une symbolique du sacerdoce" [The intrinsic connection between the ministerial priesthood and the common priesthood of the faithful: The symbolic meaning of the priesthood]. *Nouvelle revue théologique* 131, no. 2 (2009): 211–24.

Horn, Stephen Otto. "The Petrine Mission of the Church of Rome: Some Biblical and Patristic Views." *Communio* 18, no. 3 (1991): 313–21.

Jáki, Stanislas. *Les tendances nouvelles de l'ecclésiologie*. Rome: Herder, 1957.

Johnson, Luke Timothy. *The First and Second Letters to Timothy*. Anchor Bible. New York: Doubleday, 2001.

Journet, Charles. *The Theology of the Church*. San Francisco: Ignatius, 2004.

Jungmann, Joseph. *The Early Liturgy to the Time of Gregory the Great*. Notre Dame: University of Notre Dame Press, 1959.

Käsemann, Ernst. "Paul and Early Catholicism." In *New Testament Questions of Today*, 236–51. Philadelphia: Fortress, 1969.

Kasper, Walter. *Jesus the Christ*. New York: Paulist Press, 1976.

———. "Das zweite Vaticanum weiterdenken: Die apostolische Sukzession im Bischofsamt als ökumenisches Problem" [A further implication of Vatican II: The apostolic succession in the episcopacy as an ecumenical problem]. *Kerygma und Dogma* 44 (1998): 207–18. Condensed in *Theological Digest* 47 (2000): 203–10.

———. *Harvesting the Fruits: Basic Aspects of Christian Faith in Ecumenical Dialogue.* New York: Bloomsbury, 2009.

Kellner, Menachem. "How Ought a Jew View Christian Beliefs about Redemption?" In *Christianity in Jewish Terms*, edited by Tikva Frymer-Kensky, David Novak, Peter Ochs, David Fox Sandmel, and Michael A. Signer, 269–75. Boulder, Colo.: Westview Press, 2000.

Kelly, Gerard. "The Roman Catholic Doctrine of Papal Infallibility: A Response to Mark Powell," *Theological Studies* 74, no. 1 (2013): 129–37.

Kereszty, Roch. "The Unity of the Church in the Theology of Irenaeus." *Second Century* 4 (1984): 202–18.

———. "'Bride' and 'Mother' in the *Super Cantica* of St. Bernard: An Ecclesiology for Our Times?" *Communio* 20, no. 2 (1993): 415–36.

———. "Why a New Evangelization? A Study of Its Theological Rationale." *Communio* 21, no. 4 (1994): 594–611.

———. "A Catholic Response to W. Pannenberg Regarding the Petrine Ministry of the Bishop of Rome." *Communio* 25, no. 4 (1998): 619–29.

———. *Jesus Christ: The Fundamentals of Christology*. Updated ed. New York: St. Pauls, 2011.

———. *Wedding Feast of the Lamb: Eucharistic Theology from a Historical, Biblical and Systematic Perspective*. Chicago: Hillenbrand Books, 2004.

———. *Christianity among Other Religions: Apologetics in a Contemporary Context*. New York: Alba House, 2006.

———. "The Infallibility of the Church: A Marian Mystery." *Communio* 38, no. 3 (2011): 374–90.

———. "'Sacrosancta Ecclesia': The Holy Church of Sinners." *Communio* 40, no. 4 (2013): 663–79.

Koester, Helmut. *From Jesus to the Gospels: Interpreting the New Testament in Its Context.* Minneapolis: Fortress, 2007.

Koschorke, K. *Die Polemik der Gnostiker gegen das kirchliche Christentum* [The gnostics' polemics against the ecclesial Christianity]. Leiden: Brill, 1978.

Küng, Hans. *Unfehlbar? Eine Anfrage* [Infallible? An inquiry]. Zürich: Benziger, 1970.

Lamb, Matthew L., and Matthew Levering, eds. *Vatican II: Renewal within Tradition.* Oxford: Oxford University Press, 2008.

Lanne, Emmanuel. "L'Église de Rome 'a gloriosissimis duobus apostolis Petro et Paulo Romae fundatae et constitutae ecclesiae.' Adv. Haer. III.3.2." *Irénikon* 49 (1976): 275–322.

Levenson, Jon D. *The Death and Resurrection of the Beloved Son: The Transformation of the Child Sacrifice in Judaism and Christianity*. New Haven: Yale University Press, 1993.

Lohfink, Gerhard. *Jesus and Community*. Minneapolis: Fortress, 1984.

———. *Does God Need the Church? Toward a Theology of the People of God*. Collegeville, Minn.: Liturgical Press, 1999.

Lohfink, Norbert. *The Covenant Never Revoked: Biblical Reflections on Christian-Jewish Dialogue*. Minneapolis: Fortress, 1991.

Lubac, Henri de. *The Splendor of the Church*. New York: Paulist Press, 1963.

———. *The Church: Paradox and Mystery*. Translated by James R. Dunne. Staten Island: Alba House, 1969.

———. *Les églises particulières dans l'Église universelle*. Paris: Aubier Montaigne, 1971.
———. *The Splendor of the Church*. Translated by Michael Mason. San Francisco: Ignatius, 1986.
———. *Paradoxes of Faith*. Translated by Paule Simon, Sadie Kreilkamp, and Ernest Beaumont. San Francisco: Ignatius, 1987.
———. *Carnets du Concile*. 2 vols. Paris: Cerf, 2007.
Luther, Martin. *Briefwechsel 1509–1522*. WA 9.
———Luther, Martin. *Galaterbriefvorlesung von 1535*. WA 40/2.
———. "Luther at the Diet of Worms." In *Luther's Works: Career of the Reformer II*. Edited by George W. Forrell and Helmut T. Lehmann. Fortress: Philadelphia, 1970.
Lutheran–Roman Catholic Study Commission. *The Gospel and the Church—The Malta Report*. February 9, 1972. http://www.prounione.urbe.it/dia-int/l-rc/doc/e_l-rc_malta.html.
Lyonnet, Stanislas. "The Redemption of the Universe." In *Contemporary New Testament Studies*, edited by M. Rosalie Ryan. Collegeville, Minn.: Liturgical Press, 1966.
Mansini, Guy. "Ecclesial Mediation of Grace and Truth." *The Thomist* 75, no. 4 (2011): 555–83.
Marlé, René. "L'Église, quel type de communion?" [What kind of communion is the church?]. *Etudes* (October 1993): 371–79.
McBrien, Richard P. *The Remaking of the Church*. New York: Harper and Row, 1973.
Mersch, Emile. *Theology of the Mystical Body*. St. Louis: Herder, 1951.
Meyer, Ben F. *The Aims of Jesus*. London: SCM, 1979.
———. "The Expiation Motif in the Eucharistic Words: A Key to the History of Jesus?" *Gregorianum* 69, no. 3 (1988): 461–87.
Meyer, Harding. "Das Papstamt—ein mögliches Thema evangelischer Theologie?" [Is the papal office a possible theme of evangelical theology?]. *Freiburger Zeitschrift für Philosophie und Theologie* (2005): 42–56, condensed in *Theology Digest* 52 (2005): 225–30.
Möhler, Johann Adam. *Die Einheit in der Kirche oder das Princip des Katholicismus, dargestellt im Geiste der Kirchenväter der drei ersten Jahrhunderte*. Tübingen, 1825. English translation: *Unity in the Church or the Principle of Catholicism: Presented in the Spirit of the Church Fathers of the First Three Centuries*. Translated by Peter C. Erb. Washington, D.C.: The Catholic University of America Press, 1995.
———. *Symbolik oder Darstellung der dogmatischen Gegensätze der Katholiken und Protestanten nach ihren Öffentlichen Bekenntnisschriften*. Mainz, 1832. English translation: *Symbolism or, Exposition of the Doctrinal Differences between Catholics and Protestants as Evidenced by their Symbolical Writings*. Translated by James Burton Robertson. London: Charles Dolman, 1843.
Mühlen, Heribert. *Una mystica Persona: Die Kirche als Mysterium der heilsgeschichtlichen Identität des heiligen Geistes in Christus und in den Christen* [The church as the mystery of the identity of the Holy Spirit in Christ and in the church in salvation history]. Paderborn: Bonifatius, 1968.
———. *Una mystica Persona: Eine Person in vielen Personen* [One mystical person in many persons]. Munich: F. Schöning, 1968.
Mussner, Franz. "Petrusgestalt und Petrusdienst in der Sicht der späten Urkirche. Redaktionsgeschichtliche Überlegungen" [The figure and service of Peter in the late subapostolic church. Editorial-historical reflections]. In *Dienst an der Einheit:*

Zum Wesen und Auftrag des Petrusamts, edited by Joseph Ratzinger, 27–45. Düsseldorf: Patmos, 1978.

Neuhaus, David. "Engaging the Jewish People: Forty Years since *Nostra Aetate*." In *Catholic Engagement with World Religions: A Comprehensive Study*, edited by Karl J. Becker and Ilaria Morali, 395–413. Maryknoll, N.Y.: Orbis, 2010.

Noll, Mark A. "Martin Luther and the Concept of a 'True' Church." *Evangelical Quarterly* 50, no. 2 (1978): 79–85.

Novak, David. *The Natural Law in Judaism*. New York: Cambridge University Press, 2008.

O'Meara, Thomas F. "Theology of the Church." In *The Theology of Thomas Aquinas*, edited by Rik van Nieuwenhove and Joseph Wawrikow, 303–25. Notre Dame: University of Notre Dame Press, 2005.

Orbe, A. "La definicion del hombre en la teologia del s. II" *Gregorianum* 48 (1967): 522–76.

Otto, Rudolf. *The Idea of the Holy*. 2nd ed. London: Oxford University Press, 1958.

Pagels, Elaine. *The Gnostic Gospels*. Minneapolis: Fortress, 1989.

Pannenberg, Wolfgang, "A Lutheran's Reflections on the Petrine Ministry of the Bishop of Rome." *Communio* 25, no. 4 (1998): 604–18.

Pelchat, Marc. *L'Église mystère de communion: L'Ecclésiologie dans l'oeuvre de Henri de Lubac*. Paris: Les Éditions Paulines, 1988.

Perkins, Pheme. *Hearing the Parables of Jesus*. New York: Paulist, 1981.

Powell, Douglas. "Ordo Presbyterii." *Journal of Theological Studies* 26, no. 2 (1975): 290–328.

Powell, Mark E. "The 'Patient and Fraternal Dialogue' on Papal Infallibility: Contributions of a Free-Church Theologian." *Theological Studies* 74, no. 1 (2013): 105–18.

Rahner, Hugo. *Symbole der Kirche: Die Ekklesiogie der Väter*. Salzburg: O. Müller, 1964.

———. *Our Lady and the Church*. 1965. Reprint, Bethesda, Md.: Zaccheus Press, 2005.

Rahner, Karl. *Über die Schriftinspiration* [On the inspiration of the Scriptures]. Freiburg: Herder, 1958.

———. *Zum Problem der Unfehlbarkeit* [On the problem of infallibility]. Freiburg: Herder 1971.

Rahner, Karl, and Joseph Ratzinger. *Episcopate and Primacy*. New York: Catholic Publications Society, 1962.

Ratzinger, Joseph. *Das neue Volk Gottes: Entwürfe zur Ekklesiologie*. Düsseldorf: Patmos Verlag, 1969.

———. *Called to Communion: Understanding the Church Today*. San Francisco: Ignatius, 1996.

———. *Many Religions, One Covenant*. San Francisco: Ignatius, 1999.

———. "The Ecclesiology of the Constitution *Lumen Gentium*." In *Pilgrim Fellowship of Faith: The Church as Communion*, 123–52. San Francisco: Ignatius, 2005.

———. *The Spirit of the Liturgy*. San Francisco: Ignatius, 2005.

———. "Thoughts on the Place of Marian Doctrine and Piety in Faith and Theology as a Whole." In Hans Urs von Balthasar and Joseph Ratzinger, *Mary, the Church at the Source*, 19–36. San Francisco: Ignatius, 2005.

———. "The Ecclesiology of the Second Vatican Council." In *Joseph Ratzinger in Communio*. Vol. I, *The Unity of the Church*. Grand Rapids: Eerdmans, 2010.

———. "Luther and the Unity of the Churches: An Interview with Joseph Cardinal

Ratzinger." *Joseph Ratzinger in Communio*. Vol 1, *The Unity of the Church*, 44–61. Grand Rapids: Eerdmans, 2010.

———. "What Unites and Divides Denominations? Ecumenical Reflections." In *Joseph Ratzinger in Communio*. Vol. 1, *The Unity of the Church*, 1–9. Grand Rapids: Eerdmans, 2010.

———. *Jesus of Nazareth*. Vol. 2, *Holy Week: From the Entrance into Jerusalem to the Resurrection*. San Francisco: Ignatius, 2011.

———. "The Primacy of the Pope and the Unity of the People of God." *Communio* 41, no. 1 (2014): 112–28.

Ratzinger, Joseph, and Hans Urs von Balthasar. *Mary, the Church at the Source*. San Francisco: Ignatius, 2005.

Rengstorf, Karl Heinrich. "Ἀπόστολος." In *Theological Dictionary of the New Testament*, edited by Gerhard Kittel and Gerhard Friedrich, 1:407–445. Translated by Geoffrey Bromiley. Grand Rapids: Eerdmans: 1999.

Paul Schottenboer, ed. "An Evangelical Response to BEM." *Evangelical Review of Theology* (1989): 291–313.

Reynders, B. "Premières réactions de l'Église devant les falsifications du dépôt apostolique: Saint Irénée: L'infaillibilité de LÉglise." In *Journées oecuméniques de Chevetogne, 25–29 septembre 1961*, edited by O. Rousseau et al., 48–50. Chevetogne, 1962.

Richardson, Cyril C., ed. *The Early Christian Fathers*. New York: Touchstone, 1996.

Rigal, Jean. "Trois approches de l'ecclésiologie de communion: Congar, Zizioulas, Moltmann" [Three approaches to the ecclesiology of communion: Congar, Zizioulas, Moltmann]. *Nouvelle revue théologique* 120, no. 4 (1998): 605–19.

Schillebeeckx, Edward. *Christ the Sacrament of the Encounter with God*. New York: Sheed & Ward, 1963.

———. *The Church with a Human Face*. New York: Crossroad, 1985.

Schlier, Heinrich. "Ekklesiologie des Neuen Testaments: Das Heilsgeschehen in der Gemeinde Jesu Christi." In *Mysterium Salutis*. Vol. 4/1, Das Heilsgeschehen in der Germeinde, edited by Wolfgang Beinert et al., 101–221. Einsiedeln: Benziger, 1972.

Schmidt, K. L. "Ἐκκλησία." In *Theologisches Wörterbuch zum Neuen Testament*, edited by Gerhard Kittel and Gerhard Friedrich. Stuttgart: Kohlhammer, 1933.

Schoedel, W. R. "Theological Method in Irenaeus." *Journal of Theological Studies*, 35, no. 1 (1984): 31–49.

Semmelroth, Otto. *Die Kirche als Ursakrament* [The Church as the primordial sacrament]. Frankfurt: Joseph Knecht, 1953.

Stewart, Alistair C. *The Original Bishops: Office and Order in the First Christian Communities*. Grand Rapids: Baker Academic, 2014.

Sullivan, Francis A. *Creative Fidelity: Weighing and Interpreting Documents of the Magisterium*. Eugene, Ore.: Wipf & Stock, 1996.

———. *From Apostles to Bishops: The Development of the Episcopacy in the Early Church*. New York: Newman Press, 2001.

———. "Response to Karl Becker, S.J., on the Meaning of *Subsistit In*." *Theological Studies* 67, no. 2 (2006): 395–409.

———. "The Meaning of *Subsistit in* as Explained by the Congregation for the Doctrine of the Faith." *Theological Studies* 69, no. 1 (2008): 116–124.

———. "Further Thoughts on the Meaning of *Subsistit In*." *Theological Studies* 71, no. 1 (2010): 133–47.

Teilhard de Chardin, Pierre. *Hymn of the Universe*. New York: Harper and Row, 1965.

Tillard, J.-M. R. *L'évêque de Rome*. Paris: Cerf, 1982.

———. *The Bishop of Rome*. Wilmington, De.: Glazier, 1983.

———. *Church of Churches: The Ecclesiology of Communion*. Collegeville, Minn.: Liturgical Press, 1992.

Vajta, Vilmos. *Communio: Krisztus és a szentek közössége Luther teológiájában*. Budapest: Magyarországi Luther Szövetség: Budapest, 1993.

Van Unnik, W. C. "An Interesting Document of Second Century Theological Discussion. Irenaeus, *Adv. Haer.* I.10.3." *Vigiliae Christianae* 31 (1977): 196–228.

Vandevelde-Dailliere, Guy. "Nécessité de l'Eglise, salut des non-chrétiens, théologie des religions: options et enjeux" [The necessity of the church, the salvation of non-Christians, theology of the religions: options and stakes]. *Nouvelle revue théologique* 123, no. 2 (2001): 204–17.

Vanhoye, Albert. "Le ministère dans l'Eglise: réflexions à propos d'un ouvrage récent." Part 1, "Les données du Nouveau Testament." *Nouvelle Revue Théologique* 104 (1982): 722–38.

Vries, W. de. "Das Mühen des Papsttums um die Einheit der Kirche." In *Dienst an der Einheit: Zum Wesen und Auftrag des Petrusamts*, edited by Joseph Ratzinger, 66–80. Düsseldorf: Patmos, 1978.

Weigel, Gustave. "Contemporaneous Protestantism and Paul Tillich." *Theological Studies* 11, no. 2 (1950): 177–202.

Werfel, Franz. *Die wahre Geschichte vom geschändeten und wiederhergestellten Kreuz* [The true story of the twisted and restored cross]. Berlin: Verlag Haude/Spener, 1965.

INDEX OF NAMES

SUBJECT INDEX

The Church of God in Jesus Christ: A Catholic Ecclesiology was designed in Quadraat with Quadraat Sans display type and composed by Kachergis Book Design of Pittsboro, North Carolina. It was printed on 60-pound House Natural Smooth and bound by Sheridan Books of Chelsea, Michigan.